THEY CALL ME
MOSES MASAOKA

Other Books by Bill Hosokawa

JACL IN QUEST OF JUSTICE
EAST TO AMERICA
(WITH ROBERT A. WILSON)
THIRTY-FIVE YEARS IN THE FRYING PAN
THUNDER IN THE ROCKIES
THE TWO WORLDS OF JIM YOSHIDA
NISEI
THE URANIUM AGE

THEY CALL ME MOSES MASAOKA

An American Saga

Mike Masaoka
with Bill Hosokawa

WILLIAM MORROW AND COMPANY, INC.
NEW YORK

To Etsu, and all those
who share our dream
of the promised land

Library of Congress Cataloging-in-Publication Data

Masaoka, Mike M. (Mike Masaru), 1915–
  They call me Moses Masaoka.

  Includes index.
  1. Masaoka, Mike M. (Mike Masaru), 1915–
2. Japanese Americans—Biography.   3. Japanese Americans
—Politics and government.   4. United States—Relations—
Japan.   5. Japan—Relations—United States.   6. Lobbyists
—United States—Biography.   I. Hosokawa, Bill.
II. Title.
E184.J3M366   1987   973'.04956024 [B]   87-11120
ISBN 0-688-06236-9

Printed in the United States of America

First Edition

1 2 3 4 5 6 7 8 9 10

BOOK DESIGN BY PATTY LOWY

Preface

by Bill Hosokawa

Among the dozens of photographs, scrolls, and certificates that grace the walls of Mike Masaoka's tastefully furnished office in downtown Washington, D.C., are two memorable documents framed and preserved behind glass. One, dated a few days after conclusion in 1951 of the treaty that formally ended the state of war between the United States and Japan, is a telegram. It is signed by Hayato Ikeda, deputy leader of Tokyo's delegation to the San Francisco peace conference and later the prime minister who led his country through nearly a decade of astonishing economic recovery.

The telegram, addressed to Masaoka, reads: "Please accept the gratitude of the eighty million who have just regained sovereignty."

The other document, also addressed to Masaoka, is notable as much for its six signatures as its content. The signatories are the heads of six major religious organizations headquartered in Kyoto, Japan's ancient cultural and religious capital. These are strong-minded men who rarely find it possible to agree wholeheartedly. But they are united in expressing in the eloquent words below their appreciation and that of their millions of followers:

> This is to acknowledge with a profound sense of gratitude your significant contribution to the preservation of the religious and cultural heritage of Japan.
>
> We feel deeply indebted to you for the sacrificial efforts which you made during World War II to preserve the innumerable cultural assets, of worldwide importance, in Nara and Kyoto, from bombardment. Your action was a demonstration of your genuine concern for the religio-cultural assets of Japan and of your humanitarian spirit, which transcends all racial differences and national boundaries.

We take great joy in the fact that, to this day, these invaluable cultural properties in Nara and Kyoto remain intact.

We hereby acknowledge your contributions, and take great pleasure in recording them permanently in presenting you with this citation.

It is signed by Josen Kenchu, Archbishop, Horyuji Temple; Joshun Tagawa, Archbishop, Kofukuji Temple; Jitsudo Matsumoto, Archbishop, Saidaiji Temple; Kaiun Kamitsukawa, Archbishop, Todaiji Temple; Kyojun Morimoto, Archbishop, Toshodaiji Temple; and Koin Takada, Archbishop, Yakushiji Temple.

What had Masaoka done to deserve such accolades?

Hayato Ikeda's lavish praise was in reference to the part Masaoka had in the shaping of the peace treaty. Realistically, in the overall picture that part was minor. Policy was set by President Truman in collaboration with other Allied leaders, and details were hammered out by experts in the State Department. But there is little doubt that Masaoka did have a significant role in determining the direction and tone of the treaty.

Early in high-level Washington discussions about the nature of the proposed treaty, Masaoka was consulted a number of times. On the table were two strongly held and diametrically opposed schools of thought.

At one end of the philosophical spectrum were supporters of the harshly vindictive Henry Morgenthau position—that both Germany and Japan should be stripped of industrial potential and reduced to third-rate agricultural economies for many decades to come. Thus would the Allies punish them for their aggression.

At the other were those who saw the need for a strong, industrialized, democratic Japan rising out of the ashes of defeat to become the cornerstone of future American policy in the Far East. To achieve this goal, the peace treaty would have to be conciliatory, but this was not a popular position among those who found it difficult to forget the treachery of Pearl Harbor and the bitterness of the war.

There was no doubt in Masaoka's mind: if we failed to extend the hand of friendship to the defeated Japanese people, if we failed to help them establish a democratic nation after destroying their war-making potential, then the sacrifices of nearly four years of death and devastation would have been in vain.

Because Masaoka represented the Japanese American Citizens

League (JACL) in Washington, and perhaps because he was the only visible Japanese American on the scene, he was asked to contribute to thinking about the shaping of the peace. Would Japanese Americans, who certainly were among the indirect victims of Tokyo's military aggression, resent a soft treaty with Japan? Or would they oppose a harsh treaty? And what, in the long run, would be the most advantageous stance for the United States?

JACL had no official position. In fact, the organization was under membership mandate to take no stand on international affairs until it could get its domestic agenda in order. As a group, Nisei—"second-generation" Americans whose parents had come from Japan—could not forget that it was Japanese militarism that had led ultimately to mistreatment in their native America. But individually, many Nisei harbored sentimental ties to the ancestral homeland, particularly to its people and culture as differentiated from Japan as a political entity. When officials and opinion-makers asked for his input, Masaoka, speaking as an individual American citizen rather than a spokesman for JACL, had counseled an enlightened attitude toward postwar Japan.

This, of course, was much the same position taken by other Americans with knowledge of the Far East. Among the more influential was a group called the Strategic Lobby for the Pacific, headed by Eugene Dooman, a former high State Department official. Included in its leadership was Kay Sugahara, a Los Angeles Nisei who during the war had served in the Office of Strategic Services, predecessor of the Central Intelligence Agency. Sugahara, incidentally, went on to become owner of a fleet of international oil tankers.

One of the earlier voices raised in favor of an enlightened postwar policy was that of John F. Aiso, a brilliant California-born attorney and one of the organizers and later academic director of the U.S. Military Intelligence Language School, which trained thousands of Nisei interpreters and translators. Aiso expressed his ideas in a historic speech he delivered in 1943 at the New York Herald Tribune Forum, a platform from which opinion-makers discusssed important global issues for worldwide dissemination.

Looking to the world after the defeat of the Axis, Aiso said: "The peace must not be based upon vengeance engendered of wartime prejudices, but upon the fundamental principles of justice and equity. . . . The first step in the reconstruction of Japan is to get what Ambassador [Joseph] Grew has called the cancerous growth that has poisoned and contaminated everything healthy in the Japanese people out of their system. We must cast Japan into a crucible, smelt out the bad and refine the metal with which to recast a new Japan. Without one moment's hesitation we must smash Japan's military might.''

To build a new Japan, Aiso proposed constitutional and judicial reform, freedom of the press, and a revised educational system. ''In order to let the liberal elements in Japan lead that nation back to peaceful ways of living and friendly international intercourse,'' Aiso asserted, ''we must extend to the Japanese freedom from fear, fear of oppression and discriminatory treatment from the white man.''

Despite the credit Ikeda gave Masaoka, it is important to remember that numerous points of view went into formulation of U.S. postwar policy toward Japan. Masaoka was only one of many advocating a liberal treaty, a true treaty of peace which enabled Japan to become the Free World's second-largest economy and a staunch democratic ally of the United States. Yet the importance of his role is indicated by the fact that Masaoka was among a small handful of nonofficial observers invited by the United States government to attend the signing of the treaty in San Francisco in September 1951.

Of that occasion, Masaoka says: ''As I watched Prime Minister Shigeru Yoshida affix his signature to the document that would chart Japan's course into the future, I could not escape a deep sense of the drama between the country of my ancestry and the country of my birth and citizenship, a drama into which my life had been drawn and in which I had been privileged to play a part.''

In that context, it is possible to understand and appreciate Hayato Ikeda's telegram.

The part Masaoka had in sheltering Japan's cultural and religious treasures was even less direct. But there is no question that he took a strong, and not particularly popular position at a critical time. Early in the war, while the United States was still struggling to seize the offensive, strategists already were making plans for the aerial bombardment of the Japanese homeland. Lieutenant Colonel James H. Doolittle, whose carrier-based pilots bombed Tokyo, Nagoya, and Kobe on April 18, 1942, demonstrated that Japanese targets were vulnerable. As little as Masaoka knew about Japan at the time, he was aware of the priceless historic value, and the total absence of strategic value, of places like Kyoto, Nara, and Nikko, and of the Imperial Palace grounds in Tokyo. It did not seem likely that American generals in their determination to bomb Japan into submission would hesitate to destroy such cultural treasures, if indeed they were aware of their historical significance. There was also the possibility that our strategists had overlooked, or were unaware of, the likelihood that wanton destruction of the cultural heart of Japan would steel the determination of the people to resist to the death.

One day Masaoka brought up his concerns with Senator Elbert D. Thomas, a friend from Utah and by then chairman of the Senate Military Affairs Committee. Senator Thomas had lived in Japan as a Mormon missionary. He quickly agreed that he and other influential Americans should encourage the president to spare nonmilitary targets. It was an audacious thought, for American hatred of anything Japanese was running high. Because of the racist component in American patriotic fervor, it was hardly prudent for any Nisei to advance the idea publicly. On the other hand, there was no better person than Senator Thomas for broaching the idea. As the high priests noted, their religious and cultural treasures were preserved for all humanity, and they recognized Masaoka's role.

In the long view of history, however, the events commemorated by the framed documents may be overshadowed by the product of Masaoka's six lonely years of quiet, persistent lobbying in the halls and offices of Congress. After World War II, Masaoka was eminently successful in gaining legislative redress for inequities suffered by Japanese-Americans. In fact, *Reader's Digest* magazine had recognized him as Washington's most successful lobbyist. But his mission went beyond the pleas of one minority group. It was a quest whose success reversed America's centuries-old legalized discrimination against the peoples of Asia, forced Americans to live up to the spirit of the ideals expressed in the nation's founding documents, and vindicated the sacrifice accepted by Japanese-American soldiers and civilians as their contribution to victory in war. In a broader sense, what Masaoka was able to achieve in the way of justice for Japanese Americans helped raise the consciousness that made possible the sweeping civil-rights revolution of the late 1950s and the 1960s.

Masaoka's crusade on behalf of Japanese Americans reached a

peak one climactic day in 1952 when, after a raging political battle in which he helped stoke the fires, the United States Senate overrode a presidential veto. By that action America was ushered into a new era of understanding about human equality.

What the Senate did that rhetoric-filled day was to pass Public Law 414, 82nd Congress (HR 5678), 6 Stat. 163, the Walter-McCarran Bill, which brought vast changes to U.S. immigration and naturalization policy and, more specifically, eliminated race as a consideration in determining whether a person was worthy of sharing the American dream. For the immigrant parents of Japanese Americans, it simultaneously made citizenship possible and rendered moot hundreds of statutes directed specifically against them as "aliens ineligible to citizenship." For Japan, it wiped out the stigma of undesirability inherent in the exclusion provisions of the 1924 Immigration Act, a racist insult that well may have sown the seeds of war. For all Asians, it was a belated but appreciated demonstration of American recognition of their worth.

And when key domestic battles for justice were won, Masaoka turned his attention to helping Japan realize the promise inherent in the treaty of peace. Early on, he realized that both the United States and Japan would benefit from a resumption of vigorous trade relations, but that for Japan a foothold in the American market was critical to recovery. He was also aware that disagreements and misunderstandings over trade had been basic to the souring of relations between the two countries. He decided to apply his knowledge of Washington to help Japanese business through the tangle of regulations and restrictions that inhibited commerce. In this new role he became a valued consultant sought after by Japanese and American businessmen alike.

Who is this Mike Masaoka who helped bring all this to pass?

Mike Masaru Masaoka is an American only one generation removed from the muddy rice paddies of Japan. His father, Eijiro, had left his native Hiroshima Prefecture in 1903 to seek his fortune in the United States. Mike, Eijiro's fourth child, was born in Fresno, California, in 1915, and he grew up in Utah. In the summer of 1941, just months before the outbreak of war in the Pacific, Mike was hired as JACL's first executive secretary, and in that role he found himself in the middle of the chaos, confusion, and heartbreak of the evacuation and imprisonment of 115,000 Japanese Americans. Despite the burning injustice of the federal action, Masaoka demanded for Nisei the right to serve their country in uniform. He reasoned that the United States after the war could not deny justice to men who had shed blood in its defense, and in demonstration of this conviction he was the first to volunteer after President Roosevelt authorized formation of the Nisei 442nd Regimental Combat Team.

In most respects, except that his travails were more difficult, the experiences of Mike's boyhood and youth were not unlike those of other Nisei. Yet, in some remarkably different way, they prepared him to play an enormously significant role in the history of two great nations and their relationship with each other.

Today, although grown gray and hampered by health problems, Mike Masaoka still exudes flashes of the vitality, strategic genius, and bulldog determination that made him one of the striking figures of a turbulent time. Mike asked me to help him tell his personal story, and I was honored by the request. This book is the result.

Together, he and I and his wife, Etsu, who has devoted her life to the causes that were important to him, have reexplored his origins and experiences, his doubts and triumphs, the physical hunger and disappointments of childhood, the devastation of losing a brother in combat, the circumstances that demanded critical decisions and the reasons for shaping them the way he did, and the exhilaration of victory in the nation's ultimate forum, Congress. As best we could, we have tried to assess his achievements honestly in the context of their times.

Americans and Japanese alike will be the richer for getting to know the story of Mike Masaoka, American, which begins one angry day on the shores of Great Salt Lake, a desert sea more salt than the ocean, more bitter than tears.

Denver, Colorado
May 9, 1987

Contents

Introduction

I have waited a long time for this book and the story it tells. In the bicentennial year of our Constitution, *They Call Me Moses Masaoka* takes on even more significance, because it is the story of how one man can make a difference, how he can fight injustice within the system and emerge victorious. As sad and frustrating as many of Mike Masaoka's battles were, he taught us all something — that a true democracy must be strong enough to admit a mistake, learn from it, and work toward a better future for *all* its citizens.

When I was serving in the U.S. Congress, we prided ourselves on always "speaking to the issues." Mike spoke to the issues then and continues even today: racism in property ownership and immigration/naturalization regulations, denial of due process of the law, arbitrary suspension of the writ of habeas corpus, discrimination in all its forms.

Soon after the attack on Pearl Harbor in 1941, 120,000 Japanese American citizens and resident nationals were evacuated from their homes and moved into relocation camps. They became, in effect, our prisoners of war. How easy it would have been for them to turn their backs on America forever!

But they didn't. Because Mike Masaoka had a larger vision, a vision that said being an American was a matter of mind and heart — not of skin color or ethnic origin. Thousands of other Japanese Americans agreed with him. It is to their eternal credit that they loved the United States — with all its faults — enough to fight and die for the rights and privileges that had been summarily denied them. I pay, again, my deep personal respect, high esteem, and profound admiration to the 442nd Combat Regiment Team.

The wartime internment of our fellow Japanese American citizens has only recently gained public attention. As we mark our Constitution's bicentennial this year, we should stand reminded that men created the Constitution; men gave it life; men must ensure that its promises and guarantees do not go unfulfilled. Reading this book has reminded me that Moses Masaoka, in fighting to protect the rights of Japanese Americans, fought to protect the rights of all of us.

All of us Americans.

> — MIKE MANSFIELD
> Ambassador of the United States
> of America, Tokyo
>
> May 1987

Chapter 1

Moses in Mormonland

Then Moses climbed from the plains of Moab to Pisgah Peak in Mount Nebo, across from Jericho. And the Lord pointed out to him the Promised Land, as they gazed out across Gilead as far as Dan:
"There is Naphtali; and there is Ephraim and Manasseh; and across there, Judah, extending to the Mediterranean Sea; there is the Negeb; and the Jordan Valley and Jericho, the city of palm trees; and Zoar," the Lord told him.
"It is the Promised Land," the Lord told Moses. "I promised Abraham, Isaac and Jacob that I would give it to their descendants. Now you have seen it, but you will not enter it."

—Deuteronomy 34, in The Way, the Living Bible

My name is Mike Masaru Masaoka. Mike, not Michael. If that's an odd collection of names, it reflects both my American citizenship and upbringing and the Japanese part of my heritage.

Some of my friends, and some who are not my friends, also call me Moses. Moses Masaoka. They say that like the Biblical prophet, I have led my people on a long journey through the wilderness of discrimination and travail. They say that I have led them within sight of the promised land of justice for all and social and economic equality in our native America, but that we will not reach it within my lifetime.

That is not a happy prospect, but perhaps it is a realistic one. We have come so far toward fulfillment, and yet we have a long way to go.

Despite America's proud claim to world leadership in espousal of human rights, American history in this area is checkered at best. World War II marks a monumental watershed. It was as though Americans, realizing the sacrifice they had made to defend the rights of the oppressed throughout the world, had made up their collective minds that it was time to do more than pay lip service to the ideals emblazoned in the nation's founding documents. And so during the two decades after the Axis tyrants had been toppled, Americans made unprecedented progress in extending basic human rights to all. But old customs and habits die hard. Much remains to be done before we cross into the promised land.

The chief beneficiaries of change were the blacks, the historical victims of the darker side of the American character. But some of that malevolence also was directed against Asians, a facet of history not well understood outside the West Coast. This was the arena in which I was privileged to have a part.

Oddly enough, it is possible my concern for justice was predestined by a family tragedy at a time when I was worried about nothing beyond dry diapers and my next feeding.

The setting was not many miles from the spot where Brigham Young had first looked out over the harsh sands of the Great Salt Lake Basin at the foot of the Wasatch Mountains in Utah. There, one day in 1916, a lean, work-hardened Japanese immigrant named Eijiro Masaoka stared into the shimmering distance. "This is the place," the Mormon prophet had announced to his travel-weary flock. This, too, was to have been the place for Masaoka, his wife, Haruye, and their four children, the oldest of whom was only seven years old.

But where Masaoka thought he had bought land waiting to be broken by the plow, land he hoped to coax into production by sweat and love and timely rainfall, he saw only the lapping waves of a briny lake. For a long time he stared in silence at the desolation, and then in anguish he uttered one bitter word in Japanese: *"Yarareta!"*—"We've been had!"

The promoter who had sold him the land had seemed so helpful, so anxious to be accommodating. He had come to California's sweltering Central Valley with glowing reports of virgin acreage that could be bought cheaply in a lovely Utah valley blessed with plenty of cool, sweet water. And Eijiro had believed. In California, because he was an alien from Asia, the white man's laws had prevented him from owning land. The law also refused him citizenship because of his race. Permanently denied citizenship and landownership, in California he was doomed to life as a farm laborer or, at best, a sharecropper. It was a dismal outlook for an ambitious man with a growing family. So, moved by hope of an opportunity to work soil of his own in Utah, where the laws were different, he had borrowed heavily from friends to purchase property he had never seen.

Why had he alone, of the many Japanese laborers around Fresno where he worked, succumbed to the promoter's wiles? Perhaps because he was more adventurous than most, or more willing to take risks to improve his status. Perhaps he saw himself as a pioneer, exploring opportunities that his fellows might enjoy later. Or maybe he was just more naive. Whatever the case, now he owned a farm many feet under water saltier than the ocean he had crossed in search of a better life.

Eijiro Masaoka was my father. I was at the time the youngest of his four children, an infant in arms unaware of his unhappy experience until long after he was dead.

My mother, Haruye, happened to tell me the story of the land fraud one day after I had reached adulthood. She related it without bitterness, recounting it only as just another incident in a long life buffeted by the winds of adversity and misfortune.

"That man was a crook," I exclaimed in belated outrage. "Couldn't you do anything about it?"

She shrugged.

"Why didn't you go to the authorities?" I demanded.

"You must understand what it was like to be a Japanese immigrant in those days," she replied. "People like your father and me had no rights. They called America a democracy, but its benefits were not for those who were not white. Our testimony would have had no weight. We would have been laughed out of court had we dared to complain. So we swallowed our anger and persevered."

The Japanese have a word for that: *gaman*. It means to hang tough, endure, stick it out. That is what my parents did, and by example that is what they taught their family, which ultimately included six sons and two daughters. Our parents were good teachers, but I learned more than the virtue of enduring. I learned to fight for my rights. That was the American part of my heritage.

We would need the toughness acquired in childhood during the trauma of World War II when 115,000 Japanese Americans were imprisoned in U.S. detention camps. President Truman's Committee on Civil Rights termed that episode "the most striking interference since slavery with the right to physical freedom." There was much more than physical freedom involved, something precious called principle. The United States, while combating the savage intolerance of Nazi Germany, itself violated the constitutional rights of an American minority on the basis of its race. Our country had established the principle that a person is innocent until proved guilty. But in 1942 it took the position that all Japanese Americans, simply because of their ethnic heritage, should be assumed to be security risks in the war then raging and must be imprisoned without charge of any crime until they could prove their loyalty.

Does this sound impossible? Many Americans, even those who were adults at the time of the outrage, were unaware of it. But under prodding from the aggrieved, three presidents—Harry Truman, Gerald Ford, and Jimmy Carter—expressed regret that it had happened. The blue-ribbon Commission on Wartime Relocation and Internment of Civilians, appointed by Congress, said of this historical episode in its report in 1982:

> The promulgation of Executive Order 9066 [by President Franklin Delano Roosevelt] was not justified by military necessity, and the decisions which followed from it—detention, ending detention and ending exclusion—were not driven by analysis of military conditions. The broad historical causes which shaped these decisions were race prejudice, war hysteria and a failure of political leadership. Widespread ignorance of Japanese Americans contributed to a policy conceived in haste and executed in an atmosphere of fear and anger at Japan. A grave injustice was done to American citizens and resident aliens of Japanese ancestry who, without individual review and any probative evidence against them, were excluded, removed and detained by the United States during World War II.

Much of my story will deal with this unfortunate aberration in United States history, and how it affected my people as well as all Americans.

Unfair as this discriminatory action was, our national leaders laid down another condition: since we were untested as Americans, only in blood could we demonstrate loyalty to our country in its hour of peril.

I was the spokesman as we Japanese Americans, determined to prove our right to unblemished citizenship, demanded that we be allowed to fight, and if necessary to die, for our country—as many did. When at last President Roosevelt acceded, thousands of Nisei volunteered for the Army, which was the only service opened to us. Our first objective in enlisting was to have a part in defending our nation. But equally to the point, we sought to gain for our parents, our peers, ourselves, and our children the right to be treated as American equals under the law.

The Army organized Japanese Americans into the 442nd Regimental Combat Team, which fought as shock troops in eight major campaigns in Italy and France. Although the 442nd never numbered more than 3,000 men at any time, it won 18,143 individual decorations, including 9,486 Purple Hearts, and it suffered 680 dead. Five thousand other Japanese Americans, trained in classes organized by John Aiso's teachers, served as translators and interpreters in the Pacific Theater, the "eyes and ears" of Allied military intelligence.

Five of us Masaoka boys were in uniform, and we too paid a price. My next older brother, Ben Frank, died in action on a frozen French battlefield. Ike came home 100 percent disabled from combat wounds. Tad was left with a permanent limp. All five of us started with the 442nd, but Iwao Henry, the second-youngest, went into the paratroops—the infantry must have been too tame for him. All of us had something to prove, and it might be called our right to share the American dream.

The bloody sacrifice of Nisei on the battlefield underscored the unfinished fight for justice at home, and I was to have a role in toppling one after another the discriminatory statutes that had frustrated my parents. It gave me particular satisfaction that Mother, more than three decades after she was defrauded in Utah, was the principal in a landmark court decision that affirmed her right to own property in California.

What we accomplished was achieved through "the system." We struggled for our rights at a time before demonstrations and sit-ins and loud protests in front of news cameras had become acceptable. We sought redress by direct appeal to Congress and state legislatures and the courts. In short, we made the democratic system work.

But that is getting ahead of my story, which begins with my birth on October 15, 1915, in Fresno, California.

Actually, it goes back a bit further. My father, Eijiro Masaoka, was born in Aki-gun, Hiroshima Prefecture, January 10, 1878. As a younger son he had little hope of inheriting any of the Masaoka family's limited landholdings. At age twenty-five he left to seek his fortune in the United States, landing in Seattle, Washington, in 1903. Like the tens of thousands of Europeans arriving in America during that period, he was searching for economic opportunity. That search was made particularly elusive for Japanese immigrants by cultural and language differences. Yet he was confident enough about his future to marry Haruye Goto, among the few unattached Japanese women in the United States at that period of history.

Haruye had been born February 11, 1889, in Shimomashiku-gun, Kumamoto Prefecture, in southern Japan. Her father was a sometime labor contractor, supplying farm boys for jobs in the United States, and his work apparently took him back and forth across the Pacific. Haruye was a girl of sixteen when she landed in San Francisco with her parents on November 3, 1905. I never learned how she met her husband-to-be, or what attracted them to each other. Probably the introduction was through the good offices of a family friend of the Gotos, a Christian minister, the Reverend Kengo Tajima, who married the couple in Riverside, California, on July 3, 1908.

Their first child, Joe Grant, was born at Riverside in 1909. By 1911, when Ben Frank came along, the family had moved to Fresno. Sister Shinko was born there in 1913, and I was born in 1915, just a short while before our father loaded all of us aboard a train and headed for Utah. Virtually everything he owned or could borrow had gone into buying the useless land on the bed of Great Salt Lake. That left him no choice but to support his family as an itinerant farm laborer in Utah and eastern Nevada. We were living in Murray, a small smelter town south of Salt Lake City, where father Eijiro was working as a handyman when my brother Ike Akira was born in 1918.

Soon afterward we moved to Salt Lake City. With five children to feed and clothe, Eijiro worked at two janitorial jobs, one in the Beason Building downtown—which years later was to have special meaning for me—and the other at the nearby Walker Bank. There had to be a better way to make a living. He found it in a tiny fresh fruit and vegetable stand on West First South Street at the edge of Japantown, which consisted of a cluster of small shops, restaurants, and rooming houses.

Eijiro added a fresh fish department and called the store Mutual Produce in anticipation of happy relations with his customers. The idea was that my mother and the older children would operate the produce stand while he concentrated on the fish business. Because there was another fish market in Japantown, his intention was to develop out-of-town customers. He arranged to have fresh fish packed in ice and sent by rail from Seattle, Monterey, and San Pedro. With an assortment of fish loaded on a newly acquired half-ton Model T Ford truck, he would call one day a week on Japanese farmers north of Salt Lake City, bringing back seasonal produce to sell in the store. Another day he would head for Japanese farms south of the city. And Sundays, when the Japanese smelter workers had a day off, he would drive to Murray, Magna, and Garfield. I accompanied him on these trips before enrolling in school, and after I began classes I would go with him on his Sunday rounds. I would make myself useful by running up to the farmhouses, bunkhouses, and shacks in the smelter towns to invite inspection of our merchandise. Apparently I had a loud voice excellent for peddling fish. As we drove through the mill towns I would shout, *"Sakana, sakana"*—"Fish, fish"—at the top of my lungs.

After a time I noticed that toward the end of each working day Father would insist on going by himself into certain farmhouses and he stayed inside for what seemed longer than necessary. Eventually I discovered that he was enjoying nips of bootleg sake brewed by the farmers. One cold day while I was waiting outside the Inouye farmhouse, Yukus, a boy about my age, came out to play. Yukus grew up to become the first Nisei to be elected county commissioner in Utah, and later went to Japan as an official of the Mormon Church. At the time, however, he was just a youngster intrigued by the steam rising from the Ford's radiator.

"Yukus," I said, "the man at the garage told me the car

steams when the engine gets the water too hot. Maybe it would be a good idea to change the water.''

Somehow we found the petcock, drained the radiator, and re-filled it with cold water. But in draining the radiator, we let the alcohol antifreeze pour out on the ground. That night the radiator froze. Father began to ask questions, and I had to admit that I had been trying to be helpful. But he said no more about it, maybe because I never told my mother about his long visits in the Inouye kitchen.

Before long our good supply of fresh fruits and vegetables built up a clientele. One of our first regular customers was a young man named Wallace Bennett, who worked in his family's Bennett Paint and Glass Company store directly across the street from our stand. Years later Wallace Bennett was named president of the National Association of Manufacturers, and then he was elected to the first of three terms in the United States Senate. I had occasion to see him frequently in Washington, but when he left the Senate we lost touch until in 1976 he and I were two of five graduates honored as dis-tinguished alumni of the University of Utah.

When the fish and produce business began to make a little money, the family moved into some rooms above an auto-repair shop just a block from the store and almost in the shadow of the Mormon Temple. We had more room than in the flat where we had been living, but facilities were still primitive. Since there was no bathtub, we bathed in a galvanized-iron tub with water heated on the coal-burning kitchen range. The toilet was on the ground floor in the garage, and we shared it with the customers and the mechanics. In the previous place I had slept three in a bed with Joe Grant and Ben. Now Ike and I shared a bed, and that was a big improvement.

There was an empty lot alongside the repair shop, and it be-came our baseball field. Because of the field, and because there were so many of us Masaoka kids, other youngsters in the neigh-borhood made our place their hangout, and we had many noisy, exciting ball games. All our friends were Nisei—American-born children of Japanese immigrants. One of them was Sen Nishiyama, a tall, thoughtful boy the same age as Ben. He went on to earn a graduate degree in electrical engineering at the University of Utah but couldn't get a job in his field and finally went to live in Japan, where his talents were recognized and his race was no handicap.

After the war, Sen joined the staff of the United States Embassy in Tokyo, and for many years he was the ambassador's trusted interpreter. Another friend was Edward Hashimoto, who became a physician and professor of medicine at the University of Utah. Another of the group, Yasuo Sasaki, also became an outstanding physician and practiced for many years in Cincinnati.

The Masaokas certainly were the poorest of the lot, but we didn't know it. We just assumed that every kid but the eldest in a family wore hand-me-down clothes. There was always enough to eat if we weren't picky, and we were taught not to be. Often our meals consisted of unsold fish and vegetables from the store; turnips every night for a week could prove a bit tiresome. Nonetheless, our evening meals were happy affairs, preceded not infrequently by everyone joining in a hymn. I was too young to remember many details, but Sen, who frequently ate with us, recalls my father's voice rising loud and clear. I remember Father as a tall man, unusually tall for a Japanese, robust and jolly but a strict disciplinarian at home. He had to be, with a house full of children, and we learned to respect him. Mother, by contrast, was tiny and self-effacing, and always seemed to be working at something or other. She exuded a quiet dignity. Even though she never learned much English, she could meet Caucasian customers—and later our Caucasian friends—on their own terms.

The Reverend Mr. Tajima, who had married my parents, was now in Salt Lake City, and Mother faithfully attended his Japanese Union Church, which met in the living room of a rented home. I attended Sunday school there briefly. My most significant discovery was that I had not inherited my father's singing voice. Mr. Tajima assigned me to sing "America the Beautiful" for a church program. After one brief off-key practice he decided to forget the whole idea. Father seldom went to services, but it was his habit to rise and give the blessing before our family supper when we didn't sing a hymn.

These were happy times, and every two years another little Masaoka arrived to share what little we had. A sister, Kiyoko, who became known as Koke, was born in 1920. Iwao Henry came in 1922, and Tadashi (Tad) in January of 1924. Now there were eight of us children, and Joe Grant, the oldest, was only fifteen.

Then everything changed. The date was October 13, 1924. I remember it precisely for reasons that will become clear. My father set out as usual that day on his fish route. He had never failed to come back in time for dinner, but that evening he did not return. We waited awhile, then proceeded with our meal in worried silence. He hadn't come home when I went to bed. Next morning he was still missing. If Mother was worried, she didn't show it to the children. As usual, she went to open the store before we left for school. Soon after she left we heard a knock on the door. It was a tall, distinguished-looking Caucasian man. He identified himself as James Wolfe, and later we learned he was a justice of the Utah Supreme Court. He asked if we were the Masaoka family and said he wanted to talk to our mother. Then he told us that our father was dead.

One of the boys, it was probably Ben, ran to get Mother. Judge Wolfe told us that the previous evening he had been driving on the lightly traveled highway between Salt Lake City and Bountiful when he found Father lying unconscious on the road near his truck. Judge Wolfe took him to a hospital in North Salt Lake, where he was pronounced dead of multiple injuries. Father had carried no identification. Next morning they had been able to check the vehicle registration, and Judge Wolfe, taking personal responsibility, located us. We never learned the exact circumstances of Father's death. The authorities listed it as a hit-and-run accident.

I remember all this very vividly because we learned of Father's death on the day before my ninth birthday. We had never been able to make much of birthday celebrations, but Mother, sensing my desolation, put aside her own grief long enough to get me the only cake she could afford at the time—a loaf of raisin bread she topped with melted sugar for frosting and decorated with candles.

After the funeral, older members of our family met with friends of the Japanese community. Grandma and Grandpa Goto came from Fresno to help out. Everyone was deeply concerned about our future. Despite all his hard work, Father had been able to leave his wife only a very modest business, debts from the ill-fated land-buying venture that had brought us to Utah, and the responsibility of rearing eight young children. He had never been able to afford life insurance. And Social Security assistance for widows and orphans was still decades in the future. Some friends wanted Mother to let the boys be adopted, or to live temporarily with other families. But she was adamant, she would keep the family together. And she did. In a sense, then, I was the product of a broken home, a family shattered by a tragic accident but mended and held together by a mother's love and courage and the loyalty and selflessness of eight siblings.

We had to drop the fish routes, because there was no one to make the rounds, but Mother put a fish counter in the store. Joe, Ben, and even I worked in the produce stand after school and on weekends. Shinko took on a larger share of household duties. Ike and I often walked up and down the alleys behind stores to collect discarded wooden boxes and crates that could be sold to farmers for marketing their produce. On Sunday mornings, no matter how cold it was, Mother would scrub out the fish display cases. She would take the planks out to the curbing and wash them down even when there was ice on the streets. How could the rest of us goof off when she worked so hard to keep us fed and clothed?

Judge Wolfe, who went on to become chief justice of the Utah Supreme Court, took a personal interest in our welfare. In the best Mormon tradition of looking out for one's neightbors he dropped in frequently to see how we were getting along. Almost like a surrogate father he encouraged the boys to join Boy Scout Troop 46 sponsored by the Mormon 14th Ward. He watched in great satisfaction as, working together, sacrificing for each other, the Masaoka family learned to make ends meet.

It was in the Scouts that I acquired the name Mike. Until then I was known by my Japanese name, Masaru, which meant "victory" in Japanese, but which the other Scouts found difficult to pronounce. They called me Mississippi, Missouri, even Rosey, and I didn't like that much. Our scoutmaster, Bert Willis, suggested that each of the boys write a name on a slip of paper and put it in a hat, and I'd pick one out. If I liked it, they would call me that. I drew "Mike." I liked the name. When I went to college I had my named legalized, not to Michael, but to Mike Masaru Masaoka.

On special occasions, such as when one of us did particularly well at school, Judge Wolfe would bring us a cake or some similar luxury to celebrate. As I remember, Judge Wolfe was the first Caucasian to come into our home, and his was the first non-Japanese home we visited. By comparison to our crowded quarters, his home was spacious and luxurious. When we ate at his home he corrected our table manners as though we were his own grandchildren. Thanks to the judge we Masaokas began to learn what life was like outside Japantown.

Later on I discovered that the Mormon Church, the Church of Jesus Christ of Latter-Day Saints, had a particular interest in Japan and the Japanese. They had maintained missions in Japan until 1924, when Congress passed a law ending immigration from the Orient. Finding their welcome had cooled, the church brought its missionaries home. I was told that the Mormons believed the Japanese were among the lost tribes of Israel and were privileged to sit at God's right hand. Eventually I was baptized into the Mormon faith. Someday, it was suggested, the church might send me to Japan for the usual missionary tour expected of all devout young Mormons, but I never made it. Not even Mormon good works could overcome the implied insult of an American law that said the Japanese were unworthy of being allowed into the United States as immigrants.

Despite the official position of the Mormon Church, discrimination against Japanese existed in Utah, and I began to become aware of it. I knew, for example, that on the rare occasions we went to the movies we Nisei were shunted up to the topmost seats in the balcony—then known as nigger heaven—along with the blacks. One day Judge Wolfe invited me to have lunch at the exclusive social club to which he belonged, but even his prestige was unavailing. We were stopped at the door and he was told that his guest could not enter. I also learned that the Hotel Utah, the finest in Salt Lake City, would not accept Japanese guests. Japanese were allowed to enter it only through the employees' entrance as busboys. This sort of treatment, I learned after reaching adulthood, was not uncommon throughout the West.

Sen Nishiyama told us of his encounter with racial discrimination in junior high school. The pupils were told they could choose any sports activity they wished, and Sen signed up for swimming. When the class went to the municipal pool Sen was told he couldn't go in because he was Japanese. "But I'm American, just like the rest of the guys," Sen protested. "Yeah?" the gatekeeper said. "Show me your citizenship papers." Sen didn't know what the man was talking about. He went home nearly in tears.

Next day Sen was ordered to the principal's office. Wondering what he had done wrong, Sen, with knees shaking, reported to Miss Gertrude Arbuckle. Her eyes were misty as she told Sen: "I'm so ashamed of what happened to you yesterday. I have ordered the class never to go to that pool again. We will use another pool where you will be welcome.''

Sen's father reacted to this incident in a curious manner. As Sen related it to us, his father said: ''Sen, this trouble is all your fault.''

When Sen protested that he had done nothing wrong, his father replied: ''You had no business trying to get into that pool. You should have known they would not admit you, and you should not have tried to break custom. You know very well how the Japanese are treated in this country.''

We were learning. Young as I was, this incident gave me an insight into Japanese immigrant psychology, which was to avoid trouble by keeping a low profile. That's how they were able to survive in a hostile environment. I could understand the necessity, but I didn't like it. Eventually I would be able to do something about it. Just then, however, I could only listen and think. Perhaps partly because of Sen's experience I never learned to swim. But a larger reason was that I was beginning to develop other interests.

Thanks to some enlightened teachers we were encouraged to participate in all activities and to achieve as much as we could regardless of whether we were the children of immigrants or descendants of the original Mormon pioneers. Joe Grant set an example for the rest of the family by not only doing well in class but joining the staff of the high school newspaper and yearbook. Mother was greatly pleased. Also anxious to please her, I plunged into school activities. What interested me most was public speaking. At that stage of boyhood I was both shy and forward. I had always been articulate. Sometimes I was contentious. The thought of standing before an audience and speaking was both exciting and frightening. Oratory at that time in Salt Lake City, when radio was just beginning to come in, was a major youth activity. The Mormon Church encouraged public-speaking contests with representatives of the various wards competing against each other. Even junior high schools had oratorical contests. A good speaker was looked up to, like a football or basketball star. I played a little baseball and basketball in the Mormon Church's leagues and with the Japanese Union Church teams and became a fairly good tennis player, but it was obvious I was never cut out to be an athlete. (Ike was the family's best in sports. He made the lightweight all-city teams at quarterback in football and was center fielder in baseball at West High.) So I concentrated on public speaking as soon as I entered junior high school.

About that time we were able to move out of the rooms over the garage into an apartment, equipped with a genuine bathtub, in a considerably better neighborhood. C. Clarence Neslan, whom I had met through Judge Wolfe and who was to become mayor of Salt Lake City, was bishop of the ward. Like Judge Wolfe he took a lively interest in our family and encouraged my desire to speak. Some excellent teachers stirred my curiosity about history, literature, and the world around me. Teachers didn't have first names when we were children; I remember them only as Miss Chugg, Miss Creer, Mrs. Thomas, and Miss Franke. They taught me the pleasure of reading, and I devoured books voraciously—the classics, the Bible, current fiction, anything—and my vocabulary grew rapidly. Lincoln was one of my favorite subjects. The first book I ever bought was Lord Charnwood's *Abraham Lincoln*. The teachers taught old-fashioned grammar, and we learned to analyze syntax by diagraming sentences. These tedious classroom exercises helped me to acquire a knack for speaking in properly organized sentences.

In 1929 I moved up to West High School and lost no time in becoming involved in debate and oratorical competition. My first debate teacher was a Mrs. Van Winkle, who had been graduated from Cornell University with a law degree, an unusual accomplishment for a woman in those days. She taught me the rudiments of team debating, always emphasizing the importance of being better prepared than one's opponent. She also taught me that a speaker who made his presentation without notes was more likely to impress the judges than one who kept referring to them. These were lessons that stood me in good stead in four years of debating in college, and later in pushing for various causes in Congressional hearings. It was also at West High that I met Joseph Curtis, a political science teacher who introduced me to the exciting world of liberal ideas. He was a freethinker and he dared the ire of Mormon conservatives by throwing his classes open to freewheeling discussions of political and social issues. As much as anyone, he helped lay the foundations of a political philosophy, based on a liberal interpretation of traditional values, that was to guide my career.

Under Mrs. Van Winkle's coaching I surprised everyone, including myself, by winning the prestigious Stephens Oratorical

Contest and the state high school competition. Our West High debate team placed second in the state meet. The coaching I received
certainly honed and polished my speaking techniques, but in fact it
was mostly in jobs outside of school that I had picked up the ability
to persuade.

At the produce stand I wasn't content simply to bag what the
customers asked for. I sold. I developed an ability to move merchandise we were trying to get rid of, perhaps to avoid having to eat
the stuff. Kidding nice old ladies who came to shop, I could get
them to buy two heads of lettuce when they had intended to take
only one, a dozen oranges rather than six, the celery that I convinced them wasn't really as badly wilted as it seemed. It took a
certain amount of brass to do this, and I had it.

While in junior high I also had worked summers as a barker at
an amusement park named Lagoon between Salt Lake City and
Ogden. I don't recall how I happened to get the job, but I remember
very well what I did. Wearing a little happi coat, which always
embarrassed me, I would tease and cajole customers into buying
three balls for a dime to toss into numbered holes. I would tug at the
sleeves of young fellows out with their girls and shout something
like this: "Hey, hey, hey, how about spending a dime to win a
kewpie doll for your girlfriend? What's the matter? Scared you'll
lose? Too cheap to spend a dime? Come on, come on, three balls for
a dime, nine for a quarter, the more you buy the better your chance
to take home this grand prize dinnerware set."

Of course, few ever won the big prize. If someone got lucky
I'd find a way to sidetrack him into taking a lesser prize. The boss
was an older Japanese who spoke little English, so I was the front
man responsible for getting a crowd excited about the game and
anxious to spend their dimes and quarters. I learned a lot about
motivating people.

While still in high school I got an unexpected opportunity to
practice my persuasiveness in an arena that counted. Henry Kasai,
well known in the community as an insurance agent, liked to fish but
was denied a license because he was an alien. He had persuaded an
attorney to draft a bill ending the discrimination and asked me to
help him get it through the legislature. It was my first experience as
a citizen pleading for the rights of alien parents. Unlike most Issei—
first-generation immigrants—Henry spoke excellent English and no

doubt could have carried on the campaign himself. But he saw special merit in me, a citizen, approaching lawmakers who represented me. We were received cordially at a committee hearing and assured that the state law denying game licenses to "aliens ineligible to citizenship," which meant the Japanese, was not so much racial discrimination as a conservation measure. We were told that the state simply wanted to limit the number of licenses and seized on federal guidelines to bar certain aliens. That, of course, was absurd. I argued that there were only a few hundred Japanese aliens in the entire state, that only a handful of them had the time to fish and none was interested in hunting, and certainly they weren't going to endanger the game population. We got the law changed.

I came away from the experience feeling good about the American system and brimming with confidence that justice always triumphs. That confidence was to be sorely tested, but it was a great introduction to the way legislation was shaped. Since this was one of the very few legislative victories for Japanese aliens, it was given much publicity in the Japanese-language press on the West Coast.

It was about this time that I became acquainted with a remarkable man named Elbert D. Thomas. He was a professor of political science at the University of Utah and was serving as a judge at a state high school speech and debate contest sponsored by the university. I must have impressed him, because he came to talk to me after the tournament. I learned that he had been a Mormon missionary in Japan from 1907 until 1912, that his first daughter had been born there and was given a Japanese name, Chiye. He mastered Japanese and even wrote a book in that language. It was called *Sukui no Michi*—"Road to Salvation." He had taught Latin and Greek at the University of Utah before joining the political science department. He spoke at meetings of Nisei groups on several occasions and invited me to stay in touch with him.

School activities claimed so much of my time that I wasn't putting in my share of hours at the store. My brothers showed no resentment. In fact, they encouraged my interests. But it never occurred to me that they were doing me favors. I made it a point to work more than my share of Saturdays and Sundays to compensate for the time I missed during the week. Weekends were when Japanese-American young people met for social functions. Joe especially became active in the community while I tended the store. It wasn't that I was uninterested in our own community doings. I simply found what was going on at school more exciting.

Joe, six years my senior, attended the University of Utah for one year before dropping out, partly because of lack of funds and partly to concentrate on supporting the family. Ben, always steady and dependable, finished high school before joining Joe full-time. Joe, who had been a fairly good amateur boxer, was ambitious and energetic. He had big ideas for making money. The original store did so well under his full-time management that he proposed opening other outlets. The rest of us weren't sure it was a good idea, for we had experienced too many hard times. But he was the oldest, commanded a certain respect as nominal head of the family, and was anxious to try his wings. Recognizing his role, Mother was inclined to support his decision. In 1930 we opened a new store on Second South Street opposite the bus station. Some time after that we opened a third stand on South State Street near the City and County Building. Ben and Ike were made responsible for the original Mutual Produce store. Joe operated the one on Second South and I spent what time I could at the South State place.

I was graduated from West High in June of 1932, four months before my seventeenth birthday. My ambition was to study law at the University of Utah. I also nursed vague ideas of going into politics, and even fantasized about becoming the first Japanese American in Congress. But financing my education would be a problem.

Then without warning one day another of my Mormon benefactors, Mrs. Burton W. Musser, wife of a prominent oilman and in her own right a lecturer and former diplomat, offered me a four-year tuition scholarship at Harvard. It was a stunning opportunity, but of course I was in no position to go so far from home and pay my living expenses. Mrs. Musser then said she would underwrite those costs, too.

In great elation I went to discuss the offer with Mother. She still understood little English and I spoke almost no Japanese, but somehow we could communicate. She listened in silence as I explained the advantages of going to Harvard. Mrs. Musser, I explained, was wealthy and wanted to help me with no strings attached.

Finally, Mother shook her head. To accept Mrs. Musser's generosity, she said, would put not only me but the entire family under too much of an obligation. There was no reason for her to extend such generosity, she said, and therefore no reason that I should accept it. Involved in Mother's decision was an intense Japanese sense of independence that I could understand, plus pride in her ability to take care of her own without accepting help. The family was the center of her life, and its honor and integrity were paramount in her thinking. "Do nothing that would bring shame to yourself or dishonor to your family," she would tell her children. "To bring dishonor to your family is to damage all Japanese."

Did Mother understand the value of a Harvard education? I doubt it. Perhaps I had been unable to explain it clearly. Even I was not fully aware of what a degree from Harvard could mean. But I believe that even had she understood, she would have made the same decision, and I did not question it. Without further argument it was decided that I would thank Mrs. Musser, live at home, and attend the University of Utah. But there was one other condition. Mother said I was too young and immature to benefit fully from college. She suggested that I work a year, save some money, and then enroll at Utah. And that is what I did. If we could not communicate easily with Mother, neither did we argue with her.

Chapter 2

Collision Course

In the spring of 1932, the year I was graduated from high school, Prof. Elbert Thomas announced his candidacy for the United States Senate on the Democratic ticket. The incumbent was Reed Smoot, Republican and the first Mormon elected to the Senate, who had held the seat since 1902. In 1930, Smoot had joined Congressman Willis Hawley of Oregon to persuade Congress to pass what became known as the Smoot-Hawley Tariff Act. That law established tariffs equal to 59 percent of the value of imports and was a well-intentioned but disastrous effort to keep out foreign goods and save U.S. jobs and industries. The result was that our overseas trading partners retaliated and world commerce ground to a virtual halt. Professor Thomas contended that the trade war was crippling the American economy, and he made Senator Smoot's tariff one of his primary campaign issues.

After graduation I answered Thomas's call for volunteer campaign workers. I stuffed envelopes at his headquarters, manned the telephones, ran errands. As the campaign progressed, he began using me for minor leadership positions, even assigning me to speak on his behalf before small groups. That was quite a shock for me, and it must have been a shock for some voters to see a high school boy with a Japanese face representing the senatorial candidate.

It was a great experience, for I learned the rudiments of precinct-level campaigning. I also learned about the damage a high tariff policy had caused, a lesson that was doubly important because I was so young and impressionable. Thomas was swept into office in the Roosevelt landslide. As a gesture of appreciation, the senator-elect included me among the volunteers invited to go to Washington by chartered bus to witness his swearing-in.

The capital fascinated me. I was a wide-eyed small-town boy overwhelmed by the sight of the Capitol dome, the White House, the Washington Monument, and of course the Lincoln Memorial—places I had read about but hardly expected to see. Sometime during the visit, Senator Thomas took me aside. "Mike," he said, "I know you intend to go on to the University of Utah, and that's wise. But if you'd like to join my staff in Washington, I think we can find a place for you. You could continue your studies at night."

I often wonder what my life would have been like if I had joined the senator's staff. But reluctantly I went home to spend the rest of the year working at the family store on South State Street, taking a few postgraduate courses at West High, and helping to coach the school debate team.

In the fall of 1933 I enrolled as a freshman at the University of Utah with a tuition scholarship and threw myself enthusiastically into the debate and oratorical program. My reputation as a speaker had preceded me, but I quickly realized I had much to learn. The debate coach, C. Laverne Bane, was an excellent teacher.

In oratory and extemporaneous speaking my subjects had been much the same as would be chosen by other students of that period—war and peace, President Roosevelt's New Deal schemes for restoring the national economy and promoting social justice, the Kellogg-Briand Pact of 1928 renouncing war, the role of the League of Nations and the effectiveness of the World Court. One day Professor Bane asked why I didn't talk about what it was like to be a Japanese American, about the discrimination we faced, and what Americans ought to be doing about it. I replied that of course I was aware of discrimination but hadn't spent much time thinking or worrying about it. It seemed I was just too busy with other matters.

Bane made me aware of the kind of discrimination Nisei like me and Issei like my mother faced on the West Coast. He provided me with material for study about the racially discriminatory immigration law Congress had passed in 1924 and the California alien land laws, which I realized for the first time had been responsible for my father's move to Utah. It sounds strange, but Laverne Bane was the first person to explain to me how a Japanese American ought to feel about racial discrimination, and why I ought to feel that way.

And he went further. He helped me to realize that if the Nisei could make the nation understand the injustice of racial discrimination, we would be helping all Americans. Inspired, I prepared an oration on this subject titled "Yellow Shadows" which won first prize in the Rocky Mountain Forensic League contest. I was also a member of the team that won first place in the Utah-Idaho Debate Tournament. For these achievements I became the first freshman to be elected to Tau Kappa Alpha, the national honorary forensic society.

I usually was the second speaker on the debate team, which means that I presented the rebuttal, that I would respond to what my opponent had said and build a case that would impress the judges. This called for a good memory and a quick mind. There was no way to prepare a presentation; it had to be organized at the moment by picking flaws in the opposing team's logic. Debate provides an enormous challenge for one's reasoning and speaking abilities, and the training I received at the University enabled me in later years to speak on almost any occasion without a text. The only time I write speeches is when it is required, as in testimony before a Congressional committee. Even though I would speak extemporaneously whenever possible.

But while I was enjoying university life, the family faced new problems. The Great Depression was deepening. And a new idea in food marketing, supermarkets, was taking hold and forcing out mom-and-pop neighborhood grocery stores and specialized fruit and vegetable stands. Our three little stores were in trouble. That trouble was compounded by some overly optimistic investments Joe had made in the stock market. With the encouragement of brokers who genuinely hoped we would make money, Joe had begun to dabble in securities. At first he made some modest profits. That gave him the confidence to buy promising stocks on margin. The market was in turmoil, with sharp ups and downs. We got caught in a down and not only lost the original investment but owed the brokers for the margin purchases. Before we knew what was happening the family was just as broke as when we had arrived in Utah nearly twenty years earlier. But Mother refused to declare bankruptcy. It took many years, decades in fact, but she insisted on paying our debts, a few dollars at a time, to the brokers as well as to the people who had lent my father the money to move to Utah. These were debts of honor that she could not forget until they were completely wiped out.

Like the people of the Dust Bowl and other depressed areas of the nation, we looked westward. We had heard reports that the full impact of the Depression had not hit California and that there were still opportunities to be found there. Joe and Mother agreed it would be wise to salvage what we could and move the family to Los Angeles. Joe left in 1935 on a scouting trip and found a little fruit and vegetable stand near the western end of Wilshire Boulevard which he could take over for a low down payment. Mother and the rest of the family joined him as soon as he was established. Mother had agreed that I should stay in Salt Lake City and do what I could to complete my remaining two years at the University of Utah. Now, at nineteen, I was on my own.

For a youngster who had grown up in a crowded home with five brothers and two sisters, the most difficult part of striking out was living alone. I moved into a dingy little room at the Colonial, a cheap hotel in the middle of Japantown, which was all that my budget would allow. The lack of elegance didn't bother me, since I returned to the room only to sleep, and I was doing little of that. To meet living expenses I got a night job as waiter at the State Noodle House, a restaurant about as nondescript as the name indicates. My hours were from 9:00 p.m. until we closed at 3:00 a.m. Waiting tables in a noodle house wasn't much of a job, but I could eat there, and the wages, such as they were, enabled me to pay the rent, buy a few clothes, and stay in school. The owner was an Issei named Imamura. His wife was a Hawaii-born Nisei. I never learned their first names. I knew them only as Imamura Ojisan (Uncle Imamura) and Imamura Obasan (Aunt Imamura). They were kindly people, tolerant of my need to be away frequently on school activities, and they did much to help me overcome the loneliness of being separated from my family.

Traveling with the university forensics team took time away from the job, but the Imamuras raised no objection as long as I worked extra when I got back. The late-night hours made it difficult to stay awake in class sometimes. Still, there were compensations. Nisei my age would drop in for a snack after a movie, a dance, or a poker game, and I got to know many of them for the first time. I found them to be a congenial bunch. I became good friends with fellows like Shigeki (Shake) Ushio and Yukus Inouye, of the drained-radiator episode, whose families farmed near Murray. I had known them slightly when my father was peddling fish, but had lost touch after his death.

Another friend was Bill Yamauchi, who was two or three years older than I. Bill had been graduated from the University of Utah with a degree in business, but he wasn't able to find a job. He helped his father on the family farm during the week and cooked at the State Noodle House weekends. After a while he became a full-time cook and we shared a room at the Colonial. Shake, Yukus, and Bill got me involved more and more in the Japanese-American community. Bill had a girlfriend in Idaho. Sometimes he took me along when he visited her, and I became acquainted with a number of Nisei in that area. Before long I found I was being looked on as a leader and spokesman for Japanese Americans.

At school I plunged even more enthusiastically into debate and oratorical competition. The University of Utah had an exceptional squad at that time—David S. King, Frank E. Moss, Calvin Rampton, Bill Richards, and I, among others. Of that group Bill Richards and I were the only ones who did not go on to gain considerable eminence in politics. We were all close, but my closest friend was Richards, with whom I had debated in high school. He chose a business career and did very well. David King was a law student and became president of the senior class. His father was U.S. Senator William H. King. In 1958, David was elected to the first of three terms in the U.S. House of Representatives. He served for a time as ambassador to the Malagasy Republic and Mauritius and became a director of the World Bank. Frank Moss, whom we knew as Ted, went into law and in 1958 he was elected to the first of three terms as U.S. senator from Utah. Cal Rampton was at the university only two years. Then he went to Washington to join the staff of Congressman J. W. Robinson; he studied at George Washington University at night and earned a degree in law. He returned to Utah to practice and eventually became a three-term governor.

Traveling to various parts of the Intermountain West to debate, we shared dreams and hopes of the future. All my teammates had excellent minds and were stimulating company. Despite the differences in backgrounds, I was fully accepted. In fact, I might have been considered their leader. I was welcome in their homes and became acquainted with their girls. Because of my work schedule my social life was limited. But for a fellow who had to wait on tables to stay in school, I was traveling in some rather impressive company. I wasn't aware of it at the time, but Utah had an anti-miscegenation law, which meant that a man and a woman were not permitted to marry if one was white and the other was not. I did not fall in love with any of the girls we knew, but if I had I would have had to challenge the law. That opportunity, although I was not personally involved, was not to come for more than three decades.

In the spring of 1936 the University of Utah debate team traveled to Denver for the National Invitational Tournament. It was the biggest challenge we had faced. Coach Bane had prepared us well. I was fortunate to win all-American ratings in both debate and oratory. That a student of Japanese ancestry was able to express himself so well in the English language seemed to amaze the *Salt Lake Tribune,* the leading newspaper in the Intermountain West. It published an editorial titled "An Example to American Students" which was laudatory and well-meaning but painfully condescending by present-day standards. The editorial erroneously referred to me as an alien and piously expressed confidence that if Masaoka could learn to express himself in English, any real American boy should be able to do as well. The inability among many to understand that a native-born person does not have to be white to be an American is, unfortunately, a problem that has remained with Japanese Americans to this day. No matter what we do to demonstrate our Americanism, no matter how many generations we have been in the United States, many see our nonwhite faces as evidence of alien status. The editorial read:

> This Republic is a land of liberty, democracy, and equal opportunity. Malcontents may blame their failure to an economic system, political corruption, or racial discrimination, but excuses, like good intentions, make good paving material. In an oratorical contest held recently in Denver, a young Japanese student of the University of Utah carried off the honors as the most effective speaker at the conference. Mike Masaoka is to be congratulated on his victory over native orators representing seventy-five universities and colleges, and the state university is to be felicitated on having such a champion.
>
> When an alien of Asiatic parentage is able to master the intricacies and absurdities of our orthography and to overcome lingual handicaps in pronunciation and articulation, to acquire an ability to

think, to arrange his ideas in logical sequence, and to express them
clearly and forcefully, there is no excuse for failure among American
students.

Boys and girls with inherited aptitude, with mental and physical
adaptation transmitted by successive generations of ancestors, with
the incalculable advantage of always having heard the tongue in
which they plead every cause from infancy to age, have little excuse
to complain and fail in competition depending on talents bestowed
and developed by such origin and environment.

What Mike Masaoka has done any American boy ought to be
able to accomplish. His achievements and the honors accorded him
should serve as an inspiration to every boy and girl in every educational institution in this republic. It should also remind the world that
neither race, nor creed, nor color constitute a bar to advancement
here when merit asserts itself.

In a later period of my life I would have contacted the editor to help
him, in one way or another, to improve his understanding about
citizenship. When an editorial writer of an important metropolitan
newspaper was so ignorant about Japanese Americans, it was no
wonder that the public was equally uninformed. But at the moment
I was not inclined to protest.

The following year, when the tournament was held in Pasadena,
California, I repeated my double victory. I crowned my senior year
by being elected to Skull and Bones, a scholastic and activities
honorary; making the Beehive Society, limited to the top five students in the entire class; and serving as chairman of the Founders
Day program, treasurer of the senior class, and salutatorian at my
graduation in 1937. I was then twenty-one years old, still boyish in
appearance, slight of build and of medium height, with rimless
glasses then in style and a shock of thick black hair.

With graduation my world changed abruptly. Most of my school
friends went their separate ways. I wanted to go on to law school but
didn't have the money. My decision was to continue working for a
year at the State Noodle House and at whatever other jobs I could
find to save up a nest egg.

It was about this time that Tamotsu Murayama came to town.
Tamotsu was a stocky, muscular Nisei with a loud voice and a
bombastic style. He had gained most of his education in Japan and
was working for a Japanese-language newspaper in San Francisco.

His mission was to recruit membership in a young West Coast Nisei organization called the Japanese American Citizens League. It was the first time I had heard of it.

At a meeting of Salt Lake City Nisei, Murayama explained that the league, which he called JACL, was a national organization of Japanese Americans founded in Seattle in 1930. By "national" he meant that there were a dozen or so chapters in California, one in Oregon, and a couple in Washington. JACL, he said, was a civic and patriotic group concerned with the well-being and political and economic progress of American citizens of Japanese ancestry. He told of the legal, social, and economic discrimination faced by Japanese Americans on the West Coast and described JACL's program, which was expressed by its motto, "Security Through Unity." But that security was tenuous at best with only a few hundred members in the entire organization. JACL badly needed dues-paying recruits in Utah.

I couldn't see any reason for forming a JACL chapter in Salt Lake City and said so bluntly. I argued that while discrimination did indeed exist in Utah, our problems were different from those of West Coast Nisei. I told Murayama that he had not given us any incentive for joining his movement because he hadn't been able to demonstrate how we would benefit by becoming members. The majority seemed to agree with me. Mumbling about kids who thought they were so smart, Murayama left town and I promptly forgot about JACL.

I was in a no-win position as I waited to enter law school. Because law school was my goal, I was unable to look for a permanent job. The Depression made even part-time work hard to find. The noodle-house job kept me fed and paid my rent but left almost nothing to add to my savings. Joe sent me encouraging letters but no money; he was having a hard time, too.

With time on my hands, I found myself mixing more often with fellow Nisei. For some reason I could not explain, I felt comfortable and completely at ease with them even though I knew few well. I attended social functions at the church and went to community picnics where Issei ladies outdid themselves in preparing Japanese delicacies, and I quickly made friends with the most accomplished cooks.

About this time, Mrs. Kuniko Terasawa, publisher of a little triweekly Japanese-language newspaper called the *Utah Nippo,* decided to start an English section for the benefit of Nisei, most of whom, of course, could read no Japanese. She asked me to edit the one-page section, which I did for several years. Aside from items about local community activities, most of the news consisted of stories rewritten from West Coast Japanese-American journals. The job took little time and paid virtually nothing, but it was useful in giving me knowledge about Nisei activities elsewhere.

In the spring of 1938, Bill Yamauchi and Yukus Inouye convinced me that there was quick money to be made in growing summer lettuce on rented land in a high valley of the Wasatch Mountains. The way they explained it, lettuce, a cool-climate crop, would do well long after lower areas had become too hot, and could be marketed for a handsome price. So, although I knew nothing about farming, I became their partner in my first and only farm venture. We plowed and leveled and planted and hoed and irrigated and counted our anticipated profits as it grew warmer and warmer in the flatlands. But that year the heat rose into the mountains, too, and the irrigation ditches soon ran dry. We worked desperately to save the crop, toiling endless hours in the fields. And because we didn't have money to buy adequate food we ate what was most accessible—lettuce.

Fresh lettuce, lettuce fried with bacon, boiled lettuce, salted lettuce, lettuce three meals a day until I was sick of it. Despite everything we could do, our lettuce went to seed early and there was little to harvest. Bill and Yukus were farm boys accustomed to the disappointments of a business that was at the mercy of the weather's vagaries and uncertain market prices. I wasn't. About all I got out of the experience was a bumper crop of blisters.

Meanwhile, JACL hadn't forgotten us. Our next visitor was Tom Yego, a husky farmer from the orchard country of Placer County in the Sierra foothills east of Sacramento. He came to Utah as president of the California Federation of Nisei Farmers and presented JACL as an organization concerned specifically with protecting Nisei rights. Yego established an easy rapport with Utah's Nisei farmers, and his presentation, unlike Murayama's, stirred my interest in learning more about JACL. As a result we asked JACL to send an official representative to talk to us. The man chosen was Walter Tsukamoto, a personable young Sacramento attorney who was

JACL's unpaid executive secretary. He had been one of the organization's founders, and his fervor and idealism intrigued me. When I kept asking questions, Tsukamoto invited me to attend JACL's fifth biennial convention, scheduled in Los Angeles over the Labor Day weekend of 1938.

I accepted readily, since the trip would give me an opportunity to see Mother and the rest of the family. But the convention proved to be as dull as I feared it would be. There were interminable discussions about such earthshaking issues as whether serving refreshments would result in better attendance at meetings.

There are two versions about how I exploded onto the JACL scene. The popular version is that I, a brash young outsider at my first convention, became so disgusted with the proceedings that I jumped up, demanded the floor, and then in forceful tones told the members what was wrong with their organization. This perception is understandable, because Nisei of that time were not accustomed either to hearing or delivering blunt talk. But I cannot believe that I, a guest, would have been so ill-mannered as to direct harsh criticism at my hosts, although some of my older friends say I am perfectly capable of such behavior.

My own recollection is that Jimmie Sakamoto, a blind newspaper publisher from Seattle who was retiring national president of JACL, was in the chair during a general discussion of the organization. After a while Walter Tsukamoto told the group that I had expressed some interesting thoughts when we met in Salt Lake City, and he asked me to share them with the delegates.

I said that while I endorsed JACL's goals, I felt it lacked a viable program. Instead of spending so much time on petty, parochial matters, I said, it should become active nationally. But since it lacked political influence, such efforts would be ineffective. The only way to acquire that influence, I said, was to build JACL into a truly national organization by picking up membership wherever Japanese Americans were to be found, particularly in inland areas like Utah, Colorado, Idaho, and Nebraska, where they had achieved a measure of integration. In that way, I said, JACL would have the support of a wide cross section of political figures like mayors, state legislators, governors, and members of Congress when it went out in search of support for its objectives.

As I continued to speak in terms of a broad national program,

I got a vague feeling that most of the delegates had no idea what I was talking about. At that point Susumu (Sim) Togasaki stood up. Sim was a merchant, member of a distinguished San Francisco family and veteran national treasurer of JACL. He indicated he was anxious to settle some budget matters and obviously was irritated that I was taking up valuable time prattling about influencing national figures.

"What the hell," he complained. "This young fellow is talking about getting congressmen to act for us when we can't even get the mayor of Los Angeles to address our convention. Let's be realistic." Sim, who later became a valued friend and loyal JACL colleague, thought I was talking through my hat, and it was obvious many others agreed with him. But one who didn't was Saburo Kido, a dapper Hawaii-born attorney who had come to San Francisco to get his degree and stayed to launch a modest practice. He had been one of JACL's founders. Early on, he had recognized the need for an organization like JACL to cope with Nisei problems. Although he said nothing at the moment, he had listened carefully to my comments. No one could foresee it at the time, but before long he, JACL, and I were to be deeply involved with high-level political leaders.

At Togasaki's insistence, Jimmie Sakamoto ruled that since I was not a member, I was not entitled to speak and it was time to get back to the issues at hand. I sat down amid good-natured joshing. But I knew right then that JACL had great potential value, that it needed a lot of help, and that I wanted to be part of its future.

I realized I could help JACL extend its geographic boundaries and simultaneously become part of its leadership by organizing a new District Council in my part of the country. JACL at the time had three District Councils—Northern California, Southern California, and Pacific Northwest. The constitution provided that three chapters in an area could petition for their own District Council, and its chairman automatically became a member of the National Board that governed JACL's affairs. There already was a nucleus of a chapter in Salt Lake City, where Joe Grant had founded a Nisei organization in 1935. There was another group in nearby Ogden, and I knew Nisei in southeastern Idaho around Pocatello, Blackfoot, Rexburg, and Idaho Falls who could be persuaded to form the third chapter. These groups were primarily social clubs, and we gathered from time to time just to get together. I figured it would be easy to sell them on JACL. Before long JACL had three new chapters in the Intermountain District and I became its chairman and a member of the National Board.

In the fall of 1938 I enrolled in several prelaw courses at the University of Utah. Through the National Youth Administration, a federal aid program, I also got a part-time job as Mrs. Van Winkle's assistant coaching the West High debate team. Senator Thomas was running for reelection, and he welcomed me to his volunteer staff again, this time with greater responsibilities. During this period I also became more active in the broader community. I joined fund-raising efforts for the State Committee on Infantile Paralysis, the Red Cross, and the Community Chest, and became the youngest member of the Utah Conference on Human Relations. I even made time to write a manual, *Outline of Debate,* which was published by the Mormon Church for use in its speaking programs. Ultimately, more than 5,000 copies were distributed. The manual established for the first time uniform rules for churchwide competition in public speaking.

I was busy, and the months sped by. Another year passed and I was no closer to being able to attend law school. In the fall of 1939, Laverne Bane was able to get me hired, again through the National Youth Administration, as his part-time assistant to coach the university's freshman debate team while I also continued to help Mrs. Van Winkle at West High. The income was a pittance, but at least I was being paid to do what I enjoyed.

Over Labor day of 1940, JACL held its biennial convention in Portland, Oregon. I attended as the official representative of the Intermountain District, which was formally accepted into the organization. It was somewhat more subdued than the gathering two years previously in Los Angeles. War raged in Europe. President Roosevelt was being urged to declare at least a limited national emergency, and it seemed that soon the nation's young men, including Nisei, would be drafted for a year of military training. In the Far East, continued Japanese aggression in China strained relations with the United States, and there was much speculation that sooner or later Japan and the United States would clash.

Walter Tsukamoto, by then national JACL president, took note of the ominous outlook in his keynote address:

It is the duty of every American, and that means all of us who cherish the ideals of our democratic institutions, to be prepared to protect, defend and perpetuate our form of government and our way of life. . . . This love of country and duty is not, and must not be, colored by any thought of foreign ties. . . . The JACL—skeptics, ill-wishers, and minority opposition groups to the contrary notwithstanding—makes no compromise on the one and only reason for the existence of this organization: the maintenance and direction of every effort, program and activity as a patriotic body of American citizens to perpetuate forever our American ideals and institutions.

The possibility of war with Japan was something Japanese Americans did not want to think about. But the threat could not be ignored. As Tsukamoto had asserted, JACL loyalties were entirely with the United States. There was no question about that. Still, Japan was the land of our ancestry and our parents remained citizens of Japan because American laws denied them the right of naturalization. Obviously, sentimental ties existed. But I was pleased to hear Tsukamoto's address and even more encouraged that with no hesitation at all the convention passed strongly worded resolutions demanding that the Nisei be given equal rights with other Americans in serving their country.

Tsukamoto was succeeded as president by Saburo Kido. I knew no more about Kido than what I had been able to learn in Los Angeles two years earlier, but he seemed to be a popular choice. With Tsukamoto's warning still on my mind, I went home to lay the groundwork for a district convention in Salt Lake City over the Thanksgiving weekend.

That convention inadvertently gave me the opportunity to compose a document that gained more attention than anything I have ever written. We were putting together a souvenir program and found ourselves with a blank page. Unable to sell an advertisement to fill the space, I groped for an idea. I suppose I could have dreamed up something safe, like that old standby "Compliments of a Friend," but in the back of my mind was a thought that needed developing.

What I had in mind was a statement about what my country meant to me. In these cynical times such a statement might appear maudlin. In those days love of country was taken seriously. What I came up with in one furious writing session was a credo, a statement from the heart that told what Americanism meant to a Japanese American. This is what I wrote:

The Japanese-American Creed

I am proud that I am an American citizen of Japanese ancestry, for my very background makes me appreciate more fully the wonderful advantages of this nation. I believe in her institutions, ideals, and traditions; I glory in her heritage; I boast of her history; I trust in her future. She has granted me liberties and opportunities such as no individual enjoys in this world today. She has given me an education befitting kings. She has entrusted me with the responsibilities of the franchise. She has permitted me to build a home, to earn a livelihood, to worship, think, speak, and act as I please—as a free man equal to every other man.

Although some individuals may discriminate against me, I shall never become bitter or lose faith, for I know that such persons are not representative of the majority of the American people. True, I shall do all in my power to discourage such practices, but I shall do it in the American way: aboveboard, in the open, through courts of law, by education, by proving myself to be worthy of equal treatment and consideration. I am firm in my belief that American sportsmanship and attitude of fair play will judge citizenship and patriotism on the basis of action and achievement, and not on the basis of physical characteristics.

Because I believe in America, and I trust she believes in me, and because I have received innumerable benefits from her, I pledge myself to do honor to her at all times and in all places; to support her Constitution; to obey her laws; to respect her flag; to defend her against all enemies. foreign or domestic; to actively assume my duties and obligations as a citizen, cheerfully and without reservations whatsoever, in the hope that I may become a better American in a greater America.

The idealism of youth runs like a golden thread through the credo. Some of what I had to say was more in hope than reality. I was barely earning a livelihood, and certainly I was in no position to build a home. But I had hopes, I was looking into the far future, I wrote in all sincerity; and never have I had occasion to change my mind about the meaning of America. Senator Thomas entered the creed into the *Congressional Record*. The *Record* has become a catch-all for everything from newspaper editorials to prize-winning pickle recipes, but in those days it was a great honor to be recognized. In his introduction Senator Thomas said the creed "has come to be accepted as representing the true sentiments of American citizens of Japanese ancestry . . . and reflects the true American spirit and the American way." The creed has been widely reprinted. Years later Masao Satow, who worked closely with me as national secretary of JACL, hand-lettered it in elegant Old English script and copies were presented to persons the organization wished to honor.

1940 was also the year I was picked for the Yamagata Award, presented to the "Nisei of the Year" for "meritorious achievement" by the Japanese Young People's Association of Chicago. S. Yamagata, for whom the award was named, was an Issei who had been a successful Chicago businessman and had taken a deep interest in the Nisei. Walter Tsukamoto had been the first winner the previous year. I was the second and last, for the war years caused the award to be discontinued. (In 1950 JACL began its "Nisei of the Biennium" award and I was fortunate enough to win it.)

As much as the Yamagata award meant to me, I was even more moved by the endorsements written on my behalf by so many friends. Among those who submitted letters to the selection committee were Senator William King, Senator Elbert Thomas, and Chief Justice William Folland of the Utah Supreme Court. Some of them noted that I had been chosen as one of two outstanding citizens of Salt Lake City by the Junior Chamber of Commerce at its Americanism Week program. Mrs. Musser, who had offered me four years at Harvard, wrote that I was an "outstanding example of a youth born in America of alien parentage who has assimilated himself into the American cultural pattern." Mayor Ab Jenkins of Salt Lake City, better known as holder of numerous automobile speed records set on the Bonneville salt flats, said: "It is rare indeed that any young American regardless of parentage renders the service to his community that Mike Masaoka has done in Salt Lake City." Since I couldn't go to Chicago to claim the trophy, Bill Yamauchi, my onetime roommate, organized a testimonial banquet in Salt Lake City and Governor Herbert B. Maw made the presentation.

But none of these honors was helping me get into law school. Without money my prospects were no brighter than they had been three years earlier, and I couldn't continue as I had been. I sent out a feeler to Senator Thomas to see whether he could find a place for me on his staff. I also sought a full-time position with the University of Utah. Hanging over all my plans was the possibility of being drafted for military service. Like other young Americans I had registered for Selective Service in the summer of 1940. About a year later I was called up for induction, but doctors found I had flat feet, a small heart murmur, and bad teeth resulting from long neglect. I was classified as physically unsuitable for military service, but assured that I would be summoned again if the international situation became worse.

Early in February 1941 I received a telephone call that led to an inexplicable incident, one that continues to baffle me. The caller identified himself as a member of the Japanese consulate staff in San Francisco. He said that the new Japanese ambassador to the United States, Admiral Kichisaburo Nomura, had just reached the city from Tokyo en route to Washington and had expressed a desire to see me. Could I go to Ogden and meet him there when the Union Pacific train passed through?

I thought it was some silly joke. Why would an ambassador want to see me? Besides, I wasn't much impressed by the importance of an ambassador. I told the official I was too busy to go to Ogden, which was less than an hour's drive north, but if he wanted to come to Salt Lake City I could be found at the Colonial Hotel. Then I promptly forgot about it.

Several days later two long, black limousines, drew up to the Colonial. A tall, heavy man, unusually large for a Japanese, climbed out of one of the cars, waved aside an aide, and made his way into the fly-specked lobby. I recognized him immediately from his pictures as Admiral Nomura. After I introduced myself, he glanced around, and I sensed he was looking for privacy. In some confusion I escorted him up to my room. He took the only chair, and I sat on the bed. In halting but adequate English, the ambassador explained he was going to Washington on a solemn mission to try to avert the war that even then seemed inevitable. He said he understood I had traveled widely as a debater and he wanted to hear my assessment of Japan's problems with the United States.

Something about Admiral Nomura told me he was sincerely interested in hearing my opinions. I told him I thought the United States and Japan were on a collision course and war was inevitable unless Tokyo withdrew from China. He shook his head sadly. I told him that if there was war, I was sure America would prevail, and that the Nisei and most of the Issei would be loyal to the United States. He peered at me solemnly through his glasses, and I remember his words: "Masaoka-san, you are right. Whatever the circumstances, you must be loyal to your country. That is bushido, the way of the samurai." We spoke awhile longer, and then he made his way heavily down the stairway. He and his entourage reentered the limousines and headed back to Ogden to resume the rail trip to Washington. We know now, of course, that the good admiral did indeed strive mightily to prevent war, and that he was made a scapegoat by Tokyo's militarist government, which attacked Pearl Harbor even as he was talking peace in Washington.

The mystery is why he would go out of his way to see me. It was a great inconvenience for him to leave his train in Ogden, rent cars, and drive down to Salt Lake City. If I had known that he really wanted to talk with me, I would have found a way to go to Ogden. And what could I tell him that he and his aides didn't already know? But I have never forgotten his assurance that the Japanese understood we owed our total allegiance to the United States. The next time I saw Admiral Nomura was more than a decade later in Sugamo Prison in Tokyo, where he was being held by the Allied Occupation powers as a war criminal. I went to see him, and he remembered our earlier meeting. I assured him that so far as I was concerned, he was no war criminal but a man who loved peace.

At the end of the visit I asked the admiral if there was anything he wanted. He thought for a moment, then said: "Yes, there is one matter. I have heard the *Mikasa* is being desecrated by the Americans. Perhaps they do not understand. I would appreciate it very much if you could ask them to stop."

At the moment I had no idea what he was talking about. After several inquiries I learned the *Mikasa* had been Admiral Heihachiro Togo's flagship in the historic battle of Tsushima in 1905, when, to the world's astonishment, his command annihilated the Russian fleet. When she became obsolete the *Mikasa* was embedded in concrete at the Yokosuka naval base and preserved as a shrine. The U.S. Navy was using it for an enlisted men's beer hall. I made a few discreet calls. Presently the Navy found more suitable quarters for the men's relaxation.

The summer of 1941, as both Admiral Nomura and I had feared, was a time of steadily deteriorating relations between the

United States and Japan. Following a massive German invasion of the Soviet Union, Japan demanded military control over all French Indochina, and the Vichy government acceded. The United States retaliated on July 26 by placing an embargo on oil, freezing Japanese assets in the United States, and suspending shipping between the two nations. An economic boycott is the last step before outbreak of war; I sensed a complete rupture was coming but didn't know what to do about it.

Kido understood the seriousness of the situation much better than most other Nisei. JACL's Northern California District Council had scheduled a convention in Monterey the first week of August. Kido asked members of the National Board to meet with him to discuss some critical issues. I took a bus for California. What I encountered was vastly beyond anything I, or anyone else, could have anticipated.

Chapter 3

Anxious Times

I cannot vouch for the authenticity of the following anecdote but since the other principal vows it is true, and I have never known her to lie or even exaggerate, I must accept it as having happened.

My Greyhound bus from San Francisco to the JACL convention in Monterey stopped at San Jose to take on passengers. The bus was only partly filled, so I was sprawled out over two seats and engrossed in a newspaper. Two young Nisei ladies came aboard. I failed to notice them. That in itself makes the story suspect, for certainly I would have been aware of two pretty girls. One, I learned later, was named Etsu Mineta. The way she tells the story, my feet were thrust out into the aisle. To reach seats farther back, she and her friend had to step over my shoes, complaining under their breaths about inconsiderate, ill-mannered men.

That evening Dr. George Hiura of Sebastopol, whom I had met at the Portland convention, suggested we go to the mixer. I told him I didn't have a date and didn't know any girls. He said he'd arrange for a couple of blind dates at the convention dating bureau. His date turned out to be a very slim, comely girl who attracted me immediately. I hardly noticed my date. George, who as I recall was married, was simply looking for congenial companionship, so it wasn't difficult to persuade him to trade. She told me her name was Etsu Mineta, that she lived in San Jose, where her father was an insurance broker, and that we had shared the same bus earlier that day. I had to confess I hadn't noticed her. Two and a half years later we were married.

There was a great deal of conversation at the convention about worsening relations between the United States and Japan. War was no longer something vaguely on the distant horizon. It seemed to be a definite possibility. For most Nisei there was no question of divided loyalties. But it disturbed me to see some JACL leaders articulating their loyalty in such an awkward manner as this statement published as an interview in a Los Angeles newspaper:

> I am myself certain that we will be loyal to America. My faith is that when the supreme moment arrives we shall make a definite decision that our first call is America. I recognize that a certain percentage of our people are pro-Japanese. Whatever feeling we may have for Japan we have to obliterate.

To me, it was outrageous that Nisei spokesmen should be talking about making a "definite decision" when the "supreme moment" arrives. They should have been speaking out strongly in condemnation of Japanese aggression on the Asian mainland and supporting American preparedness measures. Thus I am pleased that the convention passed two strong resolutions:

> Whereas the loyalty and allegiance of the American citizen is of such vital importance at this time, be it resolved that the JACL reaffirm its allegiance to the Constitution of the United States of America and the nation for which it stands.
>
> Whereas it is the duty and the obligation of every citizen to support and participate in the various national defense activities, be it therefore resolved that the Northern California District Council urges all chapters and their members to do everything possible to assist in any activities in the promotion of national defense and its welfare.

Kido was apprehensive about the problems that Japanese Americans might face if war should break out. He was also aware that JACL was ill prepared to meet those problems. His immediate objective was to strengthen JACL by increasing its membership, establishing new chapters, and through them, working with government officials in various parts of the country to safeguard the rights of Issei. I doubt that anyone had serious fears about what might happen to the Nisei; after all, we were American citizens with all the rights and obligations that that implied, our Nisei buddies were serving in the nation's armed forces, and if we had to go to war with Japan, our hearts would be heavy but there was no reason to question our loyalty.

To help overcome JACL's shortcomings, Kido felt it was time for the organization to hire an executive secretary. Since a majority of National Board members were present, Kido polled us informally about qualifications desirable in such an employee. We were basically agreed a JACL employee must be fluent in Japanese as well as English, have good rapport with the Issei, have a knowledge of Japanese community affairs and JACL history, be able to speak in public, and have the poise and experience to meet with government officials on their own terms. In other words, he must be an articulate leader who could deal with both Issei and American communities. I was acquainted with only a few Nisei, but I was aware of one who met all the qualifications. That would be Togo Tanaka of Los Angeles, a Phi Beta Kappa graduate of UCLA. He was working in the English section of *Rafu Shimpo,* a daily newspaper, and obviously destined for more important things.

But Kido stunned me when he asked me to take the job. I pointed out that having grown up outside the West Coast's Japanese-American communities I was totally unable to meet most of the requirements. Besides, I said, I was still hoping to get into law school and had applied for a full-time job at the University of Utah. Kido asked me to join JACL for just one year. He said he and the organization needed help desperately and promised to tutor me on the fine points of Japanese-American psychology and Japanese community politics. In the end I agreed only to give his request serious consideration.

I took my dilemma to Senator Thomas and asked his advice. He knew little of JACL itself, but he had vivid memories of the harsh treatment German Americans experienced in the hysteria of World War I. He had fears about what might happen to Japanese Americans in case of war, and he urged me to do whatever I could to head off problems. In the end, the opportunity to be of service to the Japanese-American community won out over my personal plans, and I told Kido I would sign on for just one year.

Kido underscored the urgency of the situation by summoning an emergency meeting of the National Board only a week after the Monterey convention. It was held in his San Francisco office, which also served as National JACL headquarters. It was the first time I had seen the place where Kido worked. His office was in an old clapboard house on Webster street on the edge of Japantown. Like other San Francisco homes of that vintage it was in need of paint, and the bay windows did nothing to give it dignity. Kido's office, incredibly cluttered, was up a half flight of stairs from the street. I got the impression his family lived on the top floor.

Ten members of the National Board and five invited guests were present. The officers were Kido; Ken Matsumoto of Los Angeles, vice-president; James Sugioka of San Benito, California, secretary; the four District Council chairmen, Yoshio Nakaji from Southern California, Tom Shimasaki from Northern California, Tom Iseri from the Pacific Northwest, and I from the Intermountain District; and the three past national presidents, Dr. Tom Yatabe, Jimmie Sakamoto, and Walter Tsukamoto. The guests were Togo Tanaka, chairman of the public relations committee; Kay Hirao, chairman of the next convention to be held in Oakland in 1942; Evelyn Kirimura, who was editor of JACL's monthly *Pacific Citizen;* the newspaper's business manager, Vernon Ichisaka; and JACL's historian, Teiko Ishida.

Quickly disposing of some minor matters, Kido outlined the need for a paid, full-time national secretary to help the elected officers meet the problems that loomed ahead. He explained that he had talked with me and that I had agreed to take the job. Kido then proposed that the four districts be assessed a total of $5,000 to pay my salary and expenses for a year. While the National Board had authority to hire me, the District Councils had to confirm my appointment by raising the necessary funds, which they soon did.

In accepting the job I laid out a five-point program: to make JACL a truly national organization, to establish channels of communications with government officials, to launch a program to demonstrate to the public that Japanese Americans were indeed unhyphenated Americans, to open job opportunities for the Nisei, and to expand JACL membership. It was an ambitious agenda, but the members of the National Board agreed enthusiastically that it was needed.

Like most Japanese Americans of that time, the members of the National Board were reluctant to talk about salary, and I didn't press the matter, since I wasn't taking the position for the money. It was only after I had started work that Kido told me my pay would be $125 a month, which I calculated would be barely adequate to live on if I was frugal and could cadge some free meals. In any event, it was less than I was earning from my various part-time jobs in Salt Lake City. To make up for the inadequate salary, Kido gave me a fancy title: National Secretary and Field Executive. He explained that as field executive I could make independent decisions in the field, but I was never sure what that meant.

There was a lot more about JACL that I learned quickly after I packed up my few belongings in Salt Lake City, said goodbye to my room in the Colonial Hotel, and moved into equally small and drab quarters in the Aki Hotel in San Francisco's Japantown.

The first day at work I noted that Kido's office had only two rooms and asked him where my office would be. He cleared off a little desk next to where his secretary sat and said I could use it and share her telephone. After I got over that I suggested it might be a good idea if he could introduce me to the mayor, Angelo J. Rossi, to let him know I was on the job. Kido thought that was funny. "I've never met the man," he said when he'd stopped laughing. "We've been trying for ten years to get him to come out to one of our dinners, and he never shows up. Sometimes he'll send us a message for one of our convention programs, but he won't see us."

I couldn't believe it. In Salt Lake City I knew almost everyone who counted. It was no problem to reach them by telephone. "Look," I told Kido, "you're the president of a national organization and you can deliver a lot of votes. You're an important attorney. Why don't you call him up and tell him you want to see him?" Kido just shrugged, so I telephoned the mayor's office for an appointment. I couldn't get past the second assistant secretary. I called Governor Culbert Olson's office in Sacramento. I couldn't even get through to his appointments secretary. So that was the reality of life in the big city. For the first time, the magnitude of my job sank in. JACL talked big about civic responsibilities, but Japanese Americans were political nonentities. It was obvious that organizing new JACL chapters would be only a small part of what I had to do.

To begin with, JACL played only a minor role in most Japanese-American communities. The Issei, who as aliens could not belong to JACL, since membership was limited to citizens, were still the community leaders. They controlled the purse strings and many were unfriendly toward JACL, fearing it as a threat to their political power. The Issei worked through the various Japanese

Associations which, in a perfectly legitimate way, had ties to the Japanese consulates. In various communities the churches, both Christian and Buddhist, wielded greater influence on Nisei than JACL even on matters outside of religion. JACL had a loyal core of members, but their numbers were small and few chapters were well organized.

Before I had time to feel frustrated, Kido suggested I go to Long Beach for a Southern California District convention over the Labor Day holiday. As it turned out the main speaker was not a government official, as one would expect in a time of rising international tensions, but Leo Carrillo, a movie actor of some prominence who specialized in Mexican dialect roles. In his speech Carrillo made a big point of asserting that since he was of Mexican descent he was aware of discrimination and promised to help the Nisei fight persecution. That was the kind of assurance the Nisei wanted to hear, and the applause was vigorous.

Four months later, a month after the attack on Pearl Harbor, Carrillo was one of the first to demand that Japanese Americans be chased off the West Coast. In a well-publicized telegram to Congressman Leland Ford of Los Angeles County, Carrillo said: "I travel every week through a hundred miles of Japanese shacks on the way to my ranch, and it seems that every farmhouse is located on some strategic elevated point. Let's get them off the coast into the interior. You know and I know the Japanese situation in California. The eastern people are not conscious of this menace. May I urge you in behalf of the safety of the people of California to start action at once." Ford did, although he didn't need much urging. But that's getting ahead of the story.

The first few weeks on the job were spent being tutored by Kido, getting acquainted with San Francisco Nisei, and going out to nearby North California chapters to meet JACL members. On the whole I was well received, but I never seemed to be able to bring out the kind of crowd I thought a JACL meeting deserved. Very few businessmen of the community would show up. Caucasian community leaders—members of town councils and state legislators, with whom the Nisei should have been well acquainted—were conspicuous by their absence. Obviously we had a lot to do to establish pipelines to the establishment.

Kido's tutelage was invaluable. He gave me a crash course on

Japanese-American history—how the Chinese had been recruited as laborers in California starting about the time of the gold rush, and how the Japanese replaced them beginning about 1890 after Chinese immigration was prohibited. He reminded me that the citizenship of the Nisei was their most precious possession. It distinguished them from the Issei, who were legally barred from naturalization and understandably maintained their links to Japan. He told me that he was convinced JACL would be wise to demonstrate its independence from Japanese influence by keeping its distance from Issei organizations like the Japanese Associations, and that we should steer clear of relationships with the Japanese consulates and representatives of the banks and big trading companies stationed in the United States.

Kido emphasized that impoverished as JACL was, under no circumstances should it accept money from Japanese groups no matter how innocently it was offered. Later, when any links with Japan were held suspect, JACL's record gave it priceless credibility with government officials.

Kido also filled me in on the Nisei. Los Angeles Nisei, he said, were generally more aggressive than their San Francisco counterparts, more forward-looking, more inclined to be innovative. If they were for me, they would give me complete support. If not, watch out. There were so many Nisei in Southern California that they had numerous organizations and were inclined to be even less dependent on JACL than Nisei in other areas. JACL had been founded in the Pacific Northwest, Kido said, but he was dubious about the area's dedication to the movement if it weren't for a few influential individuals like Jimmie Sakamoto and Clarence Arai. This was Kido's way of saying grass-roots support must be developed.

JACL itself was not a monolithic body. It was a relatively loose confederation of local chapters. The national body was divided into four District Councils, the Northern California District being the most strongly organized. A regional rivalry existed between the Northern California and the Southern California districts, with the Pacific Northwest District usually allying itself with Northern California, and my Intermountain District all by itself. It would be necessary to build a more unified national organization.

One of my pet ideas was that JACL should encourage Caucasians to join, so that it wouldn't be a strictly racial organization.

Kido argued that the Nisei had special problems which could best be addressed by a racially restricted organization. Bringing others into the membership, he contended, would dilute Nisei ability to work on those problems, and he even expressed concern JACL might be made the tool of some ambitious politician if it became an integrated group. In view of JACL's disorganized state, that seemed to be a remote possibility. I felt there were many Caucasians interested in our problems and they could be helpful working inside the organization.

On weekends when I wasn't traveling on JACL business I'd try to get down to San Jose to see Etsu Mineta. For many reasons she attracted me in a way that no other girl had. She was aware of JACL's goals and approved of what I was trying to do. She was well-read and could discuss national or world affairs. She obviously was from a cultured and well-educated family. She was pretty. And she paid me the ultimate compliment of being interested in what I had to say.

The Mineta family was as close as my own had been, but in quite a different way. Etsu's father, Kunisaku, had been able to give his family many amenities. He was a man of culture and considerable intellectual achievement and was highly regarded in the community. Etsu's mother, Kane, was a quiet woman who reminded me in many ways of my own mother, although her well-ordered home, decorated with Japanese antiques and *objets d'art,* reflected a genteel background that I had not known in Salt Lake City. And she was an excellent cook, a talent that did not go unnoticed by a young fellow existing largely on cheap restaurant food.

Etsu was the second of five Mineta offspring. Her older sister, Aya, was working in San Francisco. Etsu was clerking in a small Japanese gift shop in San Jose. The third sister was Helen, a secretary in the speech department at San Jose State College. All three girls were college graduates and had musical training. Etsu's degree was in home economics and she had studied piano. While going to college Etsu had worked as the bread girl in the dining room of San Jose's leading hotel. Later I was to learn that this experience gave her a certain poise; she wasn't shy about talking to strangers, as many Nisei girls were. Then came two boys, Albert and Norman, with whom I became good friends. (Albert served in military intelligence during the war, was stationed in Japan during the Occupation, earned his medical degree at the University of California, and now is a pathologist in San Jose.) Norman was nine, going on ten, when I began to visit the Mineta home. He was a mischievous sort, and sometimes I had to bribe him to go away so I could visit undisturbed with Etsu. (In 1974 Norman, who had grown up to become mayor of San Jose, ran for a seat in the United States House of Representatives, won handily, and became the first mainland Nisei to be elected to Congress. In 1986 he was elected to his seventh consecutive term.)

Before long I began to think of asking Etsu to marry me eventually, if and when I could support a wife, but the war came before we could get really serious. She and her family were evacuated to Heart Mountain, Wyoming, and I went to Washington, D.C. Despite the pressure of my duties, somehow we kept in touch, but that, too, is getting ahead of the story. Once, late in the fall of 1941, I mentioned casually to Kido and Walt Tsukamoto that I was interested in one of the Mineta girls.

"Fine family," Kido observed. "Which one?"

"Etsu," I said.

Kido shook his head. "Etsu is a fine girl and pretty, too," he said. "But you'd be smarter to marry Helen."

I wanted to know why. Kido said: "Helen is a trained secretary. She can take dictation and be a lot of help to you."

I looked sharply at Kido. He was serious. I realized some time later that he was thinking in terms of getting two people to work for JACL for the price of one.

Not long after I returned from Los Angeles, Kido received a somewhat puzzling call from a man who identified himself as Curtis B. Munson from Washington, D.C. He said he wanted to see Kido about some rather important official business. I accompanied Kido to the meeting. Munson turned out to be an ordinary-looking individual with some impressive-looking State Department credentials. And we soon perked up when he began to talk. He made it clear that federal officials feared war with Japan was imminent. His assignment, he said, was to anticipate the problems Japanese Americans might face if war did come. Munson asked a good many questions about the attitudes of Japanese Americans, and he inquired about specific individuals. I knew few of them, but many were familiar to Kido. However, most of our conversations, which stretched out over three or four days and several times late into the night, had to do with the possibility of hysterical violence against Japanese Americans, and what sorts of precautions should be taken to protect them. We talked about many subjects, like Japanese aggression in China and the discussions going on in Washington between Secretary of State Cordell Hull and Japanese envoys, but always we would get back to problems Japanese Americans might face in case of war.

Kido was most concerned about what might happen in rural areas where there was still much resentment against Japanese farmers and urged that sheriff's offices be warned about possible trouble. I suggested that President Roosevelt get on the radio, perhaps in one of his popular fireside chats, and explain to all Americans that we were loyal citizens and not to be confused with the enemy, if it came to that, and that the nation was at war with Japan and not with Japanese Americans. Both Kido and I emphasized the need to get the message out to the American public, and we suggested that federal authorities get in touch with governors and mayors wherever numbers of Japanese Americans lived and solicit their understanding. Munson agreed these were good ideas and indicated he would see what he could do.

Munson asked about JACL, and after a while it became obvious that somehow he knew much about us already and was simply double-checking his impressions. He wanted to know about certain JACL leaders, not about their loyalty but whether they were strong individuals who could be depended on for leadership in an emergency. He mentioned specific names—Jimmie Sakamoto and Clarence Arai in Seattle, Mamo Wakasugi and Howard Nomura in Portland, Fred Tayama, Kay Sugahara, Joe Shinoda, Masao Satow, John Ando, and a host of others in Los Angeles, Franklin Chino in Chicago, George Yamaoka in New York. I had never heard of many of these people, but Kido was familiar with most. Munson seemed to understand our concerns, and both Kido and I felt that he was genuinely anxious to help us.

Throughout these meetings ran an unspoken theme: the federal government is concerned about the welfare of its citizens, but at the same time the citizens must cooperate with their government. These meetings no doubt had a great deal to do with our decision to work in every way possible with the federal authorities.

But many years were to pass before I really understood the

importance of our sessions with Munson. He, it turned out, was a well-to-do Chicago businessman who had been recruited into what might be described as President Roosevelt's personal intelligence network. His assignment was to assess the problems Japanese Americans might pose, and face, in the event of war. After his West Coast tour he filed a confidential report that did not surface to public view until long after World War II. In one section of his report he said:

> Nisei . . . are universally estimated from 90 to 98 percent loyal to the United States if the Japanese-educated element of the Kibei [citizens whose parents were Issei but who were educated largely in Japan] is excluded. The Nisei are pathetically eager to show this loyalty. They are not Japanese in culture. They are foreigners to Japan. Though American citizens they are not accepted by Americans, largely because they look differently and can be easily recognized. The Japanese American Citizens League should be encouraged, the while an eye is kept open to see that Tokyo does not get its finger in this pie—which it has in a few cases attempted to do. The loyal Nisei hardly knows where to turn. Some gesture of protection or wholehearted acceptance of this group would go a long way to swinging them away from any last romantic hankering after old Japan. They are not oriental or mysterious, they are very American. . . .

In another part of his report Munson wrote:

> For the most part the local Japanese are loyal to the United States or, at worst, hope that by remaining quiet they can avoid concentration camps or irresponsible mobs. We do not believe that they would be at the least any more disloyal than any other racial group in the United States with whom we went to war. Those being here are on a spot and they know it.

And in still another section Munson said flatly: "There is no Japanese 'problem' on the Coast."

Unknown to us in San Francisco, although he was well known to some JACL leaders in Southern California, Lieutenant Commander Kenneth D. Ringle of Naval Intelligence was on a similar intelligence assignment and making the same kind of reports attesting to the loyalty of Japanese Americans if war should come. Tragically, these reports apparently were given scant attention in

Washington while the decision was made to oust Japanese Americans from their homes "as a matter of military necessity," and they remained buried in the archives until postwar scholars dug them out.

What would JACL have done about resisting evacuation, which resulted in the arbitrary suspension of constitutional rights and the imprisonment of 115,000 Japanese Americans on the basis of race, if we had been aware of Munson's and Ringle's reports? That's a good question that deserves discussion in subsequent chapters. At the time, however, we had only an inkling of the importance and scope of Munson's mission, and no idea what he was reporting to Washington. After he completed talks with us, he vanished as mysteriously as he had arrived. Kido and I reviewed at length our experience with him, but generally we observed his warning to tell no one about our meetings and make no notes about what had been discussed.

Even so, his visit caused Kido and me to ponder JACL's organizational position and stance if war should come. We knew, of course, that the membership was totally behind our motto: "Better Americans in a Greater America." The big question was how to get this truth across to our fellow Americans.

The Nisei of our generation were the products of an educational system that promoted Americanism by rejecting one's ancestral heritage. Youngsters were told in grade school to speak English, to forget the alien tongue. The popular reasoning of the times was that if the old-country culture was so good, why had immigrants left it to come to the United States? In America, it was important to reject the past and embrace the present. The thrust of this kind of schooling resulted in rapid cultural if not racial assimilation. In any event, Kido and I agreed that one important way to combat the public hostility that Munson anticipated was to demonstrate how completely American we were. But in a society accustomed to seeing only stereotypes, it was easier to proclaim our Americanism than to convince the public that Orientals who looked like the enemy could indeed be Americans. So long as American society considered racial differences a problem, so long as it hadn't gotten around to recognizing the reality of a multiracial and multicultural society, it was wiser for us to focus on the similarities rather than the differences between us and the Caucasian majority.

We discussed this thesis with thoughtful white friends, and

nowhere did we hear conflicting opinions. JACL had been founded on the principle of militant Americanism, and that's the way it would continue, war or no war.

Some time in November I received a call from Senator Thomas. He said the federal Fair Employment Practices Commission headed by Mark Ethridge, editor of the two newspapers in Louisville, Kentucky, was conducting hearings in Los Angeles into job discrimination in defense industries. Senator Thomas said he understood many qualified Nisei were being denied employment, and he offered to get me scheduled as a witness if I wanted to testify. I hurriedly gathered some information and took the bus for Los Angeles, and for the first time JACL was represented in a federal hearing. The testimony must have done some good, since a small number of Nisei soon were hired for work in Southern California aircraft factories and other defense plants. But they failed to reap the benefits of the breakthrough. Within a few weeks Japan would attack Pearl Harbor, war would be declared, and the Nisei would be quickly fired even as tens of thousands of others were being recruited for work.

Late in November, Kido and I agreed it was time for me to head inland to organize new JACL chapters. Right after Thanksgiving I packed a suitcase and took the train for Salt Lake City en route to Denver, Greeley, Cheyenne, and points east. The reaction I encountered among Nisei in those towns was widely mixed. In some areas there was virtually no real awareness even among Nisei of worsening U.S.–Japanese relations, little concern about what might happen to Japanese Americans in case of war. That was understandable. The integration of Nisei in many communities was well advanced, and many felt no need for JACL, which of course had been my position in Salt Lake City some years earlier. In Denver's small Nisei group, I found it difficult to stir up much interest in JACL.

Disappointed but not discouraged, on Saturday, December 6, I headed for North Platte, Nebraska. The Reverend Hiram Kano, an Issei Episcopal minister who farmed on the side to support himself and his family, had promised a large gathering the next day of Nisei from eastern Colorado, eastern Wyoming, and western Nebraska. Isolated from other Japanese Americans, they were flattered to be getting some attention at last, and anxious to know what was going on. No one, least of all I, was prepared for what would happen.

Chapter 4

Friend or Foe?

The fifty or sixty Japanese Americans who greeted me in the basement meeting room of the North Platte Episcopal Church the morning of Sunday, December 7, 1941, made up probably the largest gathering of Nisei in the history of the area. Some of them had driven several hundred miles to attend. I never did learn how the sponsors spread the word that I would be speaking. There were only a few Japanese families in North Platte itself; most of the others farmed in scattered parts of the High Plains.

About 11:00 a.m. the meeting was called to order. At that hour, unknown to the nation's 130 million citizens, squadrons of Japanese carrier-based planes were droning through the predawn darkness toward the slumbering Hawaiian island of Oahu. At that hour they were less than sixty minutes from destiny. Blissfully ignorant of the onrushing tide of history, I rose after a brief introduction to speak of the heightening tensions in the Pacific and our government's concerns about the public's reaction toward Japanese Americans if war should come. I spoke about the Japanese American Citizens League's efforts to make the public aware that we were Americans, and about our need to win the recognition and backing of officials at all levels of government. On a map tacked to a wall, I pointed out the location of JACL chapters already in existence in inland areas and the places where I hoped new chapters would be formed, drawing circles of emphasis around places like Cheyenne, Denver, Pueblo, Scottsbluff, and North Platte. Inadvertently I was also outlining potential military targets—Cheyenne and Denver were the sites of air bases, Pueblo had a strategic steel mill, and North Platte was a railroad center.

The meeting had been going on for some time when several husky Caucasians quietly entered the room and approached the podium.

"Yes?" I inquired. "Anything we can do for you?"

"Are you Mike Masaoka?" one of them asked.

"Yes, I'm Masaoka."

"Would you mind coming outside with us for a minute?"

I assumed these were reporters from the local newspaper seeking an interview. A bit impatiently, I said: "Well, as you can see, I'm in the middle of some important business now. I'd be happy to talk to you when I'm finished. Would you mind waiting outside for a while?"

"This is urgent," one of them replied. "I'm afraid it can't wait." With that the two men pinned my arms to my sides and escorted me out of the room while the audience watched dumbfounded. My protests went unanswered as they escorted me to the city jail. I wondered whether I had been picked up for failing to get a license for a public meeting. Before locking me in a cell they told me of the attack on Pearl Harbor, where at the moment American ships were burning and American men dying. I stared at the officers in total disbelief. Even though I had been prepared for the possibility of war, the manner of its arrival made the news a ghastly, unbelievable joke. I said that I was an American citizen and demanded to know by what right they had seized me. They said they were acting under federal orders.

I spent a sleepless night in the jail cell as questions raced through my mind. What really had happened at Pearl Harbor? How had Japan dared to launch such a foolhardy attack? Were we now at war? I wasn't allowed to listen to a radio or read a newspaper. What was happening back at JACL headquarters, and in the Japanese-American communities in San Francisco, Los Angeles, Salt Lake City, and elsewhere? Were Mother and Joe and the rest of the family all right in Los Angeles? What about Etsu? And when would I get out of jail? Over and over, I kept asking myself how the authorities had known where to find me and why they wanted me. Eventually I figured the FBI had been tracking the progress of my eastward travels, although I had no idea why they would want to do that.

A long time later I learned that someone got around to telling the Nisei at the meeting that war had broken out, and they quietly dispersed to their homes. They didn't know where I had been taken and thought it wiser not to ask; no one came to the jail to inquire about me.

The next morning I was finally allowed to telephone Kido in San Francisco but warned not to reveal that I was in jail. When the connection was finally made I told Kido I had been unavoidably detained. He asked where I was staying, and I made up the name of a hotel. He urged me to get back to San Francisco as quickly as possible, and I told him I would try. Now Kido knew my general whereabouts, but I had been unable to tell him of the trouble I was having. Eventually he would find out. Until then I could look forward only to more time behind bars.

Help came more quickly than I expected. After getting my call, Kido went to an emergency meeting of the International Institute, which had been called to see what kind of help Japanese Americans might need. When Kido told the members of the board that I was stranded in Nebraska, they suggested they telephone to cheer me up. Annie Clo Watson, a YWCA executive, tried unsuccessfully to reach me, became more and more puzzled and alarmed, finally called the police in North Platte for help and located me. This time I was allowed to talk, and I asked Kido to get in touch with Senator Thomas. He must have reached the authorities quickly, for presently I was taken to the railroad station and put on a westbound train without so much as an apology.

That was the first of eighteen or nineteen times that I wound up in police custody for no reason other than that the country of my birth and citizenship was at war with the country of my ancestry. Never once was I charged; I was merely detained until unreasoning apprehensions about my identity and intent could be laid to rest. The second time was just a few hours after leaving North Platte. When the train stopped at Cheyenne, local lawmen walking through the cars spotted me and decided I needed looking into. This time I was wise enough to ask that the nearest FBI office check with Senator Thomas. Kido had instructed me to take a plane back, but there were no seats to be had. Finally, on Thursday, December 11, I reached San Francisco by train without further incident.

San Francisco's Japantown was strangely quiet, as though everyone was walking on tiptoe to avoid attracting attention. Fortunately there had been no violence against Japanese Americans anywhere in the country, perhaps because of precautions Munson had urged on local officials, but more likely because the entire country had been stunned by the attack on Pearl Harbor. Wisely, Japanese Americans kept a low profile. In San Francisco, patrol cars cruised the streets to keep order, but they were hardly needed.

Beneath the calm was anxiety and uncertainty. On Pearl Harbor day, FBI agents accompanied by uniformed police officers appeared at the homes of scores of Issei community leaders and took them into custody. These individuals, we were to learn, had been on the FBI's surveillance list for months, perhaps years, not because of any evidence of disloyalty, but because they held leadership positions in the community, or had business, cultural, or other ties with Japan. The majority were regarded by other members of the community as nice old men who might have strong sentimental attachments to Japan but wouldn't raise a finger to harm anyone. Some stores had been padlocked by the authorities. After dusk the streets of Japantown were deserted as everyone disappeared behind locked doors and drawn blinds. Thousands of miles away the Pearl Harbor attackers were racing for home. But West Coast cities were blacked out in fear of air raids.

Kido had been at a meeting in Japantown the morning of December 7 when they got word of the Pearl Harbor attack. He hastened to his office and turned on the radio for the frantic news flashes that were filling the air. When he was certain there was no mistake about the Japanese raid he reached into his files and found a brief statement which had been drafted at the suggestion of Curtis Munson. It was addressed to the president of the United States. Kido picked up the telephone, dialed Western Union, and dictated a message:

"In this solemn hour we pledge our fullest cooperation to you, Mr. President, and to our country. . . . we are ready and prepared to expend every effort to repel this invasion together with our fellow Americans." He signed it as president of the National Japanese American Citizens League.

When I reached San Francisco I found Kido being driven almost frantic by the demands of his clients and his JACL responsibilities. Families of Issei seized by the FBI pleaded with Kido to help get them released. Of course, he could do nothing for them. Japan's act of war had made them "enemy aliens," even though it was discriminatory American laws that had kept them in noncitizen status. And even though they were the parents of citizen Nisei, technically only the provisions of the Geneva Convention protected them. For the time being these Issei simply disappeared into protective custody behind the bars of city and county jails and Immigration Department holding pens while their families agonized over their fate. Businessmen found their credit curtailed or bank accounts tied up and came to Kido for help. Authoritative information about emergency regulations was lacking. I pitched in to try to bring order out of the near-chaos of Kido's office. City and federal authorities were busy, harassed, and confused, and it was almost impossible to sit down and talk with them. But that changed abruptly.

One morning soon after my return, Kido received a call from the FBI office asking him to come in with me. I didn't concern myself greatly about the summons, because we had become acquainted with some of the special agents before war's outbreak. Several of them were acquaintances from University of Utah days who had gone into the Bureau after getting their law degrees. Perhaps because of these contacts, Kido and I, as well as other JACL leaders, were to be accused by some Japanese Americans of being informers for the FBI—*inu,* "dogs," in the Japanese vernacular—who betrayed our people. I do not hesitate to say that I cooperated with the FBI to the best of my ability; the FBI was the federal agency entrusted with internal security, and it was the patriotic duty of all citizens to cooperate with any law enforcement agency. But we were never informers in the sense that we ran to the FBI with information in hopes of currying favor.

When we were questioned, which was often, we gave forthright answers. On these occasions Kido and I were able to assure FBI agents of the reliability of individuals they asked about, to assure them that drastic measures were unnecessary to maintain peace and order in the community. But some of the questioning could be nettlesome. For example, we might be asked how many Shinto shrines were in the area. I had no idea, and neither did Kido. When we said we didn't know, we would be accused of being uncooperative and evasive.

Nonetheless, I am certain that our contacts with the FBI and other government officials did much to ease the plight of many members of the community. As for the FBI's suspicions of disloyalty, what could we say? What we said was that we had no such fears about the Japanese Americans as a group, and history has vindicated the confidence we expressed to the federal agents.

On this particular occasion, we were ushered into a small conference room and left to cool our heels while waiting for N.J.L. (Nat) Pieper, the agent in charge. He entered alone. Businesslike but not hostile, he asked us questions of no great significance about the Japanese-American community, some of its members, and conditions in the East Bay Area, and we responded as best we could.

Abruptly Pieper's manner changed. His face hardened. He rose from his chair, leaned over the table, pointing his forefinger at us as though he were aiming a pistol, and rasped in a voice harsh with menace: "I expect you to answer my questions completely and accurately and without evasion. Do you understand? If I don't get the answers I want, I promise, neither of you will leave this room alive."

Pieper caught me speechless. The shoulder holster under his coat was clearly visible. I shot a quick glance at Kido. He was pale. Pieper continued to glare at us for what seemed a long time. I didn't know what to say. I didn't know what he was talking about. A sharp knock on the door snapped the tension. Someone stuck his head in and said: "Sir, Washington's on the phone." Without a word Pieper stalked out, slamming the door behind him. Kido and I looked at each other in silence. After a while another FBI agent opened the door. "Mr. Pieper says you may leave now," he said. We left quickly, knees trembling, indignant, angry, and more than a little frightened, not for ourselves so much as for all Japanese Americans, for it seemed the federal law enforcement agency had adopted Gestapo tactics against citizens. I realized with a sense of helplessness that aside from Senator Thomas, who had his own problems, there was no one in high places that we could go to for help and advice.

Once outside the Federal Building it took a while to regain our voices. "What do you suppose that was all about?" I asked.

"I don't have the slightest idea," Kido replied. "Pieper's always been cooperative up to now. Mike, I don't think we'd better say anything about this until we find out what's happening. No use getting people more worried than they already are."

We never did find out. After a while I began to believe that Pieper had staged a carefully scripted drama for our benefit. He had given us the old nice-guy-bad-guy treatment; he was showing us that he could be pleasant toward us or he could be tough, and we'd better cooperate. That, of course, is what we had intended to do all along. That was only natural. We had nothing to hide, and nothing to gain by being uncooperative. We needed their help as much as they needed ours. But Pieper's performance raised some troubling doubts.

Years later, after I had an opportunity to exchange notes with some Nisei leaders, I learned that other FBI agents had put on nice-guy-bad-guy performances for their benefit. Was it something they learned in the FBI academy? For the uninitiated like Kido and me, Pieper had staged a thought-provoking performance.

The burdens placed by community needs on JACL headquarters were much too heavy for Kido and me to handle, even with plenty of volunteer help. The San Francisco chapter's response was to hire Henry Tani as its full-time executive secretary, with offices in the Kinmon Gakuen, the Japanese language school, which had been closed after war's outbreak. There was enough room in the chapter's offices for me, and I gratefully moved in next door to Tani. Much the same sort of activity was going on in other centers of Japanese-American population. The Seattle chapter opened a full-time office. So did Los Angeles. In smaller communities, volunteers manned service centers. Nisei men and women who had lost their jobs in the nervousness that followed Pearl Harbor showed up unbidden to help answer inquiries, gather and distribute food to families whose breadwinners had been picked up by the FBI, seek out employment opportunities, and help in whatever other ways they could. But in many areas they were hardly prepared to take on these responsibilities.

The reality was that the FBI had seized more than a thousand prominent Issei within hours after the outbreak of war, stripping Japanese-American communities of their leaders. Most of the remaining Issei were understandably reluctant to step forward. The result was a gaping leadership vacuum into which JACL, as the only organized civic organization left, was inevitably drawn. And oddly enough, Nisei by the hundreds rushed to join JACL. Those who had been indifferent or even hostile became members of local chapters. Some realized for the first time that JACL's goals were worth supporting and wished to be part of it. And some came into JACL's fold in the hope that membership would serve as proof of their loyalty.

Immediately after the outbreak of war, the Federal Reserve

Bank froze the accounts of everyone with a Japanese name, citizens and aliens alike. This posed an enormous problem for families as well as businessmen. I brought the situation to the attention of Senator Thomas. What he was able to do I don't know, but several days later the rule was eased to enable people to withdraw $100 a month from savings accounts for living expenses.

That emergency taken care of, I turned my attention to two areas of public information, internal and external.

Federal authorities had clamped down on Japanese-language newspapers to prevent possible subversive use; what they didn't realize was that the press was necessary for getting information out to the Issei, an important segment of the population that read nothing but Japanese. Without reliable information the Issei could not understand what the government wanted of them, and damaging rumors could flourish. The *Nichibei* in San Francisco, headed by Yasuo Abiko, a Nisei, was permitted to publish, but other newspapers were shut down. I assembled a team of translators to produce news bulletins which were mimeographed and airmailed to the fifty-odd JACL chapters, which in turn reproduced them for local distribution. As simple as this project was, it kept the communities from disintegrating.

The external education program involved getting our story out to the American public—announcing that we were outraged by the attack on Pearl Harbor, that we would do everything in our power to bring about victory for our country, that we would do nothing to hurt America. This was easy enough to say, but more difficult to demonstrate, particularly to people who saw only our Japanese faces.

We could profess loyalty to the United States, but it was our burden to prove it. JACL urged its members to cooperate with the authorities, buy war bonds, volunteer for civil defense units, sign up for first-aid classes and donate blood, look for good newspaper publicity, and, in short, do everything to project a favorable patriotic image and to counter rumors about Japanese spies, mysterious radio signals, and flashing lights along the coast presumably signaling enemy submarines offshore. (In one widely circulated story, signal lights were reported on a bluff overlooking the ocean. They turned out to be a kerosene lamp used by an elderly Japanese farmer on his way to the outhouse in the middle of the night.)

Our strategy appeared to be working. In the waning days of

December 1941, the hostility toward Japanese Americans seemed to have stabilized, if indeed it was not fading. One reason may have been that Munson and Commander Ringle had recommended that someone high in government tell the nation that it was confident of the loyalty of Japanese Americans. In fact, Attorney General Francis Biddle had gone on the radio to urge calm.

I was encouraged enough to issue a message—and warning—of my own to JACLers on the eve of the new year:

A year ago, although dark clouds loomed on the horizon, few—if any—of us anticipated a war, least of all with Japan, the land from whence our parents came. We stoutly and vociferously insisted that we were all 100 percent Americans and that we only wanted a chance to prove it. Today we are at war. Today, the chance to prove that boast is ours. Today, we are on the proverbial spot.

Since Japan's treacherous attack upon American lives and territory some four weeks ago, the American public at large has been most considerate and sympathetic of our precarious position. The time has come when we must show our appreciation to our government and our true friends who went out of their way to demonstrate their trust and confidence in us as 100 percent Americans. We cannot let them down. We cannot let America down—for those people exemplify the finest spirit of American goodwill and sportsmanship. America is our only home. We are pledged to her preservation and perpetuation.

Just because many of the restrictions against the Japanese are being relaxed and conditions seem to be returning to normalcy, we must not dismiss the troubles of the past month as a horrible nightmare and confidently await a return to our former status. Actually, conditions are becoming worse. The longer the war drags on—and casualty lists are published, West Coast cities are shelled or bombed, atrocities are committed—the tougher our situation will become. Public sympathy may wear away and, perhaps, hate and prejudice will replace the present tolerance and forbearance.

We must gird our loins, as it were, tighten our belts, and prepare for the hardest fight in our generation—a fight to maintain our status as exemplary Americans who, realizing that modern war demands great sacrifices, will not become bitter or lose faith in the heritage which is ours as Americans in spite of what may come; a fight that will not be won in a week, or a month or even a year, a fight which will test our mettle and our courage; a fight in which we must not only make heroic sacrifices equal to or greater than those made on the battlefield but also a fight in which we will be subjected to suspicions, persecutions, and possibly downright injustices.

Ours is a difficult task, and yet the very tragedy of our position becomes a great challenge, a challenge to win our way through the ordeals ahead in such a commendable manner that we shall win for ourselves and our posterity a pinnacle in American society from which no one can ever dislodge us, or question our loyalty or doubt our sincerity. . . .

This was a message far more prophetic than anyone could possibly realize as the year 1942 dawned. In our relief that America understood us, we had failed to understand the virulence of the anti-Orientalism that for half a century had underlain the West Coast's psyche, and how close it was to the surface. The wound was opened by the attack on Pearl Harbor, and it took only a little scratching to cause it to fester into something ugly and dangerous.

The attack were minor in the beginning. Perhaps the first important blow against our integrity was an item in Damon Runyon's column, "The Brighter Side," syndicated in Hearst and other newspapers. Early in January, Runyon reported that health inspectors had found a powerful radio transmitter in a Japanese rooming house and warned of the ever-present danger of enemy agents in the United States. The report was totally without foundation, but it was enough to touch off new rumors about Japanese spies and saboteurs. The next day, John B. Hughes, a popular Mutual radio network commentator stationed in Los Angeles, began a series of broadcasts attacking the Justice Department for its alleged failure to root out Japanese Americans loyal to Japan. Syndicated Hearst columnist Henry McLemore took up the cry, demanding a roundup of Japanese Americans and injecting a new element of racial hatred by urging the nation to have no patience "with the enemy or with anyone whose veins carry his blood." Scripps-Howard columnist Westbrook Pegler wrote: "The Japanese in California should be under guard to the last man and woman right now and to hell with *habeas corpus* until the danger is over."

What should not be forgotten is that 1942 was an election year. The call for unity behind the war effort was likely to eliminate most domestic issues as political footballs, but the Japanese Americans proved to be a convenient target. As someone remarked, they were a minority big enough to be kicked around, but not so big that they would kick back effectively. And so the hate campaign picked up momentum with politicians at all levels suddenly discovering Japanese Americans were an extraordinary danger to the national security. And they made it their political and patriotic duty to remind the public of it as often and as forcefully as possible.

It was a terribly frustrating feeling to watch the hate building up on the basis of lies, distortions, and half-truths, fabrications that fed on old prejudices and nurtured latent fears. After Pearl Harbor there had been stories of Nisei acts of disloyalty during the attack; the truth was that Nisei had joined in the defense of the islands, lined up to donate blood for the wounded, shouldered rifles to patrol the beaches. Now on the mainland there were widespread stories about arms caches which turned out to be sporting guns and ammunition in hardware stores, and hidden stocks of explosives which in reality were small amounts of dynamite farmers kept for blasting stumps. JACL began getting threatening telephone calls. Anyone who looked Asian could expect to be stared at, jostled, intimidated, spat on. Japanese merchants and restaurant operators reported a sharp drop in business.

I wanted to fight back with the truth that America had nothing to fear from Americans with Japanese faces, but there was no way to reach the media as effectively as the rabble-rousers could. As Hitler had demonstrated, the truth never quite catches up with a lie, especially when the media were more interested in the sensational than the unexciting facts.

But there were exceptions. Chester Rowell of the *San Francisco Chronicle* was one of the few editorial voices of fair play. Another was Lawrence Davies, West Coast correspondent of the *New York Times*. Upton Close was the voice of reason on the radio. These were journalists of principle who refused to be caught up by the hysteria, but there were not enough like them.

In an effort to counter the rising hostility, Harry Kingman, YMCA director at the University of California in Berkeley, and his wife, Ruth, organized what was called the Fair Play Committee. A number of educators, churchmen, and civil-rights leaders lent their names to it, but they were no more effective than an earthen dam before a flood.

In the beginning the talk was of moving Japanese aliens, the Issei, out of sensitive coastal areas and from the vicinity of airports, aircraft factories, power plants, and military installations. This concern was at least understandable, since they technically were enemy aliens. But advocates of such a program sought to justify their positions by distortions. They found a sinister conspiracy in the fact that many Japanese were farming near sensitive areas, whereas the truth was that they had settled on cheap, isolated, unwanted land and had been followed there by factories for an expanding industrial establishment along with the necessary highways, bridges, and power lines.

Talk of relocating the Issei raised many fears. Where would they go? Voluntary relocation appeared to be an impossibility for most families, and the alternative had to be detention camps. Concentration camps for our alien parents, many of them elderly, was abhorrent. And what about their citizen children? Certainly many Nisei would want to accompany their parents into confinement to make sure they were taken care of. Would families be permitted to stay together? Kido and I took these questions and doubts to trusted Caucasian friends like Annie Clo Watson, Galen Fisher (who headed the Institute of Pacific Relations and had been a missionary in Japan), Monroe Deutsch (who was provost of the University of California), attorneys James Purcell and A. L. Wirin, and many others. These were courageous individuals who dared criticism and even ostracism to stand up for justice, but their influence was limited in the face of rising public anger and hysteria. Perhaps if they had been aware of the report Munson had filed, they might have been more effective in their efforts to help us.

During this early January period virtually the entire focus was on the alien group. After all, the Nisei were citizens, and who ever heard of a democracy treating its citizens like prisoners of war? Along with meetings with friends, Kido and I were involved in a series of conferences with various security officials, some initiated by us, others by the authorities. I remember in particular one session with military officers in San Jose where the mass internment of aliens was brought up. I tried to impress on them the faith we had in the loyalty of the parent generation. Let them stay in their homes, I urged, and we Nisei will volunteer for a combat battalion to fight against the Japanese. We'll vouch for their loyalty by our willingness to fight and die for our country if necessary, and they in turn would serve as hostages to guarantee our loyalty.

One of the generals waved me off. "The Army's policy is opposed to segregated units except in the case of Negroes," he said, "and we certainly don't believe in keeping people as hostages. And of course we cannot use you people in the Pacific; the danger of confusing you with the Japs would be too great." But the government in time would reverse that policy on all three counts.

Late in January the press carried disturbing news from Washington. Congressman Leland M. Ford, Southern California Republican and friend of actor Leo Carrillo, announced he was urging federal officials to move "all Japanese, American-born and alien," into concentration camps. This was the first indication that responsible individuals were advocating action against citizens. The congressman advanced a strange piece of logic: if the Nisei were loyal, they should accept internment as their contribution to the war effort. In other words, they should cooperate in the violation of some of America's fundamental principles in order to safeguard those principles. In a later time American troops in Vietnam would follow the same logic to destroy a village in order to save it.

Ford had no trouble getting the California congressional delegation to support his idea, and together they posed a powerful pressure group in Washington.

It was also about this time that California's Governor Culbert L. Olson summoned thirty or forty Nisei to a meeting in Sacramento. Kido and I attended as representatives of JACL. I knew only a very few of the others, and not even Kido recognized many of them. They seemed to have been assembled from all parts of California. Governor Olson chaired the meeting. He recognized the mounting demand that something be done about the Japanese in California, and then he dropped his bombshell. The Nisei, he said, could demonstrate their loyalty by voluntarily moving into what amounted to concentration camps, which the state would set up in various areas. Emphasizing the need to grow food, he said the men would leave the camps each morning to work on farms, their own farms if they were nearby, while their parents, wives, and children remained behind, and each night the men would return to join them.

Most of the Nisei at the meeting listened in silence, but not Kido. He raised the matter of citizenship rights and demanded to know what was being done to provide the Nisei with the equal protection under the laws which the Constitution guaranteed. To suggestions that Japanese Americans might be endangered by vigilantes and hoodlums, Kido asserted it was the governor's responsibility to provide us with protection and make it safe for law-abiding Japanese Americans to remain in their homes. I asked Olson whether other governors were making similar plans for their states. He said no, this was a program he had devised for California. The meeting broke up with Kido muttering that the Japanese Americans would never submit to a cockeyed scheme that was worse than peonage.

What was particularly disturbing about all this was that while the United States was at war against Japan, Germany, and Italy, almost all the domestic pressure was directed against the Japanese. There were more Italian aliens than Japanese aliens in San Francisco, more German aliens than Japanese aliens in Los Angeles. The German and Italian aliens had been eligible for naturalization but hadn't bothered to apply for citizenship. The Japanese were aliens because the law prohibited their naturalization. There was no pressure for mass incarceration of Germans and Italians.

Almost overnight the emphasis changed. Where the demand had been for the removal of Japanese aliens, the difference between citizens and noncitizens became blurred. We, Issei, Nisei, and Sansei (third-generation Japanese Americans) alike, were simply "Japs" no different from the people of the enemy nation. Japanese Americans were referred to as "Japs" in newspaper headlines adjacent to other headlines about Allied forces retreating in the face of "Jap" attacks. Unfortunately there was no short, snappy headline word for Japanese Americans, or Americans of Japanese ancestry. We tried to coin one. "Japyank" was awkward and contrived. "Jays" meant nothing. "AJA" for Americans of Japanese Ancestry was too obscure, and besides, the Allied Jewish Appeal had preempted those initials. "Nisei," which won a measure of acceptance years later, was at the time just another alien word. So Japs we remained, day after day, locked with the hated enemy in a devastating semantic trap. Even today we don't have an adequate word to describe Americans of Japanese ancestry.

Our unwilling headline association with the enemy created a state of mind that affected the press, the politicians, the public, and eventually the highest federal officials. If Munson's findings had been released by the president at this time with adequate emphasis on its importance, perhaps the tide could have been stemmed. But Roosevelt, for whatever reason, did nothing, and we knew nothing about what Munson had reported.

Chapter 5

Decision to Cooperate

Sometime during the early part of February 1942, John H. Tolan, an obscure Democratic congressman from Oakland, California, announced formation of what was grandiosely called the Select Committee Investigating National Defense Migration of the House of Representatives, Seventy-seventh Congress, Second Session. As it turned out, its primary function was not to investigate "migration" but to provide a platform for those advocating the removal of Japanese Americans from the West Coast.

At first, however, it appeared the committee was established in a genuine effort to determine the facts about a confused situation. I thought it was the best news we had heard in a long time, and our advisers, Nisei and Caucasian alike, agreed. The Tolan Committee, as it became known, seemed to offer us a forum before which we could make our case for fair treatment and marshal witnesses to testify as to their faith in our loyalty, to give us a direct pipeline to members of Congress, and to provide an opportunity to get the kind of media treatment we needed to rally public support. I arranged for JACL representatives to appear before the committee and urged JACL chapters in other cities to present testimony when Tolan and his cohorts arrived for hearings. Kido as national president was the logical spokesman for JACL, but he insisted that I could make a more eloquent presentation and would be a better witness than he.

I believed my appearance before the committee was critical to JACL's hopes of forestalling further evacuation talk. No extemporaneous speech would do. I dropped all other activities and set to work to write a statement. Drafts were read and criticized by our advisers as I edited and rewrote and polished the text.

All of us were concentrating so intensely on preparing for the Tolan hearings that an event of far greater significance almost escaped our notice. That was the signing, on February 19, of Executive Order 9066 by President Roosevelt. The first we knew of EO 9066 was when Lawrence Davies of the *New York Times* called to get our reaction. It was all news to me, and I had to ask what it was all about. Davies said he understood Roosevelt had given the secretary of war authority to designate military areas "from which any and all persons may be excluded."

My first impression was that it had been a predictable move, something we had expected, and nothing to be really concerned about. There had been considerable agitation for removing enemy aliens from sensitive areas adjacent to aircraft factories, airports, military installations, power plants, and the like. The Justice Department had pressed for authority to get the job done, and we assumed EO 9066 simply provided it. At the time it was only mildly disturbing to us that the Army had received the assignment rather than a civilian agency.

What the Army then proceeded to do was to use EO 9066 as a device for overriding the constitutional rights of citizens. Within weeks the Army's Western Defense Command under Lieutenant General John L. DeWitt employed its new power to incarcerate Japanese Americans en masse on the basis of their ethnicity, depriving them of rights guaranteed even petty criminals.

The press failed to catch the alarming significance of EO 9066. This assault on the Bill of Rights passed virtually unnoticed and provoked little if any editorial comment. Civil libertarians, what few there were in those days, were silent. Imagine what the press would do today if a president attempted to issue such an order.

What we had no way of knowing was that on February 11, eight days before the president signed EO 9066, Secretary of War Henry Stimson had received Roosevelt's approval to prepare for a general evacuation of Japanese and Japanese Americans from the West Coast. That same day General DeWitt was notified and told to be prepared to get the job done.

Thus the decision on mass evacuation had been made a full ten days before Congressman Tolan opened his hearings in San Francisco on February 21. As the book *Nisei* has stated, "the hearings were a sham, a forum for expressions of opinions and prejudices, for the voicing of pleas for justice as well as the cries of bigotry, none of which could have any effect on the issue.'' We had approached the hearings in the belief that the democratic system was working. In reality we were participants in an exercise in futility.

A parade of city and state officials appeared to dredge up tired old myths to justify their fears that Japanese Americans were a security risk and should be moved off the West Coast for the nation's and—voiced piously—their own safety. Significantly, no one said anything about detention; the entire focus was on removal, although no one seemed to have any idea where the displaced should go or what they should do to support themselves.

I was the first Japanese-American witness, and I took the stand still firm in the belief that what I was about to say would have an influence on the government's decisions. Congressman John Sparkman of Alabama took a prominent part in the questioning. I felt he was more sympathetic than the others.

(Elected to the Senate years later, Sparkman headed both the Foreign Relations and Banking committees before Adlai Stevenson picked him for his running mate in the 1952 presidential race. I happened to meet Sparkman during the campaign. He recalled the Tolan Committee hearings, then asked for my backing. Even though it appeared Dwight Eisenhower would win over Stevenson, I gave Sparkman a letter of support.)

The members of the Tolan Committee obviously were unfamiliar with Nisei, displaying the kind of ignorance that was to make the Evacuation acceptable to the American public. They appeared surprised that I could speak English without an accent, that I was a Mormon and not something they considered ''subversive'' like a Buddhist, that I had never been to Japan to fall under the evil spell of militarism and emperor worship, that I understood virtually no Japanese, that I was solely the product of the American educational system. The essence of my testimony was that we as loyal Americans had no choice but to bow to military necessity if that was the case, but would resist evacuation demands based on political opportunism or economic greed. I said:

> With any policy of evacuation definitely arising from reasons of military necessity and national safety, we are in complete agreement. As American citizens we cannot and should not take any other stand.

But, also, as American citizens believing in the integrity of our citizenship, we feel that any evacuation enforced on grounds violating that integrity should be opposed. If, in the judgment of military and federal authorities, evacuation of Japanese residents from the West Coast is a primary step toward assuring the safety of this nation, we will have no hesitation in complying with the necessities implicit in that judgment. But if, on the other hand, such evacuation is primarily a measure whose surface urgency cloaks the desires of political or other pressure groups who want us to leave merely from motives of self-interest, we feel that we have every right to protest and to demand equitable judgment on our merits as American citizens.

I concluded with these words:

In this emergency, as in the past, we are not asking for special privileges or concessions. We ask only for the opportunity and the right of sharing the common lot of all Americans, whether it be in peace or in war.

Although I spoke in broad terms, at this point in history the only real issue was removal of persons, primarily aliens, from militarily sensitive areas. There were rumors of wholesale evacuation of all Japanese Americans from the entire West Coast, but no one with the administration had said anything publicly about that possibility. Certainly there was no responsible reference to imprisonment of Japanese Americans in detention camps.

We know now that there was no military necessity to justify any of these possibilities. As I have noted earlier, the congressional Commission on Wartime Relocation and Internment of Civilians found after lengthy inquiry that "racial prejudice, war hysteria and a failure of political leadership" were responsible for what it termed a "gross injustice." In 1942 we sensed this to be true, but how could we prove it when we knew nothing more than what was published in the newspapers and broadcast by radio? Congressmen on the Tolan Committee insisted there were photographs proving Japanese Americans had sabotaged defense efforts in Honolulu during the enemy attack. We Nisei didn't believe it, but had no way of disproving such stories. Only much later did we learn that Nisei in Hawaii had responded magnificently in defense of their homeland. At the time there was little we could do other than to try to make our case before forums like the Tolan Committee, where, without our knowledge, the cards were stacked.

The situation was so confused that even federal officials weren't sure of policy. About the time EO 9066 was being drawn up, Kido and I met with Richard M. Neustadt, regional director of the Federal Security Agency, which had been made responsible for the welfare of those who might be forced to move by government order. He told us that the government did not contemplate either wholesale or indiscriminate evacuation of Japanese from the West Coast. Curtis Munson had given us similar information. Neustadt said only Japanese nationals living in areas specified by the Justice Department, if it came to that, would have to move out. He also assured us that Japanese nationals would be treated no differently from other enemy aliens like Germans and Italians, and that American citizens of Japanese descent would not be involved in any of the contemplated evacuation movements. Tom Clark of the Justice Department, later to become a Supreme Court justice, told us much the same thing.

Their assurances did not hold up, of course. I have no reason to believe that Neustadt and Clark were other than sincere, speaking on the basis of information available to them at the moment. And we had no reason not to believe them. At the worst, we thought martial law might be declared on the West Coast as had been done in Hawaii, placing some restrictions on a few civilians living in particularly sensitive areas. Even that seemed to be a remote possibility so far from the war zone. Under the circumstances the terrible danger to Constitutional rights inherent in EO 9066 was not apparent.

Some time later, when at last we saw the text of EO 9066, we were amazed by the sweeping powers granted the military. EO 9066 was posed as a military measure, declaring that "the successful prosecution of the war requires every possible protection against espionage and against sabotage." Authority was given "any designated commander," when he "deems such action necessary or desirable," to designate military areas "from which any or all persons may be excluded." The key words in that infamous document were "any or all persons." Roosevelt by a stroke of his pen granted the military the power to disrupt the lives and violate the rights—if it alone deemed it "necessary or desirable"—of any or all persons be they civilians or soldiers, citizens or aliens. In the absence of a declaration of martial law this was a clear violation of guarantees specified in the Bill of Rights.

There is no way now to tell what Stimson and Roosevelt had in mind when they first devised and the second approved EO 9066. I would like to believe they intended cautious use of its powers. However, the fact that General DeWitt was alerted to carry out a mass evacuation before that document was made public indicates that the president and his secretary of war had a clear idea of how the power would be used. DeWitt took advantage of the broad language of EO 9066 to force the wholesale *removal* of an entire racial minority and, in two subsequent steps not specified in the order, *imprisoned* them and *continued to exclude* them from the West Coast long after there was any possible necessity. There was nothing in EO 9066 to indicate that the government was contemplating other than removal. Not once in the many conversations Kido and I had with military officials was detention suggested.

When legal tests finally reached the Supreme Court, the justices were troubled by the arbitrary extension of military power. Frank Chuman writes in *The Bamboo People,* his legal history of Japanese Americans:

> Justice William O. Douglas declared that "detention in Relocation Centers was no part of the original program of evacuation." He pointed out that the legislative history of the act establishing the War Relocation Authority and the Executive Order 9066 authorizing the evacuation was silent on the power of WRA to detain the evacuees. He delineated Executive Order 9066 and Executive Order 9102, and all the public proclamations including the 108 civilian exclusion orders issued by General DeWitt, as being war measures put into effect only to "remove from designated areas . . . persons whose removal is necessary in the interests of national security."

Yet, somewhere along the line, the Army changed its objective and mission from simple removal to confinement, and a civilian agency, the War Relocation Authority, was given the job of jailkeeper. The Army reinterpreted its powers under EO 9066 to mean it had total authority over the freedom of Japanese-American civilians. The nation, and later the courts, sanctioned that action without really acknowledging the terrible precedent it established.

Late in February, even as the Tolan Committee continued its

hearings, Kido and I were summoned to Western Defense Command headquarters in the San Francisco Presidio. We were ushered into the presence of General DeWitt, a short, stocky, gray-haired man with the three stars of a lieutenant general on his shoulders. DeWitt was surrounded by a bevy of lesser officers, all cold and stern. He did not introduce them. DeWitt made a brief statement making it clear that we had been called in to hear what the Army had to say, not for discussion or negotiation. With that he left the room.

Another officer broke the news. In a few days the Western Defense Command would issue Public Proclamation No. 1 announcing that "all persons of Japanese ancestry"—we were referred to as "aliens" and "nonaliens"—would be required to get out of the western half of California, Oregon, and Washington and the southern one-third of Arizona. The Japanese Americans would be urged to move out "voluntarily." If "voluntary" departure didn't work, the alternative would be transfer to temporary havens until the government could map the next move. It was obvious no one had any idea what that would be. But there was no doubt that the Army intended to proceed without delay; the removal of 115,000 men, women, and children, citizens and aliens alike, voluntarily or otherwise, would begin just as soon as arrangements could be made.

I heard all this in utter disbelief. I cannot remember ever feeling so desperately let down. What we in moments of doubt had feared might happen was about to take place, and there was nothing more we could do to try to prevent it. There was no more room for argument or reason, only the cold reality of military orders. On top of it all, the Nisei were being lumped together with enemy aliens. We had been prepared for drastic restrictions on the freedom of the Issei generation. But we had remained confident in the sanctity of our rights as citizens. I felt I had failed JACL and its members. What made it even worse was that the generals now were asking JACL to cooperate with them—to cooperate like Judas goats—in the incarceration of our own people. I gagged at the thought.

But in my desperation I could see another side. If mass evacuation was inevitable, the Army's request also confronted JACL with the responsibility to help minimize the pain and trauma of the ordeal ahead.

For the moment, Kido and I could not go beyond saying that we represented only our membership and that we had no authority or right to speak for the entire Japanese-American community. Even as representatives of JACL the decision as to its role was too important to be made by just the two of us. We asked for and received permission to call a conference of league leaders to discuss our response.

Kido and I left the Presidio in silence, but that was a prelude to many agonizing discussions about principles involved, the leadership obligations to the people that we had assumed involuntarily, and the new obligations the Army was asking us to accept. What an anomalous position we were in. Our government was asking us to cooperate in the violation of what we considered to be our fundamental rights. The first impulse was to refuse, to stand up for what we knew to be right.

But on the other hand there were persuasive reasons for working with the government.

First of all was the matter of loyalty. In a time of great national crisis the government, rightly or wrongly, fairly or unfairly, had demanded a sacrifice. Could we as loyal citizens refuse to respond? The answer was obvious. We had to reason that to defy our government's orders was to confirm its doubts about our loyalty.

There was another important consideration. We had been led to believe that if we cooperated with the Army in the projected mass movement, the government would make every effort to be as helpful and as humane as possible. Cooperation as an indisputable demonstration of loyalty might help to speed our return to our homes. Moreover, we feared the consequences if Japanese Americans resisted evacuation orders and the Army moved in with bayonets to eject the people forcibly. JACL could not be party to any decision that might lead to violence and bloodshed. At a time when Japan was still on the offensive, the American people could well consider us saboteurs if we forced the Army to take drastic action against us. This might place our future—and the future of our children and our children's children—as United States citizens in jeopardy. As the involuntary trustees of the destiny of Japanese Americans, Kido and I agreed that we could do no less than whatever was necessary to protect that future. I was determined that JACL must not give a doubting nation further cause to confuse the identity of Americans of Japanese origin with the Japanese enemy.

The officers had made it clear to us that we could cooperate or they would do it the Army way. Anxious to avoid panic, the military did not make that threat public, nor were we in position to do so. Only when the evacuation was well under way did Colonel Karl R. Bendetsen, who has been described by the Army's official historian as the "most industrious advocate of mass evacuation," reveal in a blood-chilling speech to the Commonwealth Club of San Francisco that he had been prepared to complete the evacuation "practically overnight" in an emergency.

Reluctantly, we concluded there was no choice but to cooperate. We talked over the decision with friends and advisers, who, once over their shock, agreed we had no other choice. The few Issei community elders who hadn't been imprisoned counseled cooperation.

For several nights, after Kido had gone home to his family, I could not sleep. I tried to read and was drawn time and again to the Bill of Rights, particularly the due-process and equal-protection provisions in the Fifth and Fourteenth Amendments to the Constitution. "No person shall be deprived of life, liberty, or property without due process of law," the Fifth Amendment says. Due process meant the right to be presumed innocent until tried and found guilty by a jury of one's peers. Yet, the government was presuming our guilt without ever filing charges and putting us away until we could prove our innocence. Could anything be more wrong?

And the Fourteenth promises this: "No state shall make or enforce any law which shall abridge the privileges or immunities of citizens of the United States; nor shall any state deprive any person of life, liberty, or property, without due process of law; nor deny to any person within its jurisdiction the equal protection of the laws." Generations of Americans had fought and died to defend those rights. Now we were being asked to yield them peacefully in the name of national defense. I would toss and turn for hours until exhaustion claimed me.

The Army had taken the racist position that because we were not white, it was impossible to tell the loyal from the disloyal. Earl Warren endorsed this position in his Tolan Committee testimony. In England, at the beginning of the war with Germany, 117 hearing boards were set up. In six months more than 74,000 enemy aliens were summoned before these boards. Some 2,000 were interned, 8,000 were made subject to special restrictions, and the rest were allowed to go their way. My suggestion for similar boards to clear the loyalty of Nisei fell on deaf ears.

By contrast, hearing boards were established for Issei who had been picked up as possible security risks, and virtually all of them were cleared. A member of one of the boards was a young professor from Montana State University named Mike Mansfield who was destined to go on to a long and distinguished career in Congress followed by appointment as U.S. ambassador to Japan. He found nothing in the background of the Japanese he interviewed to justify continued detention. Recalling this experience, he once told me he wondered why similar boards hadn't been established to investigate Nisei instead of simply letting them sit in camps.

Because of the emphasis being put on loyalty and the difficulty of demonstrating it, I designed a JACL membership card which included a loyalty oath. It had no official or legal standing, but at least it would be a visible assertion of our fealty. Hundreds of Nisei joined JACL to get the cards.

Once Kido and I had determined that cooperation was the proper course, we went to work to convince others. The reality of the situation was that virtually every element of the Japanese-American community was looking to JACL for leadership. Buddhist and Christian churches, the only other organizations with more than local affiliates, sent telegrams to headquarters expressing support.

Kido summoned JACL representatives to a conference in San Francisco on March 8, 9, and 10. The discussions were unexpectedly subdued. I realized that everyone was in a state of shock, hardly able to comprehend that the justice they had believed in had been destroyed. Public officials who had called for fair play the week after the Pearl Harbor attack were now joining the clamor for our ouster.

Without dissent the National Board voted JACL officers extraordinary powers for the duration of the war to carry out these objectives:

1. To urge all JACL members to cooperate with the duly constituted authorities in the struggle for victory, and to recommend the same course for others.
2. To assist Japanese Americans in every way possible, help maintain morale, and ease the impact of the evacuation.

3. To keep in touch with federal authorities to ensure just and humane treatment for the evacuees.
4. To carry on a public relations program to demonstrate that Japanese Americans are good citizens.

On my recommendation, the board voted to move headquarters to Salt Lake City, which was out of the evacuation zone and where we had friends. Then the board instructed me to go to Washington, where I would have access to federal decision-makers and could lobby for justice as the evacuation program proceeded. In view of the ignorance about Japanese Americans in the nation's capital, I knew I had my work cut out for me. Kido gave an emotional and moving concluding address:

> It has been our constant fear that race prejudice would be fanned by the various elements which have been constantly watching for an opening to destroy us. They included many of our economic competitors and those who believe this country belongs to the whites alone. Many of them wanted to indulge in the unpatriotic pastime of using us as a political football in this hour of America's greatest peril. . . . We were counting on the better understanding we thought we had created. We all had expected that the public officials, at least, would serve as a buffer against possible mass hysteria. We never dreamed that such a large number of them would ride on the bandwagon, to reap political benefit out of this abnormal condition. . . . When we hear our erstwhile friends of peaceful days, those who praised us to the skies as model citizens, brand us more dangerous than the so-called enemy aliens, we cannot help but wonder if this is all but a bad dream.

Kido went on to say:

> No matter whatever we may do, wherever we may go, always retain your faith in our government and maintain your self-respect. . . . We are going into exile as our duty to our country because the president and the military commander of this area have deemed it a necessity. We are gladly cooperating because this is one way of showing that our protestations of loyalty are sincere. We have pledged our full support to President Roosevelt and to the nation. This is a sacred promise which we shall keep as good patriotic citizens.

It is significant that while Kido spoke of exile, not once did he mention the possibility that we were going into detention. Nor did anyone else. Kido and I were surprised and relieved that there was practically no outcry from the Japanese-American community against the decision to cooperate in the evacuation. We had to believe the lack of adverse reaction indicated general agreement that cooperation was indeed proper under the conditions we faced. Many besides me must have hoped that if we demonstrated our ultimate faith in the nation, the people of the United States after the heat and hysteria of war was over would somehow more than make up for what we had sacrificed.

Kido and I never doubted the necessity of JACL's decision. Yet there were times in private when we discussed violating the military's edicts, first as a gesture of outrage, and second to provoke a court test of the constitutionality of the orders. Kido had an unshakable faith in the sanctity of law and had no doubt that a challenge would be upheld. There were other JACLers who felt the same way. Walter Tsukamoto was prepared to go to jail to test the order but decided against it when he was warned he would jeopardize his captain's commission in the Army Reserve and perhaps face a court-martial on charges of disloyalty.

I was a logical candidate for a legal test, being without dependents. However, Kido insisted I would be of greater use to Japanese Americans outside of prison. Besides, Kido pointed out, any court test surely would be dragged out for months and perhaps years, and while a decision on constitutional issues was critical in the overall picture, it was not likely to be rendered until long after the immediate crisis was over. In short, there was no prospect of winning a judicial judgment in time to do anybody any good. In view of the urgencies of the moment he saw a court challenge at that time as little more than a futile, quixotic gesture that would demand more of our resources than JACL could spare. Thus we put aside thoughts of provoking a test and focused on the immediate problems. JACL, however, did become involved in a basic court challenge involving a young lady named Mitsuye Endo, about which I will have more to say.

The government lost no time in demonstrating that it meant business. On February 27 it ordered the evacuation on two days' notice of several hundred Japanese Americans remaining in the fishing village of Terminal Island in Los Angeles Harbor. The result was near-panic, heartbreak, and heavy economic loss. This action was dramatic warning of difficulties to come. Less than a week later, when the evacuation zones were announced, the Army simultaneously urged Japanese Americans to move out of them voluntarily.

Many Nisei did their best to comply. Henry Mitarai, a prosperous farmer from Mountain View near San Jose, was ready to buy land in Nevada or Utah to which he and his friends could move their operations. I accompanied Henry and several others on a scouting trip. Few landowners would even talk to us, and we came back empty-handed. Fred Wada of Los Angeles was a bit more successful. He found some land near Keatley, Utah, and settled a dozen families there in a "Food for Freedom" farming colony. Jimmie Sakamoto and other Seattleites entertained serious thoughts of moving into the Moses Lake district of eastern Washington with anyone willing to break the sod of a new area. But there was neither enough time nor enough capital to get projects like these under way, much less to meet the needs of tens of thousands of persons. The federal government, which was spending millions to train women for war work and opening up job opportunities for minorities other than Japanese Americans, failed to lift a finger on our behalf. In Congressman Tolan's words, we were part of the national defense migration program, but all it meant for us was that we had to get out.

DeWitt's voluntary removal plan was in reality a tragic farce. Most Japanese Americans had never been east of the coastal states. Few had friends inland on whom to depend for shelter, jobs, and other help. Moreover, the federal government and the Army guaranteed the failure of voluntary evacuation by doing nothing to explain to residents of interior areas why they should accept people considered too much of a security threat to be left on the West Coast. Many of the hardy souls who loaded cars with family and possessions and headed east ran into hostility. JACL headquarters heard reports that in some towns they were denied food, gasoline, and shelter. They encountered armed vigilantes and roadside signs ordering them to move on. Some had windshields smashed and tires slashed. Local law enforcement officials were getting calls that "Japs" were "escaping" from California and ought to be apprehended at the state line. It was only too obvious that unrestricted and unsupervised movement inland was fraught with danger.

I must also fault the general body of the Christian churches, including my own Mormon Church, for failing us in a time of need. Understandably they did not speak out when the issue was relocation of aliens from militarily sensitive areas. But with few exceptions, churchmen continued their silence when citizen rights were being trampled. Except for a handful of notable exceptions, West Coast churches did nothing to prepare their inland brethren to assist voluntary evacuees seeking only to obey military orders. So rampant was the fear and hysteria that some Christian ministers said that while they could vouch for most Japanese members of their denominations, they would have nothing to do with Buddhists. In time the churches became strong supporters of Japanese Americans attempting to start new lives in the interior, but that was much later.

DeWitt's headquarters ignored my pleas for protection for the voluntary evacuees. There was a war to be fought, an officer reminded me harshly, and there was no way he would detach troops to escort a bunch of Japs. I was relieved when the Army ordered voluntary evacuation halted on March 24. DeWitt thus made it illegal for Japanese Americans to leave their homes, and soon it would be illegal for them to remain.

March 24 also was the date that an 8:00 p.m. to 6:00 a.m. curfew on enemy aliens was extended to all Japanese Americans. It was a further erosion of our rights, given legitimacy by Congress a few days earlier when by simple voice vote it passed Public Law 503, making it a misdemeanor to violate orders of military commanders prescribed under Executive Order 9066. In that august body, where in the memorable past great debates about freedom had been heard, citizen rights were casually suspended. A routine, little-noticed voice vote had put our future in cold storage.

It was this sort of unthinking and outrageously callous action by the government that caused Joe Shinoda, a well-to-do nursery operator from Southern California, to offer to pay my expenses if JACL would dispatch me to Washington immediately to lobby Congress. That we turned down the proposal is a measure of our naiveté. Everyone we consulted said that in view of the national temper it would be a waste of time to go to Washington in hopes of influencing Congress.

Now it is obvious we were wrong, because of two things we didn't realize. In the Midwest and East there was relatively little concern about the Japanese Americans, little knowledge about what was going on. If the American public had been aware of the lasting constitutional implications of a hasty wartime measure, we might have been able to stir up enough concern to blunt the injustice. Second, we didn't need to influence a majority in Congress to have an impact. It did not occur to any of us that if one senator, just one, could be persuaded that we were being treated unjustly, he could bring Congress up short with a filibuster that would focus national media attention on our plight.

Under the circumstances, could we have found such a person? Would an old friend like Senator Thomas have risked his career to come to our aid? We will never know, because we didn't try to find out. But in retrospect it is difficult to believe there wasn't at least one member of Congress who would have had the courage to stand up and stir the conscience of the nation. For an example, we need only to look at Congresswoman Jeanette Rankin, the Montana Republican. She voted her conscience and alone among all the members of Congress cast a ballot against a declaration of war on Japan. When it was time to act against Germany and Italy, she voted only "present." While she was an ineffective minority of one in the House, a dissident could delay action in the Senate by the filibuster, a frequently used tactic. If I or someone had come up with the idea of convincing some senator that the principles involved in our cause were important enough to filibuster for, history might have taken a different course. We had so much to learn in 1942.

One morning about this time I read that Minoru Yasui, a young Nisei attorney in Portland, Oregon, had violated the curfew to invite arrest so that he could provoke a court test. Yasui ultimately took his case to the Supreme Court in an unsuccessful appeal. He has become a genuine Japanese-American folk hero, a tireless fighter for human rights and a JACL stalwart who deservedly won its two most prestigious awards, Nisei of the Biennium in 1952 and JACLer of the Biennium thirty years later. In 1942 I knew nothing of Yasui except that he was considered an important JACL leader in the Pacific Northwest. The news stories about Yasui's arrest made it appear that he was just a maverick publicity-seeker. There was nothing to indicate Yasui's genuine concern for constitutional safeguards or the deep thought that had preceded his decision to defy the government order. Without this knowledge I was profoundly disturbed by what seemed to be his unwise and unwarranted action.

Many years later, Yasui told me he had written to express his feelings and outline his intentions. I never received that letter. Completely in the dark and fearful that Yasui was endangering the delicate unwritten understanding we had with federal authorities, I issued a strong statement criticizing him.

Even today that statement is cited as proof of my shortsightedness in failing to oppose the Army's evacuation order. I do not apologize for it. Under the circumstances that existed in 1942—and it is important not to judge long-past decisions by contemporary values—I could not have done otherwise. There is no doubt in my mind that even had I known Yasui's thinking I would have opposed his action, morally defensible as it was, because of my conviction that it would hurt the majority. Today, Yasui is hailed for his courage. At the time he was a Lone Ranger widely criticized by his peers. Realistically, he was not the best possible candidate for a test case, since he had been an employee of the Japanese consulate in Chicago until war broke out. In the final analysis, my disagreement with Yasui was less over policy than timing. He wanted an immediate challenge. I had been convinced the challenge must come later. Over the years Yasui and I were good friends and coworkers in behalf of many good causes until his death late in 1986. I respected his dedication, integrity, and talent, just as I'm sure he respected me.

Yasui was no more successful in stemming the tide of evacuation than anybody else. As Kido had prophesied, the evacuation was a *fait accompli* long before the courts reached a final determination on Yasui's challenge, and on the suits involving Gordon Hirabayashi, Fred Korematsu, and Mitsuye Endo, which also went to the Supreme Court.

Like Yasui, Hirabayashi and Korematsu had invited arrest on their own. Yasui had challenged the Army's right to impose a curfew on citizen civilians in the absence of martial law. Hirabayashi, a University of Washington student, refused to obey curfew and evacuation orders as a matter of conscience. Korematsu evaded evacuation because he did not want to give up his freedom. JACL did not become involved in these cases until it filed *amicus curiae* briefs when they reached the U.S. Supreme Court, which was after I had left for military service.

Because of violation of law, the cases of Yasui, Hirabayashi, and Korematsu were criminal cases. Mitsuye Endo's was a civil case in that she had violated no law. She was invoking the time-honored writ of *habeas corpus,* providing citizens protection from illegal imprisonment, to demand her release from evacuation camps. Through Kido, JACL had asked James Purcell, a San Francisco attorney, to look into the legal aspects of the evacuation, and he came up with the strategy. There are many who believe the Supreme Court was wrong in upholding the convictions of the three men, but the fact remains that Miss Endo was the only one to win her case.

Peter Irons in his book *Justice at War* observes:

> Of the two pending cases (Korematsu and Endo), the *habeas corpus* petition filed by Purcell offered the best chance for an early judicial decision. It also promised (assuming a favorable decision by the Supreme Court) practical benefits to the Japanese Americans. A decision that detention was unlawful would force open the gates of the internment camps, whereas the evacuation program at issue in the Korematsu case had long since been completed. At the least, a favorable decision would require the release of those Japanese Americans certified by the WRA as "loyal" and willing to remain away from the West Coast. It was possible, in addition, that a sweeping decision against detention might strike down the WRA's restrictive leave regulations and the Army's refusal to permit the return of Japanese Americans to the "restricted zones" on the West Coast.

While there was no doubt whatever in 1942 that legal tests had to be part of our long-range strategy for seeking justice, the immediate problem involved the grim realities of evacuation. General DeWitt's headquarters posted notices that cleared, one after another, sections of the coastal states of Japanese Americans. In trains and long, dismal bus caravans the evacuees made their way to imprisonment in crude holding pens set up in fairgrounds and racetracks. Horse stalls reeking of their previous occupants became homes for people who had been proud, free, native-born Americans.

If the Army showed a certain efficiency in transporting us into confinement, it was far from prepared to meet human needs. Health precautions were minimal. In many areas it was JACL that organized public health clinics in which volunteer Nisei physicians and nurses provided free typhoid inoculations. One day I received word that sanitary napkins were unavailable at some of the assembly camps. The Army obviously hadn't anticipated this need. In desperation I called Senator Thomas again and asked him to get in touch with Mrs. Roosevelt, or anybody else in authority, to do something.

With heavy hearts we prepared to close up JACL's headquarters. Larry Tajiri, a brilliant Nisei newspaperman who had joined the staff to convert the sporadically published *Pacific Citizen* into a hard-hitting weekly newspaper, headed for Salt Lake City with his wife, Guyo, and Teiko Ishida, who had taken charge of all secretarial functions. There were many who felt Kido ought to move with the headquarters staff. However, he insisted that he and his family should share the evacuation experience with other Japanese Americans, even though he was aware of possible danger to himself at the hands of dissidents, a premonition that unfortunately came true. At first Kido had sent his wife, Mine, and their three young children to Lancaster in eastern California, where the Army had said they would not be disturbed again. But before long all of California was made a prohibited zone, although the eastern half of Oregon and Washington were not affected. What was the military necessity in eastern California that did not exist in the other two coastal states? Kido and his family wound up eventually in the Poston War Relocation Camp in Arizona, where he nearly lost his life in a brutal attack.

Even though voluntary movement out of the evacuation zones was prohibited, the Army gave me permission to head directly for Washington without going through the evacuation process. Thus, although I visited many of the relocation camps, I was never an inmate. This later led to complaints from some quarters that while I, the Nisei Moses, led my people into concentration camps, I had guilefully managed to escape imprisonment myself.

The matter of detention—and for how long?—was deeply troubling. Given the temper of the times, evacuation I could understand. But there could be no justification in logic or under law for continued imprisonment—without charge or trial—after removal from the West Coast. I vowed that freedom for the evacuees would have the highest priority.

After San Francisco was cleared of Japanese Americans, I stayed behind just long enough to tie up loose ends at JACL headquarters. Before starting out for Washington I made what turned out to be one of my wisest decisions. I asked George Inagaki to go with me as companion, assistant, consultant, driver, and all-around good fellow. I had known George only slightly, but he came highly recommended by my brother Joe Grant. Perhaps Joe sensed that Inagaki would be of value to me as a balance wheel. I was inclined to be mercurial. George was steady. He spoke Japanese fluently. He was a good listener and invariably exhibited sound judgment. He had been employed as general manager of a large floral nursery in the Los Angeles area. He owned a car, which was a critical asset. Even more important, he had many farmer friends who were willing to give him their gasoline ration coupons, which we would need for the transcontinental drive. After talking things over with his wife and father, Inagaki, who had no children, agreed to join me. We were to become closer than brothers.

Chapter 6

Assignment in Washington

George Inagaki met me in Reno, Nevada. Together we headed east toward no one knew what, overcoming the boredom of travel at the federally mandated 35-mile-per-hour speed limit by bouncing ideas back and forth as we planned our strategy, discussing what had happened and trying to foresee the future. We stopped in Salt Lake City just long enough to see that Tajiri and Teiko had found modest downtown office space for JACL in the Beason Building, where, so long ago, my father had been a janitor. Then we resumed our eastward trek. Cleveland, on the far side of the Great Plains, was our first destination on the road to Washington. A group called the American Committee for the Protection of the Foreign-Born was holding a convention, and I had been invited to speak. JACL was desperate to get the Japanese-American story told, and I welcomed an opportunity to appear.

One day, while we were traversing a particularly dreary stretch of the Midwest, George asked who I thought was most to blame for the evacuation. Secretary of War Henry Stimson had sought the power to oust Japanese Americans from their homes, and President Roosevelt by a stroke of his pen had granted it. But without hesitation I pointed the finger of responsibility at three other men, two of whom history will judge to have been great civil libertarians despite their role in our imprisonment. I remember naming these same three men when Walter Cronkite asked a similar question while filming the CBS documentary *Pride and the Shame*, after the war, and decades later I have no reason to change my evaluation.

In laying the blame, it is also important to explain the context in which the three men acted, the influence that was theirs to exert, and the circumstances that led each to make a faulty judgment.

The first was Earl Warren, then California state attorney general, later Republican governor of California, unsuccessful candidate for vice-president of the United States, and an outstanding chief justice of the U.S. Supreme Court.

Because his position as California's chief law enforcement officer gave him great credibility, Warren did more than any other person to spread fear of subversion by Japanese Americans. He had a record as an honest, hardworking political moderate. People took him seriously. Thus he was believed when he produced maps purporting to show how Japanese farmers had located near every important military installation, around airports, along railroad rights-of-way, near dams and powerlines, and in coastal areas which might serve as invasion beaches, and he cited this evidence as proof of a sinister Japanese conspiracy. He failed to recognize or admit that many Japanese had settled in isolated areas, on land no one wanted, long before California's anti-alien land laws prohibited Japanese from owning farms. Before the Tolan Committee he testified with no proof other than his personal bias that Nisei citizens, because of their American education, were more dangerous to the national security than Japanese aliens. He contended that Nisei had worked their way into strategic agencies, like the Los Angeles water department, so they would be in position to sabotage the system. His most astonishing charge was that the fact there had been no sabotage was proof Japanese Americans were waiting for orders from Tokyo to rise up in treachery. And because Earl Warren was an important public official with a fine record of service, even open-minded people were willing to believe his wild warnings of impending Japanese-American perfidy.

Many observers believe that the concern Warren exhibited for civil rights as chief justice can be traced to his realization of the tragic wrong he had done the Japanese Americans. In his posthumously published biography he expresses great remorse for the part he had in the evacuation, but that doesn't erase the enormity of his earlier actions.

What was the reason for his faulty perception? Since I never talked to him about it—I had many occasions to see him in Washington, but no opportunity to ask him direct questions—I must make some assumptions. I must assume he believed, in view of California's long, bitter history of anti-Orientalism, with which he grew up, that Japanese Americans couldn't possibly be anything but hostile to the United States. I believe he was caught up in the post–Pearl Harbor hate-the-Japs fervor, forgot his obligation as an attorney to seek out the facts, and performed as a California politician would be expected to do. The consequences were ghastly.

The second man would be Walter Lippmann, the highly respected journalist who played a brief but critically important part in the national drama. To appreciate his role it is necessary to understand the great influence he wielded. His columns were published in hundreds of newspapers. Opinion-makers in all parts of the country started their day by studying what appeared to be the infallible wisdom expressed in his column. Lippmann lunched regularly with captains of industry and the power brokers of Congress, and not infrequently with presidents. His opinions were highly regarded in Washington government circles. In February of 1942, before the evacuation decision had crystallized, he traveled to the West Coast to look into the rising feeling against Japanese Americans.

Lippmann spent considerable time with Earl Warren, which was proper in view of Warren's position. But his mistake was in accepting Warren's entire thesis about the potential disloyalty of Japanese Americans. He did not talk to Kido or me or, to the best of my knowledge, any other Japanese American. On the basis of incomplete research he wrote two columns saying Japanese Americans must be removed from the West Coast as an imperative defense measure. And because of Lippmann's stature as reporter and commentator, many accepted his recommendation without further question. There had been lesser columnists and radio commentators, some on the lunatic fringe, who had railed hysterically against the Japanese Americans. Lippmann from his Olympian pedestal gave legitimacy to the cries for getting rid of the "Japs."

Unlike Warren, Lippmann never admitted he had been wrong, that he had failed his obligation to gather all the facts before arriving at a position which he urged upon the nation. He continued to defend that position by asserting that the Japanese Americans were in danger of mob violence and it was for their safety that he reluctantly had urged they be locked up. Imprison the innocent to protect them from the rabble; that is logic unworthy of the great Lippmann but a measure of the irrationality that prevailed.

The third man would have to be General DeWitt, responsible for the Western Defense Command. He was a weak man to whom circumstances had given enormous power. No doubt he believed there had been sabotage in the Hawaiian Islands during the Japanese attack and he feared the possibility of sabotage on the Pacific Coast, particularly when he heard Earl Warren's warnings. DeWitt had only shallow convictions and he allowed himself to be influenced by what he called California's "best people," like Warren and the man he put in charge of the evacuation, Colonel Bendetsen, who in civilian life had been an ambitious young Stanford-educated attorney. DeWitt was a racist who complained about black troops being placed under his command. He saw the war in the Pacific not as conflict between governments or ideologies, but as a race war. DeWitt's "Final Report" of the evacuation includes this damning passage:

"In the war in which we are now engaged racial affinities are not severed by migration. The Japanese race is an enemy race and while many second and third generation Japanese born on United States soil, possessed of United States citizenship, have become 'Americanized,' the racial strains are undiluted." And Bendetsen, who curried DeWitt's favor (and was swiftly promoted from major to colonel), went on to brag in his *Who's Who in America* profile about the efficiency with which he carried out the removal of Japanese Americans. DeWitt was responsible for the ouster of, in the words of the Army's official report, "persons who were only part Japanese, some with as little as one-sixteenth Japanese blood." In this he outdid the Nazis, who did not persecute those with less than one-eighth non-Aryan ancestry.

While DeWitt was urging the Pentagon to let him clear the West Coast of Japanese Americans, Nisei volunteers in a makeshift classroom only a few feet from his Presidio headquarters were being prepared for military intelligence service against Japan. Long after the Japanese Americans had been driven out of the three Pacific Coast states, while Nisei volunteers for the U.S. Army were training for combat, DeWitt appeared before a Congressional committee to testify: "A Jap's a Jap. They are a dangerous element. . . . There is no way to determine their loyalty. . . . It makes no difference whether he is an American citizen; theoretically he is still a Japanese and you can't change him. . . . You can't change him by giving him a piece of paper.'' That was the mentality of the deskbound general who led the assault on our constitutional rights, and because of his position he, too, was believed. Colonel Bendetsen was the architect of the military's harsh evacuation program. But he was executing DeWitt's orders.

The tragedy is that great men like Roosevelt and Stimson, and others in position of power, listened to the faulty reasoning of Warren, the incomplete reportage of Lippmann, and the racist fears of DeWitt, accepted their counsel, and ultimately committed what legal scholars have condemned as America's worst wartime mistake. Completely ignored were reports from Navy Intelligence, F 131, the Federal Communications Commission, the State Department (Munson Report), and the Army's Chief of Staff (General Mark Clark) that the wholesale eviction program was not necessary as a military expedient!

In Cleveland I started on the first of the three missions Kido had given me. That was to tell as many people as would listen about what was happening to America's Japanese minority.

The second assignment was to get the people out of the camps as quickly as possible. President Roosevelt on March 18 had created the War Relocation Authority to assist people removed from their homes by the military and named Milton Eisenhower, a career Agriculture Department administrator, to head it. Eisenhower made it clear when we first met him in San Francisco that his idea was to establish scores of temporary havens in various parts of the West and in the mountain states to shelter the evacuees until they could be resettled. But the hostility expressed by Western governors at a meeting in Salt Lake City caused Eisenhower to think in terms of detention.

This became evident as WRA began to float ideas about establishing factories in the camps and undertaking large-scale farming projects to help the war effort. Both Kido and I saw the danger of these inland colonies becoming little more than new Indian reservations, peopled by individuals and families who were losing their initiative and independence and becoming increasingly bitter and dependent on the federal government. So the long-range welfare of our people, as well as immediate freedom, was involved in our desire to get them out of the camps without delay.

And third, Kido wanted me to lay the groundwork for a sweeping postwar campaign to rid the nation of the social and legal discrimination and prejudice that had helped to make the evacuation possible. That was a tall order. The initial step, I felt, was to convince the nation that we deserved to enjoy in actual practice the full, unabridged citizen status we were entitled to by law. Logic alone wasn't likely to swing public opinion in our favor. The most dramatic demonstration of our worthiness was to establish a record of having fought and bled in defense of our country in its time of peril. That meant we had to seek restoration of Selective Service responsibilities for the Nisei. George and I listed it high among our priorities when we reached Washington. Ironically, Japanese Americans had been placed in a position where military service was not a duty, but a privilege.

Meanwhile Inagaki and I were finding that simply traveling across the country had its problems. Two men with Oriental faces in a station wagon with California license plates were bound to attract attention. In a small town somewhere in Iowa a police officer stopped us on the pretext that George had failed to come to a complete halt before entering an arterial street. Instead of ticketing us for that offense, he took us to the nearest office of the state patrol. We were held several hours without charge, then released with no explanation. It was the first of several such experiences.

My speech in Cleveland probably was one of the most eloquent I have ever given. I pulled out all the emotional stops in a rip-snorting attack on American intolerance and anti-Orientalism, pleaded for understanding, and received a tumultuous ovation. George and I were delighted that the convention passed several strong resolutions on our behalf.

That support was to prove embarrassing if not damaging. Some time after we were established in Washington I received a letter from the Committee for the Protection of the Foreign-Born offering to sponsor a speaking tour. My name was on the letterhead as a member of the national board. I had never been approached about accepting a seat. Then I learned that the committee was on the attorney general's list of Communist-front organizations. I demanded that my name be removed, but there were to be a number of times when I was quizzed about links with the committee. It was obvious the committee had sought to use the plight of the Japanese Americans to embarrass the United States, and JACL could not be a party to that.

From Cleveland we drove to Cincinnati, where Ken Matsumoto, one of JACL's national vice-presidents, had moved from California. We rested at Ken's home for several days, took advantage of his hospitality, filled him in on what was happening back on the West Coast, and heard some horror stories about civil-rights violations in the South. That caused some genuine concern about being lynched when, a few days later, we were stopped en route to New Orleans by a hard-faced lawman in Harlan County, Kentucky, notorious for labor violence in the coal fields. As it turned out, even though we were jailed for several hours the encounter was more frightening but no more dangerous than our Iowa experience.

Our real fright was still ahead of us. The National Conference of Social Workers was meeting in New Orleans, and Annie Clo Watson had managed to get me scheduled as a speaker. This was a sympathetic group that wanted to know what it could do to help us. George and I arrived a little early on a stifling hot day. To kill time, see the sights, and get a little air, we drove out to what was called St. Bernard Parish. Unknown to us, there had been a scare a few days earlier about a German submarine having been sighted in the Mississippi. We were cruising about idly when the perfect stereotype of a Southern lawman stopped us.

"What are you Japs doing around here?" he demanded. We tried to explain that we weren't "Japs" and were in the city as guests of the social workers' convention. He wanted to know where we lived. It was a mistake to tell him California. We could see the cogwheels turning in his head as he tried to figure how law-abiding citizens could get enough gasoline to drive all the way from the West Coast to New Orleans. Suddenly he whipped out a pistol. Never before had I faced the business end of a firearm. At gunpoint he ordered us to the dirty little parish jail and locked us in separate cells where we couldn't see each other. Apparently the word spread quickly that a couple of Jap spies had been picked up. I could hear the sounds of a gathering crowd—a lynch mob, I feared. The murmuring outside grew into angry shouts, and my imagination ran wild. I could almost hear the baying of bloodhounds, and dimly recollected scenes of movie lynchings flashed through my mind. To let George know I was all right, I would flush the toilet in my cell periodically, and he would respond by flushing his.

Meanwhile the convention program committee became alarmed when we didn't show up. They telephoned Annie Clo in San Francisco. She advised notifying the FBI, and before long they tracked us down and arranged for our release. George's cell was closer to the entrance, and the sheriff let him out first. When he approached my cell accompanied by several large men I was convinced we were about to be thrown to the mercy of the mob outside the building. "Don't let them take you out," I shouted to George as I clung fearfully to the bars. It took a while for him to assure me that we were safe.

The social workers proved to be kind and helpful. I told them of the urgent need to get the evacuees out of the camps, of the need to persuade the government to change its policy of detention, the need for jobs and houses to rent and sponsors to help those seeking to make a new life for themselves in inland America. In the long run they proved to be strong allies.

En route to Washington we were stopped and jailed again in West Virginia, even though George was making absolutely sure he was observing traffic laws to the letter. Perhaps a California car carrying two Orientals couldn't help but attract attention. But by now we knew enough to ask the officers to check our identity with the FBI in Washington. I suppose it would have been simpler in these encounters with the law to say we were Chinese, as some Nisei were doing to avoid harassment. How would anyone have known the difference? But it seemed important to identify ourselves correctly as Japanese Americans, with emphasis on the American.

Driving into Washington from the west, the highway leads through the gentle beauty of the Blue Ridge Mountains and on into the lush countryside of historic Virginia. We crossed the Arlington Memorial Bridge over the Potomac into the District of Columbia and found ourselves directly in front of the Lincoln Memorial. It seemed only proper to stop before the brooding statue and pay our respects to the memory of the martyred president to whom human freedom had meant so much. Then we set off in search of a cheap hotel.

The first one we found was a little place called the Pennsylvania not far from Union Station and the Capitol. We registered and had barely washed when two FBI agents showed up to ask who we were and what we were doing. The agents were satisfied with our answers, but the incident only served to alarm the desk clerk. In some agitation he asked us to leave. Do cheap hotels have some kind of warning system linking their front desks? Not a single hotel we went to would take us. Maybe a better class of hotel would have given us rooms, but we didn't have the money to spend.

Finally we stopped at a service station and George thumbed through the telephone directory in search of Japanese names. There weren't many, but whenever he found one he would call, explain our plight, and ask whether they could put us up. No one could, and no doubt they were telling the truth when they said they themselves were jammed into crowded apartments. Then George came across a familiar name.

"Jack Murata," he exclaimed. "Why didn't I think of him before?" Jack Murata was a Sacramento Nisei who had a civil service job in the Interior Department. George had known Jack's wife, Betty, and her sister, Yvonne Kozono, when he lived in Sacramento. George called and found the Muratas and Yvonne, a nurse, were living in a two-bedroom apartment. When he related our problem Yvonne generously agreed to sleep on the living-room couch and let George and me use her room. We made the Murata apartment our home and base of operations for the next few months until George and I found a small, dark basement apartment. How the Muratas put up with us I'll never know. Nor will I ever forget their kindness and generosity. What sustained them must have been a sense that accepting an inconvenience was their contribution to the cause that George and I were pursuing. In Yvonne's case her contribution even extended to getting the hot water to soak my feet to ease the pain from a touch of gout.

George and I began a seemingly endless series of meetings, interviews, and conferences that led to various government agencies in Washington, then up to Philadelphia and then to New York (where Mr. and Mrs. Mervyn Suzuki provided the same kind of generous, uncomplaining logistic support as the Muratas) and back again. We talked to anyone who would listen, expounding our views, seeking advice, asking for help, laying plans. We found many friendly and helpful people—Roger Baldwin, national director of the American Civil Liberties Union; Reed Lewis, director of the

Common Council for American Unity; Clarence E. Pickett of the American Friends Service Committee; John Thomas of the Baptist Home Mission Society; Norman Thomas of the Post-War World Council; Roy Wilkins of the National Association for the Advancement of Colored People; Les Granger of the Urban League; leaders of a number of Jewish groups, including Rabbi Steven Wise, president of the American Jewish Congress; and countless other influential Americans of various faiths and political persuasions who were moved by the story of racial injustice.

Baldwin went out of his way to open doors and introduce us to important and influential people among his vast circle of associates. Over his objections, the national ACLU board had voted not to condemn the civil-liberties violation of the evacuation on the ground that it was a military decision necessary for national security. As if in atonement, Baldwin gave us unstinting support and made a sizable contribution from his own pocket to Gordon Hirabayashi's defense fund.

The friendship and support of nationally prominent liberals was a morale-booster. It gave us hope for the future, but it saddened me that we had reached them too late to prevent the evacuation. What would have happened had I been able to carry our message to them earlier? I asked myself that question often.

Our first meeting with officials in Washington was with Milton Eisenhower. Ken Matsumoto came in from Cincinnati and joined me and Inagaki in a long conference with the director of WRA. I asked Eisenhower's aid in realizing JACL's goals—to let the nation know that our evacuation was a military decision not connected with any acts of disloyalty so that we could eliminate public suspicions about where our commitment lay, to launch a vigorous resettlement program that would get the evacuees out of the camps and back into the nation's mainstream, and to work for elimination of discriminatory laws and practices after the war was won. Eisenhower admitted he knew little about Japanese Americans, expressed support for our objectives, and in turn asked our assistance in carrying out his difficult assignment.

After the meeting I headed alone for the Hill. Senator Thomas was not in his office. Without making an appointment I went to the Old House Office Building to call on Utah Congressman Walter W. Granger. A guard stopped me at the entrance and escorted me firmly into a side room, where he demanded to know my business. It was a jolting experience to realize that a peaceful American citizen on his way to see his own congressman could be halted by a security guard if he happened to look Japanese. Unfortunately, no one in Granger's office at the moment knew me by name. Finally the guards checked with Senator Thomas's office for assurance that I wasn't a saboteur before they let me go.

The War Department held at least two keys to the realization of our goals. One, of course, was rescission of the evacuation order, which, realistically, didn't seem likely to be an early possibility. The other was reopening of military service for the Nisei. Assistant Secretary John J. McCloy was our primary Pentagon contact, although more often we saw his aide, Colonel William Scobey, and Colonel Campbell Johnson, a black who was assistant to the director of the Selective Service System, General Lewis Hershey.

At first we failed to get much support for our proposal for restoring our Selective Service responsibilities. Frankly, we were told, aside from the matter of citizenship rights the government had no expectation of finding good soldiers among a people who had been displaced from their homes and penned up in camps under guard and behind barbed wire. What the Army was saying was that the government had been suspicious of our loyalty in the first place, and after the bitterness provoked by the evacuation there was even less reason for it to trust us. It would take a long time to convince McCloy and the brass of our sincerity. Moreover, there was no unanimity among friends and advisers about the wisdom of seeking military service. The Quakers, of course, were dedicated pacifists. Roy Wilkins, among others, counseled strongly against pushing for the right to fight. He pointed out that the blacks had been shedding blood for America since the Revolutionary War, and asked rhetorically, "Where did that get us?" Still, I was convinced that military service must be the foundation of our fight for justice. One problem of the blacks was that the story of their sacrifice had never been told or exploited adequately. That was a weakness the Japanese Americans would have to avoid.

George and I also made frequent visits to congressional offices in an effort to head off hostile measures that were being talked about. The mildest were proposals to deprive Nisei citizens of the right to cast absentee ballots. They ranged upward in malevolence to demands that Japanese Americans be prohibited from ever returning to the West Coast, that they be deported—how can a native be deported?—after the war, that men and women be kept in separate camps to prevent reproduction, and even a proposal that all the men be sterilized to take care of the "Japanese problem." Fortunately few of these proposals ever reached the floor of Congress, but lunatics were on the prowl and we could not afford to take lightly any threat, no matter how preposterous.

One day not long after we reached Washington, Milton Eisenhower told me he was leaving WRA for a post with the Office of War Information. This was alarming news. We had established good relations with Eisenhower and he was beginning to understand our goals and problems. Eisenhower perceived our concern and assured me his successor, Dillon S. Myer, a colleague from Department of Agriculture service, was a humane, understanding person.

After the war there were reports that women in the camps had been subjected to indignities by some WRA employees during the early period when Eisenhower was in charge. I suppose this was a possibility. WRA was hurriedly staffed, and it is likely there were some bad apples among the majority of decent and dedicated employees. Before the camps settled down to an orderly routine, it was inevitable that something of a jailor-prisoner mentality should exist. But at the time I heard nothing of sexual harassment, and I would like to believe top-level WRA officials would never have tolerated it.

I liked Myer from the moment I met him. He was open, direct, and frank, a tall man with a warm smile. A soft-spoken, gentle manner concealed an inner toughness and dedication to justice and humanitarian principles. Early in our association we established mutual trust and respect. Some latter-day historians have wrongly accused Myer of being responsible for the evacuation and continued imprisonment of the Japanese Americans. The facts, of course, are that he had nothing to do with the evacuation itself. He was an unwilling jail-keeper, and within a week or two of taking the WRA job, he made restoration of freedom his top priority.

Myer had an extremely difficult job. On the one hand was his deep concern for human rights. On the other were the pressures exerted on him by the more rabid members of Congress, a hostile press, and California-firsters, all of whom accused him of "coddling the Japs," and the Army, which stubbornly clung to the myth of military necessity to justify its actions. While long federal service had taught him the realities of Washington, he was not one to compromise his principles. Despite the enormous demands on his time, Myer made himself available for meetings at which we discussed policy and strategy, and frequently he ran his own ideas past me for comment before implementing them.

We worked particularly closely with three members of Myer's staff—Tom Holland, John H. Provinse, and John Baker. One of Holland's main responsibilities was helping to find job opportunities for evacuees leaving the camps. A major part of the relocation program depended on his success. Provinse headed community services in the camps, that is, the operation of the camps. We had many discussions with him about the harshness of camp life and shared with him reports of problems such as unpalatable food, inadequate medical care, and, when winter came, lack of heavy clothing. One recurring theme was the unfairness of evacuee doctors, dentists, nurses, teachers, and other professionals working for $16 and $19 a month alongside—and sometimes supervising—Caucasians drawing full government pay and benefits. Provinse agreed this was unjust, but there was nothing he or anyone else could do without stirring up critics in Congress who were searching not for ways to protect the rights of the Japanese Americans but for opportunities to discredit WRA. Baker was in charge of WRA's public information program. Given the mood of the times, it was virtually impossible for him to present WRA's program in a good light; about the best he could do was to try to put WRA and its responsibilities in true perspective, and we did what we could to help him.

While I had headed for Washington, the rest of my family with the exception of my next younger brother, Ike, had been evacuated from Los Angeles to the Manzanar WRA camp in the desert Owens Valley of southeastern California. Ike had been drafted into the Army before the outbreak of war, was among the Nisei who were not discharged after Pearl Harbor, and was stationed in South Carolina. But the family didn't stay together for long. When a call came for volunteers to help save the sugar-beet crop in the intermountain area, Ben went to Idaho to work as a field hand. Iwao Hank went off to Nebraska on a similar assignment. Shinko married. That left Joe as head of the family, Mother, sister Koke, and the youngest, Tad, at Manzanar. Etsu Mineta and her family were at Heart Mountain camp near Cody, Wyoming. I was writing to her much more often than to members of my own family.

As the hot, humid summer of 1942 slipped by, WRA instituted plans to get at least some of the evacuees out of the camps. Prominent educators saw the tragedy of denying schooling to college-age Nisei and persuaded many inland colleges and universities to accept them, and WRA permitted them to take advantage of these offers. Other Nisei men were encouraged to leave the camps on "temporary leave" for field work at the going rate of pay in the sugar-beet harvest. Thousands like my brothers responded. Many were city boys with little farm experience, but they helped save the crops of farmers who at first had been hostile to their arrival. To make sure that these men were not being exploited, I asked George Inagaki to drive back west and tour the beet states. He and Scotty Tsuchiya, who had been the owner of an Oriental antique store in San Francisco, visited scores of farms throughout the Mountain states and found generally that the program was working to the advantage of both volunteers and farmers.

Meanwhile, Tom Holland and others were trying to liberalize leave policy so a greater number of evacuees could take jobs in interior states, where the demand for them grew as word of their abilities spread. But none of this raised hopes that the camps could be emptied anytime soon. Detention, on top of evacuation, had become a *fait accompli*. There was need to plan for the long run, and I felt it was necessary for JACL to meet once more, particularly since I had begun to get troubling reports of growing unrest in the camps. During the confused and uncertain pre-evacuation period the vast majority of Japanese Americans had looked to JACL for leadership. But now that the emergency was over, now that there was time to think and brood and grow angry, it was understandable that many would seek a scapegoat on which to vent their frustrations. At this point in history for the people locked up in the camps, the federal government and the Army were still unassailable. But JACL was vulnerable. In some camps a few of the more vocal malcontents were vilifying me as "Moses" Masaoka who had escaped to the comfort and safety of Washington. Consultation with the JACL leadership about our next steps seemed to be imperative.

From his home in the Poston WRA camp in Arizona, Kido issued a call for a conference in Salt Lake City over the Thanksgiving weekend. Myer granted permission for two JACL representatives from each of the ten camps to attend. The regulations covering their travel illustrate the irrationality of the restrictions against them. Delegates from the far-inland camps like Rohwer and Jerome in Arkansas, Heart Mountain in Wyoming, and Granada in Colorado were free to travel as they pleased as soon as they passed through the camp gates. Delegates from the two camps in eastern California, Tule Lake and Manzanar, and the Poston and Gila camps in Arizona, which also was a prohibited area, had to be accompanied to the state line by government escorts before they were placed on their own.

Since JACL's funds were extremely limited, everyone, even I all the way from Washington, traveled by bus. Delegates from the camps were joined by JACL leaders from chapters in Utah, Idaho, Wyoming, Arizona, and other parts of the so-called free zone.

The reunion of men and women who had parted after the emergency conference in San Francisco in March was warm and emotional, but there was little time for sentiment, particularly when we learned that there had been a disturbance in Poston and Kido's arrival would be delayed.

I had prepared a vast agenda for the conference covering virtually every aspect of life in the camps, our relationship with the War Relocation Authority, the experiences of evacuees who had already left the camps, the status of JACL's programs and our extremely shaky financial situation, my activities in the East, and our ultimate goals. All these items deserved discussion in depth, but from my point of view all of them paled before what I wanted most from the leadership—a ringing, unequivocal resolution demanding restoration of Selective Service responsibilities for the Nisei. I believed such a resolution would go a long way toward persuading the Pentagon to restore the right. Prior to the outbreak of war, Nisei had the same Selective Service status as other Americans. Nearly 5,000 of them were in uniform at the time of Pearl Harbor. Then, abruptly, many of them were discharged. As a group, Nisei civilians were reclassified 4-C, the category for declared and nondeclared aliens and enemy aliens. After we protested, Nisei were again reclassified as registrants "not acceptable to the armed services because of nationality or ancestry."

I was convinced that without a military record, JACL would face virtually insurmountable obstacles in attaining its goals, particularly its postwar goals. In fact, I felt so strongly about the need for a JACL resolution demanding military service that I had confided to Inagaki, and later Kido, that I was prepared to resign unless I got the support.

But I wasn't quite prepared for the depth and sincerity of the opposition. Something profoundly disturbing, but fully understandable, had happened to the Nisei under the pressures of unjust imprisonment. Men who under normal circumstances would have been proud to volunteer for military service were now expressing doubts about endorsing the proposed resolution. As persuasively as I could, I argued the case for service in uniform as a stepping-stone toward our postwar crusade for equality. Just as persuasively, many of them contended that it was insanity to expect Nisei to enlist while their citizen rights were suspended, while they were barred from their homes on suspicion of possible disloyalty, while they were under racial attack in Congress and the press. "We want the government to let us out of the camps, to let us go home as full-fledged citizens, before we offer our lives in defense of our country," one of them cried with passion. Another contended that we were making our war sacrifice by accepting the evacuation and that the government had no right to demand more until it restored our rights.

These were powerful arguments, difficult to refute. We had indeed been mistreated, and resentment was natural. But I was convinced we had to walk the extra mile, to make the grand sacrifice, to offer to do the unthinkable if our ultimate goals were to be achieved. The discussion stretched out for several hours. Finally, I felt that everything that needed to be said had been said. The conference minutes show that I called for a vote with this speech:

> I have come to the inescapable conclusion that this matter of Selective Service is the cornerstone of our future in this country. Perhaps we may be somewhat shortsighted today in view of what we have gone through, but let me ask you to think of your future—and that of your children and your children's children. When the war is won, and we attempt to find our way back into normal society, one question which we cannot avoid will be, "Say, Buddy, what did you do in the war?" If we cannot answer that we, with them, fought for the victory which is ours, our chance for success and acceptance will

be small. We need Selective Service, the least we can do is to ask for it. As for the work of the Washington office, such a resolution from this body will go far in carrying on our public relations work. Gentlemen, in order to bring this discussion to a head, I call for a resolution to the President and the Army of the United States asking for a reclassification of the draft status of the American-born Japanese so that we shall be accorded the same privilege of serving our country in the armed forces as that granted to every other American citizen.

The man who stood up to make the motion was Sim Togasaki, the same fellow who asked the chair to deny me the floor in my first JACL convention in Los Angeles four brief years earlier. So much had happened in that time. Togasaki, his bulldog head thrust forward, his voice raspy with emotion, declared:

> I feel strongly that most of us desire to be treated in the same way as all other Americans, both as to sacrifices and benefits. This is a matter which vitally affects our very lives. Even though we have gone through so much, I am confident that most of us are willing to forget and forgive, and join the Army and fight for our country and our future. Mr. Chairman, I move that the resolutions committee be instructed to draw up a resolution embodying the wishes of this assembly.

There was applause, and Henry Shimizu spoke: "I second the motion. I believe we have made a most significant decision, and one which we will be proud to recall in the years to come."

The motion was passed unanimously in a loud, dramatic voice vote. A sense of relief seemed to settle over the gathering. Some of the delegates came up to shake my hand. I did not try to conceal my elation.

I had won my resolution, but the next step still posed enormous problems. Somehow the Pentagon had to be convinced of our sincerity. Additionally, I knew, as did the delegates, that our position would not be popular in the camps and that violence at the hands of angry, resentful dissidents was a real possibility.

As we prepared to adjourn, Kido warned: "Some of us will have to go back to a pretty bad situation, but it is our duty to go back and face the music. I hope it will not be bad music. But as long as we have assumed the responsibility as leaders of the JACL, the fact that we may be criticized should not bother us. We have sacrificed enough, but we will be sacrificing more by returning to the centers and assuming our responsibilities and duties.''

The music was worse than expected. Within days, rioting broke out at Manzanar. Dissidents, not necessarily pro-Japan but angry over their treatment by the United States, struck out against authority and those who cooperated with WRA officials. Fred Tayama, a JACL stalwart who had taken a key role in the Salt Lake meeting, was beaten badly enough to be hospitalized. When rioting got out of hand, WRA officials summoned troops, whose fire killed one youth and injured several others. Admitting it couldn't keep the peace, WRA hustled a number of JACL leaders, including my brother Joe and the remaining members of the family, to the safety of an abandoned Civilian Conservation Corps camp in Death Valley. The unrest spread. At Poston, Kido's barrack apartment was broken into at night while he slept and he was severely beaten. At the Rohwer camp in Arkansas, the Reverend John M. Yamazaki was attacked and Dr. Tom Yatabe, one of JACL's original founders and another Salt Lake meeting delegate, was brutalized by toughs who invaded the hospital.

George Inagaki and I didn't do much talking on our drive back to Washington. We had too much to think about.

Chapter 7

First to Volunteer

Early in January 1943, thirteen months after war's outbreak and nearly a month and a half after JACL passed its Selective Service resolution in Salt Lake City, Colonel Scobey asked me to come to his Pentagon Office. There was nothing in his manner to indicate a decision had been reached. Inagaki and I hurried to the appointment.

Without preliminaries, Scobey said the Army was thinking favorably of letting Nisei serve in combat. My face lit up. Then Scobey dropped a bombshell. What did we think of an all-Nisei volunteer force led by white officers?

There was a long silence, and then my protests began to flow. That wasn't what I had in mind at all when I was pushing for restoration of Selective Service responsibilities, I said. We Japanese Americans were demanding equal rights, not special status. I reminded Colonel Scobey that before the evacuation I had proposed formation of an all-Nisei unit and had been turned down with the argument that only Negroes were confined in segregated outfits. I also told him that while Nisei would have rushed to volunteer before the evacuation, now there was much festering bitterness in the camps about the way they had been treated. And while I had no doubt whatever that they would respond to restoration of Selective Service, it was difficult to predict Nisei reaction to a call for volunteers for a segregated unit.

Scobey explained the Pentagon's thinking. The Army was sympathetic with the Nisei's desire to demonstrate their loyalty through military service. But there were millions of Americans in uniform and millions more would be called up, and a few thousand

Japanese Americans dispersed among all those men would be virtually invisible. But a regiment-size outfit of Japanese Americans fighting as a unit was bound to attract attention, and win sympathy and admiration, particularly if it set the kind of heroic record that could be publicized.

Scobey also pointed out the hazards of organizing such a unit. If it failed to perform adequately—if the Japanese Americans did not volunteer in adequate numbers, or if they proved to be poor soldiers—the Nisei faced criticism, derision, scorn. On the other hand, their desire to distinguish themselves could lead to heavy casualties and charges that they were being used as cannon fodder. He urged us to think over the proposal, consult our friends, and report back to him within a few days.

Kido was in Poston and out of touch. Hito Okada at headquarters wasn't of much help. Gee, he said, you fellows are right there on the scene and know the score. You do what you think best and we'll back your decision. Larry Tajiri had serious doubts about the principle of segregation. He felt strongly that to accept segregation would negate everything JACL stood for. But he could also see the practical public relations advantages of an all-Nisei unit performing with great valor. Most of the other Nisei whom Inagaki and I talked to endorsed the segregated unit, but there was no way of telling whether their thinking was typical. These Nisei had already left the camps, or had never been in them, so their outlook could well be different from that of the fellows still behind barbed wire.

The reaction of our Caucasian friends was predictable. This was the breakthrough Dillon Myer was seeking, and a segregated unit didn't bother him. The pacifists were dismayed that we would feel the need to fight to prove our loyalty. The idealists were repulsed by segregation. The pragmatists saw definite advantages. There was no practical way of polling JACLers who had been at the Salt Lake City conference. It would be fatal to let Scobey get the impression by delay that we were waffling, that our demand had been a charade. Under the circumstances the ultimate decision had to be mine. And I was prepared to make that decision on the assumption that JACL's Selective Service resolution could be extended to cover any combat service.

In my lifetime there have been many decisions I agonized over, that kept sleep away for long restless nights. The decision to agree to a segregated combat unit was not one of them. It was far from an easy call, but it was not something I stewed over even though it was obvious the decision would shape the futures of all Japanese Americans, one way or another. If I endorsed a segregated combat unit, many of us might never come back and, in a way, I would be responsible for their deaths. Still, every soldier faced the possibility of death or injury no matter what kind of outfit he served in. Realistically, I knew I could not consider myself any more responsible than a commanding officer would be responsible for the deaths of men he led into battle. The only real question in my mind was how much the bitterness of the evacuation had sapped Nisei will.

The alternative to combat could well mean the Nisei might spend the war in service units, on permanent KP, and that would hardly dramatize our loyalty. Would the Nisei make good soldiers? The 100th Battalion, whose core was a Nisei National Guard outfit from Hawaii, was setting an outstanding record in training at Camp McCoy, Wisconsin, astonishing its white officers by its discipline, intelligence, and intensity. There was no reason that mainland Nisei, although they had no military background, could not perform as well as other American citizen-soldiers. Besides, the Nisei had something to prove, and that dedication could make up for whatever shortcomings as fighting men they might have at first.

I was convinced that to pass up an opportunity to prove ourselves, no matter how unfair or hazardous, was unthinkable. I knew we must accept the challenge. My conviction that I was right, and George Inagaki's solid support, lightened my burden.

A short time later George and I met with Assistant Secretary of War McCloy and Scobey. McCloy went over the proposal that Scobey had outlined in our previous meeting. He explained that volunteers would be sought, one-third from Hawaii and two-thirds from the mainland, to form a regiment-sized combat team, and if the experiment worked out well, all Nisei would be made subject to Selective Service. (As it turned out, the ratio was reversed. In Hawaii, where there had been no mass evacuation, some 10,000 Nisei volunteered, while the response on the mainland was much less enthusiastic, for reasons that will be gone into later.) McCloy showed no surprise when I told him JACL would back his plan fully. He seemed to expect it.

In the twilight years of his distinguished career, McCloy has been roundly criticized for saying in the Redress Commission hearings that he thought the evacuation was justified and there was no need for either a public apology to Japanese Americans or for paying them compensation. I regret that he feels this way. I believe he is wrong. I also believe that he endorsed the evacuation in 1942 not for political motives, but because he honestly—but wrongly—believed it was a necessary national defense measure. On the other hand, McCloy more than any single person was responsible for the Army's decision to give Nisei an opportunity to fight for their country. As we shall see, it was an opportunity that we seized with profoundly significant results for all Japanese Americans. McCloy has avowed many times, including in testimony before Congressional committees, that he was as proud of the part that he had in the formation of the 442nd as of anything he had done in a lifetime of public service. Nor should it be forgotten that when extremists were demanding WRA be abolished and the camps placed under total Army jurisdiction, McCloy insisted on continued civilian control.

As McCloy stood up to indicate the end of our meeting, I said: "Sir, I think it is only proper that I should be the first Nisei to volunteer." McCloy smiled broadly and patted me on the back as George broke in: "And I the second."

Only half in jest, Scobey said he supposed we would want commissions and a soft Pentagon assignment. "No, sir," I replied. "We've been pleading for an opportunity to fight, and now that we have it, I don't expect any favors." I knew then that wherever my military career might lead, I would serve it as an enlisted man, and that was fine with me. What I did not know was that even then McCloy was thinking of a specific assignment for me.

McCloy indicated the announcement about the combat team would be made in a few days, after details were worked out. Inagaki and I hurried back to Salt Lake City to be on hand when it hit the fan; we didn't know what might happen, but in view of the violence after our meeting in November we expected a certain amount of resentment in the camps. The decision to leave Washington turned out to be a grievous error.

In carrying out its plans for Nisei troops, the federal government scored a great coup. Simultaneously, it committed a dumb mistake that touched off anger and violence in the camps and nearly destroyed everything WRA was trying to do to help the Japanese

Americans. There is no doubt that if Inagaki or I had remained in Washington we could have averted the trouble.

But first the coup. On January 28, 1943, Secretary of War Stimson announced plans for formation of an all-volunteer Nisei fighting unit that came to be designated as the 442nd Regimental Combat Team. President Roosevelt, who so callously had signed Executive Order 9066 imprisoning Japanese Americans, now was persuaded to issue a statement which said in part:

> The proposal of the War Department to organize a combat team consisting of the loyal American citizens of Japanese ancestry has my full approval. The new combat team will add to the nearly five thousand loyal Americans of Japanese ancestry serving in the armed forces of our country. This is a natural and logical step toward the reinstitution of Selective Service procedures which were temporarily disrupted by the evacuation from the West Coast.
>
> No loyal citizen of the United States should be denied the democratic right to exercise the responsibilities of citizenship, regardless of his ancestry. The principle on which this country was founded and by which it has always been governed is that Americanism is a matter of the mind and heart; Americanism is not, and never was, a matter of race or ancestry. . . .

The statement had been drafted by WRA. Later, Dillon Myer told me that Elmer Davis, head of the Office of War Information, had penciled in the last sentence that appears above. It was quoted often to underscore the point that there were Americans of many backgrounds, including Japanese, eager to fight for their country.

Generally, the press applauded Roosevelt's decision. The *New York Times* said editorially of the Nisei: "The episode touches one's sympathies. These Japanese are American citizens, just as are the young men of German and Italian descent who are loyal members of our fighting services. . . . Their eagerness now to be in the nation's battle may ameliorate their rather lonesome lot in this country." The *New York Herald Tribune* said: "That the restrictions on loyal Japanese should now be eased to permit them to serve in the nation's war program seems only just. . . . It should serve to cement the loyalty of those who have been patiently living in internment and who now voluntarily accept the opportunity to work, or fight, for Uncle Sam." Perhaps most significant was the *San Francisco Chronicle*'s comment: "The decision of the War Department to treat them [the Nisei] like other citizens in the mustering of men for the armed forces will gratify all who have felt that the only proper test in their case is loyalty, not racial origin.''

Despite the persistent reference to us as ''Japanese,'' the public relations aspect of the combat team was under way.

However, in retrospect it is curious how the U.S. press accepted Roosevelt's complete flip-flop without question. Imagine what the reaction would be today if the White House had done such an about-face on a human-rights policy. Reporters at a televised press conference would be jumping up to ask questions like this: ''Mr. President, if as you say no loyal citizen of the United States should be denied the democratic right to fight and perhaps die for his country, why are so many of these 'loyal citizens' continuing to be imprisoned in detention camps? What has been done to ascertain the loyalty of these citizens since they were so summarily uprooted from their homes by the same Army that now invites them to volunteer for service?'' The press at the time was somnolent, perhaps lulled by the assumption that the government could do no wrong in the name of national defense.

However, the wisdom of our military-service decision was confirmed by the opposition that sprang up outside the camps. Various groups hostile toward Japanese Americans condemned the plan to open the armed forces to the Nisei for the very reason that JACL in Salt Lake City demanded it—it would be impossible to deny full citizenship rights to any American minority which had fought and shed blood for their country. In California the Native Sons viewed with alarm the decision to give Nisei an active part in the war. The Oregon senate passed a resolution opposing Nisei entry into the armed forces. The Idaho legislature demanded immediate discharge of all Nisei from the military. These were unmistakable indications of the way our status as Americans had been eroded by the evacuation. I was more sure than ever that our decision to demand combat service had been correct.

The dumb mistake was further evidence of the government's continued ignorance about Japanese Americans.

It was committed inadvertently by WRA when that agency sought to expedite release of evacuees from the camps by piggybacking a ''loyalty'' questionnaire on an Army questionnaire used to determine who would be willing to serve. WRA had been under great pressure to separate the "loyals" in the camps from the so-called "disloyals." Evacuees seeking to leave the camps had been subjected to a time-consuming investigation which was something of a sham. The gist of it was that they were certified as loyal if none of the national security agencies—the FBI, naval intelligence, etc.— had anything derogatory about them. The irony of this preposterous procedure seemed to escape everyone.

Why was it preposterous? Because the Army, while it was demanding mass evacuation, had insisted that it and the other national security agencies did not have the competence to separate the sheep from the goats. But after the Japanese Americans were locked up, the until then inadequate records of those very same agencies suddenly became quite adequate for determining loyalty.

The Army's enlistment questionnaire was designed for Nisei men of military age. Simple-mindedly, WRA retitled the questionnaire "Application for Leave Clearance" and distributed it to all men and women, alien and citizens, age seventeen and older. Two of the questions in particular created serious problems.

Question 27 asked: "Are you willing to serve in the armed forces of the United States on combat duty, wherever ordered?"

Question 28: "Will you swear unqualified allegiance to the United States of America and faithfully defend the United States from any or all attack by foreign or domestic forces, and foreswear any form of allegiance or obedience to the Japanese emperor, to any other foreign government, power or organization?"

Even under ordinary circumstances such questions would have posed problems if asked a wide cross section of adults. But it was obvious to anyone in touch with the situation that a paranoia had gained a foothold in the camps. People felt abused, deceived, betrayed, unfairly treated. Many had come to mistrust and expect the worst of their government. Thus, when WRA asked women and elderly men whether they were willing to go into combat, wherever ordered, many had visions of being rounded up into suicide battalions. Some youths interpreted the question to mean they were volunteering for the Army if they answered affirmatively.

Question 28 was even more troublesome. The United States literally was asking Issei, who by law had been denied American citizenship, to renounce the only nationality they could claim. And many Nisei were convinced that the question was designed to trick them into admitting they owed allegiance to the Japanese emperor. The agitators in the camps lost no time in provoking doubts and fears, and there was no effective way to combat them because WRA had blundered badly.

Confused and angry, many answered "No" to one or both questions. Many Nisei, who under other circumstances would have volunteered proudly, now hesitated. Some demanded restoration of their rights as a precondition of military service. The questionnaire had no provision for qualified answers. A "No" was interpreted as *prima facie* evidence of disloyalty.

As little as I knew about Issei and Nisei psychology, the pitfalls inherent in the questionnaire were immediately apparent. But they escaped the notice of Washington officials. If they had intended to stir up suspicion and unrest in the camps they could not have done a better job. By the time the blunder was discovered and the questions were rephrased, the camps were in a high state of agitation. Mass meetings raged day after day. The questionnaire split families, alienated friends, and badly damaged enthusiasm for military service.

The Army didn't help matters when it sent inadequately briefed teams of a Caucasian officer and several Nisei noncoms into each of the camps to try to answer questions and sign up volunteers. The officers may have been good soldiers, but they had little knowledge of Japanese Americans. The Nisei in uniform had gone into the Army before the evacuation and had no experience with camp life. They had little idea of how to respond to the bitterly ironic questions the evacuees fired at them about the justice and logic of asking them to step out from concentration camps to fight for the kind of democracy that had put them behind barbed wire. The American public, helped by the press, wrongly interpreted the turmoil as evidence of disloyalty and anti-Americanism. Still, it is a great tribute to the loyalty of the Japanese Americans that well over 1,000 in the camps ignored the agitation, overcame their doubts, resisted the pressures, and pledged their faith in America by volunteering in the first wave to serve without preconditions. (Later, when the draft was restored, thousands of other Nisei were inducted, and many of them served as replacements in the 442nd.) To help meet the mainland quota these volunteers were joined by hundreds of Nisei who earlier had been permitted to leave the camps. And when that was not enough to fill out the ranks, Hawaii's quota was doubled.

I have never found anyone willing to accept responsibility for the questionnaire blunder. The original probably was prepared for the Pentagon in either the State or Justice departments, and its implications escaped everyone in WRA. This was just another example of the insensitivity resulting from ignorance and the failure of bureaucrats to even understand they were on dangerous ground.

I had urged WRA to undertake some kind of segregation program in the camps, separating the agitators from those who wanted to cooperate with the government. Loyalty to the United States was not the main issue at this point; we were looking for a way to halt intimidation of the peaceful evacuees and violence against certain JACL leaders so the people could live without fear while waiting to be relocated or simply sitting out the war. We had never discussed with officials anything so drastic as the mass questionnaires.

I was visiting Mother in the Topaz camp in southern Utah, to which she had been moved, when I heard about the controversial questions. By the time I was able to reach Dillon Myer in Washington, reports of resentment in other camps had reached him and he was hurriedly trying to revise Questions 27 and 28. But by then serious damage had been done.

Immediately after Stimson announced formation of the combat team, I sent him a telegram from Salt Lake City to formalize my decision to volunteer. Then I set out to take care of a personal matter too important to be entrusted to the mails. As I often did when I wanted to talk to Etsu, I sent a telegram to the Heart Mountain camp asking her to telephone me at a specified time. Camp residents were not permitted to accept personal calls, but they could use the one pay telephone available to call out. Late at night, clutching a handful of coins and bundled against the cold, Etsu would trudge through the dark from the Mineta barracks unit to the administration building to try and reach me.

Even with night rates, long-distance calls were not inexpensive. Without wasting time in preliminaries, I asked her to marry me. With equal directness she accepted. I said I'd like to schedule the ceremony as soon as possible. She suggested Valentine's Day, February 14. I said I'd come up to Heart Mountain a day or two before that and have the ceremony conducted there. No, she said, feeling was running high about the call for military volunteers and I was being blamed for the whole problem. It might be wiser if I stayed away. She said she would come to Salt Lake City. It didn't seem right to have to disrupt our plans simply because some guys were unhappy about what I had done, but there were other disquieting reports reaching WRA about small groups of camp dissidents burning me in effigy, and threatening to "get" me and other JACL leaders. I yielded reluctantly to Etsu's concerns.

Etsu didn't have much to pack aside from a powder-blue suit that her father had suggested she take to camp so that she'd have at least one nice outfit in addition to the rough outdoor clothing that was standard camp dress. The suit was to serve in place of a wedding gown. Alone, carrying a single suitcase, she walked through the barbed-wire gates of Heart Mountain one early February day to share my uncertain life. A bus took her to the little whistlestop of Deaver. There she boarded the once-a-day northbound train to Billings, Montana, and thence to Butte, where she had an all-day wait for the connecting train to Salt Lake City. The train reached Salt Lake City late at night, ten hours behind schedule. Somehow we got our wires crossed. I wasn't there to meet her. In fact, no one was. Etsu had never been in Salt Lake City. She called JACL headquarters. Fortunately, Larry Tajiri was working late, as he often did, and he hurried to the depot to pick her up.

A more serious problem surfaced the next day when Etsu learned for the first time that I had volunteered for military service. I hadn't mentioned it; it hadn't occurred to me that I should, since I assumed she had read about it in the *Pacific Citizen*. She hadn't. She didn't know a thing about it. She felt I had put something over on her and was as angry as I've ever seen her. On top of that, she had no intention of getting married and then returning to the camp while I marched off to war. What a rocky way to start a marriage!

The storm passed over quickly. Etsu agreed I had to volunteer. She said she would marry me and we would be together until I was inducted. After that she would go to Chicago, where her sister Helen was working as a secretary, and get a job. Hito Okada's wife, Hana, who was meeting Etsu for the first time, was matron of honor. My brother Ben came down from Idaho, where he was working on a farm, to be my best man. Larry Tajiri gave the bride away and Hito sang at the ceremony. The Reverend Taro Goto, my cousin, was allowed to come up from the Topaz camp to conduct the ceremony, and Mother came with him. In deference to Etsu's parents and Mother, we went through the formality of naming go-betweens traditional in Japanese marriages. Henry Mitarai, an old family friend, represented the Minetas. George Inagaki stood up for my family. That must have been the proper thing to do, for our marriage has endured.

Etsu and I have shared good times and bad—there have been plenty of both—and we have let nothing come between us. To put it very honestly, it is her understanding, patience, and tolerance of my weaknesses that is the cement of our marriage. I am impetuous; she is steady. I view the broad picture; she handles details. She is the sounding board for my ideas, and I depend on her good sense. She anticipates my needs without in the least being subservient. She deserves an equal share of the credit for anything I may have been able to accomplish. We complement each other. Kido was wrong. I have never doubted that I married the right Mineta girl.

Expecting to be inducted at any time, Etsu and I began married life in Salt Lake City in a rented room—with the bath down the hall—in the home of an Issei family. There was no honeymoon. There was too much that needed to be done at JACL headquarters. One day I received orders to report to Fort Douglas, on the city's outskirts, for my physical. The commanding general must have received instructions from the Pentagon. He sent his limousine for me; I may have been the only inductee in the entire U.S. Army to be driven in the general's staff car to face the medics. Under the circumstances they couldn't flunk me, although I have extreme astigmatism and am far from being an outstanding physical specimen. After a lot of prodding and poking and thumping and filling me with all manner of shots, the medics certified me as fit for military service and told me to go home to await orders for official induction.

Meanwhile, there were JACL problems in Washington needing attention. WRA was distressed by the flap over the loyalty questionnaire and disappointed that thousands of Nisei weren't eagerly lining up to volunteer for the Army. I had suggested that I and other JACL leaders visit the camps to try to settle doubts and urge enlistment, but both WRA and the Army feared that would only aggravate a problem not of our making. The best thing JACL could do, they advised, was to have its leadership and membership set examples of good citizenship while the government agencies tried to solve their problem. Still, I felt I had miscalculated the Nisei mood badly and was anxious to do anything possible to push the volunteer program. Colonel Scobey assured me the problem would work itself out, but there were other things he wanted to talk over and he asked me to come back to Washington for consultations.

There was still another problem that needed attention. A few of the more racist members of Congress had started a move to strip Japanese Americans of their citizenship even as the government was urging them to volunteer to fight for their country. I drew some expense money from JACL, left my bride in Salt Lake City, and made the long, weary bus trip back to Washington.

There wasn't much I could do to help WRA except to encourage its resettlement program and pledge JACL support for it. But I was able to alert our influential Caucasian friends about what some members of Congress were up to, and they moved quickly to put out the fire.

Colonel Scobey, a tall, spare man with a patient expression, was disappointed but not alarmed by the reaction in the camps. He had progress to report and much to discuss. The Army had decided, he said, to use Nisei already in service—many of whom were in menial noncombat jobs at bases around the country—as cadre to train the men joining the 442nd. In deference to the large number of volunteers coming from Hawaii, I would have preferred to see men from the 100th Battalion as cadre. But Scobey said the Pentagon was so impressed by the 100th that it would be kept together as a combat unit. He also said that while a number of Nisei had been commissioned through college Reserve Officer Training Corps programs, they were considered too few and too inexperienced, and most of the 442nd's officers would be Caucasians. It was difficult to quarrel with that. Aside from the matter of experience, that decision might have been wise in view of the hostility and rivalry that erupted at first between mainland and Hawaii volunteers as a result of their different cultural backgrounds. This ill feeling turned to respect in combat and the men were quickly welded into a cohesive, dedicated fighting unit, but Nisei officers could well have been caught up in difficult problems in the beginning.

Scobey also said the nation's need was so urgent that volunteers for the 442nd found to have a working knowledge of the Japanese language would be diverted to the military intelligence program as interpreters and translators. From a public relations viewpoint it was important that Nisei should be serving in the Pacific Theater as well as in Europe. There were some racists only too ready to charge that the Nisei were volunteering so they could kill white men. I agreed that they should be sent where they were most needed. However, I said many had volunteered for battle and would not relish the idea of fighting the war from a desk. I was wrong about linguists being deskbound. Many went into combat of the most dangerous kind, in the jungles of New Guinea, Burma, and the Philippines and in the first wave of landings in the Pacific island-hopping campaign, where they provided invaluable service while sometimes subject to fire from both sides. Inagaki, who had an excellent knowledge of Japanese, was among those assigned to intelligence and wound up as personal interpreter for Admiral Chester W. Nimitz.

We had requested some time earlier that since about half the Nisei were Buddhists, provisions be made for Buddhist chaplains. That matter went all the way up to McCloy, who suggested that since there was widespread suspicion of, as well as ignorance about, Asian religions, it would be better public relations to approve only Christian chaplains for the 442nd. The Buddhist use of the swastika, which was often confused with the Nazi swastika although the arms point in the opposite direction, no doubt concerned McCloy. We compromised by providing for two Nisei Christian pastors from Hawaii, Captain Hiro Higuchi and Captain Masao Yamada. I have always regretted we lost on the Buddhist issue. In a nation based on freedom of worship, men of the 442nd brought up as Buddhists certainly were entitled to a chaplain of their faith.

But McCloy vindicated himself in part in a disagreement over the 442nd's shoulder patch. The Army's heraldic department had proposed a patch showing a yellow dagger dripping blood, and the words "Remember Pearl Harbor" under it. A later version depicted a yellow arm brandishing a red sword. I didn't like either of them, and neither did any other Nisei who saw them. Nisei were angry about the sneak attack on Pearl Harbor, perhaps even more angry than the average Caucasian American. But we didn't want to be reminded of that perfidy. We felt we were fighting for freedom and democracy, not vengeance. McCloy agreed. He ordered the offensive designs scrapped. Ultimately, Technical Sergeant Mitch

Miyamoto designed a handsome patch showing an upheld torch of freedom on a blue background with red and white borders, and the Nisei wore it proudly.

It was during this period that the Nisei unit was designated the 442nd Regimental Combat Team. Who knows how such numbers are picked? The designation had no particular meaning for me, until someone pointed out that the numbers in Japanese could be read either as *yon-yon-ni* or *shi-shi-ni*. The word *shi* in Japanese means "death" as well as "four." Some Issei saw a sinister omen. Some wondered whether the Army was trying to tell us something. With *shi* appearing twice, were we facing a double whammy? I preferred to consider the 442nd as a bad omen for the enemy.

There was much less concern about the regimental motto, "Go for Broke," a Hawaiian crapshooters' pidgin expression meaning "shoot the works." It was appropriate, catchy, and eventually became an accepted part of the nation's language.

Once more I traveled by bus back to Salt Lake City, where the days sped by as I tried to get JACL affairs in shape while waiting for induction. The Army, which had been in such a hurry to put Nisei volunteers from the mainland in uniform, was inexplicably slow about carrying out the program. The Hawaiian contingent was shipped en masse to Camp Shelby, Mississippi, for basic training. The mainlanders were called up in small groups or individually, and many found it difficult to catch up with their Hawaiian peers.

At JACL headquarters, Teiko Ishida agreed to fill in for me as executive secretary. Together with Kido, who with his family had moved out to Salt Lake City from the Poston camp, we talked about long-range plans, but since I had been improvising strategy while working toward basic goals, there wasn't a great deal I could do to help Teiko. Kido was a remarkable man. He was looking far into the future while most other Nisei were concerning themselves with day-to-day problems. He was impatient with details; he saw the big picture, and in that picture the patriotic response of Japanese Americans to the unfair sacrifices demanded of them would bring about their vindication. Just how that would be done would have to be worked out, but he was determined that it would happen.

Meanwhile, in anticipation of WRA's stepped-up plan to move evacuees out of the camps and back into the American mainstream, we hired Peter Aoki to open a JACL office in New York, Dr. Tom

Yatabe agreed to take over in Chicago, and my brother Joe Grant in Denver. Each made a personal sacrifice to go to work for JACL; all were motivated by a commitment to do whatever was needed for the welfare of the Japanese-American community. Working for scarcely more than expenses, they scouted for housing and jobs, carried on a vigorous public relations campaign, and tried to stamp out brushfires of hate and bigotry. They and the volunteers they recruited to help them were indispensable.

Then, finally, my official induction date was set for early June. I was ordered to report directly to Camp Shelby, where the 442nd was taking shape. That gave me time enough to take Etsu to Chicago and then touch bases once more in Washington. On our last night in Salt Lake City, before boarding a late-night train, we had dinner with a few friends. It was a sober affair, but it took on the appearance of a wild party when a catsup bottle was accidentally knocked off a table. The bottle broke at the neck, and a flying shard of glass inflicted a deep, bloody cut in Etsu's leg. We rushed her to an emergency hospital, where a police surgeon stitched up the wound and gave her a painkilling injection with a warning that she would be in considerable discomfort when the drug wore off. Etsu was in pain for most of the two-day trip to Chicago.

In Washington I made farewell calls on Dillon Myer and other WRA officials and met for the last time with some of our Caucasian advisers to ask for their continued support. At the Pentagon, McCloy, Colonel Scobey, and other officers warned that the Army was a great leveler, that I might have important friends in Washington but once I was in uniform I was responsible to the Army and the Army would be responsible for me.

There was plenty of time for thought on the slow train to Mississippi. I had a premonition that I would not survive the war. Having asked for combat, having urged other Nisei to volunteer for combat, I did not consider it an injustice in the great overall scheme of things that I would become a casualty. Of course, no one wants to die. I had much to live for. I looked forward to a long life with my bride, going back to law school, perhaps going into politics. But I knew I had to be ready for the possibility of battlefield death.

But before that I had to learn to be a soldier, and I wasn't sure how much support I would get from my Nisei peers. I was aware that many of them, even though they had volunteered, still believed that in some way I was their Moses responsible for leading into the detention camps. I didn't expect them to go out of their way to help me.

Of one thing I was certain. Five of the Masaoka boys would be back together. Only Joe Grant, the oldest and by then thirty-four years old, was not in uniform. He had told me he would volunteer if I urged him to, but I felt it was important that at least one of us remain to look after Mother. So he had gone to work for JACL to fight for democracy on the home front. Ben Frank, the next brother, quit his farm job in Idaho to volunteer for the 442nd. Ike, my next-younger brother, had been drafted before the outbreak of war. He had been transferred to the 442nd at Camp Shelby from his station in South Carolina. Hank had been working in Nebraska, and he too signed up when he heard about the 442nd. The youngest, Tad, was among those who volunteered from the Manzanar camp. None of them had been in touch with me before volunteering. They simply knew what had to be done and stepped forward to get it done. I was proud of them and delighted that we would be together once more. I knew I could depend on them in the tough days ahead. Moreover, with five of us in the same combat outfit, no one could accuse the Masaokas of shirking their duty.

I left the train at Hattiesburg, Mississippi, and caught a ride to huge, sprawling Camp Shelby. I had no more than checked in at the reassignment pool and drawn my uniform and other gear when I was ordered to report at once to the commanding officer of the 442nd, Colonel Charles W. Pence.

Chapter 8

Soldier Without Arms

Colonel Pence was a compactly built man of average size with a lined, careworn face and a small, close-clipped mustache, every bit the career soldier.

I was a raw, awkward recruit, uncomfortable in my brand-new uniform as I stood stiffly before him, trying my best to look soldierly and knowing I wasn't succeeding very well. "Private Masaoka reporting, sir," I said, remembering the words I had heard in some movie. He smiled and invited me to sit down.

"Masaoka," he said, "I know a great deal about you already. I have been told about your role in helping to get the 442nd authorized. I welcome you to my command. I am aware that you have asked for combat duty, and I daresay you will see combat, but that is not to be your primary job in this outfit. As you know so much better than I, one mission of the 442nd is to dramatize the loyalty of Japanese Americans, and it is essential to get their story out to the public. That will be your chief responsibility. As soon as you complete basic training, you will be assigned to the regimental public relations office, where Major Oland D. Russell is in charge."

"Yes, sir," I said. But even before I was taught how to tote a rifle, I learned there are many menial but necessary military duties. Like latrine detail. That means washing down the urinals, cleaning the toilet bowls, and mopping out the latrines. There is no chore quite so humbling for one totally without experience in household duties. I was sweating away on latrine detail a few days after I arrived when a runner came from headquarters with orders for me to report immediately.

Completely disheveled, looking like anything but a soldier, I hurried to Colonel Pence's office. I was introduced to a civilian from the Pentagon who, in a nice way, expressed surprise that I was cleaning toilets and told Colonel Pence that Secretary McCloy wanted me put to work as quickly as possible on the public relations staff.

Almost immediately I was assigned to Major Russell. Prior to joining the Army he had been an editor and columnist with the *New York World-Telegram,* a Scripps-Howard newspaper, and knew something about getting stories published. He had spent some time as a correspondent in prewar Japan and had written a book about the great Mitsui mercantile family. A bluff, friendly man, Russell gave me a desk and typewriter and introduced me to a Caucasian lieutenant and two Nisei enlisted men from Hawaii who made up the staff.

I was supposed to complete my basic training when I could, but for all intents and purposes my formal indoctrination as a soldier had ended. As a result I never learned to strip a rifle or even aim one. I never learned to make a bedroll, dig a foxhole, throw a grenade, negotiate an obstacle course, put together a field pack, or accomplish any of the other important infantry skills. When an inspection loomed, one or another of my brothers would hurry over to clean my rifle or make sure that my bed was made properly. Of all the millions of Americans who served in World War II, I undoubtedly would rank among the least qualified to be called a soldier. Most of the other Nisei had been in camp one to two months before I arrived and had taken smoothly to military training. I never caught up. The officers were aware of my shortcomings but they must have figured that if Colonel Pence was willing to let me get by, it was okay by them. And the colonel took seriously his instructions from the Pentagon.

I quickly learned the men of the 442nd respected Colonel Pence as a leader who cared about them. I never became close to him, but I think an anonymous Nisei GI quoted in the book *Go for Broke* put it very well:

> Colonel Pence was a wonderful man. He was a lonely man, but was a top colonel. He was promoted to general after the Vosges [campaign]. He was fair, stuck by us, and backed us in everything we did. He had great faith in us. Nobody could say anything bad about Colonel Pence. He was a real leader and a soldier. For exam-

ple, in Shelby, he said, "If the other troops pick on you, just get back at 'em, and don't take anything lying down." He was fair, and he trusted us.

What the colonel was saying was that Nisei should have pride in themselves, their uniform, and their outfit and didn't have to take guff from anybody. That kind of leadership was great for morale among men who had been under a shadow. Not infrequently, Nisei got into fights with men from other units who thoughtlessly had referred to them as Japs, and despite their lack of size they seldom came out second best. It was obvious Pence was proud of the opportunity of shaping a regiment of untested Japanese Americans into a fighting force, and they sensed his confidence in them.

There were about 3,000 Nisei already in camp when I reported. Virtually all the officers were Caucasians; a few of them were from missionary families and had grown up in the Far East. Many were Southerners who had less formal education than a majority of the enlisted men. As a matter of fact, about 80 percent of the 442nd's enlisted men had an IQ that qualified them for nomination to officer candidate school, and an astonishing number had college and postgraduate degrees. If everyone qualified to apply for a commission had done so, there wouldn't be enough riflemen. Early on it was decided that only the exceptionally qualified would be considered. Ironically, even though we were fighting for equality of opportunity, it wasn't possible to provide it. There were rumors that some of the white officers had been assigned to the 442nd against their will, and a few had strong reservations about commanding Nisei. The obvious misfits soon were transferred, and those who remained came to respect us, and we them. The commander of the service company, to which I was assigned, Captain Lee B. Hawkins, like most of the others was not a career soldier. He was a used-car salesman who had been in the Kentucky National Guard. He knew next to nothing about Japanese Americans, but he worked hard to learn about us and was one of the best-liked officers.

The 3,000 men were divided into three battalions, each with a headquarters company and four rifle companies. In addition there was a regimental headquarters company, an antitank company, a cannon company, a medical detachment, and a service company.

The 442nd also included the 522nd Field Artillery Battalion, the 232nd Combat Engineer Company, and the 206th Army Band. In short, we were to become one of two self-contained regimental combat teams in the U.S. Army designed and equipped to fight as part of a division, or on our own. It may be significant that our success led to the concept of combat teams being adopted more widely.

One of my first nonwriting assignments was to see Earl Finch, a Hattiesburg businessman and rancher who had taken a great interest in the men of the 442nd. I needed to ask his help in bridging a rift that had developed between mainland and Hawaii Nisei groups. Naturally he had assumed the fellows from Hawaii, being so far from home, were in greatest need of friendship and entertainment. He invited them to his ranch for barbecues and arranged trips to New Orleans and other places of interest. What he didn't realize was that the mainland Nisei were in even greater want of hospitality in that virtually all were broke.

Many of the Hawaii Nisei came into service with big rolls of money—going-away gifts from friends and families, and what they had earned in war-related jobs. On the other hand, mainland Nisei were from families that had had very little income since war's outbreak. Virtually all the volunteers from the camps had lost their resources in the evacuation, and their total income since then consisted of the $9 a month they were given for work in the assembly centers and the $12 or $16 they were paid by WRA. Some of them were sending an allotment out of their $21 monthly Army pay back to families still locked up in the camps. (One result of the relative affluence of Hawaiian kids was that they bluffed the more conservative mainlanders out of many poker pots with large bets. That led to further hard feelings.)

I explained the problem to Finch and suggested he spread his largesse a little more equally. Finch was glad to get the information, and mainland Nisei soon received their share of invitations. Finch entertained several thousand Nisei over the months at his own expense and became known as the one-man USO. We owed him much for his friendship and generosity. After the war the mainland Nisei fêted him and the fellows from Hawaii invited him to the islands repeatedly for the royal hospitality for which they are noted.

Several thousand Japanese Americans at Camp Shelby couldn't

help but attract attention both inside and outside the base. One of my duties was to visit other units in the great, sprawling camp to lecture the troops on the story of the Nisei, about the evacuation, and why we were volunteers at Shelby training as a segregated unit. It took some explaining to convince some GIs that we were not turncoat Japanese prisoners of war. I also spoke before church and civic groups in the area. As understanding spread, the Nisei began to get invitations for Sunday visits with local families. Oddly enough, I discovered that some of the growing friendliness could be traced to the Civil War. The Southerners still remembered mistreatment at the hands of the "damn Yankees" and seemed to feel a kinship for us, who also had been mistreated because of cultural differences.

Many Nisei volunteers were older than the average draftee. They had families, which they brought to Hattiesburg—and fell right smack into the middle of the South's racial problems. Since Japanese Americans obviously were not white, Sansei children weren't welcome in all-white schools. The black schools were so run-down and poorly equipped that Nisei parents were reluctant to send their offspring to them. And, of course, the Nisei parents expected their children to be treated in the same manner as other (meaning white) children. The Army solved the problem by setting up special classes for the Japanese-American youngsters. Then it became my job to explain to the townspeople why it was necessary to have three separate school systems in the land of the free where we were all supposed to be fighting for democracy. The teachers we recruited for the Army schools were the qualified women among wives of the Nisei volunteers. Generally, their credentials were more impressive than those of most local teachers. This was understandable; the Mississippi pay scale was only half as high as what the Nisei women had been accustomed to in California.

The race problem posed a delicate problem for all of us. Most of the officers—at least those who counted—insisted that we Nisei act, and be treated, as whites. That meant using the white latrines, sitting in the front of streetcars and buses when we went to town, eating inside the restaurants instead of being handed our food out in back. While we were uncomfortable with a double standard and sympathetic toward the blacks, we as a matter of principle were not going to accept inferior status. Despite the discrimination mainland Nisei had known on the Pacific Coast, in most respects we had never understood the Jim Crow prejudice that blacks, or Negroes as they were called then, faced daily as an accepted fact of life in Mississippi. Among us discrimination became the subject of many intense discussions, out of which developed a deep new sense of social justice involving others as well as ourselves.

The meaning of the South's color bar was brought home forcefully to some Nisei who had been assigned to guard German prisoners of war sent out to harvest peanuts. The Germans were allowed inside a restaurant for lunch, but the manager insisted that their guards in U.S. uniform had to eat outside like the blacks. I heard of other instances when Nisei servicemen were ordered not to use either white or black restrooms. Where could they take care of their needs? Secretary McCloy heard from me about these outrages, of course.

Meanwhile I was writing press releases about interesting members of the 442nd—men who had made extraordinary sacrifices to enlist—and escorting reporters who visited the unit, steering them to the more articulate volunteers in an effort to get as much newspaper space as possible. I had barely learned all my responsibilities as an enlisted public relations officer (PRO, an acronym sometimes confused for prophylactic station, and later changed to PIO, for public information officer) when Major Russell was transferred to the South Pacific. The lieutenant in the office was nominally my boss, but he was given other responsibilities as well, and the two enlisted men were moved out of the department. All of a sudden I found that I, a buck private, had replaced two officers and two enlisted men and was the total staff of the regimental public relations office.

My hours were long and irregular, leaving even less time for learning military skills. Realizing the importance of a friendly mess sergeant, I sought out Joe Itagaki, who ran the service company mess. He had been in charge of an officers' club at an Army base near Honolulu and was owner of a well-known restaurant when he talked his way into the 442nd so he could make sure his friends would be properly fed. We liked each other from the beginning. Being older than most of the others, he was sensible as well as amiable. He could always rustle up some food for me regardless of the hour. In return, I would write letters for Joe, who was not known for his literary skills, to send to friends back home. When several of the letters were published in the Honolulu newspapers, Joe's delight and appreciation were boundless.

I developed another good friend in Royal Manaka, a former fisherman from Monterey, California, who was my first sergeant. He understood my special responsibilities with the 442nd, endorsed them completely, and went out of his way to relieve me of the time-consuming routine chores of enlisted men. A wise and understanding first sergeant can be the difference between a happy company and a tense one. Manaka was one of the best.

The theme that I pushed constantly in my work was that the United States was not involved in a race war. I underscored the points that Japanese Americans had volunteered because we were Americans, that we believed in democracy, that we would be willing to fight against Japan as well as any other enemy of the nation, that even though our families were in detention camps as the result of a wartime aberration the 442nd was an example of democracy in action, and that in a period of hate and misunderstanding we sought only a chance to prove our Americanism.

Meanwhile the others were spending long days on the rifle range and obstacle courses, marching in the Mississippi heat under full pack and engaging in exhausting maneuvers. If any harbored resentment about my "soft" assignment it was gradually overcome as they began to see stories about their activities and aspirations appearing in newspapers around the country. When the Army set up its public information programs it had a good understanding of the effect that popular recognition has on troop morale.

But even as I was immersing myself completely in military duties, my JACL life reached out to claim me. Out of the clear blue I received military orders to proceed to Washington to appear before the Dies Committee on Un-American Activities. I knew, of course, about the activities of the committee headed by Martin Dies, the Texas Democrat, who had gained notoriety as a witch-hunter. But it was John M. Costello, chairman of a Dies subcommittee and an equally accomplished bully, who had issued the subpoena. About the time I was being inducted, native Californian Costello had opened a series of hearings on the West Coast. From what I could tell from newspaper accounts, Costello under the guise of ferreting out un-American activities among Japanese Americans was harassing Dillon Myer and trying to discredit the War Relocation Authority.

What I did not learn until later was that on June 11, representatives of the committee had invaded the Washington apartment where Joe Kanazawa's wife, Emily, lived and where JACL files had been stored after Joe, George Inagaki, and I had gone into the Army. Brandishing what they said were subpoenas, the investigators seized copies of my correspondence and reports to JACL headquarters. Costello had been gaining enormous newspaper attention in California with wild charges of WRA ineptitude and misconduct. The Hearst press, the *Los Angeles Times,* and other newspapers had published them without question. Now Costello had shifted his hearings to Washington and I had been summoned, supposedly to confess that I had dictated and manipulated government policy toward us Japanese Americans.

It was a weird hearing but typical of the Dies tactics. Joe Kanazawa was called up before I was. He had been at Camp Shelby, too, but I didn't know the committee had summoned him until I saw him in Washington. He had worked for some months in the JACL office, handling press releases and the like while Inagaki and I spent most of our time out meeting with various officials. Thus, Joe's testimony was not particularly relevant to what Costello was trying to prove. In his way Joe Kanazawa was a remarkable fellow. He was thirty-six years old when he volunteered — ten to fifteen years older than most of the others. Since he had a college degree and a journalism background and had been a free-lance writer, he would have been valuable in the PRO office. But that isn't the way the Army does things. The closest he got to communications was the job of hauling a weighty radio transmitter pack on his back as the 442nd advanced up the Italian peninsula, into France, and back again.

The questions I faced from Costello's subcommittee were based on the documents seized from JACL files. I was not allowed to examine them or refresh my memory about what they contained before taking the stand. After being sworn I was quizzed about scores of letters and reports that I had marked ''confidential'' or ''strictly confidential.'' This was a warning to the headquarters staff that the information should not be released prematurely. The chief investigator, Robert E. Stripling, tried to imply sinister motives on my part. One report in particular came in for intense scrutiny. I had written:

Myer . . . said that he and his staff deal with me on the same basis of confidence and mutual trust as they do among themselves. Up to now I have been permitted to sit down and discuss every major policy before it is finally passed on. Up to now no confidence has been betrayed. The War Relocation Authority desires to continue that fine relationship and will continue to do so as long as confidential matters are kept in confidence and as long as we sincerely try to cooperate with them on the improvement of conditions. He is afraid that certain guys in Congress would jump down their collective throats if they could only imagine a part of the part which we play in forming WRA policy. . . .

This, in Costello's view, was proof that a Jap was manipulating a government agency. When Myer got on the stand he took the position that I had been exaggerating my importance in reports to headquarters to make myself look good.

The truth was that there had been good communication and frequent consultation between me and WRA officials. Myer was wise enough to ask our opinion on many matters because his agency was groping in unfamiliar territory, and we had answers simply because we were Japanese Americans. Of course, he made the ultimate decisions. He should have been commended for his good sense rather than condemned for being conscientious.

The one time WRA did not consult us on a substantial matter was on the loyalty questionnaire, and that turned out to be a disaster. But Stripling, Costello's investigator, made it appear that I was wielding undue influence over WRA. That was not true and Myer had to deny it strongly. In fact, he delivered a memorable lecture to the subcommittee on ethics and human rights, and castigated it for its unfair and unruly tactics.

I on the other hand was in the uncomfortable position of answering sharp questions without embarrassing many influential people, including members of Congress like Senator Thomas and Congressman Jerry Voorhis among others, whose names had been brought up simply because they had helped JACL. They were exercising their obligation to support what they considered a just cause when they advised me or opened doors for me, but Costello in lifting those actions out of the context of my reports made them appear subversive and sinister.

Rather than put our friends in a difficult position, I was intentionally vague before the subcommittee; I failed to recall details and accepted the role of braggart and self-promoter which Stripling ascribed to me. It was far better for me to look foolish than risk compromising our friends and allies. Previously, I had served JACL best by being articulate; in Costello's inquisition, my most effective role was to play dumb.

In reality, what I had been doing for JACL in Washington was in the best democratic tradition. I was using my right to take a people's grievances to government, and that's what democracy is all about. It is significant that friends whose names came up in the hearings — liberals, church and human-rights leaders, political bigwigs — did not repudiate their actions and continued their staunch support. Until his death in 1982, Dillon Myer was one of my dearest friends.

The Costello hearings were a turning point in the experience of Japanese Americans. Following earlier "investigations" that were no more than a charade, Costello and his colleagues had come up with headline-grabbing charges about our disloyalty and how we were being pampered by fuzzy-headed New Deal ideologues in the Roosevelt administration. Many were willing to believe the stories. Costello had promised even more startling revelations in the Washington hearings, but he overcommitted himself. The hearings revealed his charges were without substance. Members of Congress who had been anxious to believe Costello now turned away. The press also became more fair. Reporters began to ask questions rather than accept unsubstantiated charges. The accusations that had been published without challenge appeared less frequently. Having volunteered and being in uniform with four brothers was visible evidence of loyalty that few American families could match.

There is, I think, a striking parallel between the performance of the press in this instance and in the shameful Joseph McCarthy era less than a decade later. McCarthy made sensational charges about Communist influence in the State Department, which major segments of the press accepted at face value. Only after great damage had been done did the press seek proof of those charges, which turned out to be unfounded or flimsy at best. After the McCarthy experience it is difficult to see the press being taken in by some future demagogue. But back in 1943 when we were the targets of demagogic venom, things were different.

Back at Camp Shelby, all the Nisei except me were being whipped into formidable fighting men. I learned about the duties of public relations officers at two specialized courses offered at Fort MacPherson in Atlanta, Georgia. My trips to Atlanta solidified my conviction that telling the story of the Nisei was a critically important part of the war effort. My uniform didn't save me from being sneered at as a "Jap" and jostled off the sidewalk by home-front commandos who thought they could hasten Japan's downfall by being unpleasant to me.

The same sort of stuff was going on elsewhere, even at the WRA camps when volunteers went back to visit their families. Guards at the camp gate, wearing the same uniform as the Nisei soldiers, were insulting. In one case I heard about, some punk guard ordered a Nisei corporal into the guardhouse at bayonet point for interrogation. Only quick action by others nearby averted a civil war. My brother Tad returned from a visit to Manzanar to report that he had been subjected to a body search before he was permitted to enter the camp to visit our mother. When these stories got around there was much bitterness in the ranks. It is to the everlasting credit of the Nisei that these outrages only strengthened their determination to be the best damned soldiers in the U.S. Army. There was a lot of educating that had to be done both during and after the war. For the time being, I wrote to Secretary McCloy urging him to look into the situation and take necessary action.

Presently, we five Masaoka brothers in the 442nd were reduced to four. Hank, who had been with the antitank unit, volunteered for paratroop training. He liked that duty, as well as the $5 additional pay, so much that eventually he transferred out of the 442nd. He was in combat in Italy during the same period as the rest of us, but not with the 442nd. Ironically, Hank was the only one of the five Masaokas in the service who came out of the war unscathed.

As I have indicated earlier, some of my most important public relations work involved an internal problem within the 442nd between Hawaii and mainland Nisei. They were of the same ethnic stock, but a cultural gulf separated them. The Hawaiians had grown up together in a benign racial environment. They were warmly outgoing and clannish at the same time. They considered many of the mainland Nisei stand-offish. They didn't appreciate the trauma of the evacuation experienced by the mainlanders, and they resented being ordered about by the mainland Nisei, who made up the majority of noncoms. On the other hand, mainland Nisei were inclined to look down on the islanders for what they considered their outrageous use of pidgin and the way they flashed their bankrolls.

Feelings between some members of the two groups grew worse when the 100th Battalion joined the 442nd at Shelby. Let me depart from my personal narrative for a bit to tell you about the 100th, which is one of the great stories of World War II. At the time of the Japanese attack on Pearl Harbor, hundreds of Nisei were serving as members of the Territorial Guard, the Hawaiian version of the National Guard. They rushed to Hawaii's defense on December 7, and their performance was outstanding. But as reinforcements reached Hawaii from the mainland, an increasing number of Nisei were discharged from the Territorial Guard. Some of them banded together as the Varsity Victory Volunteers, a work corps ready to do whatever the Army asked. And they worked tirelessly as a labor battalion. The dedication of the Nisei persuaded General Delos C. Emmons, commanding general in Hawaii, to recommend formation of a special Nisei combat unit. On May 26, 1942, the Hawaiian Provisional Battalion was authorized, made up of Nisei who had been in the Territorial Guard. On June 5, 1942, even as evacuation of Japanese Americans from the West Coast was under way, 1,300 Nisei soldiers and their officers sailed from Hawaii for combat training on the mainland. They landed in Oakland on June 10 and two days later were activated as the 100th Battalion.

The 100th trained at Camp McCoy, Wisconsin, and quickly demonstrated extraordinary skill, determination, and stamina as a fighting unit. After ten months of training, the 100th took part in war games in Louisiana and performed magnificently as a segregated outfit. No doubt it was the 100th's record while at Camp McCoy that helped persuade the Pentagon to approve the 442nd and soon afterward to reopen the draft to all Nisei men. The 100th was a tough, proud bunch; its men were justifiably cocky about their record when they joined the 442nd at Camp Shelby. They had a joyous reunion with brothers, cousins, and old friends. But not all of them were pleased with what they heard of the "uppityness" of the mainlanders. I had a busy time persuading both sides that mainlanders and islanders were in the same boat, and that all of us had to work together, fight together, to assure our future as Americans.

The most persuasive argument was in the form of visits to the nearby Rohwer and Jerome WRA camps in Arkansas. The men from Hawaii were stunned when they saw the thousands of mainland Japanese Americans, including women and little children who looked exactly like their friends and relatives, confined in a barracks town behind barbed-wire fences. They were angered when, despite their uniforms, they were subjected to interrogation by military police at the detention center's gates. The islanders immediately accepted the detainees as their special friendship project, and almost immediately the tension between the two 442nd groups vanished.

"Da guys," Joe Itagaki told me, "for da first time dey understand what you guys on da mainland have to go through."

At first the islanders had referred to the mainlanders as "Kotonks," *kotonk* being a reasonable approximation of the sound of an empty coconut hitting the ground. In turn the mainlanders called the Hawaiians "Buddaheads," a corruption of the pidgin "buta-head" meaning pigheaded. In time these insults became terms of affection as islanders and mainlanders became comrades in arms, each respecting the courage and strengths of the other.

The bond among various Japanese Americans was further strengthened when a company of linguists from the Military Intelligence Service Language School at Camp Savage in Minnesota came to Shelby for a period of infantry training. Their arrival gave the men of the 442nd an opportunity to see old friends and exchange horror stories about Army life. One of the visitors was my brother-in-law, Minoru Endo, married to Etsu's sister, Aya. Our men quickly learned that the translators and interpreters weren't destined only for desk jobs. They would be foot-slogging riflemen with the added responsibilities of linguists and would face the possibility of being mistaken for the enemy by their own side.

The 442nd was still an unpolished outfit when the 100th was alerted for overseas duty. It left in August 1943 for North Africa, landing on September 2 in Oran, where it was attached to the veteran 34th (Red Bull) Division. After further training the 100th sailed across the Mediterranean and went ashore on the Salerno beachhead, south of Naples, on September 26. Its first objective was the inland town of Montemarano. In two days of fighting against seasoned German troops, the 100th took all its assigned targets at a cost of two men killed and seven wounded. These were the first of nearly 9,500 casualties to be suffered before war's end by the 100th Battalion and the 442nd Regimental Combat Team of which it became a part.

For those of us back at Shelby, time sped quickly. Inspired by reports of the 100th's continued successes and sobered by the lengthening casualty lists, the men of the 442nd were welded into a cohesive unit. I kept myself too busy to enjoy trips to New Orleans. I wrote to Etsu nearly every day. And as the time to go overseas approached, I worked late every night on what has come to be known half jokingly as Mike Masaoka's last will and testament. Still burdened by the premonition that I would not come back and aware that my departure from JACL had been somewhat precipitate, I felt that I owed the organization a "final report" of my steward-ship as national executive secretary. The document, mostly typed at night "after hours," addressed to officers and the membership, runs nearly 200 double-spaced typewritten pages and is dated April 22, 1944, which was the day the 442nd boarded trains for Camp Patrick Henry, Virginia, staging area for Hampton Roads, where we were to embark for an unspecified overseas assignment.

Actually, only two-thirds of the 442nd shipped out. The move-ment included the 2nd and 3rd battalions plus the medics and head-quarters, antitank, cannon, and service companies. More than 500 enlisted men and some forty officers of the 1st Battalion had already gone overseas as replacements for the 100th, and the remainder stayed at Camp Shelby to serve as cadre for Nisei draftees to be trained as our replacements. In nine months of bitter fighting the 100th had suffered grievously while taking one objective after an-other. In the first month and a half of combat in Italy the 100th had lost seventy-five enlisted men and three officers killed, 239 wounded. Crossing the Volturno River under intense fire during the drive to take Mount Cassino Abbey, only fourteen of the 187 men in B Company made it through. There was no doubt the 442nd was likely to suffer comparable losses.

I mailed my report to JACL headquarters, and that's the last I saw of it. I have never had the urge to reread it. However, in writing this book a copy had to be dug out and reexamined. Most of the report was a review of my activities from the date I was hired, September 1, 1941, to June 22, 1943, when I was formally inducted into the Army. Much of it is ancient history now and well known. But one segment deserves reproduction here. It has to do with the reasoning behind JACL's decision to cooperate with the federal government in the evacuation. Because JACL as an organization and "Moses Masaoka" specifically have been criticized bitterly for this decision, accused of betraying Japanese Americans and "selling them down the river," I feel it is important to relate exactly how it was made at a special emergency meeting of the National Board and the National Council, JACL's two governing bodies, in San Francisco in March 1942. The meeting had been called to determine JACL's position regarding the evacuation order. Sixty-four of the sixty-six chapters answered the first roll call. My "final report" included these paragraphs:

> In the beginning three alternatives were discussed. One was an out and out opposition in every way possible to the government's evacuation program; another was to seek some compromise, using the threat of opposition as a bargaining weapon; and still another was "constructive cooperation" with the government, not because Japanese Americans conceded the constitutionality of this unprecedented action or the validity of the arguments for such a recourse, but because it was the only reasonable and realistic course at the time.
>
> Number One was ruled out as impossible. As individuals, some might oppose evacuation but, as an organization, mass resistance might result in greater evils than even evacuation.
>
> Number Two was rejected as impractical. The government was neither in a mood nor position to compromise. The Army held the trump cards as well as the aces. Seeking a compromise, haggling as it might be termed, might irritate the powers that be into overt action which might be more disastrous than evacuation itself.
>
> That left only Number Three: Cooperation.

I then listed twelve reasons that led to the decision:

> 1. As Americans we could do no less. In wartime, the military is supreme. They are charged with the responsibility of safeguarding our country from invasion. And at that moment the Pacific Coast might have been vulnerable to attack by Japan. Perhaps those charged with the defense of the Western Command had vital information which was not available to the public. If, in the considered judgment of the military commander, "military necessity" dictated the evacuation of all persons of Japanese ancestry, we as patriotic citizens and responsible people should not be disposed to question that judgment. If a military commander

had to justify his every action in court or consider every conceivable viewpoint before effecting any action, he would be hamstrung and the enemy would overcome him while he was in the midst of litigation.

This, in substance, proved to be the reasoning of the United States Supreme Court in upholding the constitutionality of General DeWitt's curfew and travel restrictions upon Americans of Japanese extraction almost eighteen months later. In this connection, it must be kept constantly in mind that at no time before, during, or since has JACL waived its right to question the constitutionality of the evacuation and exclusion orders. Actually, JACL agreed to cooperate "under protest," believing that this was a grave violation not only of the Constitution but also of human decency.

2. At that time, Japan's legions were on the offensive, America was just beginning to organize for the great task confronting her. To many, a Japanese invasion in force of the Pacific Coast was imminent. If we Japanese Americans had refused to cooperate with the government and the Army was forced to divert large numbers of its troops from preparing defenses to forcibly ejecting us from what were named as prohibited zones, the American people would never have forgiven us for such action. In America's darkest hours, we could not force her to weaken her defenses and invite invasion. And if Japan had launched a landing, timed with the Army's preoccupation with the Japanese American resistance to evacuation, the future would not be worth considering for Japanese Americans in the United States.

3. If resistance proved to be stubborn or forceful, troops might have had to resort to bayonet and rifle fire. If this proved to be the case, the blood of all the Japanese Americans killed, as well as federal soldiers, would have been on our hands.

4. If resistance became widespread, the very groups and interests which might have provoked the "military necessity" behind our evacuation might have introduced another reign of terror to drive out Japanese Americans. Some of the older delegates, remembering the race riots and night riders of another day in California when powerful interests desired to force passage of the Japanese exclusion law, advised against any move which might incite these groups into action again.

5. If Japanese-American opposition to evacuation because of race gained the attention and active sympathy of other "colored" or

California-despised minorities, these other nationalities might have joined the demonstrations. Race riots and even civil war might have been the result.

6. In any case, if violence occurred in any form to Japanese Americans or other non-Caucasian races because of the evacuation program, Japan's propagandists would have had a real holiday exploiting the doctrine of race war as against that of ideas and ideals. As it was, they did introduce arguments to that effect in their propaganda aimed at the peoples in Asia and Southwest Pacific. Just imagine what they could have done had race riots resulted.

7. The experience at Terminal Island was a shocking reminder of what might happen if resistance or threat of opposition brought about another 24-hour evacuation order. The people suffered tremendously because there wasn't an organized, supervised removal. All the fathers had been interned by the FBI for investigation, leaving only worried mothers and children. Furniture and other articles sold for only a few cents on the dollar. No packing crates, for example, were available and no fish boxes found around the wharves, and fruit and vegetable crates rushed by truck from Los Angeles by the JACL had to be used. And when they moved out, they had no place to go. Many slept out in the open. And women and children sleeping under blanket tents and crowded into church chapels were not uncommon sights in Los Angeles after that tragic event.

8. Persons of Japanese ancestry had considerable property in the prohibited zones. If some safeguards were to be provided by the government, cooperation was essential.

9. The alien Japanese would have to go as a matter of course. They did not even have the cloak of citizenship with which they might question the evacuation orders. Most of them were and are the parents of the Japanese Americans. They were and are very old as a group, averaging close to sixty years. They were heartsick over the loss of their lifetimes' achievement, for evacuation signaled their failure to be Americans and to have their children recognized as such. Many would die in the process. They were too deep-rooted to be able to pioneer again in some new clime. The least their children, the Japanese Americans, could do was to volunteer to go along with them and to help them as best they could as one way of trying to repay their parents for all the sacrifices which they had made for them. The Japanese Americans were duty bound to share the adversity and hardships of a

cruel adventure with their parents in the twilight of their lives.

10. This cooperation would be our contribution to the war effort and proof of the Americanism of the Japanese American. In the words of Edward J. Ennis, director of the Alien Enemy Control Unit of the Department of Justice: "No other group of people in the history of the United States have ever been called upon to make greater sacrifices for their country and none have responded more nobly."

11. In the long run, cooperation would make it easier for our non-Japanese friends to work in and for our behalf and benefit. They could point to the fact that we had permitted ourselves to be uprooted from our homes, our businesses, our associations, everything we knew and held dear, in order to cooperate with the government when national unity and sacrifice were the vital issues of the day. This fact of cooperation could become the most potent weapon Japanese Americans have ever had to win the goodwill and respect of all Americans all over the United States. Difficult as is the role of the so-called pro-Japanese American, imagine how impossible their position would be if critics could point to active defiance of the military by those whom they were trying to aid as an indication of their disloyalty and interference with the war effort. Cooperation was the only way to pave the road for public relations both from our own viewpoint as well as those fair-minded Americans who desire justice for Japanese Americans.

12. Finally, since the government was determined to evacuate us whether we liked it or not, common sense dictated that we try to make the most of a very difficult situation, that cooperation was the best way to secure humane treatment and consideration. Cooperation on our part would impose a moral obligation, at least, upon the government to reciprocate that cooperation by working with us in the matter of planning and administration. Arousing the antagonism and hatred of high government officials wouldn't be conductive to kindly, personal interest in our welfare. Cooperation would result in a more liberal, understanding administration as opposed to an arbitrary "prisoner of war" type of supervision. It is inconceivable to me that an agency comparable to the War Relocation Authority with such able directors as Milton S. Eisenhower and Dillon S. Myer would have been created had Japanese Americans openly challenged the authority of the military in those hours of uncertainty and fear. Cooperation, in a sentence, offered the best opportunity for Japanese Americans to regain their dignity, self-respect, and civil rights.

JACL's policy has always been to seek the greatest good for the greatest number over the longest period of time. In this case, the same yardstick applied. Aside from the considerations of patriotism, the arguments boiled down to one conclusive fact: the Army was all-powerful at that moment. Fierce, determined resistance and opposition might have been more dramatic and spectacular but "constructive cooperation" as we chose to call it would, and did, save possible bloodshed, greater economic and property losses, and considerable hardship.

If we blundered in 1942, it was in the failure to resist with all our energies *detention* after *removal*. Although at the time they seemed to merge in the public mind as a single crisis, they were two totally different issues.

Removal we could understand as an urgent military necessity demanded by the commanding general of the Western Defense Command and authorized by the president in the name of national security.

But JACL had never accepted continued imprisonment after the immediate needs of removal from endangered areas had been met. Detention ran head-on into basic constitutional rights — the right to equal protection under the law, the right to due process, the right to be informed of charges, the right to a speedy and public trial, the right to confront accusatory witnesses, the right to life, liberty, and pursuit of happiness, the right of *habeas corpus*.

We failed at a critical juncture of history to assert those rights in the strongest possible terms. Protest may have had no immediate, practical effect, but we should have made our voice of outrage heard. We had never agreed to detention, but neither did we protest it vigorously enough.

Perhaps one reason for our failure was that we had been caught off guard by consistent government assurances about the temporary nature of removal. Implicit in their demand for cooperation was the understanding that when the tide of war had turned, as surely it would before long, the evacuees could return to their homes and businesses.

But once the exodus established its momentum, there was the overwhelming problem of logistics — how to feed, shelter, relocate, and support 115,000 men, women, and children suddenly uprooted from their homes. Since they could not be turned loose across a hostile land, they had to be placed in relocation camps, which were to have been a temporary solution. When the Army ringed them with barbed wire and WRA set up bureaucratic require- ments for leaving, their function was changed abruptly from emer- gency relocation depots to semipermanent concentration camps. By then it was too late to reclaim the egg of freedom from the omelet and make it whole.

We believed, but of course we could not prove, that there was no military necessity for the evacuation in the first place. More than four decades were to pass before the federal Commission on War- time Relocation and Internment of Civilians, after exhaustive hear- ings and research, confirmed our contention that the evacuation was wrong and unnecessary. This was our position in 1942, and there has been no reason to modify it since then. The decision of U.S. District Court Judge Donald G. Voorhees in Gordon Hirabayashi's 1986 *co-ram nobis* or writ-of-error case — that the federal government en- gaged in misconduct ''of the most fundamental character'' in concealing evidence of Nisei loyalty and General DeWitt's racist mo- tivation in the Supreme Court review of Hirabayashi's conviction — further supports our contention.

But under the circumstances that existed in 1942, when we were told that it was our patriotic duty to do whatever was necessary to defend a nation in great peril, there was no choice but to coop- erate with our government. If identical circumstances should arise tomorrow — and I pray that they will never arise — chances are that I would urge the same acceptance of patriotic duty. But I would hope that we as a nation have learned from our mistakes, and that our leaders would be more sensitive, more frank, more honest with the people, more faithful to the observance and preservation of constitutional ideals.

Totally unaware of the information that had been denied us, the men of the 442nd boarded ships on May 1, 1944, to begin the long, boring voyage to somewhere on the other side of the Atlantic. That many of us would not come back, I was certain. I had not voiced my own premonitions to Etsu during a trip to Chicago on a three-day pass prior to heading overseas. On shipboard, I tried to put such gloomy thoughts aside as I pondered the long future of Japanese Americans and JACL after victory had been won. As I had written in my ''final report,'' ''JACL must maintain its leadership among the Japanese Americans to the end that those twin, yet not identical, ideals expressed in the national slogans — 'Better Americans in a Greater America,' and 'Security (from fear of violence or forcible ejection, from racial discrimination and prejudice) Through Unity (of all Americans in a common cause)' — may become living realities for all loyal Americans of Japanese ancestry.''

Chapter 9

Combat

A convoy moves no faster than its slowest members, and all our ships were slow. It took a month to cross the Atlantic, thread the Straits of Gibraltar, and finally coast into wreckage-choked Naples harbor. The date was June 2, 1944. It was our first shocking exposure to the destruction of war — rubble in the streets, shattered buildings, leaning utility poles, broken glass, dust, dirt, and grime.

"War," a combat instructor had told us, "is killing people and busting things." We didn't really understand what he was talking about until we went ashore and saw for ourselves. The fighting had moved up the Italian peninsula, but the awesome aftermath of battle was all about us. The relief at having solid ground underfoot was tempered by the knowledge that soon we would be putting our fighting skills to the test. We set up camp in a staging area a few miles inland while the troops unpacked their weapons and other gear.

A few days later we were on the move again. A fleet of landing ships took us a short distance north to the Anzio beachhead, which the Yanks had seized at enormous cost. It was a good thing the area was secure, for the 442nd was in no condition to fight. We were soft from a month at sea and wobbly from the incredibly rough overnight trip from Naples. We would need at least a couple of weeks of toughening up to get ready for combat.

But first there was an important reunion. The 100th Battalion, now a seasoned fighting outfit with a reputation forged in nine months of bloody combat, joined the 442nd as its 1st Battalion, although it kept its designation as the 100th in tribute to its gallantry when it was a fighting organization on its own. That was a happy day. The men of the 100th were as glad to see us as we were to see them. They saw us as dependable old friends and reinforcements. We saw them as trusty mentors, comrades who had been tested and whom we could count on. By this time the 100th was no longer a completely Hawaiian Nisei outfit. Many mainlanders had joined its ranks as replacements.

Back at strength with three full battalions, the 442nd became one of the regiments of the proud 34th Division, made up largely of Iowa and Nebraska National Guardsmen. During the days we were getting ready to fight, being briefed about Germans and hardening our muscles, we also had our first opportunity to encounter a few Italian civilians. Some of the dark-haired, dark-eyed street urchins reminded me of the Japanese-American kids at home. They begged for chocolate bars, chewing gum, and candy. Most GIs were generous; the Nisei of the 442nd, perhaps thinking of friends back in the WRA camps, were especially so. Italian officers may have wondered about men with Oriental faces in U.S. Army uniform. The civilians saw us only as Yanks.

The 442nd finally went into combat on June 22. Climbing into trucks, the troops were driven into the hills north of Rome, which had just fallen to the Allies. I could hear the distant rumble of cannon as the battalions took positions. The immediate objective was the town of Suvereto, en route to Belvedere. The 2nd and 3rd battalions led the advance, one on each side of a dusty, winding road, with the 100th in reserve. I had been told we were to relieve two regiments which were up ahead. This indicated the area was relatively secure. Nonetheless, there was the gut-tightening realization that what we had worked for was about to take place, that our troops would now be shooting to kill and our own men would be coming under fire. My self-assigned responsibility was to trail a safe distance behind the advance units, remaining out of the line of fire but staying close enough to pick up some eyewitness coverage of the 442nd going into its first action.

My jeep driver — even though I was only a private first class, as a public information noncom I was assigned a vehicle — and I headed up the road in pursuit of the troops. We didn't see any of our fellows, but as we passed through a little village I noticed Italian civilians waving frantically at us. I waved back, and on we went.

Suddenly a mortar shell landed in the road not far ahead. There was the heart-stopping concussion of the explosion and the whistle of shrapnel. That was the first inkling that the villagers had been warning us of danger ahead, not cheering us on. As untrained and inexperienced as I was, I knew enough to dive for cover. Even before the jeep jerked to a stop, my driver and I raced for the shelter of a mound and threw ourselves flat. Trembling on the ground, we gradually became aware the mound was a pile of moist and aromatic manure from a nearby barn. Any old port in a storm! Every time we heard a round sailing toward us, the driver and I groveled deeper into the manure.

Some time later when the shelling stopped — it seemed like hours — we heard our troops approaching. "Hey," one of them said as he spotted us, "what are you guys doing here? We're supposed to be the point."

I said I was up front to write about what the 442nd was doing in the war.

"Hell," the soldier said, "we haven't started yet."

I've been told that my driver and I were the first members of the 442nd, not counting the 100th, to come under direct enemy fire, and therefore the first to qualify for the Combat Infantryman badge. Let me reemphasize that of all the men in U.S. Army uniform, I without doubt was among the least qualified to be rated as a combat infantryman. However, there were to be many more occasions when I was under fire, or ran the risk of coming under fire, so I wore the badge proudly. When the 442nd was in the line, I left the safety of the service company area frequently to gather material firsthand for newspaper accounts. I accompanied patrols on both night and day forays into disputed territory. I carried a carbine, but it's a good thing for all concerned that I never had occasion to use it.

My brother Tad, a BAR (Browning automatic rifle) man, was the first Masaoka to be wounded. It was on the third or fourth day of action when his knee took some shrapnel. The wound was bad enough that it could have provided him a ticket home. Tad did what any number of Nisei did later on. He went AWOL from the hospital and hitchhiked his way back to his outfit, 2nd Battalion, E Company. He still suffers from a gimpy knee.

On an early visit to a forward area I made a reassuring discovery. Back at Camp Shelby I had been apprehensive about how I would be accepted by fellow Nisei who saw me excused from the hard training. I felt some of them would be envious of what they saw as my special status. But when I voluntarily shared the danger and discomfort of the dogfaces up front, often staying with them overnight when I easily could have gone back to my tent in the rear, I won a grudging sort of acceptance and respect. There was a lot of satisfaction in that, especially since some of the fellows had no idea what a PRO did. More than once someone would come into my tent after a night on the town, and confusing the PRO office for a prophylactic station, would ask the "doc" to fix him up.

I first noticed the change when an infantryman — I can't remember who it was — offered me his slit trench. "Here, Mike," he shouted, "you take it. I can dig me another one a lot quicker than you can." He was right. I was no better with a shovel than with a rifle. I accepted his hole gratefully. After that I was offered a slit trench many times. Not infrequently when we came under fire I was shoved roughly into a slit trench while its owners hurried off to seek other shelter. I'm relieved to report that so far as I know, no one was killed or wounded as a consequence of having given me his trench. Many times I was invited to share a foxhole for the night. I became one of the guys, a little less capable than they of taking care of myself and therefore needing to be looked after.

Gradually it occurred to me that they were interested in more than what I might write about them. They wanted to do everything they could to make sure that I survived. They realized that while I might have had a part in getting them into the war, I was willing to take my chances with them. But in addition, there was the matter of the work that lay ahead of us as Japanese-American veterans claiming our rights as full-fledged citizens when the shooting ended. For that, they knew it was important for me to be around to speak for them. I have never allowed myself to forget that obligation.

There were hundreds of Nisei in the 442nd whom I never got to know personally, but their attitude toward me, if not altogether warm, was at the very least pragmatic. I could not claim the kind of affection that some correspondents, like Ernie Pyle, for example, received from troops wherever he went, but it was enough that my Nisei comrades cared enough to do special things to help me.

One of my main responsibilities was to interview individual GIs and send their stories back, not to the camps from which they volunteered, but to their original hometowns on the West Coast. In all I wrote more than 2,000 stories, with many of the interviews being conducted under combat conditions. "Why are you out here fighting for your country?" I would ask these men. In other outfits the reply might be a wisecrack, like "The draft board got me before I could get away." With the Nisei the invariable answer was: "Because we want to prove ourselves as Americans." It was a stereotype, but they meant it. As we talked, more specific motives would be revealed.

Several men told me variations of a single theme: "My Dad is interned at a Department of Justice camp as an enemy alien, and I want to see him released and join the rest of the family. He's no threat to America, everybody knows that. I think that because I volunteered he now has a better chance of being paroled so he can get together with Mom and the rest of the kids in a WRA camp." Others said they hated life in the WRA camps so much they figured it was worth taking the chance of being killed just to regain their freedom.

In all of my stories I tried to make clear that volunteers from the camps were fighting for their future as Americans. And when I wrote special background features to be handed to correspondents, I made the point that the Nisei were fighting against Fascism and tyranny regardless of its face.

Almost invariably, correspondents who visited the 442nd would ask whether we would fight the Japanese. Would German Americans have any hesitation about fighting the Nazis? My answer was that we were not involved in a race war, but a war of ideologies. We would fight against Japan if we were called on to do so. In fact, there were several thousand Nisei in the Pacific Theater in hush-hush intelligence work. We happened to be in Italy because that's where the Pentagon had sent us, and we'd do our best wherever we happened to be.

The Office of War Information picked up the theme in its broadcasts to Japan. The 442nd, OWI said, in fighting Fascism was fighting for the ordinary people of Japan, who were in the grip of military dictators. There also were questions about why we were fighting as a segregated unit. My reply was that the 442nd was not the product of American racism, but an opportunity for us to demonstrate that even though we had been mistreated, we had enough faith in our country to volunteer to defend it.

In retrospect, my recollections of the fighting in that first campaign meld into a montage of blood and heat and dust and noise with few clear-cut impressions. In the drive on Belvedere, when the 2nd and 3rd Battalions ran into heavy opposition the 100th charged up between them and broke the back of the German resistance. It won a Presidential Unit Citation for that action. The regiment then pushed across the Cecina River. The 100th plunged on toward the port city of Leghorn while the other two battalions fought through rugged hill country toward Luciana in almost two weeks of constant action. The Germans fought back with artillery, mortars, and rifle and machine-gun fire, leaving mines and boobytraps as they retreated. The Nisei took heavy casualties as they moved forward, but their performance improved with the experience they gained in each successive action. I marveled at the stoicism of these Nisei citizen-soldiers pushing on from one objective to the next with enormous courage and determination — and paying an awesome toll in blood. I never overcame the cold, tight feeling in my gut when I saw Nisei wrapped in bloody bandages being carried back from the forward aid stations, the mangled bodies of Nisei dead waiting to be moved to the rear.

It was at Little Cassino, our nickname for Hill 140, in this campaign that my brother Ike became the second Masaoka casualty.

Ike was a combat medic with 2nd Battalion, Fox Company. Under fire, he went out repeatedly to aid the wounded until a mine explosion ripped his belly open and did cruel things to his insides. Ike's buddies managed to pull him back to the aid station. When I was finally able to see him in a base hospital in Rome he was in ghastly shape. His weight was down to about half of normal. A doctor told me he would be surprised if Ike lived. But Ike was tough. Word that his first son had been born in Chicago helped him to pull through. He survived but was left 100 percent disabled. Ike's company commander recommended him for a Distinguished Service Cross, second only to the Medal of Honor, for having rescued a number of men under intense enemy fire. He was awarded a Silver Star for valor plus the automatic Purple Heart.

The heat of the Italian summer set in as the 442nd took the key cities of Livorno and Pisa and reached the flat valley of the Arno River in three weeks of nearly continuous fighting. "The 100th and the 2nd and 3rd battalions came of age," Chet Tanaka has written in *Go for Broke*. At the end of July the regiment was pulled back to

Vada for a few days of rest before rejoining the push to cross the Arno.

That proved to be some of the bitterest fighting in the 442nd's experience. It was in the first days of September that the 2nd and 3rd battalions established a bridgehead while the 100th was spearheading a crossing in another sector. The German army was in broad retreat. The 442nd was sent back to the Naples area to lick its wounds, which were fearsome. Including the 100th's part in the battle for Rome, the men of the 442nd had suffered 1,272 casualties — 239 dead, 972 wounded, seventeen missing in action, and forty-four suffering noncombat injuries. Our Caucasian officers did not go unscathed. To their credit they demanded nothing of the men they wouldn't do themselves. We were becoming hardened to war, yet it never became easy to accept the loss of buddies, fellows we had grown up with, men with whom we were united in a personal crusade. Our mourning for them was mitigated only by the faith that their cause was worthy.

In mid-September, welcome replacements arrived from Camp Shelby to fill our ranks, and by month's end we were off on our second big campaign. Detached from the 34th Division, the 442nd went aboard ship at Naples and made an uneventful landing at Marseilles on the French Mediterranean coast. For the next two weeks we moved up the Rhône Valley in trucks and railroad boxcars until we joined the 36th (Texas) Division west of the town of Bruyères in the rugged, pine-covered Vosges Mountains not far from the German border.

What followed will never be forgotten by anyone who was there, nor should any American fail to remember. For the next month the 442nd fought almost continuously in bitter cold, over heavily forested terrain where both visibility and gains were measured in yards, and where everyone was in constant danger from German artillery shells that exploded when they hit the trees and scattered shrapnel in every direction along with bits of timber ripped off the treetops.

The Germans had been told to hold at any cost, and they had well-equipped crack troops in the area. The attack to take Bruyères began October 15 with the 442nd advancing in the rain through ankle-deep mud. The Germans were tenacious. If the Nisei took a position, they had to be ready for an almost certain counterattack.

Bruyères was captured. La Broquaine fell, then Belmont, then Biffontaine, but at terrible cost. After eight days of fighting the 442nd was ordered back to Belmont for rest.

Two days later we got word that another unit of the 36th Division, the 1st Battalion of the 141st Regiment, a Texas outfit, was cut off some nine miles away and unable to get back. The Nisei were assigned to rescue the "Lost Battalion."

So it was back to battle again, foot by foot against fierce German resistance, circling some strongpoints, taking others with bayonet charges in the face of point-blank fire. It took five days of the fiercest kind of combat to reach the Lost Battalion. By then one of our companies was down to eight riflemen in charge of a sergeant. Another had only seventeen men, with all their officers dead or wounded. In all, the 442nd suffered some 800 casualties in the rescue of 275 men and officers of the Lost Battalion.

Was the sacrifice worth the result? That is a hard question. When can death be justified? Years later I took many opportunities to cite that battle to promote with great effect the contention that we were deserving. There is an eloquent answer from an unnamed Nisei soldier in Chet Tanaka's book: "We rescued the Lost Battalion but the guys on the line knew it could have been us instead of them. The 100th was almost cut off in the fight for Biffontaine. Getting 'lost' was part of the chances you took in combat."

Among those who died in the operation was Ben Frank Masaoka, my next-older brother, who had been the best man at my wedding. And since this is the Masaoka story, I must tell you of the circumstances.

Ben was a rifleman in Company B of the 100th. After Tad was hit, Ike was so severely wounded, and Hank transferred to the paratroopers, someone with a sense of compassion reassigned Ben to the less hazardous duty of perimeter guard at regimental headquarters. It was after the rescue operation was under way that Ben showed up at my tent in Service Company.

"I'm going up front this morning," Ben said. "Just wanted to let you know."

I asked why, reminding Ben that men were needed in the perimeter guard, too, and he didn't have to take risks.

"Yeah," Ben replied. "That's what the colonel said. I told him we were taking a lot of casualties and I felt I ought to be up there with the guys. The colonel said I didn't have to go, but he said he wouldn't stop me if I really wanted to go.''

The sense of comradeship, Ben's sense of obligation to be with his buddies in a time of danger, was one of the secrets of the 442nd's great combat record. We cared for each other. The men knew they could count on their friends. Before he left Ben turned half shyly to me and said: "Here, Mike, this is something I made for you."

It was a ring. In his spare time Ben had carved a hole in the center of a 25-cent piece and had painstakingly beaten it into a plain silver ring with whatever crude tools he had gotten hold of. I still wear it today as a combination wedding ring and keepsake to the memory of my brother who died for a cause we both believed in.

Late that evening, long after darkness descended over the frozen forest, word filtered back from the front. Ben had gone out with a patrol. It ran into a German ambush, and as the Nisei started to pull back one of them saw Ben fall from an apparent shot in the head. They had been unable to retrieve the body.

There was nothing I, or anyone, could do in the dark. I slept little that night. Before sunup next morning my friend Joe Itagaki and I picked up carbines and ammo and started forward in a totally unauthorized two-man search operation. Joe told me afterward that I seemed to be out of my mind, but he wasn't about to let me go alone to look for Ben. We moved up through the battalion command post and through company headquarters, asking questions of everyone we saw, until we finally reached the platoon where Ben had been. We were told that yes, Ben apparently had been shot in the firefight that followed the ambush. At least two men said they had seen him fall, but no one had been able to locate his body.

Although the area where Ben's patrol had been was still contested ground, Joe and I went out into it. We searched everywhere, peering under the brush, under old logs and shattered tree trunks, and found nothing, not even Germans. For most of the day Joe and I, joined by others, beat our way back and forth through the timber, for the 442nd never left a man — wounded, killed in action, or missing in action — behind. I kept hoping that somehow Ben had been only wounded and captured. In company records, Pfc. Ben Frank Masaoka was carried as missing in action. In an effort to ease Mother's pain, I wrote that there was hope Ben was safe in a German prisoner-of-war camp. Once I was told Ben's dogtags had been found on a body in a sector many miles distant. But the tags were never delivered to me or any members of the family. There is no record that Ben was ever captured. Only after the war ended was he listed officially as having been killed in action.

Two years later we received word that a body presumed to be Ben's had been located in a grave in a part of the Vosges where the 442nd had never been. The remains were brought back and reinterred at Arlington National Cemetery. They rest today among the nation's heroes in Section 13, Grid L31, Grave 6683-17.

It was during the search for Ben that I sustained my only wound. The Germans were shelling the sector sporadically, and one tree burst was close enough to scatter shrapnel around Joe and me. A fragment sliced through my trousers and left a two-inch flesh wound near my left knee. I scarcely noticed it at the time, and only much later did I get it dressed at an aid station. Afterward, when I had a chance to think about it, I didn't feel justified in putting in for a Purple Heart.

There seemed to be something terribly incongruous and wrong about claiming a Purple Heart medal for one brother who had been killed and the same award for another brother who had sustained an inconsequential wound. There were many other Nisei who felt the same way about the Purple Heart. The official record shows 9,486 Purple Heart medals were awarded men of the 100th and 442nd, but it's a good guess that if every slight wound had been recognized the number would have been doubled. Even so, we became known as the Purple Heart Regiment, and we wore the name as a badge of honor in itself.

There's no question, however, about the cost of the month-long Vosges campaign. The regiment was cut down to half strength. More than 800 men were hospitalized, joining 1,000 who had been injured earlier, and another 140 were dead. In his autobiography, U.S. Senator Daniel K. Inouye, who was to be critically wounded in a later action, writes dramatically:

> When General Dahlquist [Major General John E. Dahlquist, commander of the 36th Division] called the regiment out for a retreat parade to commend us personally, he is reported to have said to the CO, "Colonel, I asked that the entire regiment be present for this occasion. Where are the rest of your men?" And Colonel Pence, as bone-weary as any dogface in the outfit, replied, "Sir, you are

looking at the entire regiment. Except for two men on guard duty at each company, this is all that is left of the 442nd Combat Team.'' And there we were, cooks, medics, band and a handful of riflemen, a ragged lot at rigid attention, without a single company at even half its normal strength. . . . My outfit, E Company, with a normal complement of 197 men, had exactly 40 soldiers able to march to the parade ground.

General Dahlquist responded with a commendatory letter which said: ''The courage, steadfastness, and willingness of your officers and men were equal to any ever displayed by United States troops.'' Colonel Pence was a compassionate man, a splendid soldier but perhaps too compassionate to be comfortable in the role of leader of shock troops. After the Vosges campaign, in which he too was wounded, Pence received his brigadier's star and another assignment and our executive officer, Lieutenant Colonel Virgil R. Miller, took command of the regiment.

The Vosges had been something of a forgotten front, but suddenly the press became aware of it. Reporters hurried to the area. I worked hard to make sure the sacrifice of the Nisei would be recognized. Suddenly, in newspapers all over America, readers learned about the 442nd. They learned about men fighting for freedom while their families were still in American relocation camps. They learned of Nisei gallantry in a battle that opened the way to Allied invasion of the Rhineland. A few well-placed suggestions led to the men of the 36th Division declaring all members of the 442nd ''Honorary Texans.''

You can call this a gimmick, but the plaque presentation ceremony made for more favorable newspaper publicity. Secretary McCloy's idea of an all-Nisei segregated unit was bearing fruit. But at what devastating cost!

It was inevitable that some correspondents should raise the question as to whether we were being used as expendable suicide troops, a question that may have crossed the minds of some Nisei themselves. And after the war, there were questions about the Nisei being moved by the same suicidal spirit as the Japanese kamikaze pilots who flew their planes into American warships.

Let me put those questions to rest once and for all. The Nisei were fighting for their futures as Americans, for freedom and equality of opportunity for themselves and their families. They had everything to live for, but like the Americans of the Revolution, they were willing to give their lives if necessary for their ideals. This is altogether different from the Japanese kamikaze pilots and banzai-chargers who knew they had lost the war and were trying to take as many Americans as possible with them when they died. One puts a reverence and a value on life. The other denies life has value.

I think it can be proved that of all the individual decorations the Nisei troops won for valor, more were awarded for saving the lives of comrades than for killing the enemy. That doesn't sound like throwing their lives away, does it?

Colonel Pence was not commanding cannon fodder. On at least one occasion when he was given a plan by a general officer for taking an objective, Pence replied that he had no doubt his men could carry out the mission successfully but it would be too costly and the staff had better go back and come up with another plan. I know that at lower levels Nisei sergeants told their white officers that certain plans were too risky and they could shove them up their you know what. Then, chances were that the Nisei came up with better and less costly ideas for capturing the target. Our men tried to be careful of their safety, but they also realized they had a dirty job to do.

If the Nisei were not suicide troops, why were they given so many extremely hazardous jobs? It's true the 442nd was called on to spearhead a number of attacks and assigned key roles in many other critical operations. But these assignments were given us only after we had gained a reputation as a crack fighting team. So, in a way it was an honor for the 442nd, which had been authorized only after some strong Pentagon reservations, to be called on to do the hard but important jobs. These assignments were a tribute to our reliability and our loyalty and our skill at fighting, which was our way of showing our dedication to our country. To put it another way, when we were given a particularly difficult task, it was like giving the ball to the most dependable halfback, even when he's hurting, when it is important to pick up a few yards for a first down.

These were some of the things we talked about among ourselves as we rested in the "Champagne Campaign" after the costly fighting in the Vosges. That experience had helped many of the Nisei to mature. Our original narrow point of view, which focused on ourselves, broadened as we saw the bigger meaning of the war and the postwar opportunities for creating a better world for all, even our German and Japanese enemies. We remembered how the blacks in Mississippi were treated, and having seen the equality of all men in battlefield death, we realized how important it was to recognize and implement the equality of all men in life.

When the Hawaiian Nisei went home after the war, many became politically active. They joined the Democratic Party, as opposed to the pro-establishment Republicans, and worked their way up into positions of power where they could use their influence to demand vigorous attention to human rights and racial equality. There is no doubt in my mind that even though they may not have realized it, these Nisei's concerns for the rights of all people were born on the battlefield and in the sad and contemplative hours that followed combat when the recent dead were still very much alive in our hearts.

The Champagne Campaign largely involved patrolling the mountains along the quiet Franco-Italian border just inland from the Mediterranean. The scarred 100th was given the sunny, pleasant sector nearest the sea, but because there was little action men from the other units also had an opportunity to take their turn on the Riviera for rest and relaxation. However, in addition to the three infantry battalions the 442nd had other units. The 522nd Field Artillery Battalion, the 232nd Combat Engineer Company, and the antitank company and cannon company often were detached from the 442nd for special assignments. Most of the time I stayed with the 442nd, and that caused me to miss one of the great stories of the war.

That happened when at the end of the Champagne Campaign the 522nd was sent back up into central France. Its artillery supported the crossing of the Rhine and Neckar rivers. Late in April, attached to the 4th Division, the Nisei outfit drove into southern Germany. It was during this period that a patrol, including Nisei scouts from the 522nd, reached the now infamous Dachau concentration camp. The Americans opened the prison gates and liberated the starving inmates, who were more dead than alive. No reporter or PRO was there to record the event. The Nisei role in this dramatic moment went unreported for decades. Why? For a very simple reason. GIs had been ordered not to fraternize in any way with the enemy nor share scarce rations with civilians. They assumed the prisoners were Germans. But it was impossible not to give them food, clothing, medicine. And having deliberately broken regulations, they simply clammed up. But what a story it would have made at the time to tell of Nisei, whose own families were in American-style concentration camps, helping to free the victims of Nazi inhumanity. Liberators overseas, prisoners at home, someone remarked. What wouldn't I have given to have been there to make comparisons!

Ironically, it was during the Champagne Campaign that I nearly lost my life. For days I had been feeling listless and exhausted. I couldn't seem to get warm. At sick call the doctors detected no fever, and in the absence of other symptoms they told me to go back to work. But T/4 Richard Nomura, our company medic, who had been a pharmacist in civilian life, suspected something was seriously wrong with me.

"Mike," he said, "I'm going to forge the captain's signature on these papers and send you to the base hospital. I don't know what the trouble is, but you're a sick man. You need to be checked over. I think it's worth taking the chance to get you help."

In Marseilles the doctors found I was suffering from an advanced case of pneumonia and promptly put me under an oxygen tent. Dick Nomura's alertness undoubtedly saved my life. I was still recuperating when the 442nd was ordered back to Italy; I rejoined it just in time for the Po Valley campaign.

I found the 442nd bivouacked near the 92nd Division, a segregated black outfit with white officers. In that sense the 92nd Division and the 442nd were similar, but their combat records were quite different. Correspondents who passed through the area asked why the Nisei had turned out to be exceptional soldiers while the black division was considered mediocre at best.

The answer was obvious. The blacks were not inherently poor soldiers. They had distinguished themselves in previous wars, particularly in the Indian wars, when they were feared as the "buffalo soldiers." The 92nd's problem was in training and leadership. Little had been expected of it. Most of its white officers were chosen with little thought other than the assumption that Southern whites knew how to handle blacks. The result was that the worst aspects of segregation were perpetuated. Under the circumstances, blacks had little incentive to assert themselves. The manpower they represented was largely wasted by official shortsightedness. By contrast, the Nisei felt they had something to prove. In pursuit of that objective they had the Pentagon's support. They had trained intensely, and their officers were caught up in the fervor. Above all, they had pride in themselves as Americans. I had to explain all this to correspondents without appearing to demean the blacks. It wasn't their fault, but the nation's.

So much publicity has been given to the rescue of the Lost Battalion, which I understand has been designated one of the fifty greatest battles in American military annals, that there is a tendency to ignore the 442nd's last major drive in Northern Italy, which spearheaded the first Allied victory in World War II over the Axis powers.

The Germans had spent some nine months digging into the rock of the Apennine Mountains of northern Italy and had built a virtually impregnable defense called the Gothic Line. Allied forces had been unable to dent it in five months of bombing and shelling. Somehow, it had to be breached. The strategy devised was to get the 442nd, which the Germans recognized as crack assault troops, secretly into position to spearhead a major diversionary attack on the west end of the line. Meanwhile, the main assault would take place elsewhere.

In our sector the 3rd Battalion, in absolute silence, spent two nights getting into position. The first night the men took eight hours to climb a twisting mountain trail to a village where they hid during the day from enemy observation. The next night they moved silently to a 3,000-foot ridge between two peaks.

Meanwhile, the 100th had moved secretly into position for a frontal assault on a mountain stronghold code-named Georgia. At dawn on April 5, 1945, the 100th's attack began. Simultaneously the 3rd Battalion opened up on the defenders from the right. The surprise was total, but the Germans reacted swiftly. A furious, bloody battle ensued, but it ended quickly. In a scant thirty-two minutes a stronghold that had held out for five months was seized. Meanwhile the 2nd Battalion, farther inland, was plunging ahead against fierce opposition. Suddenly what had been a diversionary attack had become a full-blown offensive. The U.S. Fifth Army poured through the breach.

This constituted a critical breakthrough, but the battle was far from won. There were other strongpoints to be eliminated and casualties to be accepted. But in a week the back of the German resistance had been broken. In three weeks the Germans were in full retreat. By May 2 the war in Italy was over. A week later Germany surrendered. The Nisei covered themselves with glory in the Po Valley campaign. Every man was a hero, but oddly there were not enough medals to go around.

I had been aware for some time that an impressive number of recommendations for the Medal of Honor had been submitted to higher levels. Certainly the extraordinary bravery demonstrated in these battlefield episodes deserved consideration for the nation's highest military award. Yet not one was approved. Every last recommendation has been downgraded to Distinguished Service Cross or Silver Star. These decorations are awarded only for exceptional valor, but they are not the Medal of Honor, which only Congress can bestow. Before the Po Valley campaign nearly forty Distinguished Service Crosses had been awarded to the men and officers of the 442nd. I had a deep, dark suspicion that some deskbound second lieutenant down the line was automatically downgrading citations a notch when he reviewed them, but I couldn't prove it and there wasn't anything I could do about it.

After the fighting ended, my old mentor Senator Thomas came to Italy as chairman of a Senate Foreign Relations Subcommittee. He visited with the 442nd, and I had an opportunity to spend some time with him. We talked about the record of the Nisei generally, and finally I got around to the matter of decorations. He promised to look into it.

Shortly, we got word that the Medal of Honor had been awarded posthumously to Pfc. Sadao Munemori, Company A, 100th Battalion. Munemori was in a forward unit for the April 5 assault on the Gothic Line. When his squad leader was wounded, Munemori took charge and led his men through a minefield. Pinned down by machine-gun fire, Munemori worked his way to within grenade range and knocked out two machine guns. A German grenade rolled into a crater occupied by Munemori and two others. Munemori dove on the grenade, smothering the explosion with his body. He died, but his two buddies escaped with minor wounds. Much later I was told that Munemori's recommendation for the Medal of Honor was the only one from the 442nd that hadn't been acted on when Senator Thomas made his inquiry, so the award was made to him.

Munemori's sacrifice certainly entitled him to the honor. But there were ten or fifteen others equally deserving. Let's take just a couple of examples.

Dan Inouye, who enlisted at nineteen and was commissioned in battle, led his platoon in an attack on Mount Nebbione on the Gothic Line. Pinned down by German machine guns, Inouye blew one up with a hand grenade and killed the crew of a second with his tommy gun. Inouye was hit in the stomach but continued to fire until his right arm was shattered by a rifle grenade. Despite his wounds he directed the final assault up the ridge. He was awarded the Distinguished Service Cross. Doctors were unable to save Dan's arm, but he went on to become Hawaii's first congressman and later its distinguished United States senator.

Sergeant Kazuo Masuda was a California farmboy whom I had interviewed soon after the action that led to his recommendation for a Medal of Honor. Crawling 200 yards through heavy fire, he picked up a mortar tube and ammunition and then crawled back to his forward observation post. Alone over a twelve-hour period, his accurate mortar fire turned back two German counterattacks. What made him perform such heroics? He told me he was convinced the volunteers of the 442nd, if they could prove they were worthy, would be able to make a better place in America for people like his family. Several days later I was stunned to see his body being brought back. He had been killed while leading a patrol.

The 442nd has been called the most decorated unit in American military history for its size and length of service. It was in seven major campaigns and won seven Presidential Unit Citations (the highest unit citation), plus thirty-six Army Commendations and eighty-seven Division Commendations. Its members won 18,143 individual decorations, including 9,486 Purple Hearts, one Medal of Honor, fifty-two Distinguished Service Crosses, 560 Silver Stars with twenty-eight Oak Leaf Clusters, and more than 4,000 Bronze Stars with 1,200 Oak Leaf Clusters. General Joseph (Vinegar Joe) Stilwell couldn't have been more right when, at the ceremony in 1945 in which the Distinguished Service Cross was presented to Sergeant Masuda's sister Mary, he said: "The Nisei bought an awful big hunk of America with their blood."

Participating in the ceremony as a representative of the American Veterans Committee was a movie star named Ronald Reagan, until recently an Army Air Corps captain. "Blood that has soaked into the sands of a beach is all of one color," he said. "America stands unique in the world, the only country not founded on race, but on a way — an ideal. Not in spite of, but because of our polyglot background, we have had all the strength in the world. That is the American way." Ronald Reagan, as we know, went on to real-life roles on a larger stage.

Just for the record, let me add that the total includes three awards I received. They are the Bronze Star, the Italian Cross for Military Valor, and the Legion of Merit. How a noncombatant won the Italian medal for military valor, I do not know. The citation reads: "Nella Campagna d'Italia Si Distingueva per Valore ed Alto Spirito di Sacrificio." Mine was one of two Italian Crosses for *valore militare* presented to the 442nd. Perhaps I happened to be standing in the right place. The 442nd received twenty-two Legion of Merit Medals, a noncombat award, and mine was one of two given to enlisted men.

My citation takes note of "exceptionally meritorious conduct" in running the 442nd's public relations office. It says I processed "more than 2,700 stories, many of which were obtained on the front lines at considerable risk of life and limb. These stories not only recited the unprecedented achievements of the organization but also demonstrated to the public at large that Americans of Japanese ancestry were worthy of equal treatment and consideration and refuted Japan's propaganda in the Far East as to the nature of this war. . . ."

My narrative has focused on the 442nd because I served with it. But we must not forget the Nisei who served in the Pacific Theater as interpreters and translators, the eyes and ears of the Allied war effort as members of the Military Intelligence Service. They fought in the jungles of New Guinea, landed with the Marines at Iwo Jima, bled at Guadalcanal, fought behind enemy lines in Burma with Merrill's Marauders, entered the caves of Okinawa in search of stragglers and civilians. Mostly they fought and worked and bled and died in anonymity, for they were America's secret weapon. Major General Charles Willoughby, General MacArthur's chief of intelligence, has credited the Nisei with shortening the war in the Pacific by more than two years, saving a million American lives, and millions of U.S. dollars.

Since Japan was unaware of the extent to which Nisei were gathering information about them, it was critical to keep their activities secret. I've wondered what the result would have been if during the war the American public had been told about the role Japanese Americans were playing in the Pacific Theater. While the damage of the evacuation had been done before Nisei linguists went into action, knowledge of their unique contribution to victory could well have blunted the shameful racism that persisted. Take the case of Frank Hachiya of Hood River, Oregon, a noncommissioned officer in U.S. Army intelligence. His was among the Japanese-American names that Hood River bigots removed from the community honor roll to demonstrate their patriotism. Hachiya died in the invasion of the Philippines. Sent behind Japanese lines on a scouting and mapping mission, he was critically wounded by U.S. troops as he was returning with vital information, which he delivered before he died. Hachiya was awarded the Distinguished Service Cross.

According to a Selective Service monograph, some 33,300 Nisei served in World War II. More than half were from the mainland; 20,000 had at one time or another been inmates of U.S. detention camps. Compare that number to the 267 who refused induction, demanding restoration of their rights before they would serve their country.

Some historians, writing from the isolation of their ivory towers, have contended the draft resisters were the real heroes of the Japanese-American story because they had the courage to stand up for a principle. These historians are wrong. The significance is in the relatively small number of dissidents in the face of gross injustice. The heroes are the men and their families who demonstrated their faith in America. In the postwar years, Congress passed one remedial measure after another to correct historical wrongs. In every instance it was the record of Nisei military valor and sacrifice that drew attention to past injustices and convinced those in power that change had to come. Without that record the fight for justice would have been infinitely more difficult. There is persuasive reason to believe that Japanese Americans, and other minorities, today would not be enjoying unrestricted citizenship rights without the Nisei record of unswerving loyalty.

Chapter 10

Postwar Mandate

The German surrender in Europe brought an eerie quiet to the Italian front. The guns were silenced. The killing stopped. The men of the 442nd didn't realize how exhausted they were, physically and emotionally, when at last they put down their arms. There was no frenzied celebration, only sober relief. Some of the men of the 100th had been in combat for twenty months. More than 600 of our buddies were dead, many more than that number scarred and maimed for life. And there was that matter of the war in the Pacific, where thousands of our Nisei friends were helping to tighten the noose around the Japanese Empire.

To a man we wanted no more of killing and being killed. We were ready to go home. But if our country needed us to fight in the Pacific Theater, we were ready. The possibility of having to kill Japanese soldiers, who sprang from the same roots as ours, entered our minds, of course, but a tragic irony of war was not something to brood over. Brothers had slain brothers before, and probably would do so again. Japan's militarists had launched the war, killing Japanese Americans in Honolulu, touching off the hysteria that had cruelly bruised all of us. Now that the Nazis were vanquished, we sought no bloody vengeance against Japan. I think it is fair to say we wanted only the kind of victory that would permit a new beginning for ourselves as Americans of Japanese descent, and for the Japanese people as well.

Colonel Virgil R. Miller, the 442nd's commanding officer, voiced our thoughts at a memorial ceremony honoring our dead: "The sacrifice made by our comrades was great. We must not fail them in the fight that continues, in the fight that will be with us even when peace comes. Your task will be the harder and more arduous one, for it will extend over a longer time." It was a sobering warning from a man who had led us well.

But first there were chores to be taken care of. German prisoners had to be rounded up, processed, confined, guarded, and taken on work details until arrangements could be made for their repatriation. Jubilant Italian villagers seeking vengeance against collaborators had to be restrained until civil order could be restored.

One day a call went out for men fluent in Japanese. Nearly 200 men and officers volunteered for transfer to the Pacific Theater after a brush-up course at the U.S. Military Intelligence Language School in Minnesota. And before long we resumed hard combat training in anticipation of taking part in the invasion of Japan. But Japan was on its last legs, and the nuclear bombs detonated over Hiroshima and Nagasaki were only the ghastly and unnecessary *coup de grâce*. Four months after the German surrender, Japan, too, capitulated and at long last we could turn our thoughts to new concerns.

Reporters came to our camp for comment. How did we feel about Japan's surrender? We were elated. The war was over, wasn't it? What about that new nuclear bomb that had wiped out Hiroshima and Nagasaki? We knew no more than what we had read in *Stars and Stripes*. It was a helluva weapon. It was just too damned bad that civilians had to be killed — we had seen too much of that in Italy and France. But if it shortened the war, we were glad we had this new weapon rather than the other guys. No one had any inkling of the immense political and social implications of the dawning nuclear age. None of us was aware of the awesome horror of massive radiation. We were just dogfaces talking of home and what we would do after we shed our uniforms.

There was a lot of fantasizing about what it would be like back in the old haunts, with unlimited beer and steaks and soft, warm, compliant girls. There was serious talk, too, about starting college or going back to complete educations, about studying law or medicine, getting married, starting families, or looking after parents who would be struggling to recover from the trauma of the evacuation.

I had much to think about. First, there was my personal future. I would be going back to a wife; I was no longer a footloose bachelor who could manage to survive on the pittance the Japanese

American Citizens League could afford to pay, provided they wanted me back. I still had ambitions to make a career in law, but now I was within a few months of my thirtieth birthday and the prospect of additional years in the classroom was not inviting. I felt an obligation to JACL and its members to help the organization complete the struggle for justice begun when it demanded the right of military service for the Nisei. Even more deeply I felt an obligation to do everything I could to make certain my buddies had not made their supreme sacrifice in vain.

On the other hand, I had my own life to lead and JACL seemed to have done very well without me. Sab Kido had kept the organization together. Hito Okada somehow had raised enough money to keep it solvent. Larry Tajiri had done a magnificent job of editing the weekly *Pacific Citizen,* which had been my one solid link with the Japanese-American community back home. Teiko Ishida and my brother Joe were among those representing JACL out in the field and had proved most effective at the kind of work I had been doing prior to induction. Through the *Pacific Citizen* I had kept myself aware of what was going on in the WRA camps, the growing public support for Japanese Americans as their loyalty was demonstrated by the exploits of the 442nd, and of the Supreme Court's ruling in the Mitsuye Endo case, which was that evacuees must not be detained against their will once it was determined they were not likely to be a national security risk.

I was more confident than ever that despite the price our men had paid, JACL's position on military service had been sound. I was also aware that, as Colonel Miller had admonished us, there was a long, hard struggle ahead to win our full rights as Americans.

Yet I was not sure there was an active, up-front role for me with JACL in that struggle. I seemed to have drifted away from the organization; I felt a closer kinship with the veterans. Kido had never said in so many words that he wanted me back, nor had he discussed his postwar agenda in his occasional letters. Given the hazards of war, I had never asked him to keep the job open for me. Perhaps, I began to think, I should be looking for other ways in which to contribute. Perhaps, since I had been away from JACL for so long, had been out of touch, it was an appropriate time to search out new challenges.

It was about this time that I heard from Oland Russell, the

newspaperman whom I had succeeded in the job of running the 442nd's public relations office. Russell said he had been aware of my record, and if I wanted to go into journalism he would be happy to find a place for me on the staff of the *New York World-Telegram,* to which he had returned. Other friends, including reporters from the *New York Times* who were in uniform, urged me to apply for a job with their newspapers when I returned to the States. The idea of a career in journalism was intriguing. Not only would it make me a decent living, but it would give me a platform from which I could work for justice and equality for all Americans.

I well might have become a newspaperman except for the fact that Etsu was waiting for me in Chicago. Under a complex system in which GIs accumulated points for time spent overseas and medals won, veteran troops were being sent home as rapidly as possible. I was with a group of fifteen or twenty Nisei among thousands of men assigned to an aircraft carrier whose ample hangar deck was converted into sleeping quarters. We sailed from Italy early in December 1945 and crossed the Atlantic in slightly more than a week in contrast to the month the eastward voyage had taken. Many of the men took their discharge as soon as we reached Fort Dix, New Jersey. If Etsu had been in New York, I too would have been discharged there, and then in all likelihood I would have crossed the Hudson to take advantage of Olie Russell's offer. But as it turned out I was still in uniform when I reached Chicago just before Christmas.

A couple of Hawaii Nisei, on a leisurely trip back to the islands, had attached themselves to me. I was anticipating a quiet, intimate dinner with Etsu on my first night home. It turned out to be a boisterous party at a restaurant with Etsu and my buddies, and I'm sure they would have followed us to her tiny apartment if I hadn't found them a room at the YMCA.

A few days later, even before I had adjusted to the idea of being home, Kido telephoned me from Salt Lake City. I don't know how he learned I was in Chicago, but he lost no time in asking when I was coming back to work.

"I didn't understand that you expected me to return to JACL," I said. "You never said anything about it in all the time I was in the Army."

Kido was not a profane man, but he came as close to profanity as I've ever heard him. "I didn't have to say anything," he sputtered across fifteen hundred miles of telephone line. "We assumed you were going to work for JACL if you made it through the war. That was understood by everybody. We're waiting for you. We have a lot of unfinished business to take care of, and you're the guy who has to get it done. You can't abandon JACL now. Do I have to get down on my knees and beg you to come back?"

I told him I'd think about it and let him know as soon as I talked to Etsu, but I knew then that I had to go back. And Etsu agreed. I must admit that I had been just a bit miffed that Kido had not been specific previously about his plans for me. But once he told me I was needed, the adrenaline began to flow. Simple lack of communication had almost changed the course of my life.

In Salt Lake City I quickly realized that in many respects JACL hadn't changed. It was being operated on a shoestring. Kido had big plans, but he wanted me to run the organization out of Salt Lake City and trot off to Washington whenever I could to lobby for the ambitious program he had in mind.

He had thought out a sweeping five-point program affecting all Japanese Americans and, in a broader sense, the basic concept of human rights of all Americans. After JACL adopted the program, which he assumed it would do, Kido wanted me to run with it. In brief, the five points were:

1. A change in federal law to give Issei the right of citizenship through naturalization. Legalized discrimination against them was based on their status as "aliens ineligible to citizenship." If Congress granted them naturalization, hundreds of discriminatory laws, including statutes denying them the right to own farmland, would be wiped off the books.

2. Revision of immigration laws to give Japan treatment equal to that of other nations. In 1924 Congress passed a law prohibiting further immigration from Asia, thus in effect labeling Asians as undesirable and inferior people. This slap in the face had been responsible in part for the ascendancy of Japanese militarism which led ultimately to American entry into World War II. During the war an embarrassed U.S. government decided our Filipino and Chinese allies were worthy of an immigration quota. Kido's intent was to eliminate all racial discrimination in immigration and naturalization matters.

3. Compensation for actual monetary losses suffered in the evacuation. Kido had contended all along that the evacuation had been unjust and unnecessary, and that the evacuees were entitled to be reimbursed at least for their financial losses.

4. An intensive and extensive public relations program. Japanese Americans, Kido felt, had been victimized because they were little known throughout the United States. Their story, their wartime sacrifices, their numerous contributions to America, all needed to be publicized.

5. A just peace treaty with the Japanese. Kido believed that Asia would play an ever more important role in America's future, and he was perceptive enough to see that Japan, our erstwhile enemy, as the Orient's most advanced nation must become the cornerstone for a stable, prosperous, peaceful western Pacific. To make this possible the United States must agree to a just peace treaty, and JACL should exert whatever influence it could to see that it was done.

These were only broad goals, and a lot of thinking would be required to refine the details and shape a workable campaign. Some of the points were not new. On many occasions before the war we had talked about the need to get citizenship for the Issei. But the entire package made sense, and I had no quarrel with the thrust of Kido's objectives other than to be staggered by their scope. In fact, I had been thinking along the same general terms, but had not had the opportunity to put my thoughts together into a specific program. Kido and I had never sat down to talk about long-range goals for JACL except in passing during the hectic pre-evacuation days. Still, anyone who stopped to analyze the basic reasons for the problems Japanese Americans faced would agree with Kido's proposals for overcoming them. What surprised me about Kido's program was not the vision involved so much as the audacity in taking on such vast goals so soon after the hostilities had ended.

JACL, even though it was the leading organization of Japanese Americans, had been unable to block the evacuation; its members were scarcely out of the barbed-wire camps where they had been prisoners of their own government, and here Kido was talking of going to Congress with an agenda that would overturn the discrimination that had been locked into the nation's laws for generations. The Japanese-American communities on the West Coast were still in a shambles. Those who had returned to them were just beginning to pick up the strings of living. Businesses had been lost, livelihoods destroyed, savings dissipated, community links shattered. The future was distressingly uncertain.

JACL itself was in extreme difficulties. Its treasury, never adequate, was empty. At the time of the evacuation it had sixty-six chapters and nearly 20,000 members. Driven from the West Coast, made the scapegoat of Nisei frustration and anger, it now had only ten active chapters, mostly in the sparsely populated Intermountain District, and 1,700 scattered members. The organization needed extensive rebuilding at a time when Nisei were deeply preoccupied with rebuilding their own lives.

My war experience must have made me more cautious than I had ever been, for I had no great confidence that I could achieve Kido's goals. What little experience I had in Washington was with the administrators, like Dillon Myer of WRA and John McCloy in the Pentagon. Three of Kido's five objectives involved direct relations with the lawmakers of Congress, a large body of diverse personalities, prejudices, interests, and opinions about which I knew next to nothing.

"Gee, Sab," I said, "what you've outlined is an impossible mission. Why don't we hire a lobbyist who's familiar with the ins and outs of Washington?"

"That's exactly what we're going to do," he said. "We don't have the money to employ a real one, so we're giving the assignment to you. Besides, we know you can do a better job than any hired hand unfamiliar with our history and our problems. Dedication to our cause and commitment to our people can make up for lack of experience."

Kido's own dedication and commitment imbued him with an irresistible persuasiveness, and I somehow had to translate his vision into action. The first step was to get a mandate from JACL's membership at a convention, the first since 1941. It was scheduled for Denver in February 1946, only six and a half months after the end of the war. To make sure we would get the mandate it was necessary to draw up a convention agenda. That was my responsibility. Dr. Takashi Mayeda, a Denver dentist, was convention chairman, but he had a busy practice and was unfamiliar with organizational matters. Min Yasui and his brother-in-law, Toshio

Ando, both attorneys, had undertaken most of the groundwork, and I found they had done an excellent job.

I met Yasui for the first time in Denver, and my respect for him grew. He held no grudge against me for JACL's failure to support him in 1942 when he invited arrest by violating the Army's curfew order, and I understood the sincerity that led him to institute on his own a legal challenge against violation of his constitutional rights as a citizen. I had no quarrel whatever with the principle involved in his action. Where we had differed was in the timing and strategy, and where we agreed was that JACL and its program were the Nisei's brightest hope. We could put our differences behind us in light of the business ahead.

But not all the delegates were willing at first to let bygones be bygones, particularly with reference to the relatively small number of Nisei who in bitterness and confusion had renounced their American citizenship and asked to be sent to the Tule Lake segregation camp as the first step to going to Japan. When war ended, most of them had had second thoughts and pleaded coercion and asked that their renunciation be canceled. Having been in service during this period of turmoil, I was not altogether familiar with the depth of the emotions that had developed. The book *JACL in Quest of Justice* contains this revealing paragraph:

> Some of the delegates charged that many of the renunciants were troublemakers who had disrupted the camps, condemned JACL stalwarts as WRA stooges, ridiculed volunteers for military service as "suckers" and opted to go to Tule Lake because they either hated America or wished to escape military service. These individuals, one delegate asserted, would be a constant reminder that there were Nisei who wavered in their loyalty to the United States and they would always be a disruptive element in Japanese American communities. JACL was urged to go on record as demanding the immediate deportation of those who failed to express loyalty, and that Tuleans allowed to remain in the United States be required to carry special identification cards. Others expressed anger that if no distinction was made between those who stood on principle and those who wavered, the disloyal Tuleans would reap the benefits won through Nisei military sacrifice.

Strong feelings indeed. The resentment of JACL members who had been abused and vilified for their loyalty was understandable, but that, too, had to be put behind us as we accepted the important challenges ahead. Once the anger had been replaced by a more tolerant attitude, the delegates buckled down to serious business while Min and I worked virtually around the clock to help committees formalize convention decisions in written reports. In addition to the five points that Kido had asked, the delegates adopted a number of other objectives, many at my urging. Among the more significant were these:

STAY OF DEPORTATION: A number of Japanese nationals, mostly international traders who had married U.S. citizens and established American families, were now subject to deportation under the law. JACL felt that in the name of justice these persons should not be deported.

MINORITIES: JACL should take the initiative in calling a national conference of minorities and urge creation of a federal cabinet-level Department of Human Relations and Minority Problems. No racial or ethnic discrimination should be tolerated in jobs, housing, or issuance of business and professional licenses.

ALIEN LAND LAWS: JACL should challenge the constitutionality of anti-alien land laws and escheat procedures.

EVACUATION: The U.S. Supreme Court's ruling of the constitutionality of the evacuation should be reexamined without the pressure of wartime hysteria. A JACL commission should be established to gather and preserve all documentary material pertaining to the evacuation.

VETERANS: JACL should extend all its resources toward helping veterans to readjust to civilian life.

AMERICANIZATION: JACL should carry out a long-range Americanization program to help Japanese Americans become, as its motto states, "Better Americans in a Greater America."

NONINTERVENTION: The organization backed off somewhat from Kido's proposal to take an active interest in the peace treaty with Japan. JACL would not intervene in the affairs of other nations unless the rights of Japanese Americans were directly involved. This resolution reflected the insecurity about their status as Americans which many Nisei still felt as a result of the evacuation, and their desire to strengthen their position in their own country before looking abroad. However, national headquarters was ordered to study and report on the status of Nisei who had been stranded in Japan during the war.

The convention, after paying due homage to Kido for his magnificent wartime leadership, elected Hito Okada to succeed him and went through the formality of appointing me national secretary. Kido still insisted that I should be based at national headquarters in Salt Lake City and make periodic trips to Washington to push JACL's program. Etsu and I rented a small apartment in Salt Lake and I shuttled off to the nation's capital, but early on it became evident I could not do justice to either the organization or my mandate under such an arrangement.

Take, for example, the return of the 442nd from Italy in July 1946. Virtually all the combat veterans had been replaced by younger men, but the unit's homecoming offered a great public relations opportunity. The original plan had been simply to demobilize the unit at Fort Dix without fanfare, but on one of my hurried trips to Washington it was not difficult to persuade the Pentagon to approve a more fitting ceremony. On a showery early summer day elements of the 442nd proudly paraded down Constitution Avenue in Washington, D.C. Secretary John McCloy's office in the Pentagon had arranged for President Harry Truman to review the troops. As the Nisei stood at attention on the Mall and photographers scurried about, their commander in chief presented the 442nd with its seventh Presidential Unit Citation.

"You fought for the free nations of the world," the president told the Nisei. "You fought not only the enemy, you fought prejudice — and you won. Keep up that fight. Continue to win. Make this great republic stand for what the Constitution says it stands for: 'The welfare of all the people, all the time.' "

The news services gave the ceremony extensive coverage, and the story of Nisei heroism and Americanism was sent around the world. It was a moment of triumph and vindication which I would have given almost anything to witness, but I was at my desk in Salt Lake City. JACL just didn't have the funds to let me go back to Washington to take part.

After some months, Masao Satow, who had taken a year's leave from the YMCA in Milwaukee to serve as JACL's Midwest regional director, was asked to come to Salt Lake City to assume the responsibilities of national secretary, freeing me to work full-time as Washington representative.

Satow agreed to work for one year. That assignment stretched out to twenty-five years. I was the outside man. Satow ran the internal organization. We didn't get in each other's way. We worked in our separate fields with full confidence in each other, and I treasure memories of that association.

Early in 1947, Etsu and I moved to Washington and rented a second-floor three-room apartment in a row house at 501 B Street (now Constitution Avenue N.E.). It had a tiny kitchen, a bedroom, and a living room. It was to be our combination home and JACL office, and often the office requirements intruded into our sleeping quarters. The rent was $125 a month, which JACL paid. Etsu was carried on the payroll as a secretary, although she was much more, and that helped pay our personal bills. In reality, Etsu and I were a team, and I could not have performed with anything approaching efficiency without the logistical support she provided in the way of research and general all-around legwork.

Our only other employee was Gladys Shimasaki, whose brand-new husband, Ira, was still in the Army. Gladys was a demon typist who turned out an astonishing amount of work. Etsu's supplementary duties included preparing lunch for us. Almost invariably it was salad. Salad was healthy, and besides it was cheap. One of the first things I had to do was to register as a lobbyist as required by a new law. There were some 225 of us who registered. Today lobbying has grown into a massive industry. There are more than 10,000 active lobbyists, many with extensive staffs, and thousands of others have come and gone. I am within the top dozen in seniority among those who have registered continuously since 1946.

How does one set about learning to become a lobbyist? I had no tutors, so I had to teach myself. Lobbying is a matter of salesmanship — to bring an important legislative issue to the attention of a legislator in position to do something about it, and provide him with the information that will persuade him to support your stand. I was totally convinced that adoption of JACL's program was critical to the future of Japanese Americans, that justice called for remedial legislation, and that the United States would be a better country if it rectified its wrongs. Fortified by this conviction, I took my cause to members of Congress, one at a time, on a one-to-one basis.

The theme common to all our goals was equality — equal treatment under the law regardless of race — and the most urgent of the goals were deeply involved in the equality issue. Basic to our concerns was equal right to naturalization for the Issei. If that objective could be achieved, discrimination based on ineligibility to citizenship would crumble, nullifying some 500 national, state, and local laws, ordinances, and regulations based on that classification.

The home in Fresno where Mike Masaoka (infant in mother's arms) was born. At left is Eijiro Masaoka, Mike's father. Children (from left to right) are sister Shinko, Ben, and Joe, with bicycle.

At father's grave. Mike and Ike (standing). Shinko, Mother, and Hank (kneeling). Tad, the family's youngest (in foreground).

*Private Mike Masaoka in June
1943 before he was assigned to
the 442nd Regimental Combat
Team's public information
office*

*At work in southern France two
years later*

*Four of the five Masaoka brothers who served in the U.S.
Army: (from left) Ben, killed in action; Mike; Tad,
wounded; Ike, completely disabled. Hank volunteered for
the 442nd but was transferred to the paratroops.*

Mike (right) with his buddy Sergeant Joe Itagaki

Mike receiving Legion of Merit from General Wood

*Mike and Etsu after
the war*

*Mike about the
time he began
working as
JACL lobbyist*

Mike with Congressman Walter Judd (right) and Robert Cullum, executive secretary of Committee for Equality in Naturalization (left)

Mike presents a vase to Dean Acheson in appreciation for carrying the Oyama alien land law case to a successful conclusion before the Supreme Court. The decision overturned discriminatory laws prohibiting land ownership by Japanese immigrants.

Japanese diplomats Kiichi Miyazawa (left); Hayato Ikeda, later prime minister; and Mike

Masaoka family: (standing) Ike, Mike, Tad, Joe, Hank; (seated) Kyoko, Mother, Grandmother Tsuru Goto (age 99), Shinko

Lobbyist Masaoka with Senator Everett Dirksen

Masaoka family in 1968: Tad, Mike, Shinko, Hank, Kyoko, Ike, Joe, and Mother (seated)

Michael, Etsu, granddaughter Michelle, Midori.

Etsu and Mike, 1987

Chapter 11

Memorable Victories

On my first trip to Washington after JACL's convention in Denver I met with Senator Thomas and Congressman Walter H. Judd of Minnesota to discuss the possibilities of getting legislation enabling the Issei to become naturalized. And somewhere down the line, I suggested, there was a need to update and revise immigration and naturalization laws to eliminate racial bias.

Both agreed Issei naturalization was an attainable goal and promised to support the effort, but they questioned the timing of a more sweeping revision. Thomas recommended that JACL wait until after a treaty of peace had been signed with Japan before taking on immigration reform, because there still remained much anti-Japan war sentiment. Judd, a former medical missionary in China, had engineered token immigration quotas for the Chinese, Filipinos, and East Indians during the war as a gesture to our allies, but he too thought broad reform was premature.

I encountered the greatest pessimism from the man I had expected to be most enthusiastic. Joseph Farrington, the nonvoting delegate to Congress from the Territory of Hawaii, considered by the Nisei vets in his constituency as a "friend" of the Japanese Americans, told me his first priority was statehood for Hawaii. Both citizenship for Issei and immigration reform would be impossible, he said, until Hawaii became a state. I disagreed thoroughly and made a small, friendly wager. As it turned out, immigration reform preceded statehood by seven years.

Meanwhile, there was a more urgent matter to take care of — blocking the deportation of certain Japanese aliens. These were individuals who had been permitted to enter the United States temporarily before the war as treaty merchants or students under provisions of the 1924 Exclusion Act. They were not permitted to become permanent residents and were subject to deportation if their status changed. The war had stranded them in the United States and changed their status. Even though many had married U.S. citizens and established American families, they faced deportation, an action that would create great hardships for them and their American dependents. JACL headquarters was being bombarded with appeals for help.

There were several ways to attack the problem. Individuals could go to court, as some did, but that promised to be a long-drawn-out and costly process with no assurance of victory. We could seek remedial legislation, but that, too, would be a slow route with the likelihood that many families would be deported while a bill was under consideration. On the advice of Washington experts I decided the best strategy was to get members of Congress to introduce private bills staying the deportation of individual Japanese. Such private bills would serve two purposes: they would provide relief for the individuals, and they would bring the larger problem to Congressional attention.

Few legislators were aware of the extent of the issue. It involved even individuals high in government. There was, for instance, the case of Edith Frances de Becker Sebald, daughter of an Englishman and a Japanese mother. Born in Japan, she was a Japanese citizen when in 1926 she married William J. Sebald, an American naval officer who later joined the diplomatic service. He was General MacArthur's political adviser in Tokyo, and his last post was ambassador to Australia. Two years prior to his marriage, Congress had passed the Asian Exclusion Act. It denied Mrs. Sebald permanent residence in the United States because she was considered to be Japanese. She could remain here as a visitor for only six months at each entry, having to leave at the end of that period to await renewal of her permit for another six months. Like the treaty merchants, Mrs. Sebald legally was subject to deportation for having overstayed her permit.

The chairman of the House Judiciary Subcommittee on Immigration and Naturalization at the time was the venerable Frank Fellows, a Maine Republican. He suggested that I was "a bit crazy" to think that with the war so recently ended and so much animosity remaining, any sweeping action was possible. But he conceded the need for changing the law to halt summary deportations. With the yeoman help of Walter Besterman, a European refugee attorney who was then the subcommittee's clerk, we were able to get a relief bill introduced.

While waiting for the legislation to work its way through Congress, selecting worthy cases for the private bills was no problem. There were many individuals with dramatic stories of wartime service — Japanese citizens who had taught their language in American military schools, men and women who had made propaganda broadcasts to Japan, who had translated captured Japanese documents for U.S. intelligence, all with the knowledge that they faced deportation after the war and uncertain treatment by Japan, whose nationals they legally were.

At first, sponsors for the private bills were difficult to find, and here we called on our friends for help. Utah Senators Thomas and Arthur B. Watkins and Congressmen Walter Granger and William Dawson were accommodating. Yet there was a limit to what we could ask of them, and it was important to reach members of committees directly involved.

Sometimes our friends in Congress would call their colleagues and ask them to see me. Associates outside Congress were extremely helpful. People like Roger Baldwin, Norman Thomas, and Clarence Pickett had influence enough to write or telephone some members of Congress and urge them to give Mike Masaoka a hearing. Still, there was a huge amount of just hard, patient work. Many times I waited for hours in a congressman's reception room until the secretary took pity and somehow managed to get me in to see her boss. In that era there were no Nisei members of Congress to open doors for me. Japanese Americans were virtually unknown on the Hill; I was the first Nisei that many of the legislators had ever seen, and I must have been something of a curiosity. But that was all right if being a curiosity helped the cause.

Eventually the effort paid off. So many bills from so many members were placed in the hopper — we filed more than 200 — that deportations were ordered halted while a general public remedial bill was placed under study.

Shortly, the proposed Soldier Brides Act of 1947 provided an opportunity to strike another blow for equal treatment. The act would enable U.S. servicemen overseas to marry and bring their brides home without regard to immigration quotas. But since Asians were not permitted to emigrate to the United States under the 1924 Exclusion Act, servicemen were in effect prohibited from marrying Japanese women. In Congressional hearings I argued that the law as proposed was discriminatory, not only toward the Asians but also toward the millions of Americans who had served in various parts of the Pacific Theater; if you fought in Europe you were free to marry a local girl and bring her back as your wife, but if you served in the Pacific, tough luck. That, of course, was unacceptable discrimination.

The House saw the logic of our argument and made Asian wives of servicemen eligible to enter the United States. But in the Senate there was a revival of fears of miscegenation and the old racist charges about Asians being unassimilable. Congress finally settled on a ridiculous compromise providing a thirty-day period during which servicemen could marry Asian girls and apply for their entry. U. Alexis Johnson, later an ambassador to Japan and an under secretary of state, was a consular officer in Yokohama at that time and recalls vividly the confusion — and the deplorably hasty marriages — the law provoked.

What Congress said by its action was that for one month Japanese women would be acceptable as immigrants, but after that they would revert to unwanted and unacceptable status. The whole idea was preposterously racist, but it was the best we could get out of Congress at the time. After the thirty-day period, private bills for the benefit of specific individuals were the only recourse. One beneficiary of a private bill was Captain William Marutani, later a distinguished judge in Philadelphia, who met his future wife, a nurse, in a military hospital in Japan, where he was hospitalized. It was outrageous that under the law an American military officer of Japanese origins was prohibited from bringing his Japanese bride home to the United States except as a temporary visitor.

The plight of soldiers with Asian brides was an issue likely to stir up useful public attention. In this case we exploited it by trying to avoid solutions through the private bill route. This created pressure on Congress that led to an overhaul of the entire law. That came in 1952, and I will have more to say about that later. Nonetheless, even the thirty-day amnesty, if it can be called that, was a victory of sorts. One small, brief breach had been made in America's racially discriminatory statutes when GIs were told they could bring home brides "irrespective of race."

Meanwhile I was working away on a wide variety of other projects encompassed by the JACL agenda. As consultant to President Truman's Committee on Civil Rights, I was able to get Japanese Americans mentioned. Its report urged naturalization legislation and compensation for material losses suffered in the evacuation. When President Truman adopted the report, the very substantial influence of the White House was thrown behind the proposals.

The compensation proposal was highly significant for two reasons. If approved, it would constitute an admission by the federal government that the evacuation was an injustice and its victims were entitled to recompense; second, it would inject funds, whatever the amount, into the economy of Japanese Americans at a time when they were still struggling to overcome the effects of the evacuation. Still, White House endorsement was a long way from Congressional approval.

Despite small victories, my efforts seemed to be producing relatively few tangible results until the early summer of 1948, when suddenly everything seemed to fall in place. First, we moved to a slightly larger apartment, which also doubled as an office, at 300 Fifth Street N.E. We were sorry to lose Gladys Shimasaki, who resigned to have a baby, but were fortunate to have a husband-and-wife team, Tosuke and Lorraine Yamasaki, come aboard. Tosuke was a former newspaperman and able to turn out a steady stream of press releases. Lorraine was a crackerjack secretary. There was a happy celebration in the office when on June 1, President Truman signed into law a bill opening citizenship to aliens, again "irrespective of race," who had served in the U.S. forces in World Wars I and II. This benefited Issei who had volunteered for special service against Japan, and those Issei servicemen who had failed to take advantage of a naturalization measure sponsored by JACL back in the 1930s.

A few days later a project of great symbolism which I had been working on for some time came to fruition. Two Nisei soldiers who died in Europe were interred at Arlington National Cemetery. They were Pfc. Fumitake Nagato of Los Angeles and Pfc. Saburo

Tanamachi of San Benito, Texas. They were the first Japanese Americans to be buried there, the first ethnic Japanese to be honored at Arlington since 1898, when seven Issei members of the crew were listed among those who died in the sinking of the battleship *Maine* in Havana Harbor. Five generals took part in the ceremony. John J. McCloy was among the honorary pallbearers.

General Jacob L. Devers, chief of the Army Field Forces, delivered the tribute, which was broadcast nationwide. He said:

> There is one supreme, final test of loyalty for one's native land — readiness and willingness to fight for, and if need be, to die for, one's country. These Americans, and their fellows, passed that test with colors flying. They proved their loyalty and devotion beyond all question.
>
> They volunteered for Army combat service and they made a record second to none. In Europe, theirs was the combat team most feared by the enemy. In the Pacific, they placed themselves in double jeopardy, facing the bullets of friend as well as foe. Everywhere, they were the soldiers most decorated for valor, most devoted to duty. Their only absences without leave were from hospitals which they quit before they recovered from their wounds, in order to get back into the fight for what they knew to be the right.
>
> These men, to two of whom we pay our heartfelt respects today, more than earned the right to be called just Americans, not Japanese Americans. Their Americanism may be described only by degree, and that the highest. The United States Army salutes you, Privates First Class Fumitake Nagato and Saburo Tanamachi. You, and your compatriots, will live in our hearts and our history, as Americans First Class.

The Pentagon about this time was renaming some of its troop transports and cargo ships in honor of war heroes. I suggested that one of them be named the *Sadao S. Munemori* to memorialize the first Nisei Medal of Honor winner. The idea took hold immediately. A troop ship was renamed in an appropriate ceremony, and the story of Sergeant Munemori was placed in its wardroom.

Despite these honors paid Nisei soldiers, there were still discriminatory barriers to be overcome in the armed forces. No Nisei had ever been enrolled by any of the military academies, and none of the services other than the Army was accepting them. In 1947 I asked Farrington, the delegate from Hawaii, to nominate a Nisei to general was authorized to pay. The name given them — pots and pans claims — was indeed appropriate. The remainder required Congressional appropriations for payment. (A study undertaken in 1983 by the Commission on Wartime Relocation and Internment of Civilians estimated property loss alone at between $810 million and $2 billion at 1942 prices.)

The first claim to be settled was that of Tokuji Tokimasa of Los Angeles. He was paid $303.36 early in December 1949 on a claim for $322.89. For the rest of December and all of 1950, only 211 claims were processed, with 137 of them receiving awards. The 137 successful claimants had asked for a total of $141,373, an average of $1,031.92 each. They were paid an aggregate $62,500, or an average of $456.20. Even more astonishing was the cost of settling what presumably were the most simple cases. It was costing the government $1,400 in salaries, investigations and operating expenses to pay each $456 claim.

The Justice Department recognized this was an impossible situation, but long meetings I had with the staff of the Japanese Claims Section produced no solutions. I suggested that since lack of documentation proving loss was the main problem, the government accept affidavits backed by hearsay evidence. The staff lawyers were horrified, citing the probability of foggy memories and the possibility of widespread perjury and collusion. We finally agreed that some kind of compromise settlement formula was desirable for those who wanted to avoid delay or a costly legal battle.

After further lengthy negotiation we agreed it was important to settle small claims first since it was likely these individuals were most in need of the money. Ultimately we agreed to a ceiling of $2,500 as the most anyone could receive through the compromise route, with settlement to be "compromised" at 75 percent of the compensable items claimed, or $2,500, whichever was less. I hated to surrender what promised to be a substantial amount of money, but I settled for the formula because it was apparent that a revised law had no chance of passage in the foreseeable future without Justice Department support.

The agreement broke the logjam, but we ran into another problem. The Internal Revenue Service proposed to tax the payments as income. The IRS backed down only when Senator Thomas Kuchel of California introduced a bill to block it, and William Rogers, who was a member of two Republican cabinets, offered to defend the evacuees without fee. By the end of 1952, 15,354 claims had been settled for a total of $18,255,768. That averaged out at $1,189 per claim. At the same time administrative expenses had been reduced to $43.27 per award.

As of May 1, 1954, a total of 3,001 large claims totaling $62,188,960 remained to be settled. Although more than 20,000 claims had been compromised in nearly five years, less than half of the amount sought had been approved. Prospects were bleak for early settlement of the remaining claims. I persuaded Republican Congressman Patrick Hillings of California, who had succeeded to the seat vacated by Richard Nixon when he was elected to the Senate, to introduce a bill to clarify issues that were blocking the pending claims. Congressman Hillings scheduled hearings in Los Angeles and San Francisco. Nearly every one of the 119 witnesses endorsed the changes. Only a dozen years had passed since the evacuation; the hearings provided dramatic evidence of the reversal in public sentiment.

As a result of these hearings the House Judiciary Committee's subcommittee on claims approved a number of provisions designed to speed up the settlement procedure. But the battle was far from over. The Hillings Bill underwent a series of changes before it was finally accepted by the House in April 1956, and by the Senate in June. Among other things, the measure provided for compromise settlement of claims up to $100,000. It also recognized claims filed after the original deadline.

On November 10, 1958, William Rogers, by then attorney general, held a ceremony marking the signing of the 26,522nd compromise settlement. That completed the program except for eight substantial cases that had been sent to the Court of Claims. A total of $36,874,240.49 had been paid, but it had taken ten years. Rogers expressed appreciation ''to Mr. Masaoka, the Japanese American Citizens League, and the claimants themselves for their helpful cooperation toward this result. . . .''

I spoke of the appreciation of the thousands of evacuees. But I also said Congress should have been more generous in determining compensable items. In retrospect, I now wish that I had been more critical of the shortcomings of the original legislation, and of the legalistic interpretations of government attorneys. It took another seven years to settle the last claim. That was a Court of Claims award of $362,500 to the rice-growing Koda family, who had sought $1,210,000. By then Keizaburo Koda, the founder of the business, and his son William were dead. The settlement went to another son, Edward, and William's widow, Jean. James Purcell of San Francisco was the attorney for the Kodas. I received a modest fee for helping in the case. It was the only compensation I received from the entire claims program, although I had helped hundreds of claimants and attorneys.

The government's fears about fraud had been totally unfounded. There was one case, involving a claim of less than $200, and the claimant was found not guilty in court.

The Evacuation Claims Act of 1948 has been cited as reason for denying further compensation sought by JACL through its legislative redress campaign and the $24 billion class action suit filed by William Hohri and twelve others on behalf of the National Council for Japanese American Redress. The original statute declared that "the payment of an award shall be final and conclusive for all purposes, not withstanding any other provision of the law to the contrary, and shall be a full discharge of the United States . . . with respect to all claims arising out of the same subject matter."

However, I have contended coercion was involved in administering the claims program. Before a House Judiciary subcommittee early in 1986, testifying on behalf of Go For Broke, Inc., then the umbrella national Nisei veterans organization, I charged that the 1948 law for all practical purposes forced most evacuees to accept compromise settlements for loss of compensable items as arbitrarily determined by the government. In effect, I said, the evacuees had to give up a 25 percent commission in order to secure relatively speedy service.

Subsequently an appellate court has described payment under the 1948 law as "bounty." The court ruled that "We are not unmindful of the hard choice to which Congress put the evacuees. By forcing them to choose between a ready administrative remedy and a costly lawsuit, Congress effectively forced the evacuees to settle for half a loaf rather than risk a fight for what the Constitution declares to be theirs by right." The payments under the 1948 act were a token sum to help meet the expenses of replacing actual loss.

A much deeper issue — redress for wrongful imprisonment — is involved in the new effort.

Even the "half a loaf" was paltry. Approximately $38 million was distributed in all. If that sum had been divided equally among the 115,000 victims, each individual's share would have been $330.43. Furthermore, the money was paid a decade after the evacuation, when inflation had slashed the purchasing power of the dollar in half. No, $165.22 was neither generous nor even just compensation. Even so, the Evacuation Claims Act was a significant piece of legislation that at the time was hailed by the Japanese American community.

Filing was a relatively simple procedure that individuals could do on their own. Most sought the help of attorneys who, under the law, were entitled to 10 percent of the award. This helped many young Nisei lawyers to establish their practices. Congressman Walter told me he had expected JACL would help the community file claims and build up its own treasury, or that I might want to go into the business myself. I considered that an improper conflict of interests. After they received their checks, many persons made voluntary contributions to JACL.

What I got out of the Evacuation Claims Act was little more than a valuable lesson. Thereafter we had our own experts draft bills precisely the way we wanted them, and then left it up to Congress to undertake the fine tuning.

During the immediate postwar years the pursuit of justice also was proceeding on legal fronts other than Congress. I was involved directly or peripherally in many of them but will mention only four of the most important — the vote on California's Proposition 15, and the Oyama, Fujii, and Masaoka court cases.

Proposition 15 was a measure placed before California voters in the fall of 1946 to validate various amendments to the racially discriminatory Alien Land Law of 1920. Its passage would lock in measures intensely prejudicial to Japanese Americans. JACL formed an Anti-Discrimination Committee which raised $100,000 — a very substantial sum in those lean post-evacuation years — to oppose it. Etsu and I went to California to direct a last-minute public information campaign for justice, basing it on the loyalty of the Issei and the Nisei war record. Leaflets were printed and Etsu and Henry

Kanegae, a farmer who flew his own plane, hopped around the state delivering them. The effort paid off. The election was in effect an opinion poll of the state's attitude toward Japanese Americans, and it showed that the California of 1946 was not the California of even half a decade earlier. Proposition 15 was defeated 1,143,780 to 797,067.

The Oyama case involved eight acres of farmland purchased near San Diego in 1934 and 1937 for Fred Oyama, a citizen and minor at the time, by his foreign-born parents, who had taken the precaution of going to court to be named his legal guardians. The state of California sought to seize the Oyama farm, and others bought under similar circumstances, contending the purchases had been made with intent to violate the Alien Land Law. In fact, the state was practicing a form of blackmail by paying a reward for information about alleged violations of the land law and offering to "sell" the escheated farms back to the owners after charges were filed.

The Oyamas had come to Kido and A. L. Wirin for legal help. Because the case involved a basic issue, and the injustice seemed so flagrant, it was a good test for JACL support. The California Supreme Court ruled against the Oyamas. We decided to appeal to the U.S. Supreme Court. Wirin and Kido, prominent in their own rights, felt a more prestigious attorney would be advantageous in presenting the argument before the Supreme Court.

Dean Acheson had resigned as undersecretary of the treasury about this time to reenter private practice, and I heard he might be amenable to taking on a case that would win him some public attention. Although none of us knew him, Wirin, Kido, and I went to see him. Acheson met us together with his associate Charles Horsky, who had a brilliant legal mind and later became a presidential aide. After I explained the details, Acheson said, "The constitutional question involved interests me very much, and it would be a good one for me to take on. But it's going to be expensive. What can your people afford?"

"Sir," I said, "the principals are not well-to-do and JACL is a small and poor organization. But I think we could come up with, let's say, five hundred dollars?"

Acheson was obviously startled but could not suppress a smile. "That, Mr. Masaoka," he said, "wouldn't even begin to pay the printing bill. I might as well take the case free of charge."

Whether he meant it or not, I couldn't miss the opportunity. "That's wonderful, Mr. Acheson," I exclaimed, jumping up to shake his hand. "You have a client."

Acheson did indeed represent the Oyamas without fee, and JACL footed the incidental expenses. In 1948 the Supreme Court ruled against California, finding the Alien Land Law violated the equal-protection clause of the Fourteenth Amendment as it related to American citizens. After the victory, we presented Acheson with a lovely Japanese vase. His only other benefits from the case were considerable public notice and a reputation as a representative of good causes.

(There were, however, two incidental developments. Acheson later represented Torao Takahashi, an alien who had sued to obtain a commercial fishing license, which had been refused him by the California Fish and Game Commission. The U.S. Supreme Court held the California action was unconstitutional because it discriminated against Takahashi solely because of his race. The two cases raised Acheson's awareness of U.S.-Japanese relations, which became extremely important in the drafting of the peace treaty ending World War II after he became secretary of state.)

The Sei Fujii case had some different implications. Fujii, feisty publisher of the newspaper *Kashu Mainichi* and an alien ineligible for citizenship, bought property in Los Angeles under his own name to challenge the Alien Land Law. This time the California Supreme Court found the law in violation of both state and federal constitutional guarantees of equal protection.

The Fujii case was a test of alien rights. While it was on appeal after losing in district court, my brothers and I instituted another suit to test citizen rights under the Alien Land Law. With the cooperation of William Carr of Pasadena, a realtor and member of the American Friends Service Committee, we contracted to buy land with money from our brother Ben's GI death benefits. Our stated intention was to build a home and give it to our mother, Haruye. Under the Alien Land Law this was illegal. The state could seize the property, our mother would lose her home, and we sons would lose our investment. To test whether this could really happen, we filed suit against the state. James Purcell was our lead attorney.

In court we argued that an act of charity on the part of the sons, an act that would be considered meritorious if performed by Americans of other racial extractions, made felons of us. "Can the state of California," we asked, "by statute relegate citizens of the United States to a position inferior to that of other citizens and, in some cases, inferior to aliens, merely because of the racial origin . . . in the matter of the right to purchase land, sell, hold and convey real or personal property, and in the personal relationship of those citizens to their own parents?"

The court's ruling in March 1950 read in part: "I hold that the Alien Land Law of California under the facts in this case is unconstitutional because it violates the Fourteenth Amendment of the United States, both as to the alien mother and the citizen sons."

In reality, Mother wasn't greatly interested in having a house. She preferred to move about visiting her children, so we did not complete purchase of the property. But remembering the discrimination that caused her and her husband to move to Utah back in 1916 and the grief of that experience, she was a willing and interested party to the lawsuit. No one was more delighted than she when the Alien Land Law was finally struck from the books.

Mother used the money from Ben's death benefits to fund a memorial scholarship each year. It was the first postwar scholarship for a worthy Japanese American going to college. The money was only $250, but in many cases it proved the difference between going to school and having to stay out a year. The first two winners became doctors of medicine. Other early beneficiaries were Kaz Oshiki, who went on to become the highly respected administrative assistant to Congressman Robert W. Kastenmeier of Wisconsin, and Cherry Tsutsumida, the highest ranking Nisei woman in civil service. Oshiki was involved in Congressional affairs even before Dan Inouye became the first elected Nisei member of Congress. At one time Tsutsumida was an administrator in what was then the Department of Health, Education, and Welfare, responsible for one-third of the nonmilitary budget of the United States. The Ben Frank Masaoka scholarship was continued for twenty-five years from Mother's own funds. Today there are more than 250 scholarships of various kinds in the JACL program, distributing tens of thousands of dollars each year to promising Japanese American students.

Perhaps my most important single public relations project also became reality in 1950. Three years earlier, friends in the American Jewish Committee had introduced me to Dore Schary, a prominent movie producer. He had gained fame for having broken a long-standing taboo in making *Gentleman's Agreement,* a frank treatment of restrictive covenants. He was thinking of making a movie speculating on the identity of the unknown soldier interred in the Tomb of the Unknowns, who might be an American of any ethnic origin. Eventually he dropped that idea and became interested in the story of the 442nd. We talked intermittently about it. Finally he announced that a film would be made about the Nisei fighting men. It was to be titled *Go for Broke* and Robert Pirosh, an Army combat veteran who had won an Academy Award for a war movie called *Battleground,* was named to write the screenplay and direct it. Van Johnson, then a popular actor, was picked for the lead. All the Nisei in the film except one were veterans of the 442nd. The exception was Henry Nakamura, who had been too young to be in the war, in the important role of Tommy. And I was asked to serve as technical consultant. With JACL's permission I took the assignment, flying out to Hollywood for about one week each month during the filming.

Schary was completely dedicated to the project, and Pirosh quickly captured a feel for Japanese Americans and the spirit of the 442nd. The story told about Nisei internees volunteering and was climaxed by the rescue of the Lost Battalion. The result was an authentic film about Nisei sacrifice and patriotism that was moving without being maudlin. "That's exactly the way it was," more than one Nisei vet told me as he dabbed at his eyes after viewing the movie. Pirosh's skill enabled the film to avoid the false notes that marred, and made so controversial among Nisei, *Sanga Moyu,* the ambitious Japanese-made television drama on the same subject.

The premiere of *Go for Broke* was held in Washington, D.C., with numerous government notables attending. It was there that I first met a young congressman named John F. Kennedy. Combining entertainment with action and a poignant message, the film enjoyed substantial box-office success and told the Nisei story to millions of Americans who could never have been reached in any other way. Occasionally *Go for Broke* is still seen on late-night television.

Go for Broke also had important personal consequences. By my standards, the consultant's fee I received was generous. For the first time Etsu and I were not totally dependent on our meager JACL salaries. Now we would be able to buy a home of our own and think about starting a family.

Chapter 12

Two Votes That Changed History

Persuading Congress of the need to strike racism from 175-year-old American immigration and naturalization laws was an awesome challenge. The founding fathers, who could not have known that one day Asian immigrants would seek and be deserving of citizenship in their country, had made no provision for naturalization of other than whites. The laws had remained that way until after the Civil War, when "persons of African nativity" were made acceptable. Some time afterward, American Indians were given citizenship.

Times continued to change, and naturalization rights for Asians, in our view, had become a matter of overdue justice. Was the nation ready to acknowledge this? Congress had to be made aware that the stigma of "aliens ineligible to citizenship" established two classes of immigrants — "desirable" and "undesirable." This was the root cause of Issei problems, and indirectly those of the Nisei, and had to be eliminated.

A companion issue was equal opportunity to immigrate to the United States. Immigration from Asia was restricted by a patchwork code starting in 1882 when Chinese were barred. The restriction was tightened over the years until the National Origins Clause of the 1924 immigration law prohibited immigration from any country within what was defined as the Asia Pacific Triangle. During World War II, limited quotas were provided for the Philippines, China, and India as a gesture to military allies.

I believed that as a matter of principle the United States must deal with all nations on the basis of equality. Equality under the law was basic to our long future as Americans as well as to the postwar relations between the United States and Japan. While I was busily working on many urgent projects, concern for a fundamental change in the way the nation regarded and treated Asians loomed always in the background.

Back in 1925, not long after Congress had passed the Asian exclusion act, a liberal Japanese statesman named Yusuke Tsurumi had given a memorable speech at the Institute of Politics in Williamstown, Massachusetts. I do not remember where I first read the speech — perhaps it was in preparation for a debate — but the force of his logic left a lasting impression on me.

Tsurumi pointed out that Japan, as a matter of good faith, signed the so-called Gentlemen's Agreement of 1907 restraining the migration of laborers to the United States. Japan, he said, understood that so long as it kept its part of the agreement, the United States would not pass an exclusion law against the Japanese as it had done against China.

Passage of the exclusionary Immigration Act of 1924, Tsurumi said, carried in addition to the idea that Japanese were undesirable the implication that Congress suspected the integrity of the Japanese government. Said Tsurumi:

> It has been said that the issue at stake, the supreme issue before Congress, was the protection of American civilization against a flood of Japanese immigrants. With all due respect, I beg to dissent from that contention. No responsible person in Japan has ever desired or now desires to force upon the United States any class of immigrants that was not wanted. . . .
>
> The issue in Japan was whether the Japanese nation was to stand on an equal footing with Western powers or to be cut off from the fellowship and be driven back upon a purely Oriental policy and theater of operations. . . . The issue was not immigration.
>
> As far as affording any outlet for the peasants and laborers of Japan is concerned, that issue was closed years ago, and any additional guarantees required for the security of American national life would have been gladly yielded. The sole issue was the method of handling an affair on which a friendly agreement already existed. . . .
>
> To my Oriental mind, the procedure of Congress is inexplicable. The grave consequences flow from the fact that it is now very difficult for any Japanese liberal to convince the conservatives and the nationalists that the process by which the Immigration Act was passed was not intended to serve notice on Japan that she need expect

no more cooperation from America and that the ruthless pursuit of
national interests without respect for the feelings of others is not a
high and noble quality of patriotism. The grave consequences to
which I refer will affect the social development of Japan far more
than the destiny of America. . . .

Tsurumi was prophetic. What he feared did indeed come to pass.
Japan's nationalists and militarists overcame the liberals and led the
nation up the bloody road to Pearl Harbor. I was convinced that
Congress must act to grant Japan the dignity of equality or our costly
military victory would have been in vain.

But the reality of the situation was that only a few years had
passed since the end of a savage war which propagandists on both
sides had depicted as a conflict between races, and less than a
quarter century had gone by since Congress had voted the 1924
immigration law. Even with justice on our side, it appeared that a
cautious, step-by-step strategy with the backing of liberal elements
willing to support us would be the prudent way to seek JACL's
objective of eliminating racism from both naturalization and immigration statutes. There were many prominent Americans that I could
go to for advice, and in planning our strategy we had held long,
earnest discussions about the wisdom of tying the two issues together. Would our chances of success be better taking them on one
at a time?

Or should we, like the men of the 442nd, "go for broke" with
a head-on assault? The ultimate decision, in the absence of specific
instructions from JACL, would have to be mine.

The end of exclusion would mean recognition that the Japanese
were "good enough" to be admitted into our country. If postwar
Japan was to emerge as a democratic friend rather than a sullen
conquered nation, its nationals could not be treated less worthily
than the nationals of other countries, including Germany and Italy.

But if it seemed likely that two goals were too much to take on
at one time, naturalization deserved first priority. Our parents were
in the twilight of their lives, the greatest portion of which had been
spent in the United States, and their contribution to its progress and
well-being had earned them citizenship. The Issei unquestionably
were our first responsibility.

We mulled over numerous ideas. One was a special measure to
give the Japanese the same privileges extended the Chinese, Filipi-

nos, and East Indians during the war. The problem with this proposal was that it was likely to run into rough seas without addressing JACL's broad goal of eliminating race and national origin as a consideration in naturalization.

A limited proposal, not likely to face much opposition, was a bill to offer naturalization to Gold Star mothers. Subsequently the measure would be extended to cover Gold Star fathers, then to parents of Purple Heart veterans. I gave consideration to this course because it would be difficult for Congress to turn down the fathers and mothers of men who had shed blood for their country. Once the principle of citizenship for worthy Asians could be established, it would be less difficult to win naturalization for all Issei. The House approved this bill, but Congress adjourned before the Senate could act.

As the weeks sped by, my reading of the Congressional mood indicated there was a fighting chance to get action on both naturalization and immigration. I met frequently in strategy sessions with Congressman Judd and Congressman Francis Walter of Pennsylvania, the lone member of the Dies Committee who had refused to be stampeded by that infamous body's witch-hunting tactics. Walter was a popular House leader who had accepted an assignment as chairman of the Un-American Activities Committee at the request of Speaker Sam Rayburn to give it credibility and respectability. A Navy veteran of both world wars, Walter was a great admirer of the Nisei military record and became a staunch supporter of JACL's goals.

We were joined in our strategy sessions by Robert Cullum, a former WRA official. He worked out of the JACL office as executive secretary of the Committee for Equality in Naturalization, made up of more than a hundred distinguished citizens who had lent names and support to the naturalization proposition. Eventually we decided it made sense to join the two issues.

Early in 1948, Congressman Judd introduced HR 6809, whose objective was to "eliminate all racial barriers in existing naturalization laws and to make it possible for Asian and Pacific peoples to enter the United States as quota immigrants."

This was the sweeping measure I had preferred from the beginning, and now we pulled out all stops to build support. The Washington office sent letters to scores of influential friends urging their help. We lined up witnesses to appear when hearings were scheduled. The lobbying effort required money. JACL stalwarts set out to raise funds on the mainland. Their vehicle was the Anti-Discrimination Committee, called Kika Kisei Domei in Japanese, and the Issei contributed generously.

With Keisaburo Koda, the venerable California rice grower, I went to Hawaii to ask for contributions. The idea of citizenship for some 85,000 Issei was so exciting that we were received everywhere with open arms. Koda was a powerhouse in our meetings with Hawaii's Issei leaders. Ben Tashiro was particularly helpful on the island of Kauai. In Hilo, James Hirano pitched in. In Honolulu, Katsuro Miho and Tets Oi threw their influence behind our efforts. Hawaii raised more than $250,000, a drop in the bucket by current lobbying standards but a substantial amount for us.

Extensive committee hearings were held in which the war record of the Nisei was cited frequently as justification for extending citizenship to Issei. General Mark W. Clark wrote in a letter presented to the hearing:

> The supreme test of citizenship is the willingness of a man to risk his life so that our country may live. Under my command in Italy the 442nd Regiment and 100th Infantry Battalion, composed of Nisei, fought the Nazi combat forces with the valor and skill characteristic of the young Americans that they are. The parents of these heroic Nisei should have the privileges of the democracy their sons helped to preserve.

John J. McCloy, the father of the 442nd, added:

> I believe legislation such as this, at least as it affects the interests of the Japanese Americans, is only an appropriate form of recognition for the loyalty which Japanese Americans as a whole evidenced to this country during the war.

I added my voice to theirs. If what I said was overly dramatic, it was also sincere:

> In the foxholes before battle we would talk about a lot of things; but the No. 1 topic was this: Sure, we wanted America to win the war, but we also wanted America to be the kind of America that it professed to be, and that kind of America would not discriminate against people like my mother, who came here early in the 1900s. When she had eight children, Dad died leaving us practically pen-

niless. Yet, my mother saw every one of us through school, a number of us through college, and when the test of supreme loyalty to
this country came it was my mother who first said, "Boys, your job
is to go out and fight for these United States, because it is my
country." Well, there were lots of other mothers and fathers like
that, and their sons and I knew each other overseas, and over and
over again they insisted that my job was to come and tell you, the
Congress of the United States, what their loyalties were — loyalties
which could not be questioned.

Despite the favorable hearings, the House failed to bring up HR
6809 for vote. In 1949, Congressman Judd introduced the bill again.
It was designated as HR 199, and in March of that year the House
passed it by voice vote after defeating a motion to recommit, 336–39.
Then I learned another frustrating lesson in politics. Senator Richard
Russell of Georgia, leader of the Southern bloc unwilling to accept
racially tinged reform, put the bill on the shelf by demanding that it
be passed over.

Despite this defeat there was much to cheer about. We had
solid support in the House. The California delegation, which in the
past usually was first to scream "yellow peril," was unanimous in
its support.

This was a period of great excitement for Etsu and me and our
associates. We were young, and it was a heady experience to walk
into the offices of the powerful and to be given attentive audience
while pleading the cause of justice. I had learned my way around the
Hill, and hard work and sheer persistence finally were beginning to
pay off.

At one stage it was important for me to meet Congressman
John Robison of Kentucky, a ranking member of the House Judiciary Committee. He continued to evade me. One day I saw him
headed for the men's room. I hurried after him. When he stopped at
a urinal, I moved alongside him and began to talk to him when he
couldn't get away. I doubt that I was able to say anything significant
in the few moments I had, but he invited me to his office for a more
conventional meeting. In time he became a strong supporter. Ed
Gossett of Texas, another member of the House, had been made
aware of the 442nd's rescue of the Texas Lost Battalion in the
Vosges, and he too became one of our most effective allies. I joined
various veterans' groups, attended their conventions, reminded them

of the Nisei role in the war, and solicited their support in putting pressure on their representatives in Congress. It is difficult to over-estimate the value of their backing, or of the support of the press.

Newspapers that had ignored our plight during evacuation days, or had endorsed our incarceration, began to take an enlightened interest in our campaign, thanks in no small part to our press releases. Dozens of journals, ranging from the *New York Times* down to little community weeklies, endorsed the Judd bill, and certainly JACL's educational program is entitled to take at least some of the credit for this change of attitude. The *Los Angeles Times,* which had pilloried Japanese Americans savagely for a generation, published an editorial beginning with this paragraph:

> Passage by the House of legislation permitting the naturaliza-tion of Japanese, Koreans and other Orientals now barred from cit-izenship is an act of simple justice. The Senate should accept the legislation without question and remove from the statute books a vestige of race discrimination and prejudice.

In June 1949, Cullum was able to write to Reed Lewis, chairman of the executive board of the Committee for Equality in Naturalization:

> As you have requested, editorial comment concerning the Judd bill for Equality in Naturalization and Immigration has been brought together and is forwarded herewith. No unfavorable editorial has been written, so far as I am able to determine. Of more than forty editorials reproduced herein, originating in fifteen states and the District of Columbia, nearly one-fourth appeared in the California press, a further proof that sentiment along the West Coast has be-come most favorable to enactment of this legislation.

Looking back, it is something of a marvel that we were able to accomplish so much with so little. Contributions to the campaign did not go far in Washington. Our pay was scarcely enough to pay living expenses. Etsu threw herself into the work with as much determination as I did. Our social life was limited, as much for lack of time as money, and our diversions simple. On many a humid summer evening we sought to escape the oppressive heat of our apartment by taking a picnic supper of rice balls and trimmings and heading for a shady spot along the Potomac. Mieko (Myke) Kosobayashi, one of our bright, dedicated, indefatigable secretaries who served the cause so well, still likes to remind Etsu and me of the enjoyment we found in such simple relaxation after a day of intense effort.

It is a credit to the persistence of Congressman Walter that the naturalization bill was taken up again in the second session of the 81st Congress, which began in January 1950. With House support apparently assured, we finally persuaded Senator Russell to propose an amendment naming only "Japanese" in the resolution. The Senate accepted this version, but now the House balked. A joint conference committee was named to work out the differences. Congressman Walter succeeded in restoring the original statement of principle eliminating race and national origin as a consideration in naturalization, but in return Senator Pat McCarran of Nevada, chairman of the Senate conferees, demanded inclusion of a number of so-called security clauses.

Both House and Senate accepted the revised resolution on August 14, 1950. However, just prior to adjournment for the day, Senate Majority Leader Scott Lucas of Illinois moved to reconsider Senate approval, thereby blocking its passage. Lucas was under heavy pressure from his ethnic constituency to oppose the security clauses. On August 23, Lucas withdrew his motion to reconsider, thereby sending the Walter Resolution as amended to the White House. President Truman vetoed the resolution and returned it to the House on September 9, indicating that while he favored the naturalization sections, he strongly disapproved of the security clauses.

That same afternoon the House overrode the veto 307 to 14 and sent the measure to the Senate, which failed to act before Congress adjourned. Meanwhile, JACL held its biennial national convention in Chicago and Senator Lucas was asked to speak. It was an invitation the senator could not decline gracefully. Before our membership he pledged to call up the bill when Congress resumed deliberations.

Lucas lost his bid for reelection that November, but he still had an opportunity to call up our bill when President Truman convened a lame-duck session. On its first day, November 27, 1950, Congressman Walter reintroduced his original resolution, and for the fourth time the House passed it. Once again Senator Russell objected, and Congress adjourned on December 15 without further action. Senator Lucas, despite his promise to JACL, failed to call up either the latest Walter Resolution or the vetoed version with its security provisions.

To appreciate the significance of the security provisions on our goals, it is necessary to be aware of a sequence of vastly significant national events which were beyond our control. The nation was in the throes of anti-Communist spy fever. Alger Hiss, a high State Department official, had been indicted for perjury after he denied giving secret information to Whittaker Chambers, a former *Time* magazine editor and admitted Soviet agent. Senator Joseph McCarthy, the Wisconsin Republican, was riding high on what had started as a one-man crusade against Communists in government, whether they existed or not.

Spurred on by McCarthy's fears, Congress earlier in 1950 had passed a harsh domestic security measure sponsored by Senator McCarran. Liberals were particularly disturbed by Title II of the Internal Security Act. It made it possible for any future president in an emergency — declaration of war, insurrection, or invasion — to suspend the writ of *habeas corpus* and imprison citizens in the same way that we had been treated in World War II. In fact, Title II codified the outrage committed against Japanese Americans, and with good reason it came to be known as the concentration-camp law. President Truman vetoed the Internal Security Act, calling it "a long step toward totalitarianism." McCarthy led a successful override and the act became law.

Senate conservatives wanted even more restrictive measures for controlling Communism. They saw our naturalization bill as likely to pass. And since there was a tenuous link between immigration and naturalization and subversive aliens, they attached their proposals to the naturalization bill. Among the more controversial points was a provision for deporting any alien endangering the public safety. Civil-rights activists saw it as a power that too easily could be abused.

Adding to the debate — and confusion — was a comprehensive study of immigration and naturalization laws begun by the Senate Judiciary Committee about the time our program was getting under way. The committee's report, delivered April 20, 1950, was a 925-page document. Whatever it purported to do, the report proposed more new restrictions than liberalizations and made no mention of extending immigration and naturalization to Asians other than those who had benefited by wartime measures.

When the 82nd Congress convened in January 1951, three omnibus bills were introduced. S 716 was offered by Senator McCarran. A companion bill, though not nearly as restrictive, was introduced by Congressman Walter. The third bill, more liberal than the others, was introduced by Congressman Emanuel Celler of New York, chairman of the House Judiciary Committee, who liked to say he was the only member of Congress remaining from 1924 when the last major revision was made.

All three bills left untouched the general immigration and naturalization provisions of existing law.

Joint Senate and House subcommittee hearings on the three bills were held in March and April 1951. Some sixty witnesses testified. JACL was among them, but it was overshadowed by shipping interests and large civic organizations who had their own concerns. Two new omnibus bills developed from the hearings, S 2055 by Senator McCarran and HR 5678 by Congressman Walter with Judd, Sidney R. Yates of Illinois, and George Miller of California among cosponsors.

It was at this stage that contacts developed over the years with subcommittee staffs paid off. We were able to get our proposals for equality in immigration and naturalization, and several other liberalizing measures, into the bills. One enabled alien males married to American women and their minor children to enter without being counted against the quota. This gave American women the same rights as American men, who, under current law, could bring in their alien wives without regard for the quota. A second liberalizing measure was of greater significance to the Japanese. It permitted Japanese who had been admitted as legal immigrants prior to 1924 to take naturalization examinations in their native tongue, which was recognition of the unfair conditions that kept many of them from English fluency.

I was aware that these issues were controversial, but they also were essential to reform. Also extremely controversial was the national-origins formula which based immigration quotas for any country on a percentage of inhabitants of the United States in 1920 who traced their origins to that country. Since the American population in 1920 was predominantly of northern and western European origin, those countries would receive the largest quotas and more recent immigration groups would be short-changed.

Many of our friends both in and out of Congress were in favor of immigration and naturalization reform but opposed the excessively restrictive security measures. They could not vote for the first without accepting the objectional amendments. That dilemma also backed JACL into a corner. We could not push for our key goals without accepting the entire package. Nor were we in a position to abandon or postpone those goals — for a decade or even longer, by best estimates — if we lost this opportunity. Whichever way we decided to go, we would be wide open for condemnation. This was a classic case of desirable and necessary legislation being burdened by amendments which were irrelevant and objectionable.

After numerous conferences with JACL leaders around the country, my decision was to push for the bills despite their faults. In the final analysis the rationale was simple: the Title II concentration-camp law was already in the statute books, and the amendments would not make them significantly more harsh; we had to win naturalization rights while the time was ripe.

I was unaware of it at the time, but HR 5678 carried Congressman Walter's name rather than Judd's because of a petty bit of partisanship. I learned much later that Speaker Sam Rayburn, realizing the omnibus bill was likely to pass with a little additional effort, persuaded Judd, a Republican, to let Walter, a Democrat and chairman of the Judiciary Subcommittee on Immigration and Naturalization, carry the ball to assure passage and, incidentally, give Democrats the credit.

Judd was more interested in seeing justice done than winning political credit and yielded to Rayburn. Be that as it may, Walter was one of the staunchest friends of the causes JACL espoused, and his key committee assignments enabled him to wield considerable influence helpful to us. Walter's secretary, Ruth Miskell, was feared and disliked by many on the Hill because of her crusty manner, but she was cordial toward me and frequently managed to get me in to see her boss even when he was busiest. In many respects Walter replaced Senator Thomas after his retirement as my principal contact in Congress.

Given a choice, I would have much preferred a simple measure that met our objectives rather than a complex and controversial omnibus bill. But since I didn't have that luxury, I supported the new Walter-McCarran Bill vigorously. Overall, contrary to the charges of our liberal friends, it would not further restrict immigration but liberalize it for the first time since 1924. It was not easy to part company with some members of Congress who had been so supportive of our position in earlier legislative battles. To them, the security provisions were anathema, and I respected them for their zealous defense against what they perceived to be a serious attack on individual rights. Under other circumstances I would have been with them. But there was another side to the controversy, and here, too, a basic human-rights issue was involved. Furthermore, I was not convinced that the dangers my friends feared were as ominous as they believed, and fortunately history has proved that their concerns were excessive.

At the request of Congressman Chet Holifield, the California Democrat, I composed a statement setting forth JACL's position to help him formulate his own stand:

> For the first time in American law, this provision would establish the principal of equal opportunity in immigration and naturalization to all persons without regard to race. . . . It is ironic that while we invest our very lifeblood in Korea to thwart Communist advances there, and labor to win the allegiance of Japan and Southeast Asia to our cause, we render suspect the sincerity of our enterprise abroad by our discriminatory policy at home. . . . The House has approved on at least four separate occasions legislation to authorize the naturalization of lawfully admitted resident aliens, but because of Senate reluctance to act upon this issue as a single and separate item, this inequity has yet to be abolished.

The legislation, a document of 300 pages, had been thoroughly revised at least six times, and I recognized it could not satisfy everyone. My statement to Congressman Holifield continued:

> A major criticism is the charge that the Internal Security Act of 1950 is made a part of the permanent immigration and naturalization law and in a far more restrictive form. In the first place, it must be remembered that this act is already on the statute books and that it affects immigration and naturalization practices. Even if the omnibus bill is not passed, the Internal Security Act remains as a serious factor in immigration and naturalization policies.

I noted various other objections, then concluded with the thought that enactment of this legislation would not preclude but would encourage later amendments, step by step, to improve the basic law.

Even among Japanese Americans, opinion on the bill was not unanimous. An organization calling itself the Nisei Progressives issued a statement urging defeat of the Walter-McCarran Bill; the statement was published in the bilingual *Hokubei Shimpo* newspaper of New York City. Charging the bill was racist while professing to wipe out racism, the statement read:

> Senator McCarran, Congressman Walter, et al., would sell us racism in the name of progress. If these gentlemen were truly dedicated to liberalizing our present immigration laws, why do they not sponsor a simple measure granting immigration and naturalization rights to those people now denied them? We who have desired those rights, especially for our parents, cannot but proclaim that the price for them is too high under the McCarran-Walter Bill. We are being offered naturalization and immigration rights in exchange for discriminatory double standards for Negro and Oriental peoples. We who want equal rights in the fullest sense cannot submit to racist and opportunistic principles. . . .

New York attorney Thomas T. Hayashi answered the Nisei Progressives with data that I had gathered, pointing out that some 88,000 resident aliens, 85,000 of whom were of Japanese ancestry, would remain ineligible for naturalization if the Walter-McCarran Bill should fail. He wrote:

> Under such disability, some eight states preclude these aliens from acquiring real property; New York State forbids them from entering into at least twenty-two professions or occupations, in New York City they are barred from at least twenty-one types of businesses, certain states will continue to deny old age assistance and assistance to the blind. Furthermore, aliens who entered the United States prior to July 1, 1924, and having no record showing lawful admission for permanent residence can ordinarily obtain a certificate of lawful entry with relative ease, however those who are ineligible for citizenship are prohibited from taking advantage of this expeditious procedure. Generally, Oriental alien wives, husbands and unmarried minor children of American citizens will continue to be barred from entering the United States.

The departments of Justice and State endorsed the measure. So did organizations traditionally hostile to us such as the American Legion, Veterans of Foreign Wars, the American Federation of Labor, and the Grange. But we lost the support of many New York–based liberal organizations and churches. They wanted broad approval for entry of displaced persons and war and political refugees. And when they couldn't get this concession they opposed the entire bill on the ground that the security provisions were unfair and McCarthyite.

Prior to the bills coming to the floor, I worked an average of ten hours a day on Capitol Hill, days that were followed by additional hours in my office studying the situation, reading and rereading the bills, developing strategies. On April 25, 1952, the House approved the Walter version of the omnibus bill 206 to 69, a not unexpected margin in view of its record.

The Senate began debate May 13, with opponents seeking to block action by proposing more than 200 amendments and demanding time to speak on each one. The first real test of strength came six days later when the Senate refused, 44 to 28, to recommit McCarran's bill to the Judiciary Committee for "further study." Two days later, May 21, the bill survived its second test when the Senate defeated, 51 to 27, a motion to substitute a bill proposed by Senator Herbert H. Lehman of New York. As I watched tensely from the Senate gallery, at 7:00 p.m. on May 22, after four of eight major amendments had been defeated on roll call votes, the Senate by voice vote passed the McCarran version.

The Senate and House versions were sent to conference the first week of June, with Walter and McCarran serving as chairmen of their respective delegations. Agreement was reached on June 9. The conference report said that in more than a hundred instances the existing law had been liberalized. What was most important to me was that the final bill provided naturalization opportunities to all legally admitted residents regardless of race or national origin, and it provided an immigration quota for all countries under the 1924 National Origins Quota Act. For Japan the number was a token 185 per year. The most significant reform in U.S. immigration policy since 1924, and in naturalization laws since the Civil War, was sent to the White House on June 13, 1952, for the president's signature.

I was elated. The joy was tempered by the fact that the White

House, under intense political pressure from all sides, had indicated President Truman would veto the bill just as he had vetoed the Internal Security Act two years earlier. But Congress was in a mood to challenge the president, and therein lay our hopes of ultimate victory.

The president vetoed the measure on June 25, sending it back to the House with a long message describing it as a step backward that would intensify "the repressive and inhumane aspects" of present immigration procedures. He noted that the bill was extremely complex, with 164 separate sections, some with more than forty subdivisions. He acknowledged that a general revision of immigration and naturalization provisions was long overdue, but charged that the bill would not provide the nation with a policy adequate for the present world situation. Significantly, Truman proposed that a new bill addressing his objections be drawn up with the help of a blue-ribbon immigration commission. He also urged enactment of legislation removing racial barriers against Asians, saying failure to do so "can only have serious consequences for our relations with the peoples of the Far East."

The veto posed a dilemma for loyal Democrats who were in favor of the bill. Congressman Yates was one of them. He didn't want to offend his Nisei constituents in Chicago, yet he was uneasy about the security provisions and felt a duty to support the president. "Congressman," I said to him, "we have the votes to override in the House. Don't worry about us. You shouldn't hesitate to vote your conscience."

Congressman Walter made a strong plea for the bill:

> The veto message before us points to many good and desirable provisions of the bill. Among them it lists the removal of racial barriers to immigration and naturalization; the removal of discrimination between sexes, and other improvements of the existing law. If the President's veto is sustained, none of these improvements will be written into the law. The old people of Japanese ancestry, 85,000 of them, whose sons covered themselves with glory on the battlefield of the last war, fighting and dying for the United States, these old people will not become citizens of the United States, and they will continue to face difficulties even in holding on to their property in the several states. . . . If the President's veto is sustained, Communist propaganda in the Far East will be given a new shot in the arm by

being permitted to spread the word that we intend to keep the Orientals out and that the words of friendship we address to them remain just empty slogans.

Congressman Judd declared the bill's good points overshadowed its shortcomings, asking:

> Is it not better to accept the bill with its real gains, even though it does not correct all that many believe to be inequities, than to reject the great forward steps which it represents in the very areas where we are sustaining our most serious losses? Is it sensible to reject those forward steps just because the bill does not achieve the Kingdom of Heaven on earth?

On June 26, a day after Truman rejected the bill, the House as expected overrode the veto 278 to 113, seventeen votes more than the necessary two-thirds.

The momentous Senate vote was scheduled for the next day, June 27. The earlier passage by voice vote was misleading. My nose-counting indicated a very close decision, a toss-up; one vote might mean the difference between victory and failure for our campaign. If we lost this opportunity to win citizenship for our parents, there was no assurance that a second chance would become available in their lifetimes.

JACL at the moment was holding its twelfth biennial convention in San Francisco, with one ear cocked for the news from Washington. After the House vote I telephoned JACL's president, Dr. Randolph Sakada, asking him to rally the organization for one last grand now-or-never lobbying effort. Sakada called a special meeting of the National Board, which moved to ask the delegates to telegraph their individual senators. At a late-night meeting the delegates were briefed by Dick Akagi of the Washington office staff and telegram blanks were passed out. It was past midnight when Mas Satow took the handwritten messages to the Western Union office for transmittal.

In Washington early the next morning I began telephoning staff members of senators we knew, making a final appeal for support. Then I hurried to the Capitol to buttonhole the senators themselves as they gathered for the session, lobbying them shamelessly. While I emphasized what the bill would do for Japanese Americans, privately I urged enactment of the legislation to make more meaningful the treaty of peace with Japan. How could we welcome Japan into the family of nations, I asked, if we continued to exclude her nationals on the basis that they were not fit to be accepted as immigrants?

In this, perhaps my most critical day in Washington, I was working alone. Bob Cullum long since had gone back to the Interior Department when the Committee for Equality in Naturalization had run out of money. Etsu and my then assistant, Dick Akagi, had gone out to the convention in San Francisco. My moral support was in the Senate gallery. My mother was there along with Mieko Kosobayashi.

Mother had come to Washington in the spring of 1952 and had followed the progress of the Walter-McCarran Bill with great interest. There was no keeping her away from the Capitol that fateful day. When Vice-President Alben W. Barkley sounded the gavel as presiding officer, I hurried up to the gallery to sit with Mother and Mieko.

The debate began at 12:00 noon, and by unanimous consent it was to end at 2:30 p.m., with the time to be divided equally between proponents and opponents. If two and a half hours seemed inadequate for considering such an important bill, it could be rationalized that everything to be said about it had been said. Senator McCarran was the lead-off speaker. He accused the president of making "unfounded and untrue" statements about the nature of the bill in his veto message. "In God's name, in the name of the people of America, in the name of the future of America to which we all look, let us have the courage today to override this unfortunate veto message," he thundered.

Senators Herbert H. Lehman of New York and Hubert H. Humphrey of Minnesota, who had come to our aid on many earlier occasions, led the fight in support of the veto. Referring to the security measures, Humphrey said the new law would bar anyone from Poland and "slam the door" on most immigrants from other Baltic states. Lehman said the bill would make immigration "a myth" by "reducing it to a trickle" in violation of the American spirit of welcoming worthy foreigners.

The national-origin provision, which continued to favor immigration from northern and western Europe, also came under heavy attack. Senator John O. Pastore of Rhode Island declared the bill was "born in bigotry, founded in hate, and sought to reaffirm the

discrimination devised in the present national origin quota system."
In truth, the national-origin provision was a difficult one for me to
swallow. Japan's quota, a meager 185 persons a year out of a
worldwide annual quota of 154,658, was a mere token. The entire
Pacific area was allotted only 2,000 immigrants, most of which slots
could not be used on racial grounds, while Germany alone had a
quota of 25,813. A more equitable system of apportioning the total
quota was necessary, and would be our next goal, but I could
rationalize that a quota of 185 was 185 more than Japan had been
allowed under existing law.

Senator Ed Benton of Connecticut expressed shock that the
State Department was in favor of the bill. Addressing our concerns,
he said he had phoned Secretary of State Dean Acheson to say he
believed "Congress would most assuredly repeal the Oriental Exclusion Act, in which the State Department is so much interested,
and that it would be willing to establish quotas for Oriental immigrants." A bill to this effect had already passed the House, Benton
said, "and I told Dean Acheson I was sure that the Congress, if not
at this session, most assuredly next year would pass such legislation."

As so often happens, both sides claimed to be on the side of
the angels. Senator Benton asserted: "A vote to sustain the veto will
be a vote to reaffirm this nation's basic humanitarianism and its
Americanism in the truest meaning of those words." On the other
hand, Senator McCarran pointed out that the bill has the "unqualified endorsement of every major Oriental group in the United
States."

With the deadline for cutting off debate fast approaching, Senator Harry P. Cain, the Washington Republican, asked for two
minutes. Cain, as mayor of Tacoma, had been one of the few
politicians on the West Coast to oppose the evacuation. Now he
waved two telegrams which he said he had just received. "They
represent one of the many reasons why I am anxious to vote to
override the president's veto," he said.

The first telegram was from Kenji Okuda, delegate of the Seattle chapter at the JACL convention. "I specially urge you to be
present on the Senate floor and cast your vote to override an action
which threatens the security of the United States," Okuda's wire
said. The second was from Thomas B. Takemura, official delegate

of the Puyallup chapter. Urging an override, Takemura declared that "this presidential veto is an insult to our ancestry."

"It is good to join hands with Mr. Okuda and Mr. Takemura in support of legislation which we believe to be reasonable, constructive and of assistance to our nation's security," Cain told his colleagues. At least some of our telegrams from San Francisco were reaching their targets.

The roll call started. George Aiken of rock-ribbed Republican Vermont was at the top of the alphabetical list. He voted to sustain Democratic President Truman's veto. Wallace Bennett of Utah was next. A Republican. He cast his vote for overriding. Mark one up for our side.

Up in the gallery, Mother, Mieko, and I tried, with no assurance of accuracy, to keep tally. We were prohibited by Senate rules from making notes, so we counted on our fingers, I tallying the "yea" votes to override, and the two women the "nay" votes. What complicated the voting was that after the roll call senators could change their vote, or declared they were paired with someone, or a colleague might rise to say that if the honorable senator from wherever were present and voting, he would vote nay.

The final vote was fifty-seven to override, twenty-six to sustain. Truman's veto had been killed by five votes. The Walter-McCarran Bill, for better or worse, was law. For the first time in history the laws of the United States specified that Asians were entitled to be treated as the equals of other immigrants. The goal that had dominated my thinking ever since coming to Washington five years earlier finally had been attained. Mother was jubilant. Brushing back tears of happiness, I hurried to phone the JACL convention on the other side of the continent.

The conventioneers already knew. Someone had heard the news on a noon radio broadcast. Pandemonium had broken loose on the convention floor. What the delegates didn't know was how desperately narrow the victory had been, and what an important role each of them had played in reaching our goal.

Despite the 57–26 margin, a switch of just two votes would have made the count 55–28, one vote short of the two-thirds majority, and sustained the president's veto. In the three West Coast states, the vote was uneven. The two California senators, William Knowland and Richard M. Nixon, both Republicans, voted against the president. In Oregon we lost liberal Wayne Morse, but Guy Cordon went for the override. In Washington State, Democrat Warren Magnuson voted with the president, Harry Cain voted for the override.

In Arizona, it is likely that Ernest W. McFarland, the Democratic majority leader, would have voted against the president in any case, but JACLer John Tadano had kept him aware of Nisei concerns. In all, thirty-two Republicans and twenty-five Democrats voted to override. Eighteen Democrats and eight Republicans supported the veto.

It is difficult to assess accurately my part in the victory. I had lobbied virtually every senator in one way or another. Thirteen senators had not voted. I had urged nine of them, generally considered liberal and opposed to the bill, to absent themselves during the voting if they could not vote to override. They were Republicans William Langer of North Dakota, Henry Cabot Lodge, Jr., of Massachusetts, Margaret Chase Smith of Maine, and Charles W. Tobey of New Hampshire; and Democrats Clinton P. Anderson and Dennis Chavez of New Mexico, Estes Kefauver of Tennessee, Brian McMahon of Connecticut, and Mike Monroney of Oklahoma. I have no way of knowing why they did not vote, but their absence had a significant effect on the outcome.

I am more confident that I had a part in persuading two Republican senators to vote to override the veto. They were Edward Thye of Minnesota and John Williams of Delaware. Their two votes could well have been the margin of victory.

Some political analysts have said Congress was looking for a fight and Truman's veto would have been killed in any event. Perhaps so. There is no way to be sure. But I am convinced that our efforts swung the balance even though the issues that were our direct interest were a minor part of the Senate debate. Without the work we had put in, we very well could have lost the two votes that were the difference between success and failure.

Two years later, when the Washington, D.C., chapter of JACL sponsored a dinner commemorating passage of the Walter-McCarran Act, some of the officials involved in the struggle gave me generous credit. Senator McCarran called me the world's champion lobbyist, like an Irishman because "Masaoka was always around when you need him and always delivered." Congressman Walter recalled that the *Reader's Digest* had called me Washington's most successful lobbyist and said that "he's still the most successful one I know." The director of the House Judiciary Committee staff, Walter Besterman, humorously accused me of wearing out the green sofa in his reception room. "For six years Mike has been on the green sofa, sitting until he got what he wanted. He and JACL ought to be charged for wearing out government property."

In a more serious vein, Commissioner of Immigration and Naturalization Argyle Mackey declared: "The Japanese people are fortunate to have such an able representative as Mike Masaoka in Washington. I know of no one more loyal and respected by Senators and Representatives. The Immigration and Naturalization Service has worked with him and we have always found his requests reasonable, though sometimes difficult to fulfill. He is a credit to all of us."

The accolades were gratifying but my real reward was in knowing that thousands of Issei, more than 6,000 in the year after the law became effective on December 24, 1952, applied for and were granted citizenship. No longer would they be subjected to legal discrimination because of race. The racism inherent in the Asia-Pacific Triangle restrictions was not eliminated until 1965, but that process was begun by the momentous events a dozen years earlier.

In the Senate gallery that day there was little time for elation. I had to hurry home and pack for the flight to San Francisco. The propeller plane droned westward through the night as, completely drained by the events of the past two days, I tried to rest. Sleep eluded me. I knew an emotional and triumphant reception awaited me at the convention for having steered our organization to its most coveted objective. Other thoughts raced through my head. We had triumphed against overwhelming odds. Our painful wartime decision to give our government complete, unquestioning loyalty in the face of injustice in return for the implied promise of redress at some later time, our decision to demand the right to serve our country in uniform, had been vindicated. The bloody sacrifice of the men who had stepped forth to serve had not been in vain. I recalled the last time I had seen my brother Ben Frank before he gave his life in battle, and I blessed the memory of all the other good men who hadn't come home.

Having helped to bring about momentous change, what was next for me? There was much left for JACL to do, but the major goals had been won. Perhaps it was time for me to seek new challenges and opportunities, to provide greater security for Etsu, wife, partner, and loyal soldier. As soon as possible, we would have to sit down and talk about our future. That was my last thought as I dropped off into a fitful sleep.

Chapter 13

Peace with Japan

Although I had never been to the land of my ancestry, did not speak its language, and knew almost nothing of its culture, Japan persistently has intruded on my life for better or worse. My ethnic background helped shape my youth as an American. Rising hostility between Japan and the United States led to my association with the Japanese American Citizens League. The Japanese navy's treacherous attack on sleeping Pearl Harbor aroused the hate and hysteria that played a major part in the West Coast evacuation, which in turn had a profound effect on my life and the lives of my Japanese-American compatriots.

Even in Italy after the German surrender I felt the influence of Japan. Australian troops, soon to be transferred to the Pacific for World War II's final campaigns, asked for briefings about Japan. And as the 442nd's public information noncommissioned officer, I was volunteered to provide them. What did I know about Japan? Nothing other than what I had read in *Time, Newsweek,* and *Stars and Stripes.* But because of my Japanese features, it was assumed I had knowledge. German Americans, Italian Americans, Swedish Americans, or Americans of any other ethnic origin aren't expected to be experts on Germany, Italy, Sweden, or whatever country their ancestors came from. But for reasons I've never been able to fathom, Japanese Americans are expected to know everything there is to know about Japan. This, of course, is nonsense that makes it difficult for Japanese Americans to be accepted as, for want of a better expression, full-fledged Americans. It is a stereotyped view that persists to this day even though these Americans may be several generations removed from Japan.

I encountered this attitude in postwar Washington when my concern was almost entirely with issues involving Japanese Americans. When I visited with members of Congress, administration officials, and even leaders of liberal organizations to talk about naturalization for the Issei or compensation for wartime losses, frequently I found the conversation being steered to postwar Japan and the shape of the upcoming peace treaty.

"Mike," they would say, "how do you think the Japanese would react if . . ." Or, "What's likely to be the result in Japan if the United States . . ."

I tried to explain I had no special insights into Japanese politics or the Japanese mind nor access to any source of information they didn't have. "Yes, of course," they would continue. "I understand that, but I'd just like to get your reaction."

I also found that wartime animosities persisted, particularly among those with friends and relatives among the casualties. Not only did I have to defend—all over again—the loyalty of Japanese Americans, but I had to overcome impressions left by propaganda during the war about the barbaric, savage, sneaky, subhuman "Jap" enemy. Americans celebrated the heroism and sacrifice of their men in combat, but the same kinds of gallantry by the Japanese had been pictured as suicidal and fanatical. A postwar study of Hollywood films made during the war years notes that "Japanese soldiers revealed loathsome buck-tooth grins as they cheerily bayoneted helpless prisoners, strafed fleeing civilians, or sniped at soldiers from the rear." Some American psychologists had explained the "aggressive" behavior of Japanese on "harsh toilet-training practices and an emphasis on shame rather than guilt."

Repeatedly I was asked whether such people—including Japanese Americans—could or would respond to a generous peace treaty or whether they would ever understand democracy.

My response was to point to the record. In Japan, the Allied Occupation was progressing smoothly. The vast majority of Japanese, freed from military domination, were cooperating wholeheartedly with General MacArthur's program of eliminating Fascism and installing a democratic civilian government. The one-third of Hawaii's population which was of Japanese origins had responded magnificently in defense of the islands after the Pearl Harbor attack. Neither in Hawaii nor on the mainland had there been a single act of sabotage or espionage by Japanese Americans or resident aliens. Rather, thousands of Japanese Americans had volunteered for military service and performed bravely in defense of the United States in Europe and the Pacific Theater.

As for the character of the Japanese themselves, I sought information from people like my old mentor Senator Thomas and Congressman Judd, who had lived in the Far East and knew Asia intimately. I also found support from Joseph Grew, who had been ambassador to Japan when war broke out, and his predecessor, William Castle. They assured me the Japanese people treasured values similar to those of Americans and other Westerners and that they had been as much the victims of Fascism and militarism as the people of Italy and Germany. Later I received additional insights in long conversations with Major General Charles A. Willoughby, General MacArthur's chief of intelligence, and Ambassador William Sebald, MacArthur's political adviser and, as it happened, Willoughby's brother-in-law. Willoughby was firm in his belief that the work of Nisei combat intelligence specialists in the Pacific Theater who translated and analyzed captured documents and interrogated prisoners had shortened the war in the Pacific by as much as two years and averted millions of American casualties and saved hundreds of millions of dollars.

(After Sebald retired in Washington he became president of the revived Japan America Society, whose primary purpose was to promote friendly cultural relations between the two countries. I served as vice-president for several terms, and when Sebald was ready to step down, he persuaded me to run for the presidency. The autonomous chapters of the Japan America Society since prewar times had an unwritten rule that only Caucasians could serve as president, even as their counterpart organizations, the America Japan Societies in Japan, restricted their presidents to prominent Japanese. I decided it was time to eliminate this minor bit of racism, ran for president, and served two terms, followed by more than ten as chairman of the executive committee.)

As I got deeper into American-Japanese relations, I became more convinced that Japan must be treated no more harshly than the other Axis nations as a matter of postwar policy. To make sure the lives and dollars spent in winning the war had not been expended in vain, the Japanese must be given equality with other peoples under

American law. Even the most liberal and humanitarian peace treaty would be misleading to the Japanese if we continued to deny them immigration and naturalization rights on the basis of race. So long as the Japanese were considered "undesirable" and "unworthy" under our laws, any peace treaty would only be a mockery and a betrayal. In this sense, JACL's mission of winning equal rights for the Issei was firmly linked to postwar Japan's aspirations.

Furthermore, in America's own self-interest, we would be foolish to lose sight of the fact that Japan was Asia's only indus-trialized nation with high standards of education and literacy. I pointed out that a people who could make the great leap from feudalism to the status of world power in three-fourths of a century could be, given the benefits of democracy, as staunch as friends and allies as they had been formidable as foes. In view of the divided status of Korea, the near-chaos in China, and the increased Soviet presence in the Pacific, we would need friends in Asia. This was not an altogether popular view. There were many influential Americans who wanted to see Japan punished by being reduced to no more than an agricultural nation.

Dean Acheson, who became secretary of state in the Truman administration, was among those who discussed these matters with me on several occasions. I didn't realize it at the time, but much of my thinking was influenced by research I had done for debates at the University of Utah on the Treaty of Versailles ending World War I. I was convinced the harsh demand for reparations by the victorious Allies had led to the resurgence of German nationalism which re-sulted in acceptance of the Nazi Party.

Beginning early in 1946, less than half a year after war's end, leaders of the new Japan began to appear in Washington with MacArthur's authorization. Many found their way to my modest office-apartment, directed there by either Washington officials or friends on the West Coast. The visitors not only told me what was going on in Japan, but wanted to discuss Japan's future and Amer-ican plans for that future.

The first Japanese to call on me was Dr. I. F. Ayusawa, ex-ecutive director of the Central Labor Relations Council and member of LARA, the Licensed Agency for Relief in Asia, the official agency for transmission of relief and financial aid to Japan and former Japanese-occupied territories. Dr. Ayusawa's tour was sponsored by the American Friends Service Committee. A graduate of Haverford College and with a degree from the New York School of Social Work, Dr. Ayusawa had been forced to go into seclusion because of his opposition to the war.

Close behind Dr. Ayusawa came Kensuke Horinouchi, Japan's last career ambassador in Washington, who had been replaced by Admiral Nomura. Horinouchi, by then president of the Foreign Service Training Institute, headed a ten-man delegation to the Moral Rearmament world assembly in Los Angeles. Horinouchi also was chairman of LARA, and we discussed private American relief efforts to help needy Japanese. He listened with great interest as I told him of JACL's efforts to persuade Congress to remove racial discrimination from immigration and naturalization laws.

"That is a very important goal," Horinouchi told me. "You are aware that Japan, even at the height of its power, could not get Congress to change its discriminatory codes. You are also aware that the 'grave consequences' of America's 1924 exclusion act led eventually to war. Elimination of discrimination would contribute substantially to a peaceful and productive Occupation and also to Japan's ability to take its rightful place in the family of nations. I am not optimistic about the chances of such a small organization as JACL, but I wish you well. Nor am I optimistic about Japan's chances for early recovery. As before the war, Japan must export to live. Japan lacks the capital to build an industrial complex capable of competing with other industrialized countries. I hope Americans will be good enough to buy some of our products."

This was the considered opinion of one of Japan's best-informed leaders. Today I look back and marvel at how much has occurred in the New Japan despite its material limitations. The progress of postwar Japan is even more impressive than the miracle of the Meiji Restoration, when Japan, awakened by the thunder of cannon aboard Commodore Matthew Calbraith Perry's black ships, made the transition from feudalism to industrialism in a few short decades.

The first Japanese mayor to visit Washington was Shinzo Hamai of Hiroshima. He came in the fall of 1946 in the first of almost annual tours to remind Americans of the horror of the atomic bomb and to raise funds for its victims. Hiroshima was my father's prefectural homeland, and I felt a special responsibility to do everything I could to help the survivors of my country's fury. I supported

Mayor Hamai in many campaigns to collect money and medicine for his people.

Also among early visitors was Takizo (Frank) Matsumoto, a member of the first postwar Diet, who had spent many summers working on California farms while pursuing an education in the United States. I had first met him in Salt Lake City about 1940 when he urged me to study in Japan while teaching English. Matsumoto was an advocate of the closest possible relations with the United States. He was the leader of a group of rising young leaders with similar ideas. We spent many hours together in Washington discussing the future of our two countries. At the time he was being mentioned as a likely choice for first postwar ambassador to Washington. He died before he could realize his potential. I've often wondered how the course of U.S.-Japan relations would have been affected if he had lived.

In 1948 and 1949 the U.S. Occupation, whose policy was to teach the Japanese as much as possible about the United States, approved American visits for a stream of newspapermen, educators, and other opinion leaders. Most of them spoke English adequately and did not require interpreters. They were followed by government officials and business leaders, and I became busy arranging appointments for them with their American counterparts. A large number of the early visitors were economists or military analysts. I could understand why economists were so prominent; Japan had to build up trade in order to restore the economy. As for the military, Japan's armed forces were in the process of being totally dismantled, but many Japanese could foresee the day when the United States would be asking them to take a role in the defense of the western Pacific.

A surprising number of nongovernment visitors claimed to be supporters of the Moral Rearmament movement. Had Christianity established such a strong foothold in postwar Japan? Not quite. In time I learned that many Japanese had discovered that the easiest way to win Occupation approval for a visit to the States was to profess conversion to the principles of Moral Rearmament.

The first official mission to the States was led by Katsuma Ohno, the Foreign Ministry's leading American expert, who later was to become ambassador to Great Britain. In several lengthy discussions with the delegation, I provided insights into what was happening in Washington and learned about Japan's developing consensus on postwar policies.

Early in January of 1950, Takizo Matsumoto returned with a delegation made up of members of the Lower House of the Diet, the more powerful arm of Japan's bicameral legislature. I was asked to lecture on the role of Congress and how it operated. William Sherman, then a junior State Department officer fluent in Japanese, was the interpreter. When Sherman retired in 1986 after a distinguished diplomatic career, he recalled that the Japanese legislators expressed surprise and pleasure at my frank explanation of the way lobbyists work to influence Congress.

I remember something else about that meeting. Shortly before I was to make my presentation I learned that after landing in San Francisco the delegation had driven to Sacramento. There, on behalf of the Japanese people, they apologized to the then governor, Earl Warren, for the difficulties he had experienced during the war with Japanese Americans.

I was outraged. I spent an hour of my time with the delegation explaining that Warren as attorney general was, as much as any individual, responsible for the unwarranted expulsion and imprisonment of Japanese Americans, aliens and citizens alike, during World War II. I told them of our wartime travail and my strong feelings about the unconstitutional deprivation of our rights, liberties, and property. I insisted that the Japanese owed an apology to the Issei and Nisei for the attack on Pearl Harbor that provoked the evacuation, not to Warren, and that the American government also owed us an apology.

Many of the Japanese were unaware, or only vaguely aware, of our experience. What gave my story credibility in their view was that Sherman translated it fully. I noticed some of the Japanese glancing his way as though expecting him to cut off my speech, and later some of them expressed amazement that I could speak so openly. After that I took every opportunity to let Japanese visitors know of the trials we had experienced during the war.

The second Foreign Ministry mission, which arrived a few weeks later, was headed by Ryuji Takeuchi, who returned in 1952 as deputy chief of mission for the first postwar Japanese ambassador, Eichi Araki. Takeuchi himself became Japan's fifth postwar ambassador in Washington. All of these delegations included bright young men on their way up the professional ladder. Without exception they reached ambassadorial rank, and of course the early acquaintanceship proved valuable when I met them later.

One point I made repeatedly to Foreign Ministry officials was that many of their prewar consular representatives had treated Japanese Americans shabbily, looking down on them as the unimportant offspring of no-account expatriates. If the officials had cultivated relations with the Nisei, I suggested, they would have had a better understanding of American attitudes. I urged them to keep in mind that in years to come Japanese Americans would be taking on increasingly more important roles in U.S. society and in local, state, and federal governments.

Early in June of 1950, Hayato Ikeda, then minister of finance, came to Washington with his personal secretary, Kiichi Miyazawa. Ikeda later was to become the prime minister who proposed, and succeeded in, doubling the individual income of the Japanese. Miyazawa, later foreign minister, finance minister, international trade and industry minister, and frequent contender for prime minister, had studied economics at the University of Chicago under Professor and later U.S. Senator Paul Douglas and spoke English as well as native-born Americans. They brought with them an invitation from Prime Minister Yoshida to visit Japan at my earliest convenience. Since Japan was short of foreign exchange, even such distinguished individuals were limited by MacArthur's headquarters to $10 per diem for expenses. This failed to cover bare needs even in those days. I was in no position to take visitors to a restaurant, but I could invite them to share *ochazuke* (rice and tea with pickles) with Etsu and me in our small apartment complex.

Something about the Japanese makes it difficult for them to be without rice for long. The Masaoka hospitality, such as it was, delighted our guests and helped to break down their anxiety at being in America and their reserve about speaking their minds. In shirtsleeves, and in the informality of our kitchen, we had many long, frank discussions about Japan and the United States and the relationship between our two countries into the long future. These talks established friendships and provided me with important insights which later I could share with American policymakers. At the same time I was helping Japan's future leaders to understand American viewpoints. The *ochazuke* session apparently made quite an impression on Ikeda. I was told that in a bedside visit with members of his cabinet during his final illness in 1964, Ikeda recalled that the only time he ate five bowlfuls in one sitting was in our kitchen.

Ikeda was followed to Washington by Kinjin Morikawa, secretary-general of the Japan Civil Liberties Union. He was returning the visit of Roger Baldwin of the American Civil Liberties Union. Baldwin, a supporter of JACL from evacuation days, helped organize a Tokyo JACL chapter during his trip in 1947 to help Nisei who had been stranded in Japan during the war for a variety of reasons to return to their homes in the States.

Newspapermen, religious leaders including Buddhist priests, educators, and businessmen continued to arrive in Washington in a seemingly unending stream. I tried to help them in every way possible, frequently allowing them to pick my brains in long, time-consuming sessions. Many businessmen suggested that I could do well for myself, and serve the cause of U.S.-Japan relations, by setting up a consulting service to help the firms that would be coming to the States before long. "Soon there will be a great need for your know-how," more than one businessman told me. "With your experience and contacts, you can provide a valuable service."

They were suggesting a role for me as a friendly advocate or expediter, or perhaps as a lobbyist, which was precisely the kind of work I was doing for JACL. For the time being I was fully occupied with JACL's objectives. Perhaps later, I told myself and my visitors, I might be in position to consider their needs.

Despite numerous conversations with both Japanese and American officials, I make no claim to having had any influence in the writing of the peace treaty. The opinions I voiced were shared by many important individuals, and my input could have been no more than a very small part of the thinking that went into formation of a policy. It may be that my greatest contribution simply was confirmation of the inclinations of more learned men. Yet there were questions that only a Nisei could answer. For example, a State Department official told me he was concerned about the reaction of Japanese Americans to a lenient treaty.

"Is there much resentment against Japan for being the cause of the unpleasantness you people experienced?" he asked. "Is there a possibility of protest demonstrations if the treaty is perceived as being too easy on the aggressors? We would hate to have anything like that happen.''

I replied that Japanese Americans were as deeply outraged as other Americans by the attack on Pearl Harbor. But I also told him that it had been their own country, the United States, that deprived Japanese Americans of their constitutional rights and confined them to detention camps, and many still felt aggrieved about that. Aside from a small minority, I said, I didn't think there would be any opposition to a conciliatory peace treaty with Japan.

"What about the leftists?" he wanted to know.

He was referring to a handful of Japanese anti-Fascists, some of them members of the Communist Party, who before the war had managed to seek refuge in the United States from the militarists. They blended into the prewar Japanese-American communities, although their radical views caused uneasiness among the Issei. Many of these political refugees had served the Office of War Information and the Office of Strategic Services on psychological-warfare projects. They were bitterly opposed to militarism but were interested in the welfare of the Japanese people and the recovery of Japan as a nation, particularly with left-leaning leadership. I did not see them opposing a liberal peace treaty.

The final peace treaty document took a remarkably enlightened position that in a very brief time made our erstwhile enemy the almost indispensable cornerstone of our Far East policy as well as our chief overseas trading partner. Perhaps Ikeda's post-treaty cablegram, mentioned earlier, speaks for itself.

In any event, I was not altogether surprised when the State Department invited me to attend the peace conference in San Francisco in September 1951 as a nongovernmental observer. It's a misnomer to call that meeting a ''conference,'' since most of the details had been worked out months earlier in quiet negotiations, ''on the basis of trust and understanding,'' by John Foster Dulles, designated as Acheson's special adviser.

I later learned that a number of prominent members of Congress had urged the State Department to invite me. They felt the presence of a Japanese American might impress on the Japanese delegates that we had had some input into shaping the treaty and generally approved of it. Interestingly enough, four junior members of the House Foreign Relations Committee with whom I had discussed the treaty went on to have great influence on relations between the two countries. Mike Mansfield of Montana, after a long and distinguished career in the Senate, became our most popular and effective ambassador to Tokyo. Brooks Hays of Arkansas became a presidential assistant. Jacob Javits of New York also moved to the Senate, where he was a liberal stalwart deeply concerned with relations with Japan. Christian Herter of Massachusetts became secretary of state and the nation's first trade representative, a cabinet post created by President Kennedy under the Trade Expansion Act of 1962.

Since JACL had an organizational policy against becoming involved in matters relating to the Japanese government, I sought permission from the national president, Hito Okada, to accept the invitation to the peace conference. He agreed that it was not only proper but a great opportunity for JACL to be represented.

President Truman set the tone for the conference in his opening speech when he said: "It is a treaty that will work. It does not contain the seeds of another war. It is a treaty of reconciliation, which looks to the future, not the past. . . . Let us be free of malice and hate to the end that from here on there shall be neither victors nor vanquished among us, but only equals in the partnership of peace." Nothing could be more magnanimous than for the winners in a bitter war to be willing to let bygones be bygones.

Glittering social events surrounded the conference itself. Early in the week, San Francisco's Japanese-American community sponsored a banquet at the Fairmont Hotel atop Nob Hill for members of the Tokyo delegation headed by Prime Minister Shigeru Yoshida. He was a short, gray man with a small mustache, a prewar envoy to Great Britain who had been imprisoned by the militarists for his opposition to war. After the surrender he had provided the leadership restoring a devastated nation to respectability.

More than 500 persons, mostly Issei, attended. There was irony in the fact that only a few years earlier the hosts had languished in detention camps as an indirect result of the actions of the government the guests represented. Keisaburo Koda, the so-called rice king from Dos Palos, California, who had suffered grievous financial loss in the evacuation, was chairman and made the opening address. I was one of three asked to extend greetings. Swept up in the spirit of reconciliation, I managed to avoid noting the irony.

Issei members of the audience told me later that Yoshida spoke movingly of the travails the Japanese had suffered because of the ruthless ambition of the militarists, and of his pride in the emerging democratic Japan. He spoke of his gratitude for the way the Issei and Nisei had conducted themselves during the war. Yoshida elaborated on this theme in an hour-long meeting with Saburo Kido and me shortly before his departure for Japan. We told him of our wartime experiences and of our postwar efforts to change discriminatory laws. Speaking in adequate English, Yoshida said we had acted as Japan would have expected us to act—as Americans and not as Japanese—in the tradition of the samurai code, which demanded absolute loyalty to one's "lords" regardless of one's origins. He urged us to continue the fight against any kind of discrimination and declared that opening of immigration and naturalization rights for Japanese nationals would give real meaning to the peace treaty.

The meeting with Yoshida was memorable, but the conference highlight was the signing of the peace document on the stage of the Opera House, where the United Nations charter had been adopted a few years earlier. Dean Acheson signed for the United States, and Yoshida, concurrently prime minister and foreign minister, signed for Japan.

In accepting the treaty, Yoshida spoke in Japanese, with Henry Toshiro Shimanouchi reading a simultaneous translation. Born in Japan, Shimanouchi had been reared and educated in the States. Denied American citizenship, he joined the Japanese foreign service after the war and served with distinction as consul general in Los Angeles and ambassador to Norway, as well as serving as the press officer when the Japanese embassy was reopened in the spring of 1952. His diction was flawless, and I listened with deeply mixed feelings—pleased that Japan was being welcomed back to the family of peace-loving nations, but sad over the staggering price inflicted by Japan's military aggression on the Japanese people and the people of the other victimized countries.

Yoshida praised the treaty as an agreement that was neither punitive or retaliatory, that restored to the Japanese people full sovereignty, equality, and freedom. He said he was happy to accept such a fair and magnanimous treaty, but felt obliged to mention three points "which cause us pain and anxiety."

First were territorial questions involving the Ryukyu archipelago and Bonins, seized by the United States, and the Kuriles and South Sakhalin, occupied by the Soviets in the last days of the war. Within a few years the United States returned the islands it held; the USSR still holds the territory it took, including islands within sight of Japan's Hokkaido.

Second, Yoshida expressed concern for the economy of his nation, battered by war and shorn of overseas assets and markets. He pledged that Japan would do everything possible to cease being a burden on other countries, and we have seen how well it succeeded.

Finally, Yoshida expressed concern for the several hundred thousand overseas Japanese who still had not been repatriated more than six years after war's end. Most of them were still imprisoned in Communist-held areas, and in time that problem, too, was resolved.

"Japan has opened a new chapter in its history," Yoshida declared, and Secretary Acheson made his agreement clear in his closing speech when he referred to "our friend Japan."

I watched as forty-nine nations, including Japan, signed the treaty of peace. The Soviet Union and its satellites did not. A treaty of commerce and navigation and the United States-Japan Security Treaty also were signed during the conference.

The security pact was formalized in the headquarters building of the Presidio overlooking the Golden Gate. This was the same building to which Kido and I had gone to be told of evacuation plans, the building from which General De Witt directed the removal of Japanese Americans from the Western Defense Command. Within a stone's throw was the old hangar where Nisei soldiers organized Japanese-language courses for the Military Intelligence Service. Coincidentally, Lieutenant General Joseph M. Swing, who now commanded the post, was appointed commissioner of the Immigration and Naturalization Service following retirement and administered the Walter-McCarran Immigration and Naturalization Act eliminating race as a factor in these areas.

The conclusion of the peace treaty was celebrated at a great banquet at the Palace Hotel, now owned by a Japanese chain. Diplomats and cabinet officers in formal attire mixed with heads of mission in their native costumes. The mood was relaxed and festive, with champagne flowing freely. An event of this elegance was a first for me. Unaware that I should have worn white tie and tails, I rented a tuxedo and escorted Etsu's sister Helen to the banquet. Etsu hadn't come to San Francisco—we could afford neither the transportation nor the formal dress she would need. So far as I know, Helen and I were the only Japanese Americans present. Guests from many lands, assuming we were members of the Japanese delegation, congratulated us profusely. I felt it necessary to explain, smilingly, that we were Americans. It was neither the first nor the last time our nationality was mistaken.

Back in Washington, I submitted a statement on behalf of JACL to Senator Tom Connally, chairman of the Senate Foreign Relations Committee, urging early ratification of the peace treaty. It also declared that American sincerity would be demonstrated by "the speedy enactment of legislation that will extend to the Japanese immigration and naturalization privileges."

There is one small footnote. Many years later, Ambassador Sebald told me that while plans for the peace conference were being drawn up, he received a State Department telegram in Tokyo suggesting "almost equal" treatment for the Japanese delegation. He responded strongly, urging the Japanese be received in a spirit of unreserved friendship and complete equality. As we have seen, Washington accepted his recommendation. But he declined to take all the credit. Sebald said he was told that State Department bureaucrats and members of Congress, who had been discussing treaty plans with a Nisei in Washington, had become convinced a friendly approach was best. I was the only Nisei talking regularly to government people at that time, and Sebald and I laughed about that, but I may have contributed unknowingly to the success of the peace conference.

Now, scarcely ten months after the signing of the peace treaty, I was flying to San Francisco again, this time to report to the JACL convention on the realization of our twin goals of citizenship for our parents and the end of racial discrimination in immigration. The outpouring of emotion and appreciation showered on me at the convention wiped out the frustration and exhaustion of the long Washington struggle, washed away the bitter memories of imprisonment and war. But as I told the delegates, the triumph was the result of group effort—the men and women who had accepted their government's unfair evacuation order as their wartime sacrifice, the courageous youths who had volunteered to fight and give their lives if necessary for the country that had doubted them, the untiring support of volunteers who had backed up my work in Washington. It had been my privilege to spearhead the campaign for justice; the victory belonged to all Americans.

Now the time was ripe for Etsu and me to step down. The two of us had talked occasionally of making a change to pursue our own lives, but never with anyone else. When we were alone in San Francisco, I brought up the matter again and she agreed there would be no better time to make our move. I owed it to old stalwarts like Sab Kido and George Inagaki to tell them of my intention. They understood. They expressed deep regret but they recognized it was unfair to ask me to remain. At a luncheon, at the end of my report on activities of the Washington office, I announced our resignation, effective at once.

There was a long moment of silence as the meaning sank in, then a chorus of "No, no." Leaving JACL was far from easy. Except for nearly three years in military service the Japanese American Citizens League had been my only fulltime employer. I had stayed with it for starvation wages because I believed in it and its objectives. In return I had found the confidence of my peers and the leadership role exhilarating.

Some critics have contended that in my Washington role I had become the JACL king-maker and enjoyed too much being the tail that wagged the organizational dog. It is true that in Washington I was regarded as Mr. JACL, and of course I had urged certain policies of the league. That was because I felt they were the only way to achieve the goals established by the membership. I also encouraged leaders who shared my opinions to seek national office. They would make my work easier than if I faced a hostile internal hierarchy. As I have related earlier, Mas Satow as national director ran the organization. He was the inside man who kept in touch with the membership. I was the outside man carrying out the organizational mandate, and I provided an important voice in shaping that mandate. When there was occasion to speak out, I was JACL's spokesman rather than Satow or the elected president. My links with JACL and the leadership role gave me a certain ego satisfaction.

Kido and Inagaki, the in-coming president, were delegated to work out some arrangement for my continuing services. When I told them of my intention of opening a consulting office in Washington, they suggested I take on JACL as my first client. We figured that with most of JACL's agenda completed, I could spend the greater part of my time serving Japanese and other clients that we anticipated would be clamoring for my services. At the time Etsu and I jointly were being paid $500 a month with JACL picking up the rent and other expenses including a secretary's salary. Under the new arrangement my firm would be paid $1,000 per month plus necessary travel and long distance telephone expenses, but I would be responsible for rent, secretarial help and everything else.

This turned out to be a much better arrangement for JACL than for me. The retainer was considerably less than it was costing by then to maintain a fulltime office. Meanwhile, I found I was spending the largest part of my efforts on JACL business. In effect JACL was getting the same level of representation at substantially less cost. Of course there were advantages to being recognized as JACL's man in Washington. As representative of the only national Japanese American organization I commanded a certain prestige which opened many doors. The position also gave me stature with the Japanese business community.

On the other hand the JACL tie limited my clientele since I could not accept accounts that might suggest any conflict of interest with JACL's overall program. I would not accept Japanese business accounts directly because that would require me to register as a foreign agent, which was incompatible with JACL's record of militant Americanism. I also found principle getting in the way of business. For example, I could not accept a very lucrative offer to represent South Korean and Hongkong textile interests because of my commitment to Japanese exporters. Because of my commitment to free trade, I could not accommodate Nisei flower growers who asked me to work toward reduction of imports from Central and South America.

Business developed far more slowly than I had been led to believe it would. When I was working full-time for JACL the Japanese had been eager to pick my brains and ask my advice. Indirectly, they were of concern to JACL, so I provided the service without charge. After I went into business for myself they continued to come to me. They rarely offered to pay for my time, and I was too inexperienced as a businessman to set a fee before we started to talk or to bill them afterward. Much to my chagrin, I found some of my "clients" were taking my ideas and my advice to Caucasian consulting firms and attorneys and paying huge fees to have them executed. The crowning insult was that sometimes the Japanese would bring me the proposals drawn up by the Caucasian firms and ask me, again without fee, to evaluate them. And I didn't know how to tell the Japanese that the original ideas were mine, that I was fully capable of carrying them out, and that I deserved a fee for my services. From their viewpoint, the Japanese were not necessarily taking advantage of me. I think they saw me as a public figure with something of an obligation to lend them a hand. The fact that I was giving advice without charge gave me a prestige unattainable had I been in their pay. Unfortunately I couldn't pay my bills with prestige.

A large part of my trouble was my own inexperience with practical matters. But I could also understand Japanese concerns. Perhaps unintentionally they practiced a kind of reverse discrimination; they realized the United States was a white man's country and found it difficult to believe that even a Nisei full of great ideas could deliver as much in the marketplace as a Caucasian. They trusted my judgment and valued my advice but wanted to be represented by the most prestigious practitioners in the business and were prepared to pay whatever price was asked. Wouldn't an American firm setting up business in Japan be likely to hire an old-line Japanese firm to handle the details even though they asked other Americans for advice? In the beginning the Japanese obviously were not impressed by my modest office and my tiny staff. There wasn't much I could do about that. Later, when I became more businesslike, I learned that some Japanese firms would not come to me because they thought I was too busy to accept them as clients. There was another important factor. My timing was bad. Many Americans serving in the Occupation of Japan had established business contacts there while I was immersed in the JACL program in Washington. When they came back the firms they joined or established had the inside track.

Chapter 14

First Visit

After the 1952 JACL convention in San Francisco, Etsu and I made two long trips, which were our first vacations in ten years of marriage. In reality they were vacations only in the sense that we were away from the office, for we were kept busy from early morning to late at night.

The first trip was to Hawaii as guests of organizations that had backed JACL's effort to win citizenship for the Issei. Among them were the Honolulu Japanese Chamber of Commerce, the Japanese Chamber of Commerce and Industry of Hawaii, the Maui Japanese American Club, the West Kauai Association, the East Kauai Naturalization Drive Committee, and the Big Island Issei Naturalization Committee.

Etsu and I flew into Honolulu the evening of September 12 and were met by what reporter Lawrence Nakatsuka of the *Star Bulletin* described as the largest and most enthusiastic group to greet a mainland Nisei. (After Hawaii achieved statehood, Nakatsuka became Senator Hiram Fong's press secretary.) Hundreds of veterans of the 100th Battalion and the 442nd who were taking an active role in civic and political affairs were among the greeters. We were given the sumptuous Queen's Suite at the Royal Hawaiian Hotel, then taken to meet old and new friends at a reception in the grand ballroom. At the risk of overlooking many, I must mention five who were particularly helpful in raising the $250,000 contribution from Hawaii that kept JACL's citizenship drive going.

From Honolulu were Tetsu Oi, secretary of the Japanese Chamber of Commerce, and attorney Katsuro (Kats) Miho. Kats attended the University of Utah in Salt Lake City in the early thirties, supporting himself with a job in a Japanese restaurant at about the time I was working at our fruit and vegetable market. Miho became Hiram Fong's law partner and later was appointed to a judgeship for Guam.

From Hilo on the Big Island was popular and respected James Hirano who, after the Walter-McCarran Act became law, personally helped more than a thousand Issei to become naturalized citizens, including himself.

From Kauai was Ben Tashiro, a veteran of military intelligence service in the Pacific. After Hawaiian statehood, he became the first Nisei appointed to a federal district judgeship. His appointment was confirmed by the Senate Judiciary Committee chaired by James Eastland of Mississippi, an opponent of Hawaiian statehood who had been quietly persuaded of Tashiro's merits.

And on Maui, there was Teichiro Maehara, businessman and civic leader.

Our hosts had arranged a heavy program of social affairs and courtesy calls along with sightseeing, which I had been too busy to enjoy on previous trips to the Islands. Five events stand out in memory:

• Laying a wreath to Nisei war dead in the Punchbowl National Cemetery overlooking Honolulu. The remains of many Nisei who gave their lives in Europe had been brought home for interment with those who died in Pacific battles.

• A luncheon reunion with Elbert Thomas, who had been named governor of the Trust Territories by President Truman after his defeat in the Senate race in 1949.

• A breakfast meeting, accompanied by Spark Matsunaga (later congressman and senator) and his wife, with Governor Oren Long, the last Democratic-appointed governor before Hawaii became a state. Spark told me he and his wife and Etsu and I were the first Japanese Americans ever invited to the governor's mansion for breakfast.

• An emotional meeting with members of the Okinawan Association, who expressed gratitude for my part in persuading the Army to allow relief and goodwill parcels to be sent to friends and relatives in Okinawa.

• A great, exhilarating community testimonial luau in Honolulu.

Everywhere we went Etsu and I were showered with affection and entertained royally. The extremely hospitable, warmhearted people of Hawaii were eager to show their appreciation for JACL's part in persuading Congress to remove racial bias from immigration and naturalization laws. The remaining item on their agenda was statehood, and I promised to do my very best to help them realize that goal.

Etsu and I returned to the mainland after twelve eventful days, full of rich memories but nearly exhausted from the "vacation." Ten days later we were on our way to Japan. Etsu had been to Japan as a third-grader. In fact the entire Mineta family had lived in Japan for a year before coming back to make their permanent home in San Jose, California. This was my first trip. Although I had learned something of Japan's economy and politics from my reading and talks with visitors, I knew almost nothing of Japanese history, traditions, and customs. The Japan that I had learned about from Mother and other Issei was the Japan of the long-gone Meiji era. Now there was a new Japan to explore.

We traveled by way of Seattle. At a reception there I met Consul (later ambassador) Shizuo Saito. He was aware that one of the objectives of my trip was to meet with Japanese interests that I might represent in Washington. When he learned that I had no meetings set up, he offered an introduction to Yasuo Tawa, director general of the Japan Cotton Spinners Association and the driving force behind the rebuilding of the Japanese textile industry, and his boss, a splendid old man named Kojiro Abe. The textile manufacturers, gearing up for exports after war's disruption, needed help in getting a more important share of the American market. Saito's introduction ultimately led to my being retained as the association's lobbyist. It became my first important Japanese client, and I feel deeply indebted to Saito for his help. Although the Japanese textile industry has yielded in importance to spinners in several other developing countries, Tawa and his successors have remained with my firm.

Travel across the Pacific in those days was by propeller plane droning along at 300 or 350 miles per hour. We had to refuel at Anchorage and then at Shemya, a desolate, fog-shrouded, treeless pinpoint of rock in the Aleutians, before making the final hop to Tokyo. I noted with awe that two other tiny islands, Attu and Kiska, were not far from Shemya, and Nisei language specialists from the initial MILS class were among the first to go ashore in the battle to retake them from the Japanese in the early days of the Pacific War.

My first sight of Japan, from three or four miles up, was of green forests and rice paddies and little towns along the coastline. Nothing of war's destruction was visible until, just before landing at Haneda Airport, we saw the hulks of several wrecked ships in Tokyo Bay. Although Tokyo had been pounded mercilessly by U.S. bombers, I saw little of the wreckage that I remembered from Naples, Leghorn, Marseilles, and other European cities. Later it occurred to me that what little remained after a firebombing of flimsy wooden Japanese homes and factories could be cleaned up more quickly than the ruins of concrete buildings in Italy and France.

Welcoming us was an escort officer from the U.S. embassy, a representative of the Japanese Foreign Ministry, and a number of others, including George Kiyoshi Togasaki and Tamotsu Murayama. Tamotsu, who had come to prewar Salt Lake City to try to organize a JACL chapter, was working as a reporter for the *Nippon Times,* the country's leading English-language daily, whose name subsequently was changed to *Japan Times*.

Togasaki, my friend Sim's older brother, was president of *Nippon Times* and undoubtedly the best-known Japanese American in Japan. Born and educated in the United States, George served with the U.S. Army in France in World War I and was among the founders of JACL. He also was a victim of his own country's racist immigration laws. He had married a delightful Japanese woman. Because of her race, she could not come to live in her husband's homeland except on visits limited to six months. Finally despairing of ever enjoying a normal family life, George had moved to Japan, where he spent the war years. Among other things, George became active in Rotary and was elected its international president.

I had met George a short time earlier at the San Francisco JACL convention, where he was among the speakers. Now he took time off to travel with Etsu and me as guide, adviser, arrangements-maker, and interpreter.

More important, he got me in to see the giants of Japanese industry, whose genius generated and guided their nation's postwar recovery. They were an impressive crew, many elderly but blessed with organizational skills and unsurpassed leadership ability. Their names are like a Who's Who of the Japanese business establishment: Keidanaren's legendary Taizo Ishizaki, Bank of Japan's Watanabe, Canon Camera's Dr. Takeshi Mitarai, Matsushita Electric's Konosuke Matsushita, Yawata Steel's Yoshiro Inayama, Asahi Steel's Shigeo Nagano, Toyo Boseki's Kojiro Abe and Toyosaburo Taniguchi, Sony's youthful Akio Morita, Suntory's Kozo Saji, Dentsu Advertising Agency's Hideo Yoshida, Sumitomo's Hisashi Tsuda, Mikimoto Pearl's Yoshitaka Mikimoto, Bank of Tokyo's Ichijiro Matsudaira and Shigeo Horie, Yanase Automobile's Jiro Yanase, and a number of others. It was unprecedented for a foreign visitor to meet all these powerful, busy tycoons in the course of a single visit to Japan. George Togasaki, himself a man of great influence, had the formula for opening doors. He told Japan's business leaders that Mike Masaoka knew more about what was going on in Washington than any other person.

These business leaders were good listeners and even better questioners. They wanted to know about American businesses, the economic outlook, my estimate of the potential market for Japanese goods. They were fairly familiar with American business practices but knew little about politics and government and the role that Congress plays in setting policy, and even less about public relations and lobbying.

I needed little encouragement to lecture my hosts. I doubt that they understood much of what I said, although they were uniformly affable, smiling and nodding and thanking me for taking the time to visit them. In retrospect, this may not have been the best way for me to sell myself as a potential Washington representative, but I thought the apparent acceptance of what I said indicated approval.

Lately Americans are being told to learn Japanese if they wish to do business in Japan. In my case, and at that time, my almost total inability to speak their language proved to be something of an advantage. Speaking in my own tongue automatically made me the dominant party in the conversation. Interpretation and translation became their responsibility. I knew what I was saying, and they had to seek out the fine nuances.

One of our first appointments was a lunch at the U.S. embassy with Ambassador Robert Murphy. After that, I embarked on the speaking schedule that Togasaki had arranged. These included engagements at the America Japan Society of Tokyo, whose president at the time was Prince Takamatsu, the emperor's brother; Rotary; the Tokyo Chamber of Commerce; the Tokyo Industrial Association; International Christian University; Japanese Press Club; Foreign Press Club; and a gathering of Nisei war veterans. At every opportunity I told of the experiences of Japanese Americans, their wartime travail and their postwar progress, urging the Japanese to utilize the unique skills of Nisei professionals in dealings with the United States.

After a speech to the America Japan Society some non-Japanese suggested that I soft-pedal my accounts of discrimination faced by Japanese Americans. I was warned of the danger of arousing Japanese resentment against Americans during a critical period of history. My response was that it was important to let the Japanese know the unvarnished truth about hate and hysteria in wartime, and also to relate the ability of a democracy to overcome abuses. Whatever they may have thought of my position, I continued to speak my mind.

Perhaps the single most enjoyable event was a reception at the Korakuen Gardens when many Issei who had worked in pioneer America and returned to Japan before the war gathered to recall their experiences. They were delighted to hear of JACL's success in overturning discriminatory laws, and many of them indicated they might have remained in the United States if they had been eligible for citizenship. They were enthusiastic that now the Japanese were considered worthy of immigrating to America and becoming citizens.

One evening we were guests of Prime Minister Yoshida; there I was responsible for a faux pas that gave me a certain friendly notoriety. In my Salt Lake City childhood it was customary to address adult males as *Ojisan,* meaning Honorable Uncle, a respectful but informal term. In English a prime minister would be addressed as Excellency, or Mr. Prime Minister. Not knowing how the dignified Yoshida should be addressed in Japanese, I called him *Ojisan.* It startled his aides but amused the old man. "Masaoka-san," he said in English, "you have taught us that Nisei are Americans. Certainly you are not Japanese."

Togasaki escorted us on a trip that stretched from the northern tip of Hokkaido to Kyushu on the far southwest, stopping at famous temples and scenic spots, strikingly beautiful Kyoto and Nara, the steel mills of Yawata, the spinning mills of Hamamatsu and the chinaware factories of Nagoya. I could not have wished for a more thoughtful, attentive, guide except for one thing. George was, shall we say, a robust sleeper, and night after night his snoring rattled the flimsy shoji screens that separated our quarters in the inns.

My most dramatic experience came at a sumptuous formal banquet in Hiroshima at which, coincidentally, Saburo Kido and his wife, Mine, and Kats Miho and his wife, Jane, also were guests. By coincidence, all of the menfolk's fathers had been born in Hiroshima. Mayor Hamai; the prefectural governor; American officials of the Joint Strategic Bombing Survey team; and a number of Issei return-ees were present along with many local dignitaries. In a question period after the usual speeches and, without rancor, someone asked a direct question: How did we Japanese Americans feel about the atomic bombing of Hiroshima?

Sincerely and tactfully, Kido and Miho recounted their horror, leaving the burden of response to me.

I explained that I was a soldier in United States uniform when Hiroshima was bombed. At that time, I said, I believed the use of a new and more effective weapon meant an earlier end to the war, saving the lives of countless Japanese civilians and soldiers on both sides, and I was relieved. I said it was months later that I learned an entire city had been wiped out and hundreds of thousands of civil-ians had been killed or permanently condemned to the living hell of radiation, and I grieved for the victims. I said I, as well as many Americans in high places, was troubled that the bomb had been used when it appeared Japan was on the verge of surrender. Although I sympathized with the Japanese and understood their revulsion, I said that as a soldier I had to agree that use of the bomb was justified because it did lead to a swift end to the war.

I went on to say that in my mind President Truman was not motivated by racial prejudice in approving use of the bomb. I told the audience about Truman's personally presenting a presidential citation to the 442nd, and of his support for many bills on behalf of Japanese Americans. The members of the audience listened in si-lence. I could sense that if they were not ready to agree with me, they appreciated a straightforward answer.

More recently, Japan scholars like Edwin Reischauer have said that in the long view the nuclear bombing could be justified not only militarily but because it destroyed the power of imperialists and supernationalists who supported the military aggression that was such a yoke of oppression on the Japanese people.

In private discussions with Japanese leaders like Mamoru Shigemitsu, who as foreign minister signed the surrender documents on the battleship *Missouri,* I suggested that it was to Japan's benefit to have lost the war because it freed the people from militarism and led to democratic government, industrialization under the capitalistic system, and extension of human rights to all citizens. Shigemitsu, and a few others, said that privately they agreed.

I left Etsu in Japan with friends while I took two side trips, to Korea and Okinawa. General Mark Clark, United Nations commander in Korea, who had become familiar with the 442nd as commanding general of the Fifth Army, saw to it that I received special permission to visit both areas. I was given the status of correspondent for the *Nippon Times,* issued a set of fatigues, and flew to Korea in a military transport.

Despite the opening of cease-fire talks more than a year earlier, fighting continued on the tortured peninsula. I saw shell-pocked roads, burned villages, and battle-scarred mountains. The unmistakable stench of war reminded me grimly of World War II in Italy and France. I saw many Nisei, career soldiers as well as World War II retreads, serving their country in combat once more. Since few Americans spoke Korean, and most adult Koreans spoke Japanese, Nisei intelligence specialists rushed to Korea from Japanese occupation duty were particularly valuable. They and others I talked to confirmed what I knew too well: War is hell. There are no winners, only losers.

Okinawa, an important base for pursuing the war in Korea, is a hot, humid island. My welcome was especially warm in another sense. Okinawans in Hawaii had written friends of my part in enabling them to send relief parcels to the homeland, and I was received royally. Reversion of Okinawa to Japanese jurisdiction was the main domestic issue being promoted by local leaders. I came away convinced they were not aware of the financial and economic problems inherent in American withdrawal. Even before the war Okinawa had been a depressed province. If the free-spending Americans left, or their numbers were drastically reduced, Japan would have to undertake heroic measures to avoid a devastating depression. Okinawa is now governed by Japan, but U.S. Marines and Air Force units continue to be stationed there, contributing to the local economy as well as the security of the Western Pacific.

During our Hiroshima visit I told a newspaper reporter that although my father was born in that area, I knew nothing about his origins since he had died when I was nine years old. The story the reporter published brought twenty or twenty-five men and women to my hotel, all strangers and all claiming kinship. They were simple country folk, bronzed by the sun, their hands cracked by hard labor, uncomfortable in their best clothing. Some of them brought photographs of my father's funeral, pictures that I recognized but didn't know existed. Meeting these people was an emotional experience. Conversations with business leaders could be conducted comfortably through interpreters, but in this meeting with relatives I regretted my inability to express my feelings directly to them. Etsu, as usual, came to my rescue and translated for me.

It was in Hiroshima that Togasaki taught me how to cope with the Japanese custom of exchanging gifts. Every visitor to my hotel, in Hiroshima and elsewhere, felt obliged to bring a gift—a basket of fruit, some local delicacies, lacquerware or porcelain, a piece of silk or perhaps a woodblock print. I could not possibly consume or take along all the gifts, and to decline them would have been unforgivably rude. George explained that etiquette required that I offer each visitor a gift in return, and that is what saved me. When someone gave me a present, I needed only to duck out, pick some appropriate item from my collection of gifts, and offer it to my visitor. Of course it would be accepted after the usual protests, and everyone would be happy.

My newfound Hiroshima kin escorted Etsu and me to the family burial plot near a bamboo grove some distance from town. In rural Japan families set aside a bit of property as a private cemetery where the ashes of many generations are interred. It was proper that we pay our respects. I viewed the moss-flecked granite tombstones, sprinkled them with water as was the custom, and felt the presence of unknown ancestors at this tranquil spot so unchanged by the years, so different from the hustle and bustle of Tokyo. Beyond the grove along a dirt road were humble thatched homes such as the one where my father had been born, and an irregular checkerboard of tiny rice paddies separated by earthen dikes. Somewhere one of the season's last cicadas sang its raucous song.

Etsu looked at me and I looked at her, and we shared the same thought without speaking: Here, but for the grace of God, go I. More than ever I was grateful that my father had had the courage to seek a better life in the land called America, despite all its faults and shortcomings.

My visit to Etsu's ancestral home in Shizuoka, in a pleasant tea- and orange-growing area south of Tokyo, evoked similar feelings. But there things were different. She remembered relatives she had met three decades previously. Many had made names for themselves. Their homes, their lands, their speech and dress indicated they were much better off than my relatives in Hiroshima. I could not help recalling, when I first began to visit Etsu, the difference I noticed between my humble home in Salt Lake and her home in San Jose, reflecting so much of Japanese culture.

On the long flight home Etsu and I had much to talk about. Everywhere we had been the people seemed happy, healthy, and busy—as though they were on a national mission to rebuild their lives and their country. Of course there were problems, too, and I could foresee many more of them arising, although their nature was far from clear. I resolved to do everything in my power to promote better relations between my country and the country of my forebears.

It had been an eminently worthwhile trip. It had made us proud of our ancestry. But Etsu reminded me of something else. We had not signed up a single paying client for my new business nor had we developed any real contacts for future business relations aside from a still tenuous tie with the textile association. At that point everything was as usual with me—*pro bono,* on the house, and in the idealistic, nonprofit interests of better relations. It was JACL all over again.

Chapter 15

What Is a Consultant?

While Etsu and I were traveling in Hawaii and Japan, Mieko Kosobayashi, who had turned out to be a remarkably capable young woman, was closing the JACL office. She had come to us from Minnesota for her first job as a nineteen-year-old. We soon adopted her as "family" and were sorry to see her leave in 1956 for a civilian job with the U.S. armed forces in Japan, where she wanted to study the language and culture. Since then she has held secretarial positions with top federal administrators. Currently she is executive assistant to the commissioner of customs.

Mieko was invaluable as we set out to establish our company, Mike M. Masaoka Consultants. In January 1953 we opened a three-room office in a converted apartment building at 1737 H Street, Northwest, within easy walking distance of the White House. It was a simple partnership, including my brothers Ike and Tad with Etsu and me. Ike, who had undergone lengthy rehabilitation for his war wounds, was managing a floral nursery in California and did not become an active partner. Tad, recently married, had been a Social Security claims examiner in San Francisco. In expectation of a better job, he had come to Washington, only to find all federal employment had been frozen. He accepted my offer to join the firm. He had studied economics at the University of California, and I knew he would be valuable in my operations.

A few months later Etsu's sister Helen became an employee under somewhat similar circumstances. She gave up a secretarial job at San Jose State College and came to Washington to prepare for a position in South Korea under the United Nations Korean Rehabilitation Act. Then she ran into a particularly irritating form of discrimination. The government of South Korea, still piqued over the years their country was occupied by imperial Japan, refused to permit entry of Japanese Americans. It didn't seem to matter that Nisei were among the American troops that rushed to South Korea's aid in 1950, that Nisei were among U.S. forces maintaining the peace. Helen and other civilian Nisei simply weren't wanted in Korea because of their ancestry. The United States, which also had discriminated against Nisei on the basis of ancestry, found it difficult to protest. Helen worked with us for several years before returning to San Jose.

In the beginning our furniture consisted of little more than the battered desks and chairs from the JACL office. We ordered stationery, and without further ceremony we were in business as consultants and advocates. Unfortunately most of our potential clients didn't quite understand what we had to offer. Nor were they aware that they were expected to pay for the advice we were prepared to give.

Meanwhile, Etsu found us a comfortable but far from elegant apartment in a new building in the Capitol Heights area of southeast Washington. It was our first real home. One of our new neighbors was a friendly young congressman from Oklahoma named Carl Albert. The Alberts and the Masaokas became good friends. On occasion Etsu baby-sat for their children. We remained friends as Albert moved up to increasingly more important posts in the House leadership. Ultimately he was elected speaker. He and his staff were always cooperative. The lucky coincidence of meeting individuals who went on to influential positions played no small part in what success I may have enjoyed.

For many months the only paying client of Mike M. Masaoka Consultants was JACL. We had agreed on a part-time retainer arrangement in the belief that the big battles had been won and there would be relatively little to do. We were wrong. In fact, there was so much to do for JACL that, if it weren't for the need to generate income, we wouldn't have had to go out looking for clients.

What kept us so busy was the need to follow up passage of the Walter-McCarran Act. Congress overrode President Truman's veto on June 27, 1952, but the law did not become effective for six months, December 24, 1952. (Until much later I did not realize how truly signficant it was for Congress to override a veto. In all the nation's history, presidents have vetoed a total of 2,438 bills, and as of September 17, 1986, only 98 of those vetoes has been overridden. President Andrew Johnson suffered 15 overrides in the turmoil of following the assassination of President Lincoln. Presidents Truman and Ford were overridden 12 times each. Only 5 of President Reagan's 49 vetoes had been overridden up to the time the survey was made.) Our concern was that the opportunities provided Japanese by the Walter-McCarran Act be expedited with sensitivity and understanding. From JACL's viewpoint, it was also important to make use of the public-relations opportunities in the new law.

The first resident alien Japanese to be naturalized was Mrs. Kimi Yanagawa of El Paso, Texas. She had entered the United States as a six-year-old, was graduated Phi Beta Kappa from Mills College in Oakland, California, and received her master's degree from the University of Texas in 1948. Even though she was not eligible for naturalization, she filed a declaration of intention to become a citizen in May 1947 to qualify under Texas law for teaching credentials. She was sworn in as a citizen on January 5, 1953, the first day that Federal District Judge R. E. Thomason heard naturalization cases after the new law went into effect. Later in January more than 200 Issei received naturalization papers in a mass ceremony in Honolulu. In various federal courts in California another 160 Issei were sworn in during January as they rushed to become citizens.

Perhaps even more dramatic is the story of the first Japanese quota immigrant to be admitted since 1924. He was Sosaburo Kujiraoka, by coincidence a nephew of Keisaburo Koda, the rice king. He received his visa personally from Ambassador Robert Murphy in a ceremony at the American embassy in Tokyo on January 21, 1953. Kujiraoka was so anxious to qualify for citizenship that he volunteered for the United States Air Force to expedite naturalization.

The Walter-McCarran Act made such an impression on Mr. and Mrs. Frank Ono of Dayton, Ohio, that they named their son, born February 6, 1953, McCarran Walter Ono. Congressman Walter and Senator McCarran appreciated the honor, but they took some ribbing from their colleagues—McCarran Walter O-NO!

While the Japanese immigration quota was only 185 a year, more than 2,400 were permitted to enter through the first eight months because of the removal of racial barriers. Most of those admitted for permanent residence were the nonquota wives of American servicemen. The quota itself was totally unrealistic and I tried to find other ways of enabling worthy Japanese to immigrate.

An opportunity arose in 1953 when the new Eisenhower administration proposed a refugee-relief act to permit entry of 214,000 victims of racial, religious, and political persecution. In the Immigration Subcommittee, Congressman Walter, now its ranking minority member, was able at my urging to amend the bill to include 3,000 Japanese, 3,000 Chinese, and 2,000 Arabs. The full Judiciary Committee refused to accept the amendment and reported out a bill benefiting only Europeans. During House floor debate Congressman Judd joined Walter and they succeeded in restoring approval for 2,000 Japanese, 2,000 Chinese, 2,000 refugees from Hongkong, and 2,000 Arabs.

When the measure reached the Senate, the Judiciary Committee reported out an exclusively European bill. On the floor Senator McCarran was able to tack on 2,000 Chinese refugees.

Meanwhile I had received letters from leading members of the Japanese Diet, including Susumu Nikaido, who later became deputy prime minister, and Takeo Miki, a future prime minister, asking what might be done for typhoon and flood victims in Okinawa, Kagoshima, and Wakayama prefectures.

The four most important members of the conference committee named to consider the House and Senate versions of the refugee bill were Senator Arthur Watkins of Utah who had defeated Senator Thomas in the Eisenhower triumph the previous November, Senator McCarran, Congressman Louis Graham of Pennsylvania, who was the new chairman of the House Immigration Subcommittee, and Congressman Walter. I had personal assurances from each of them that some accommodation would be made for Japan in the compromise bill. The formula that I proposed, and they accepted, was to include "victims of natural calamities" along with racial, religious, and political refugees, without specifically naming the Japanese.

Both houses of Congress found the measure acceptable. After receiving assurances that President Eisenhower would sign the bill, I hurried to the State Department to impress on desk officers that it was the conference committee's intention to provide relief for Japan. U.S. consular officials expedited visas for 3,000 Japanese flood and typhoon victims. Through this one bill we were able to get the equivalent of more than sixteen years of quota immigration.

How have these immigrants fared? In the fall of 1986 hundreds of members of the Kagoshima Immigrants Association met in San Jose, California, to celebrate their more than three decades of life in the United States. They included men who had become landscape architects, hotel and restaurant operators, manufacturers and merchants. Some have become leaders in the huge greenhouse floriculture business in the Salinas, Monterey, and Watsonville areas south of San Francisco. Many of their children have become architects, engineers, and teachers. I had a role in helping these refugees to immigrate to the United States, but it was their determination to succeed, plus the generous assistance of Nisei like Yoshimi Shibata, that enabled them to become valuable, productive citizens and an asset to America. And, as usual in such situations, the immigrant beneficiaries of this statute had no conception of how their special amendment became part of a law intended primarily for Europeans.

I also had a role in organizing the program that brought more than 3,500 young Japanese to the United States as temporary farm workers and trainees. The idea came up in conversations with Gen. Joseph M. Swing, the commissioner of Immigration and Naturalization. During service in Japan he became aware of the poverty of rural Japan, and he also knew of the shortage of reliable farm workers in the United States. Why not bring young Japanese to America as temporary workers so they could learn our farming techniques while earning money? At the same time they would ease the U.S. farm-labor shortage. It was a good idea that was only partly successful, mainly because of the vast differences in American and Japanese farming practices. Perhaps its greatest value was in creating a pool of rural Japanese with strong pro-American feelings. Rural Japan continues to be the stronghold of power for the ruling Liberal Democratic Party.

I found myself spending much time defending the 1952 Immigration Act, and JACL's vigorous advocacy for it, from criticism by liberal friends with whom we had fought for civil-rights gains. They did not object to the provisions for immigration and naturalization of Japanese. Rather, they were concerned that immigration would be restricted rather than liberalized by the new law, and that deportations would be stepped up. They were also opposed to the racist discrimination of the Asia-Pacific Triangle. On this last point I was in complete agreement and will have something to say about it in another chapter.

The statistical evidence is clear. Whatever the faults of the Walter-McCarran Act, it did not unfairly reduce the flow of immigration into the United States. The figures show the converse is true. As for deportees, the numbers do not indicate ideological witch-hunting despite the infrequent headline stories about foreigners being barred from attending political and other conferences.

The most compelling endorsement of the Walter-McCarran Act is that over the past thirty-five years its critics have made little effort to change or eliminate provisions they denounce. There have been hundreds of opportunities to lobby for changes, but the demands have been more vocal than meaningful. This lack of action leads me to wonder whether the charges against the act were primarily exercises in so-called liberalism. I have declared repeatedly that neither I nor JACL would object to liberalization of the 1952 law if provisions for equality in naturalization and immigration were preserved.

Because immigration matters involved so many Japanese cases, I became well acquainted with Thomas G. Finucane, chairman of the Board of Immigration Appeals. Eventually he certified me to practice before the board, making me the first and I believe only non-attorney, non-social worker authorized to appear. Largely on a *pro bono* basis I appeared in a number of cases involving interpretation of immigration and naturalization laws as they related to Japanese. When he retired as chairman in the late sixties, Finucane lauded me for not having lost a single case despite my lack of formal training.

While I continued my JACL work, I was also spending much time trying to learn about Japanese businessmen and their problems. After all, they would be my bread and butter.

Early in my association with them I became aware of an interesting dichotomy in their cultural outlook. On the one hand, they were subtle, gentlemanly, and low-key. This was their predominant side. The subtlety was evidenced in the delicacy of their paintings and exquisite carvings, the artistry in textile design and even of packaging, the fine nuances of the tea ceremony. The indirection that characterized their language was reflected in business negotiations. They hated to come out directly and say no. It took me a while to learn that if a businessman said something would be "difficult" or that he would "try" to get something done, he was signaling that I would be wise to forget about it.

On the other hand they were prone to excesses, and a good example is their drinking. Sake (rice wine) and beer flowed liberally at their dinners. It was customary for members of a party to pour for each other, never allowing the level in the glass or sake cup to fall. The apparent objective was to get everyone completely and happily pie-eyed with the least possible delay. The privileges and restrictions of rank and status vanished in an alcoholic haze. This was their widely accepted way of throwing off the inhibitions they had labored under all day.

Since I am not a drinker, I had to learn early that I must be firm about declining drinks. I found I could do this without offending my hosts provided I kept pouring for them. My Mormon background came in handy. Among my black friends I had found it prudent not to go out of my way to mention the faith of my boyhood, which discriminated against them; the Japanese not only understood but were sympathetic when I said my religion forbade alcohol. Everywhere in Japan I was the guest at loud, happy, men-only parties in expensive restaurants and geisha houses. (Some of the more considerate hosts saw that Etsu was properly entertained by their wives, but not infrequently she was left to her own devices at the hotel. As always she was a good sport about it.) The next day nothing was ever said among my associates about anyone's behavior the night before. Like the black-clad assistants of kabuki drama who flit unobtrusively about the stage, what happened at a drinking party was not to be noticed.

Generally, the Japanese are self-effacing. We Americans are in the habit of talking up our product. That's a cultural trait and our form of salesmanship. The Japanese, in offering a perfectly exquisite gift, will say something like "This is a very poor thing, really not anything at all, but will you pay me the honor of accepting it, please?" They invite a guest to a sumptuous banquet and say: "I'm afraid this is just very ordinary food, but please sit down and share it with us."

Thus when the Japanese came to my Washington office for assistance in opening up the American market, the cultural differences made it difficult to sell them on the concept of American public relations. I had no trouble selling myself. I was an American, and the Japanese knew it. My Americanism is what brought them to me for advice and assistance. Even if I could have, I would not have tried to adopt their cultural patterns. I spoke to them as bluntly as I would have spoken to Americans. I did not kowtow to rank, and I gathered that they rather appreciated my straightforward approach. But in their gentle way they were inclined to question the need for certain activities, like lobbying Congress to get favorable legislation.

That, I explained patiently to a parade of Japanese businessmen, is the seat of American political power. The Japanese government, patterned after the British parliamentary system, assigns power to the prime minister, who is the chief of the ruling party, and his Cabinet. The prime minister normally enjoys an absolute majority in the Diet, which, despite the heckling of minority members, is largely a rubber-stamp body. (The Japanese bureaucracy is another matter. Even a strong prime minister faces struggles with bureaucrats set in their ways and jealous of their authority.) The Cabinet proposes legislation for the Diet's consideration. Since members of the Diet do not have research staffs like those available to members of Congress, they seldom initiate legislation. In the United States, legislation originates in the Congress.

Members of Congress, representing the people, who are supreme, can and often do ignore the president's wishes. In fact, I told my Japanese visitors, representatives and senators of the opposition party routinely oppose the president, even on critical national matters. In trying to influence U.S. policy it is helpful to have friends in the bureaucracy and an attentive ear in the White House, but it is Congress and its committee system, and their respective staffs, that provide the action. And that was why, I told the Japanese, I concentrated my efforts on Congress.

I explained to my first clients, the textile association, that their strategy for winning a larger share of the U.S. market must incorporate the subtleness of their culture with a minimum of head-on confrontation. In practical terms, that meant letting their American associates carry the ball for them. I proposed organizing the American Textile Importers Association, made up entirely of U.S. firms. It was no coincidence that their interests were parallel to those of the Japanese manufacturers. In a vague sense, it could be said that the association, and others like it that came later, were a "front" for Japanese interests. But it also could be argued with vigor and validity that American importers and their employees were entitled to speak up for their business interests, that the vast clothing industry was involved, and that millions of Americans were being served by access to high-quality goods at reasonable prices. For me, there was another advantage in establishing these American organizations: I could represent them without becoming involved with the law requiring registration of foreign agents.

Because I was continuing to wear two hats, the registration requirement posed something of a problem. In the first place, my credibility as a representative of the red-blooded, true-blue JACL would have been shattered if I also had been registered as an agent of Japanese interests. But many of the best business opportunities that came my way would have required registration. Since I continued to regard JACL as my primary account, sentimentally if not in dollar terms, I had to watch these potentially lucrative clients go off to other American lobbyists and consultants who were without encumbrances.

Even so, there were occasions when I could not avoid the appearance of wearing two very different hats. This caused some confusion. More than once I was asked by congressmen how I could be representing both a patriotic American organization like JACL and Japanese business interests.

"Sir," I would reply, "you know that I am an American who fought for my country during the war. You also know how important a stable Japan is to the United States in the postwar world. If I can help keep U.S.-Japanese friendship strong, based on the prosperity that comes from mutually advantageous trade, that will be a very important contribution I can make to my country's welfare. I understand your concern about the effect imports will have on a deteriorating domestic textile industry, but please keep in mind that at this point in its recovery the Japanese economy depends heavily on textile exports. If Japan goes under—and at this stage this is a very real possibility without U.S. support—that would pose an enormous new problem for American foreign policy. What I am doing I consider to be a service for both the United States and Japan."

An encounter with Senator Strom Thurmond of South Carolina was more indicative of the problems an American with a Japanese face encounters in representing Japanese interests. When I approached him about the textile issue, he said, no doubt with an eye on spinning mills in his state: "Young man, I want you to know we're tired of you foreigners coming over to tell us how to run our business." Ah, me, how long would it take and what would we have to do to overcome the perception that everyone with Asian features was a foreigner? Thurmond was kind enough to listen to explanations that I was an American war veteran with American interests at heart, including those of cotton growers in the South who shipped much of their crop to Japan. But would he remember the next time I had occasion to meet him?

I never considered myself to be a hired gun willing to take any client if the fee was right. I had to believe in the client's cause. The result was that I passed up numerous opportunities to make a fast buck. On the other hand, over the years the list of clients for whom Mike Masaoka Consultants (later changed to Mike M. Masaoka and Associates) provided service of one kind or another includes the elite of the Japanese business and industrial establishment. The drought ended after the textile group hired me, and I became associated with, among others, Dentsu, which became the world's largest advertising agency; Ajinomoto, manufacturers of monosodium glutamate and other food products; Suntory, the distilling firm; Nippon Steel; Sumitomo Trading; the Japan Trade Center; Toyota, the automobile manufacturer; Japan Airlines; Matsushita Electric; and the Bank of Tokyo's wholly-owned American banking subsidiaries.

What I was able to do for them varied from firm to firm. Most of them came to me for advice when they were just entering the American market. Primarily, they sought guidance about American regulations and public attitudes. For all of them I made four points, which might not have been new to some but which could stand repeating:

• Upgrade and maintain the quality of your products. Before the war, Japanese goods had been synonymous with cheapness, flimsiness, and poor workmanship. During the war, Japan had unveiled advanced technology and superb workmanship in some of its weapons, demonstrating an ability to compete with the industrialized West. Those skills should be applied to the civilian goods being produced for export. Although it might be tempting in the interests of expediency, Japan would be foolish to try to break into postwar world markets quickly by resuming mass production of cheap and shoddy goods.

- Take pride in your products; give them Japanese names to distinguish them and make those names hallmarks of excellence. Japanese industrialists had been inclined to give their products American names in an effort to win acceptance, but I saw no reason to do that. Today names like Toyota, Nissan, Honda, Sony, Hitachi, Sansui, Seiko, Fuji Film, and Kikkoman soy sauce are American household words. One day the Suntory people asked my opinion on a name for a new green liqueur they planned to introduce in the United States. They had several suggestions, but none seemed quite right. I asked what it was called in Japan. "Midori," they said, meaning the color green, evoking visions of cool tranquility. I laughed and said there's nothing wrong with that—my daughter is named Midori. So Midori it became in the American market, and happily the liqueur has enjoyed substantial popularity.
- Be scrupulously honest. Keep all your activities aboveboard. Never even hint at offering bribes or favors, an accepted business practice in many parts of the world but very risky in the United States. Some of my Japanese friends asked about a tactic attributed to Ambassador Hiroshi Saito, one of Japan's most popular diplomats back in the 1920s. According to these stories, Saito frequently hosted poker parties at the embassy for leading Washington newspapermen. The stakes were not modest. Saito gained the reputation of being a regular and gentlemanly loser, but in return he picked up many interesting and useful bits of gossip and backstairs information to which the reporters were privy. I suppose the same sort of thing happens today when business tycoons are off by themselves on a friendly round of golf. Nonetheless, my advice to the Japanese was to keep everything strictly on the up-and-up. (If I were to relive my life, one of the first things I would do would be to learn to play golf. I am sure I missed scores of opportunities simply because I did not accompany clients and associates to the country club.)
- Study the American market. This was advice the Japanese didn't need, but I reiterated it. Most of them were extremely thorough

about investigating the needs and preferences of American consumers before they entered the market. They lacked the conceit, which some U.S. manufacturers still suffer from, that their products were so good that they didn't have to be adapted to overseas customer preferences or requirements. One example of American folly is the attempt to sell 120-volt appliances, designed for the domestic market, in Japan, where the electrical system is 100 volts and the plugs are round rather than flat. It would have been very simple to modify appliances for export to Japan if anyone had thought about it, but no one did, and Japan quickly built up its own prosperous appliance industry. American refrigerators are efficient and convenient machines that were highly regarded by Japanese visitors. Some liked the refrigerators so well that they shipped them home with their household goods. These appliances proved too large for the average Japanese home. Rooms are separated by a flimsy shoji wall; when the refrigerator motor turned on at night, the noise jolted householders awake. Japanese manufacturers soon were producing small, quiet refrigerators, which quickly took over the Japanese and Third World markets.

Before long I found to my simultaneous elation and dismay that the business of my clients was growing so rapidly and their requirements had become so diverse and complex that my little firm was unable to provide all the necessary services. Some required legal counsel, investigation of patents, or help with licensing and exclusive-agent agreements. Some needed the skills of an advertising agency. Some sought broad market and public-opinion surveys, or help with test-marketing campaigns. These were highly specialized fields that Masaoka and Associates could not expand into without vastly enlarging the staff. I knew what needed to be done, but I had worked too long on a shoestring with my personal skills as the only real asset. I did not feel comfortable undertaking a management role. So I opted to remain a modest organization specializing in the kind of work we were best qualified to do, which was consulting on legislative matters.

   To give the company more business know-how, and to be closer to Japanese corporate offices in New York City, in 1958 I took on an old friend, Sam Ishikawa, as a partner to run our new

Manhattan office. Sam had a master's degree from Harvard Business School and had worked with me in JACL. After leaving JACL he had gone to Japan to work with the English department of Kyodo News Service, had learned to read and speak Japanese, and had become familiar with Japanese business practices. Eventually he became a full partner with me and Etsu in the New York office, which we called Masaoka-Ishikawa and Associates.

As the work load demanded, we added a few research specialists to the Washington staff, and eventually Japan-born T. Albert Yamada, who is completely bilingual in addition to his other talents, became — and remains — my right-hand man. That was about the extent of our expansion and I was comfortable with it. Mike Masaoka could get things done, sometimes in forty-eight hours of nonstop activity, but he was never cut out to be a tycoon. And in our way we were effective. Our know-how was respected. Frequently we were called on to work out under subcontract the legislative strategy for other consulting firms retained by Japanese companies willing to pay them astonishingly large fees.

Why were our principal employees of Japanese ancestry? Good question in view of our insistence on equal opportunity. It was a practical matter since virtually all of our clients were Japanese. Lobbying in Congress or the administrative branch, our ethnicity presented the appearance of personal involvement; we could not be accused of being involved simply for profit. Moreover, we had credibility and we could not be ignored. With our wartime experience, we could demonstrate that we understood the consequences of strain between the land of our birth and the land of our ancestry and therefore would never advocate any policy that would endanger amicable relationships.

While our business was slow, there were many who could see big opportunities ahead. Some of them came to us with tempting proposals for taking advantage of Japanese interest in the American market. Inexperience in business made me cautious. We made only one serious attempt to go big-time, and that proved to be an expensive error. Two Manhattan-based media specialists, who had been on President Eisenhower's White House staff, persuaded Sam and me to hire them to expand our operations into television, national public relations and promotions for Japanese clients. It sounded like a good idea at the time. We soon learned the Japanese weren't ready for such costly efforts, and our two new associates really didn't have the background to carry out their grandiose ideas. I remembered this costly experience every time I was tempted to move into an unfamiliar area.

Chapter 16

Statehood and Adoption

Until I entered the Army I knew little about Hawaii's Nisei. Sab Kido was Hawaiian-born, of course, but he had spent most of his adult life on the mainland and he had better things to do than talk about his boyhood. At Camp Shelby I discovered major differences between the way mainland Nisei and Japanese Hawaiians looked at things. In the Islands they composed one third of the population compared to one third of one percent on the mainland. Even though they had faced some social discrimination, it was on quite a different scale because of their economic clout in a multiracial society. There had been no mass evacuation in the Islands. The Hawaiian Nisei at Shelby struck me at first as a happy-go-lucky bunch, speaking outrageous pidgin English, and doing little in their spare time other than playing the ukulele, singing, and gambling.

Most of us mainland Nisei had spent time in the relocation camps or still had family and friends behind the barbed-wire fences. Uprooted from the West Coast, we no longer had homes with which to identify. We were more quiet and thoughtful and spoke conventional English. The Hawaiians considered us snobbish, and even patronizing. The two groups did not get along until, as I have noted earlier, the Hawaiian Nisei visited the WRA camps in Arkansas and saw families and little children like their own relatives locked up under guard. That was shocking realization of what the war meant to mainland Nisei.

After we went overseas I had an opportunity to get to know many of the Hawaiians, particularly the older ones. We talked often about what would happen after the war. We talked about the need to get involved in politics to right what we thought was wrong in

America, and about the need to win statehood for the Territory of Hawaii. I learned that statehood was an emotional issue, and that many residents of Hawaii, particularly wealthy members of the dominant Republican Party, opposed it because of fears about a Japanese voting bloc.

"Would the Nisei vote as a bloc?" I asked Joe Itagaki, my mess-sergeant friend.

"Naw," he replied. "We disagree among ourselves all da time. But da Republicans are strong. Dey got da line of succession all set up. No place in da GOP for outsiders. I'm a Republican from way back, but most of da new guys will become Democrats, da party of da working man."

That's precisely what happened under the leadership of Jack Burns, a one-time police captain who had steadfastly defended the loyalty of Hawaiians of Japanese ancestry.

In combat there was no difference between Hawaiian Nisei and mainland Nisei. They worried about each other and sacrificed for each other regardless of background. When I went forward, the "butaheads" from the islands were as ready as the "kotonks" from the States to share food and shelter with me. I pledged to myself that if I survived, I would work as hard to get social and political justice for the guys from the Islands as for the mainland Japanese Americans. Despite differences in backgrounds, we were one.

I didn't have long to wait. In January 1946, soon after I rejoined the JACL staff, I heard some Nisei combat veterans were protesting their treatment at Camp Haan, near Los Angeles, where they were awaiting passage back to Hawaii. Their passes to town were restricted and they were being put on garbage detail in place of young recruits. Furthermore, I learned that the vets were being shipped home steerage while civilians were given cabins. I shot off telegrams of protest to Delegate Farrington and the Pentagon.

Nisei coming the other way were also having problems. For years before the war the Immigration and Naturalization Service required Nisei from Hawaii to present certificates of citizenship before allowing them to sail for the mainland. Documents issued by Hawaiian authorities were not always recognized, resulting in the need for hearings before examiners who were not always available. Mitsuyoshi Kido, executive secretary of the Territorial Emergency Service Committee of Honolulu, wrote that even war veterans were still being subjected to harassment. I sent off some more telegrams. Several months later veterans were exempted from the travel restrictions.

This discrimination could be traced to the confused pattern of immigration to Hawaii during its various political stages—from kingdom to independent republic to a territory of the United States within a decade before the turn of the century. After Hawaii became a territory, many Japanese immigrants abandoned sugar-plantation jobs, which amounted to little more than peonage, and hurried to the mainland in search of better opportunities. In 1907 President Theodore Roosevelt signed Executive Order 10009 blocking entry of Japanese and Korean aliens from Hawaii to the mainland. Ostensibly it was to prevent them from competing with Californians for jobs. In reality it was a move to maintain Hawaii's cheap labor force. The executive order resulted in the travel controls that, forty years later, still required Nisei to prove their citizenship and Issei to show they were legal residents of Hawaii.

In the fall of 1947 I learned that four elderly Issei, longtime residents of California, were being threatened with deportation, not to Japan but to Hawaii, under the 1907 executive order. They were Mr. and Mrs. Jujiro Muranaka of San Fernando, seventy-six and seventy-two years old respectively; Shinkichi Shimizu of Guadalupe and Mrs. Haru Toyama of Del Ray, both in their sixties. I took the problem to Hawaii's delegate in Congress, Joe Farrington, and he introduced a private bill on behalf of the four. Meanwhile, I got in touch with the White House staff, and a short while later President Truman revoked the executive order relating to "limited passports."

Statehood was revived as an issue within months after war's end. Farrington lobbied intensely for it in Congress, arguing that doubts about the loyalty of Japanese Americans had been dispersed unequivocally during the war. But old fears die hard. Mrs. Alice Kamokila Campbell resigned from the Democratic National Committee to oppose statehood, arguing that Hawaii's Asians could seize political control by bloc voting. If Hawaii became a state, she warned, its two senators might be used by Tokyo to influence American policies. These, unfortunately, were fears that many still shared. "We Don't Need a 50th Oriental State," declared a flyer widely distributed in California.

The issue's sensitivity can be judged by the reaction to my

suggestion that since no top federal job in Hawaii had been filled by a person of Japanese ancestry, why not appoint one of many qualified Nisei to the next territorial judgeship? My statement was picked up by the Honolulu press and the *Star-Bulletin* quickly attacked the proposal, less because it lacked merit than because the newspaper feared it might adversely affect Hawaii's chances of attaining statehood.

Perhaps a more reasonable argument against statehood was that the islands were not contiguous to the forty-eight states. Eventually, Alaska's admission destroyed that hurdle. After Farrington died, his wife, Betty, became Hawaii's delegate and continued the battle for statehood until she was defeated by Jack Burns. Much of Burns's strength came from the solid support of young Nisei Democrats, many of whom were veterans who had taken advantage of the G.I. Bill to acquire an education.

At the time the political wisdom was that Alaskans would vote Democratic while Hawaii was strongly Republican. Burns's strategy was to support Alaska's bid to become the forty-ninth state, thus pleasing the strong Democratic majority in Congress, before making the big push for Hawaii with the support of the Republican administration.

But even then Hawaii was swinging toward the Democratic Party with its young leaders working doggedly for statehood. Spark Matsunaga, later to become a U.S. senator, occasionally made the long train ride from Boston, where he was attending Harvard Law School, to help the Farringtons and Burns lobby. Daniel Inouye, first Nisei in Congress and now Hawaii's senior senator, took off from law classes at George Washington University whenever he could to help Hawaii's delegate. I had met both men in the service, but cannot claim to have known them well. They were combat officers and I was an enlisted man in headquarters. But in Washington we worked together frequently on statehood and other issues and I came to appreciate and respect their talents. After their election to Congress I was privileged to be associated with them on many matters about which I will have more to say later.

Hearings on Hawaiian statehood had been held repeatedly since prewar times. The House passed statehood bills in 1947, 1950, 1953, and 1954. Burns made his push in 1958. Since so much of the ground had been covered previously, only a few highly select witnesses appeared at the 1958 hearings. I was among those invited to testify before both Senate and House committees, mostly, I presume, to demonstrate the difference between Japanese Americans and the stereotypical Japanese soldiers of World War II.

When Hawaii finally became a state in 1959 Jack Burns sent me a handwritten note which I treasure: "Thanks, Mike. We're all going to be better for all this." Later he wrote me more formally: "We shall be forever in your debt for the vital assistance you gave us in the campaign for statehood, and it is a debt we shall not forget."

Also among my mementos is a resolution from the Territory of Hawaii's last legislature: "Be it resolved by the House of Representatives of the Thirtieth Legislature of the Territory of Hawaii that it convey, and does hereby convey, in behalf of the people of Hawaii, its deepest appreciation and heartfelt gratitude to Mike Masaoka for the major role which he played in obtaining statehood for Hawaii. . . ."

In Hawaii's first election as a state, Hiram Fong, a Chinese American Republican, and Oren Long, a Democrat, were named senators. Fong became the senior senator by a flip of a coin. At the time Dan Inouye, who had lost his right arm during one of the final battles of the war in Italy, was undoubtedly the most politically popular Nisei in Hawaii. He had expected to run for the Senate, but Democratic Party leaders persuaded him to defer to senior statesman William Heen. Bowing to seniority, Inouye then declared for Hawaii's single House seat, displacing Patsy Takemoto Mink who had her eye on the post. Heen was defeated but Inouye won easily. Jack Burns ran for governor and lost narrowly to William Quinn, the last appointed governor. Spark Matsunaga was Burns's candidate for lieutenant governor and he too was defeated. When Inouye moved up to the Senate in 1962, Matsunaga was elected to the House. Patsy Takemoto Mink joined him when Hawaii received a second House seat. Matsunaga and Mink competed for Fong's Senate seat when he retired in 1976 and Matsunaga won a hard-fought battle. Hawaii's congressional delegation over the years has been among the most effective and influential from both national and state viewpoints. Alice Kamokila Campbell and others who shared her fears had been tilting with straw men.

While all this was going on, a profound change was taking

place in the personal lives of Etsu and me. Since both of us came from large, close-knit families, we had hoped to have children when we were economically secure. But when we were ready, Etsu and I learned to our intense disappointment that we could not have children of our own.

After much deliberation we decided on adoption. We inquired at various adoption agencies and orphanages in centers of Japanese American population, but all had long waiting lists. Pearl Buck, the author, who was deeply engrossed in finding homes for abandoned Eurasian children of American servicemen and Asian women, urged us to consider some of her charges. Ultimately we decided that, inexperienced as we were at parenting, the problems that might arise as a result of a mixed heritage atop those involved in simply being parents might be more than we could handle. We asked Dr. Kazuye Togasaki, an eminent San Francisco obstetrician and sister of George and Sim, to be on the lookout for a Japanese American child we could adopt.

She called us one day in the summer of 1955 with the good news. The mother of a newborn girl was willing to give up the child. Etsu flew to San Francisco and I asked Jim Purcell to take care of the legalities. George Togasaki happened to be in San Francisco and he delivered the baby into Etsu's arms. Etsu took the infant to San Jose where her mother helped with its care for the first few weeks. It is difficult to describe my feelings when at last I saw the baby, but it is familiar to all men gazing for the first time on their first girl-child—a sense of awe and love that this tiny, sleepy, helpless being was mine to hold and love and nurture, and a staggering realization of the responsibility faced by her new parents in guiding her to adulthood. We named her Midori Marie, the Japanese name meaning green or verdant and signifying the richness of new life.

Midori came to live with us in our apartment. Strangely, one small addition to the family made what had been an adequate apartment much too small. After the formalities of adoption were completed, Etsu began house hunting. She focused on Montgomery County, Maryland, just across the boundary from the District of Columbia, because of its reputation for good schools. Eventually she found a new three-bedroom, split-level home in Somerset, a quiet, wooded area of Chevy Chase. The house was only seven miles from the office and there was plenty of open space where

Midori could play. The house was ideal but I had reservations about the cost since we also would have to buy furniture and pay for landscaping.

I was still hesitating when the sales agent warned that he might have a problem selling to us because we were Orientals. That got the adrenaline flowing. I told the agent I wanted the house and would rally my friends in Congress and elsewhere to my support if anyone attempted to block the sale. No one did. The neighbors proved friendly and helpful and today Somerset is an integrated, middle-class community, which has retained its pleasant character.

We moved in in April 1956. Etsu took her time furnishing the house, purchasing piece by piece some furniture created by George Nakashima, the world-famous Nisei craftsman. Much of the decoration consists of antiques and artifacts given us by Japanese friends and clients, sometimes in lieu of fees. The display is hardly *shibui* by Japanese standards and has caused some friends of our children to describe our home as the Masaoka museum. Etsu also found an Issei landscaper to put in small Japanese-style gardens in the back and front yards.

Even as a new father in a new home, I was hard to domesticate. Our agreement was that Etsu would be responsible for all aspects of maintaining home and family, paying the bills and arranging to keep the lawn mowed and shrubs trimmed, while I ran the office without her help. Etsu soon became known among our friends as a "demon mother," completely dedicated to the upbringing of Midori and, later, Michael. She seldom accompanied me to social events that required couple participation. On the rare occasions we went out, the baby-sitter was a trusted friend like Mieko Kosobayashi or Mary Toda.

Two years after Midori was born, Dr. Togasaki telephoned to say she had a newborn boy available for adoption. Taking Midori with her, Etsu flew to San Francisco again to receive husky, round-eyed Michael Edward Masaoka. We had gone through the formalities of adopting Midori in the District of Columbia. With Michael, we ran into complications in Maryland. An unsympathetic court officer, apparently suspecting we were involved in a California baby black market, questioned our documents. Fortunately Jim Purcell had done a thorough job. Although Etsu and I were nervous, the judge found nothing amiss and quickly approved the adoption.

It was a delight to see Midori and Michael learning to walk, starting school, developing their personalities. Midori was an extrovert, always articulate, the thoughtful sister looking out for her little brother. Michael was more restless, curious, often the loner with raw talent in music and art. Frequently on weekends the four of us would drive out to the history-steeped countryside around Washington, visiting national landmarks while I tried to impress on the children the romantic history of our country and the wealth of their heritage as Americans.

From the beginning we told our children we had "chosen" them to be our daughter and son because we were unable to have our own. They accepted the explanation. One Christmas some children from their elementary school visited an orphanage called Children's Village, and their teacher told us she overheard Midori saying to her brother: "Aren't we lucky that Mom and Daddy adopted us?" Years later, after I suffered my first heart attack, Etsu and I were discussing various physical weaknesses that we thought might run in our families. "Thank goodness," the children exclaimed simultaneously, "we're adopted."

Admittedly, Etsu and I spoiled our children because we wanted them to have all the things our parents had been unable to give us. However, because of the demands of my work, I left to Etsu most of the responsibility for their upbringing. As with so many others in Washington, I failed to spend enough time with the youngsters, excusing my neglect by rationalizing that in helping others I was making a better future for our own children.

Etsu's continued absence from the office made it imperative that I find an assistant who was more than just a secretary. After Mieko left we had several temporary fill-ins. Then I found Mary Toda, a California-born Nisei who, like so many others, had moved east as a result of the evacuation. She came to us recommended by William Marutani, the Philadelphia attorney. Mary went to work in February 1960, and has been with us ever since. She likes to remind me that I kept her working the first three and a half years without a vacation. Then, with my blessing, she took off two and a half months for a trip around the world. In addition to superb secretarial skills Mary possesses uncommon good sense, which makes her valuable in the role of executive assistant. She knows when to speak up and when to remain silent, when to push me for decisions and when to take care of them on her own. She is totally dependable and capable of enormous volumes of work, willing to stay up nights to meet a deadline. Often she was called on to take clients from Japan on sightseeing trips around Washington, and that made it necessary for her to catch up with her office responsibilities at night and on weekends.

Mary could be sharp with incompetence, but she related well with strangers, particularly those in need of help. She was also very perceptive. Often she would warn me to be careful in dealing with certain individuals, and invariably her evaluation would be accurate. She and Mieko scolded me when I charged what they considered to be excessively modest fees, or refused to send bills to people who had asked for favors. "You can't pay your bills with scrolls and plaques," they would say, "and you can't eat letters of appreciation." If I had listened to them more often, I might be better off today.

The 1960s were a time of great social ferment. Many young people were caught up in the hippie movement. Black leaders, angry over the slow pace of civil-rights progress, preached militancy. Oddly, the Japanese American community was split on the issue of civil-rights advocacy. Some of the older Nisei, having worked diligently to recover from the economic loss and psychological trauma of the evacuation, were seeking peace and tranquillity. Largely by their own efforts they had gained status and social acceptance, which they guarded jealously. Like many middle-class Americans they were repelled by the activists' first-shaking rhetoric, the torching of ghettoes, the violent confrontation between blacks and the established order. I could understand their reluctance to become involved.

On the other hand, many Nisei, I among them, could not brush aside the evacuation's cruel assault on our civil rights. Even though we had come back from our ordeal, I felt it was our obligation as Americans who had experienced oppression to fight for the human rights of all peoples. Soon after the war I had been instrumental in organizing what was called the National Civil Liberties Clearing House. This was an informational program, unable to lobby. That led in 1948 to the more active Leadership Conference on Civil Rights with Roy Wilkins as chairman. Representing JACL, I was one of the founding members. More than 150 organizations— minority groups, labor unions, churches, human-rights advocates—

joined forces to press aggressively for people's rights. Its formation marked the start of the militant civil-rights movement which ultimately led the nation to the sweeping reforms of the Civil Rights Act of 1964. For years, I was a member of its Legislative Strategy Committee.

In the summer of 1963, Dr. Martin Luther King, Jr., laid plans for a massive civil-rights demonstration in Washington. I knew JACL must take part, but this was a decision that needed organizational support. The then JACL president, K. Patrick Okura, who lived in Omaha, Nebraska, agreed. Okura called a special meeting of the league's national board, which authorized JACL participation in the rally. Several dozen of us marched together under the JACL banner. There were seats reserved for Okura and me on the platform at the Lincoln Memorial where Dr. King delivered his famous "I have a dream" speech, but the crush of the crowd was so great that we were unable to get there.

During this period I was making regular trips to Japan to consult with clients. On one of these trips, Sam Ishikawa and I paid a call on the ambassador, Douglas MacArthur III, nephew of the general. In parting the ambassador asked if there was anything he could do for me. Of course, it was the standard courtesy being extended a visitor. Jokingly I said I would appreciate it if he could arrange for me to visit mainland China, which at the time was off limits to Americans.

"I'm afraid I can't do that, Mike," the ambassador said. "But how would you like to go home by way of Russia? I'm having lunch tomorrow with the Soviet ambassador, and I could ask him about a visa for you and Sam."

A few days later we were on our way to Moscow by way of New Delhi and over the Himalayas to Tashkent, where we were met by an Intourist escort. The customs inspector at Tashkent was a hard-eyed North Korean who understood some English. He gave us a thorough shaking down, finally asking to see copies of *Time* and *Newsweek* that Sam and I were carrying. Both of them contained items not particularly complimentary to the Soviets. The airliner was held up for four hours while the officials examined the magazines line by line before returning them to us.

During the long flight to Moscow the Intourist escort quizzed me about the West Coast evacuation and the wartime treatment of

Japanese Americans. It was quickly evident he knew more about the evacuation than most people in the United States. He asked how I felt about racism in America, and the oppression of colored peoples by capitalists. He obviously was testing to see whether I might make some statements that could be used for propaganda purposes. I hope I did not give him too much to be encouraged about.

Perhaps because of orders from the Soviet ambassador, Sam and I were given VIP treatment in Moscow. But that was not enough to camouflage the squalor and harshness of life in a Communist police state, or the fact that in their supposedly classless society a few are more equal than the masses. As our Intourist escort reminded me, it is true that our government suspended citizen rights of Japanese Americans and imprisoned us in concentration camps. But it is also true that our government has recognized the error and injustice of that hysterical wartime action. There is no comparison between the Soviet and American systems, and I regret that good manners prevented me from making that clear in so many words to the gentleman from Intourist.

From Moscow, Sam and I flew to East Berlin and crossed through Checkpoint Charlie into West Berlin. We hadn't been in our hotel very long when an American official called to say he would like to talk to us about our experiences in the Soviet Union. It turned out to be an extremely thorough debriefing. One episode stands out in my mind.

"Do you recall the day in Moscow when you went to the GUM department store to look for some galoshes?" he asked. I nodded. "And do you remember that a Russian bumped into you, and then quietly offered to sell you rubles for American currency?"

Certainly I remembered, and I said I had tried to ignore him because I had heard stories of Americans who had been jailed after being trapped into making illegal currency transactions. "How do you know about all this?" I asked in surprise.

The interrogator smiled. "That man was one of our people," he said. I didn't know whether to be relieved that Uncle Sam had been looking after me even in Moscow, or to wonder whether my reliability was being tested. What would have happened if I had agreed to sell dollars for rubles at an illegal rate?

Chapter 17

Unfinished Business

Before the war three Japanese banks—Sumitomo, Yokohama Specie (now the Bank of Tokyo), and Mitsui—had branch offices in Hawaii and on the West Coast, performing the usual banking functions. A large number of Japanese Americans used these banks because they were conveniently located. For the Issei, who controlled family and business purse strings, these banks were favored because they posed no language and cultural barriers. Savings deposited in dollars could be withdrawn in either American currency or Japanese yen, so many opened accounts in hopes of taking advantage of fluctuating exchange rates.

When war broke out these banks were closed and their assets taken over by the Alien Property Custodian. After the war the United States proposed that Americans with yen deposits collect from the banks in Japan at the official exchange rate which had been fixed at 360 yen to one American dollar. Before the war the rate had been about 4 yen to the dollar. It didn't take a mathematician to figure that if someone had $1,000 on deposit in 1941, converted to Y4,000 at the time, and the deposit was returned in dollars at the new rate, the claimant would be paid all of $11.11 with no provision for the interest that had accumulated. Not many of the more than 23,000 depositors were pleased with the idea. When an examiner recommended that the claimants be paid at the prewar rate, the Justice Department requested that Congress outlaw all payments on the ground that they were administratively too costly to process.

The Senate twice passed the requested legislation by voice vote, and twice JACL persuaded the House Banking Committee not to report it to the full House. That meant no action was taken in the

House, thus killing the bill. Had we failed at the committee level, in all probability the strong Senate support would have ensured passage in the House.

As I had learned in the fight for evacuation claims, Washington moves at an excruciatingly slow pace when special money matters are involved. Several years passed before the Justice Department overruled its own examiner's recommendation for payment at the prewar rate, in effect forcing the claimants to go to court. Eventually it was agreed the claimants would be paid dollar for dollar on their original deposits. This was not as generous as it may seem because the interest that had been accumulating was approximately equal to the principal. In other words, the depositors were to get back half their money. Considering that the original offer was 360 yen to the dollar, the settlement was a windfall.

By the time some 20,000 Issei and Nisei had been repaid, the Sumitomo and Mitsui bank assets set aside for this purpose were exhausted. Yokohama Specie had about $4.5 million left. Unpaid and ineligible under the rules were some 3,000 claimants including those who had failed to turn in their claims on time, those who had been interned rather than evacuated, and former residents now living in Japan. Attorneys Saburo Kido and Al Wirin, with Katsuma Mukaeda, a Los Angeles Issei as consultant, organized these claimants into the Committee of Japanese American Yen Depositors and asked me to try for legislation that would make them eligible for payments. All the principals agreed to work on a contingency basis since few of the claimants had enough confidence to put up any money.

What happened next illustrates the importance of knowing people who can help if one does not have the power to create change. Stymied at every turn, I went to see Joe Rauh, an attorney who had been with the Justice Department at the time of the evacuation and who was deeply involved with the Leadership Conference on Civil Rights as its general counsel. Seeing no civil-rights issue, Rauh was unenthusiastic about getting mixed up with the yen claimants. Exasperated, I blurted out: "Damn it, Joe, you aren't interested in helping anybody but the blacks!" That remark hit a tender spot. He agreed to take on the case.

Our goal was to persuade Congress to amend the basic statute as to eligibility and get the Justice Department to agree to a settlement formula no less generous than that provided previously paid depositors. We argued that it was unfair to deny payment to persons for largely bureaucratic reasons. Congressman Matsunaga introduced a bill incorporating many of the precedents established in the Evacuation Claims Act and we helped push it through both houses.

After that came long and intense negotiations with the Justice Department with me at Rauh's side. I can think of no more appropriate way to describe those sessions than as a fifteen-round heavyweight boxing match. Rauh finally prevailed in the litigation that was required. The payments made to our clients came very close to that of the initial claimants. The court awarded Rauh one third of the attorneys' fee. One third went to Wirin, and the final third was divided among Kido, Mukaeda, and me. Although my share was modest compared to the huge payments common to such cases, it was the largest fee my firm has ever received. Even more satisfying was the fact that we had succeeded where few thought we had a chance.

I became involved in a somewhat less likely international matter when Tokuyasu Fukuda, a member of the Diet representing the Tokyo administrative district and former chief of the Self-Defense Forces, came to see me. His district included the tiny Bonin Islands, also called Ogasawara, specks in the Pacific hundreds of miles southeast of Tokyo. During the war the U.S. Navy had occupied the Bonins after the Marines captured nearby Iwo Jima. The Bonin Islanders, ousted from their homes and scattered to various parts of Japan, were anxious to go back. Fukuda asked me to help them. Because of the vague resemblance to the plight of Japanese Americans who had to bow to military necessity, I became interested in the matter.

Digging into the situation, I discovered the United States was reluctant to leave the islands because of their supposed strategic importance. In reality there was little strategic value other than the location. The harbor was not outstanding, and there wasn't much to support a military base. Some of the natives could trace their ancestry back to American whalers and seamen who had jumped ship and settled in the Bonins. Yet they all considered themselves Japanese and wanted to return to Japanese jurisdiction. Their association had raised some money and hired a Washington law firm to plead their case. The attorneys had used up the money with little to show for it when Fukuda came to me.

I took up his case with friends in the Pentagon, the State Department, and Congress. Eventually they got around to studying the matter and decided that the Bonins weren't important in relation to Okinawa and several other island groups. They were returned to Japanese jurisdiction in 1967. The Bonin Islanders were delighted and grateful, but they also were almost destitute. My reward for helping them to regain their homes was a handsome silver model of a boat, a beautifully carved piece of rare coral, and a very nice letter.

Fukuda wrote: "This great task [of restoring the Bonin Islands to Japan] would never have been achieved without your assistance."

While most of my business was related to the United States and Japan, we also handled strictly domestic matters. For example, one of my earliest clients were Japanese American flower growers in California. Finding the local market largely taken over by other growers during the war, the Japanese Americans utilized the expanding airline industry to ship cut flowers to eastern and midwestern population centers. The problem was that airlines refused to allow the growers to consolidate their shipments to take advantage of bulk rates. I kept working on the Civil Aeronautics Board for several years before consolidation of air freight was approved. Not only did the flower growers benefit, but the ruling contributed much to the expansion of the air-cargo business.

Another early client was the West Mexico Vegetable Distributors Association headquartered in Nogales, Arizona. Its seventy-five American members imported about 90 percent of the fresh winter vegetables and fruit grown in the Mexican states of Sinaloa and Sonora and distributed them throughout the United States and Canada. The importing season was from December through May when local produce was unavailable.

In the mid-sixties I was invited to meet with officers of the association who were seeking Washington representation to protect their interests against competitors, particularly Florida tomato growers and shippers. The association president that year was Tooru Takahashi, a Nisei whose family operated a number of produce markets in Los Angeles. Also present at the meeting held in a Washington motel were executive secretary Albert Conrad, director Angus Mackenzie, and Nasib Karam, city attorney for Nogales, where the produce was processed and prepared for distribution. Karam was a large, dark-skinned man who, I later learned, was of Lebanese extraction.

The meeting began badly. Karam fired a series of questions at me like a prosecutor in a criminal trial, hardly waiting to hear my replies. Why should an Arizona association, most of whose members were white Americans, want to hire a Japanese firm, he asked. Wouldn't Congress, already irritated by Japanese trading practices, resent being lobbied by a Japanese? What made me think I could do a better job for them than an American firm?

It had been a bad day for me on the Hill and now I was in no mood to be browbeaten. In view of my unsuccessful lettuce-growing experience I wasn't sure I wanted to get involved in produce again. But Karam irritated me and I responded vigorously, sometimes angrily, to his questions. I said I hadn't solicited their business, but had been invited to meet with them. Then I explained that my firm was not Japanese, but as American as they, and reviewed my lobbying experience for Japanese Americans, dwelling at some length on my battles against racial persecution. I also urged them to check me out with Arizonans in Congress such as Senators Barry Goldwater and Carl Hayden, and Congressman Morris Udall. That seemed to reassure Karam somewhat, but I wasn't certain he was about to change his mind about me.

As the meeting ended Karam mentioned that he was headed for San Francisco on other business. I asked casually whether he, being an attorney, had ever run across my good friend James Purcell in the Bay area. Karam stared in surprise. "Jim's wife, Helen, is my sister," he exclaimed. "I'll be seeing them when I'm out there."

If I had been aware of the connection, the acrimony of that first meeting no doubt would have been avoided. The association agreed to hire my firm for a one-year trial and the relationship has now continued for more than two decades. Fresh produce used to be too expensive in winter for all but the wealthy. Now, thanks to imports, tomatoes, green beans, bell peppers, snow peas, cucumbers and other salad vegetables, and a wide variety of fruits are available and affordable throughout the cold months. The association's business has more than doubled during the period of my employment, with imports amounting to between 1.2 and 1.4 billion pounds a year with a value of $200 million to $250 million.

I soon discovered the produce business involves much more than simply harvesting and selling crops. I became involved in problems relating to government inspections, packaging, use of pesticides, customs procedures, trucking rules, laws regarding foreign carriers crossing international borders, antidumping regulations, and even container restrictions.

In every term of Congress we could expect Florida tomato growers to seek restrictive legislation aimed at West Mexican imports. Mexican tomatoes are vine-ripened, carefully graded and hand-packed to avoid bruising during transport, which is the same way California tomatoes are handled. But about 85 percent of Florida tomatoes are picked while green and hard for ease of transportation. Regardless of size, the green tomatoes are dumped loose into containers for shipment to plants where they are "degreened," that is, given a red color by exposing them to a gas in a special chamber. The Florida system is less expensive but of course adding color to green tomatoes does nothing to enhance their flavor.

It was important to demonstrate the difference in the product to the eleven members of an agricultural marketing subcommittee who were being asked for special consideration by the Florida interests. I knew that none of the congressmen came from a tomato-growing area and somehow the problem had to be dramatized for their benefit. My solution was to have crates of Mexican, California, and Florida tomatoes shipped to Washington. The association representatives who had come to testify stored the tomatoes in their hotel rooms and turned on the air conditioners to keep them cool. Just before the subcommittee met we carried the crates into the hearing room and our witnesses made a convincing presentation. The subcommittee was so impressed it decided against reporting any restrictive packing or packaging bill for the full committee's consideration.

Another agricultural problem led to my involvement in a much broader issue. One day in the 1960s S. John Nitta, head of the American Chick Sexing Association of Lansdale, Pennsylvania, came to see me. Prior to the war Nitta had gone to Japan to study the science of chick sexing, which is extremely important to the chicken- and egg-producing industries. An expert chick sexor can examine from 800 to 1,500 day-old chicks per hour and separate males from females with virtually 100 percent accuracy. Segregation is important because if you are in the egg business, you don't want to be feeding vast numbers of chicks that will never grow up to lay an egg until they develop distinguishing sexual characteristics.

Nitta had taught the skill to a number of Nisei as his business expanded after the war. The demand for their services became greater than the number of Americans willing to undergo the demanding training course. Nitta soon saw that the only way to serve his network of clients was to recruit experienced sexors from Japan. That's when he ran into visa problems. I went to Frank Auerbach, by then in the State Department's visa section, to explain that there was a critical shortage of sexors in the poultry industry, which could be relieved only by easing immigration regulations.

Auerbach acknowledged that the poultry people had a legitimate problem and promised to do something about it. Then he asked what I was doing about the discriminatory Asia Pacific Triangle matter. It was a nagging problem left over from the passage in 1952 of the Walter-McCarran immigration reform. In effect, the Asia Pacific Triangle was an extension of the Asiatic Barred Zone in the Immigration Act of 1917. The triangle was a geographic area including the continent of Asia with the exception of Soviet Siberia, and most of the western Pacific outside of Australia and New Zealand. Twenty independent countries, with half the world's population, were within the area. The law held that even though a person was born outside the triangle, if his racial ancestry could be traced to that area he would come under the ancestral country's quota for immigration purposes. For example, it meant that if a person of Japanese ancestry born in Canada (and therefore having Canadian citizenship) sought to emigrate to the United States, he would have to apply for entry not as a Canadian but under Japan's quota of 185 per year. The Asia Pacific Triangle clearly was designed to restrict Asian immigration even more severely than the meager quotas provided.

The authors of the Walter-McCarran Act retained this discriminatory provision, while providing token quotas, to appease Pacific Coast politicians who otherwise might have opposed the entire immigration reform effort. At the time I had disagreed strongly with this political strategy, but accepted it in order to win support for the omnibus legislation. There would be, I figured, other opportunities to eliminate the triangle. Now Auerbach was giving me a signal.

That opportunity came when the Kennedy administration set up as one of its goals what was called an "overhaul" of the 1952 legislation. An interagency immigration-policy committee was set up with Auerbach, representing the State Department, as chairman. Auerbach was in complete sympathy with JACL's opposition to the Triangle and in committee deliberations he lost no opportunity to raise the issue of equality for Asians.

I had a hand in lobbying all three Kennedy brothers on this issue—John in the White House, Robert in the Justice Department, and Ted in Congress. The Kennedys favored elimination of the Triangle as a matter of fairness and justice, but being politicians they were inclined to listen to certain western members of Congress who warned there was still strong opposition to Japanese immigration.

To present another view, I enlisted the support of Senators Inouye and Fong, and Congressman Matsunaga. Fong was then serving on the subcommittee on immigration. There he argued that the Triangle was an affront to all Asians, and that West Coast opinion was ready for an end to that kind of racism.

Kennedy and Phil Hart of Michigan were other members of the subcommittee. I testified for more than an hour, repeating the story of the contribution made to America by Japanese and Chinese immigrants, for the benefit of Kennedy and Hart who knew little about Asian American history. But probably the most important part I played in passage of the reform bills (S 500 and HR 2580) was a 155-page brief submitted in JACL's testimony. Frank Chuman in his book *The Bamboo People* calls it "perhaps the most comprehensive report extant concerning our shameful history of discrimination against Orientals in the areas of immigration and naturalization." As a matter of fact, I have submitted many statements of equal or greater length in testimony about Japanese American and civil-rights matters. I have been kidded about my long-windedness, but it isn't unintentional. My statements were purposely detailed, because people have short memories and members of Congress and their staffs change regularly. I have learned it is essential to give each new generation of the Washington power structure a comprehensive review of the past.

But without doubt the greatest part of the credit for finally wiping out the Triangle goes to Auerbach. Robert Kennedy told me the president had decided to make elimination of the Triangle an important part of the package because of Auerbach's persistence.

President Kennedy did not live to see the Asia Pacific Triangle eliminated. President Lyndon Johnson signed the bill into law on

October 3, 1965, at the Statue of Liberty. I was among the guests invited to the ceremony in recognition of the part I played in its passage. Rather than an overhaul of immigration laws, the bill was an amendment to correct flaws in the Walter-McCarran Act. For the first time in history Asians would be treated under American immigration and naturalization law in exactly the same way as Europeans—without regard for race, creed, or nationality.

The restrictions against immigration from Asia had been the product of West Coast racism fanned by fears of invasion by hordes of yellow-skinned people. That fear never materialized. Prior to World War II, the largest number of Chinese to appear in the U.S. Census was 107,488 in 1890. The highest population of Japanese on the mainland, including the American-born, was 138,834 in 1930. Ten years later the number had dwindled to 126,947 as substantial numbers of aliens left the United States.

By the time the immigration laws were reformed, Japan's standard of living had reached such a level that emigrating to the United States was no longer attractive. Today Asia's share of the world immigration quota of 290,000 annually is taken up largely by Third World nations, primarily South Korea, the Philippines, Taiwan, and Hong Kong. The image of Asian immigrants also had changed. Once they were seen as coolie laborers. With the exception of refugee "boat people" from the Indochina peninsula, most of the new Asian immigrants have the education and the skills to make their way in American society, many as professionals and highly successful entrepreneurs. It was JACL's concerns with justice that helped open the door for them.

Immigration reform, unfortunately, did nothing to eliminate the objectionable security provisions of the Walter-McCarran Act, which reiterated Title II of the Internal Security Act of 1950 that etched into law the 1942 imprisonment of Japanese Americans. Its repeal was a critical item of unfinished business.

Chapter 18
The Repeal of Title II

In the late sixties, when civil disobedience in opposition to the Vietnam War became widespread, we began to hear disquieting reports that the Justice Department was building concentration camps at six out-of-the-way locations. Adding to the poignancy was word that one of the camps was at Tule Lake, California, where Japanese Americans had been imprisoned only two decades earlier. Presumably these new camps were to become holding pens for street demonstrators who could be detained under Title II of the Internal Security Act of 1950.

In brief, Title II codified the 1942 imprisonment of Japanese Americans. The Supreme Court had ruled in the Yasui, Hirabayashi, and Korematsu cases that even in the absence of specific laws, our evacuation and detention were justified because of the war emergency. Title II spelled out those government powers. It provided the legal basis for locking up, without trial, persons suspected of posing security risks in time of war, insurrection, or invasion. Not many Americans were aware of this law, which on the face of it would seem to violate various provisions of the Bill of Rights. Now, growing opposition to the Vietnam War, unrest on college campuses, and the anger of blacks impatient to win civil rights caused some government figures to dust off Title II. We were at war, and they saw civil disobedience as tantamount to insurrection. Japanese Americans viewed with alarm the prospect of a new wave of hysteria leading this time to legalized imprisonment without trial of a different unpopular minority.

Title II came into being in a curious way after World War II when American concern turned from Fascist militarism to Communist subversion. Senator Joseph McCarthy of Wisconsin was the chief Communist-hater. He teamed with the Democratic chairman of the Senate Judiciary Committee, Pat McCarran of Nevada, to push for what became known as the Internal Security Act of 1950. Title I had to do with its so-called internal security provisions. Title II had to do with its so-called emergency authority. President Truman vetoed the bill. JACL joined the Leadership Conference on Civil Rights in urging that the veto be sustained, but Congress overrode it easily. Thus, the onerous provisions of the Internal Security Act were already law when they were incorporated into the Walter-McCarran immigration reform. By advocating the Walter-McCarran Act despite this flaw, JACL found itself at odds with our liberal colleagues. My position was that since Title II did not change existing law, we could pursue the benefits of immigration and naturalization reform without compromising principles. As a practical matter, no one's rights seemed to be unduly endangered by Title II's authoritarian provisions so long as they were not invoked. But that was before barbed-wire fences began to go up around new concentration camps.

In August 1968, JACL at its convention in San Jose, California, voted to make repeal of Title II its next major goal. The principle was laudable but I had reservations. There is no bad time for attacking repression, but widespread American fear of subversion would make it extremely difficult to get rid of what many saw as an internal-security safeguard. Realistically, lobbying Congress on such a controversial issue in behalf of a part-time client would overextend the limited resources of my office. But once the decision was made, I prepared for yet another battle on the Hill, fortified by JACL's commitment to reopen a full-time office in Washington and hire a trainee to help me.

Title II had special importance to Japanese Americans but it also had broad national implications. Thus I had no hesitation about asking for the assistance of the Nisei members of Congress. In April 1969, Senator Inouye and Congressman Matsunaga introduced identical bills calling for repeal of Title II. Inouye's bill had 23 co-sponsors, Matsunaga's 157. With that kind of support, smooth sailing might have been expected. But that was not to be.

In the Senate the bill was referred to the Judiciary Committee's internal security subcommittee. In the House an independent Internal Security Committee, headed by Richard Ichord of Missouri, took jurisdiction. Both committees held extensive hearings in which the Japanese American experience was cited at length. There was a clear consensus that we had been detained illegally, that due process had been denied us, that the precedent should not be repeated, and that Title II should be repealed. The Senate subcommittee cleared the bill without delay and the full Senate approved it unanimously. But a majority of Ichord's House committee took the position that some safeguards should be retained to protect the public safety from civil disobedience. To avoid the kind of incarceration Japanese Americans had suffered, the committee proposed that a mechanism be set up for expeditious personal hearings.

In light of the JACL mandate, the Ichord formula was unacceptable. What we feared was that if the Ichord proposal was put to a vote, both houses would approve it in the face of the increasing violence of street protests. Congress adjourned before anything could be done.

In the next Congress, the 92nd, Inouye reintroduced his bill, and Ichord his committee-approved bill. Matsunaga and I put our heads together and devised a new strategy. His bill, HR 234, was revised to address a change in the United States Code as it pertains to imprisonment of prisoners. That made it possible to take that new bill out of Ichord's Internal Security Committee. With the blessings of the speaker, the new bill was referred to the Judiciary Committee, which in turn referred it to a subcommittee chaired by Robert Kastenmeier of Wisconsin, a Democrat.

This was a tremendous coup. Kastenmeier's views of human rights ran parallel to ours. His able, popular administrative assistant was Kaz Oshiki, who had gone through the evacuation and incarceration. Kastenmeier once observed that he and Oshiki were the same age, both had been born in the United States of recent immigrants, both were in college when World War II broke out, but he had been allowed to remain in school while his future aide was imprisoned as though he had committed some heinous crime. He said this was an outrage and he wanted to do everything he could to make up for that failure of democracy.

The Ichord committee's bill wasn't all bad. Its proposal for boards to provide speedy hearings after detention was, in effect, the same one I had made as a way of determining loyalty after the evacuation. But our goal, of course, was to eliminate laws authorizing any kind of detention in violation of First Amendment rights.

Kastenmeier, together with Illinois Republican Tom Railsback, wanted to proclaim that no citizen shall be imprisoned or otherwise detained by the United States in situations such as those covered by Title II except pursuant to an act of Congress.

Kastenmeier explained to me that a mandate for prior congressional authorization possibly would not be respected in a national crisis. But, he said, it might cause the president to think about the consequences before acting precipitously. "It might not do much," Kastenmeier said, "but it just might give us time to rally common sense." President Roosevelt in 1942 was not subject to such constraints when he signed Executive Order 9066 and made the evacuation a *fait accompli* before anyone could say "Hold on, let's think about it a minute."

Would anyone have said that? I don't know. The situation in 1942 was altogether different from that of the sixties. A new generation of Americans had become more sensitive to human-rights issues. The presence of Japanese Americans was a reassuring guarantee that Congress would be made aware of minority rights.

The Judiciary Committee accepted Matsunaga's bill incorporating Kastenmeier's thinking. The next battle was in the Rules Committee, which determines whether or when a bill will be considered by the full House, and under what conditions. In this case there were two proposals—Matsunaga's and Ichord's—addressing generally the same subject with each supported by a senior committee chairman. At one point in the deliberations over whether to send one or both bills to the floor, the venerable Congressman Emanuel Celler came out of the committee room to talk to me.

"Mike," he said, "both the Matsunaga and Ichord proposals have strong backing. What do you suggest? Should I continue to fight for the Matsunaga bill? Or do you think we should send both versions to the House and let them take their choice?"

I pleaded that he give Matsunaga one last try.

Fifteen minutes later he emerged, smiling. "Congratulations," he said. "Now it's up to you to get the votes on the House floor."

The story ended happily. The Matsunaga version passed, 356 to 49, on September 14, 1971. Senate Majority Leader Mike Mansfield scheduled early consideration of the House version, and it was accepted without opposition. On September 25, 1971, President Nixon, on his way to meet Emperor Hirohito in Anchorage, Alaska, signed the bill that wiped Title II off the statute books. Many JACLers say with great sincerity that we must make sure the travails of 1942 are never repeated, but few know the whole story of the struggle to include safeguards in addition to simple repeal of Title II.

With extremely few exceptions, my relations with JACL were smooth, although many of the issues we worked on were controversial even within the Japanese American community. There were times, I admit, when I was somewhat ahead of the organization's thinking. At those times it seemed the Washington tail was wagging the JACL dog, and one of them led to my most unpleasant experience involving the organization.

Early in the first Nixon administration, William (Mo) Marumoto, who had grown up in a Los Angeles barrio and spoke Spanish fluently, was named to the White House staff to handle minority affairs. Marumoto was looking for ways to recognize minorities and involve them in government, such as by appointment to important regulatory or oversight bodies as well as to the literally scores of commissions and committees whose duties were mainly honorary. He asked me to suggest some potential candidates. I knew a number of well-qualified Japanese Americans, but obviously there were many, many others I hadn't heard about. I sent a memo to the presidents of JACL's ninety-odd chapters across the country asking them to suggest names and professional backgrounds of Japanese Americans whose talents and qualifications might be of interest to Marumoto but without mentioning either the White House or Marumoto by name.

Shortly afterward I found myself savagely pilloried in a letter to Japanese American newspapers signed by some of the same young activists with whom I had worked on JACL's human-rights campaigns. They charged that I had sold Japanese Americans down the river in 1942 when I urged them to cooperate with the government in the march into concentration camps, and now, they said, I was in the process of betraying them again by gathering information for use by national-security agencies. The charge was so preposterous that at first I was inclined to ignore it as the delusion of sick minds. For the record, let me repeat that detention camps had not entered the

picture when JACL took the position that it was our patriotic duty in
wartime to obey government orders no matter how repugnant. I do
not apologize for having advocated 100 percent Americanism. Japanese Americans in 1942 agreed almost unanimously with JACL's
actions. Hindsight has a remarkable way of sharpening wisdom and
distorting judgments.

The paranoia of some individuals who see conspiracies everywhere, and decades later remain blindly critical of JACL and its
early leadership while ignoring the facts, is deplorable but can be
understood. What upset me most was reference to me in the published letter as a Judas. I could accept being called a Moses leading
his people, if not entirely successfully, in search of the promised
land. But to be likened unto the disciple who betrayed Christ was
intolerable. I considered a lawsuit charging defamation of character,
but was dissuaded by attorney friends who convinced me that nothing was to be gained by going into court against individuals seeking
to overcome their lack of credibility with notoriety.

In the long run, what was damaged most by this attack was not
my reputation but the opportunity for Japanese Americans to gain
recognition on the national level. Marumoto had been hired specifically to find members of minority groups who could help enrich the
American cultural and political tapestry. He had access to the seats
of power. While many Japanese Americans hold important positions
in Washington, Marumoto was with one exception the first to be
named to the White House staff. The exception was Yoichi Okamoto,
who was President Johnson's personal photographer. Marumoto's
efforts were blunted by the Judas controversy. The spite of a small
group destroyed a once-in-a-lifetime opportunity for numerous deserving Japanese Americans.

What little remained of the bad taste in my mouth was eliminated at the 1970 JACL convention in Chicago, when I was honored
at an unforgettable testimonial banquet for my years of service to the
organization. Mother was flown from Los Angeles to share the
limelight. The accolades showered on me that night were elabo-
rately generous; I could not hope to deserve them all if I lived
another lifetime. One I found particularly moving was from Takito
Yamaguma, vice-president of the Bank of Tokyo in California:
"Thousands of my Issei contemporaries feel as I do, but perhaps
cannot adequately express their gratitude and appreciation for your

role in making possible the realization of their lifelong dream of truly becoming a part of America as American citizens.''

The toastmaster was Congressman Matsunaga. Tributes were delivered by Edward J. Ennis, my friend and chairman of the board of the American Civil Liberties Union; Roy Wilkins, chairman of the Leadership Conference on Civil Rights; Congressman Sidney R. Yates of Illinois, representing congressional friends; and U. Alexis Johnson, undersecretary of state, who spoke of my efforts to improve U.S.-Japanese relations. Jerry Enomoto, then president of JACL, presented me with a bulging album of friendship letters. Then Katsuma Mukaeda and Yamaguma gave me tickets and a check, a gift from Issei all over the country, to take Etsu, Midori, and Michael on a leisurely trip around the world.

There was more. Approximately $70,000 had been contributed to establish a Mike M. Masaoka Trust Fund, to be used as I saw fit. My decision was to establish a Distinguished Public Service Award. It would be presented at JACL's biennial conventions ''to an individual or organization, other than Japanese American, that has contributed outstanding and significant public service in (a) promoting friendship, understanding and cooperation with Japan, and/or (b) improving the quality of life for all Americans, and especially those of Japanese ancestry.'' The award was to be $1,000 and a suitable plaque. Dr. Thomas T. Yatabe, one of the founders of JACL, was the first trust-fund chairman. The current chairman is Shigeo Wakamatsu, a former national JACL president and longtime colleague.

Although it wasn't intended to be that way, the award with one exception has gone to American or Japanese diplomats. The first honoree was Prof. Edwin O. Reischauer, the Harvard Japan scholar who also served as ambassador to Japan. An organization, the National Leadership Conference on Civil Rights, was next to be recognized, with Joe Rauh accepting. Then, in order, were U. Alexis Johnson, ambassador to Japan and under secretary of state, who with me helped organize nationally the Associated Japan America Societies; Nobuhiko Ushiba, Japanese ambassador to the United States and Japanese chairman of the Joint U.S.-Japan Economic ''Wisemen's'' Committee, and the first and only cabinet minister for external economic affairs; Mike Mansfield, ambassador to Japan and former U.S. Senate majority leader; Robert Ingersoll, ambassador to Japan, deputy secretary of state, and American chairman of the ''Wisemen's'' Committee; James Day Hodgson, ambassador to Japan, president of the Associated Japan American Societies of the United States; and Yoshio Okawara, Japanese ambassador to the United States, deputy vice-minister of foreign affairs. In 1986 the award went to Philip H. Trezise, former ambassador to the Organization for Economic Cooperation and Development in Paris, and Senior Fellow at the Brookings Institution, who during his tenure as minister for economic affairs at the U.S. embassy in Tokyo helped lay the foundations for Japan's economic recovery.

The gift from our Issei friends enabled my family to take a leisurely trip around the world, which the children helped to plan in detail. I decided we should fly eastward with the thought that after viewing Europe and southeast Asia, Midori and Michael would be able to appreciate their heritage more fully when we reached Japan. We flew to London, then on to Paris, Rome, and Athens. The Asian portion started at New Delhi, with stops at Bangkok, Hong Kong, and Taipei before flying to Tokyo. We were both tourists and explorers, leaving the big cities for the countryside whenever we could. We stayed in a shabby Paris walk-up and a splendid old Japanese inn. We also stopped at some lavish hotels and met important personages. Michael was the family photographer, Midori our interpreter in areas where French was spoken. Midori and Etsu rode on camels, elephants, and water buffaloes, and I tried to keep track of the luggage. We tasted native foods and each of us became ill at one time or another. We visited Kyoto and Hiroshima and I cannot recall how many other Japanese tourist spots. We carried home some great memories, and the conviction that there is no place like home.

After the Chicago convention I gave JACL formal notice that the time had come for me to relinquish the part-time job as Washington representative which I had accepted in 1952. I set 1972 as the date for my departure and urged JACL to name my successor without delay so that I could spend as much as possible of my two remaining years to help my successor learn about the intricacies of Washington. These were hard and priceless lessons I had learned in six years as a full-time JACL employee, and twenty years as consultant and watchdog when I was being retained for what amounted to virtually full-time work.

After more than a quarter century, the time was opportune for severing JACL ties. For one thing, my Japanese business was keeping me as busy as I wanted to be. For another, the times and JACL were changing. Sansei, members of the third generation, were moving into leadership roles at national and local chapter levels, advocating a level of activism that made people of my generation uncomfortable. It seemed only proper that a younger person take over the watch on the Potomac.

Chapter 19
Redress

JACL's choice as my successor in Washington was a remarkably talented young man named David Ushio. More accurately, he was my choice. The organization selected several candidates and left the final decision to me. Ushio, coincidentally, was Utah-born and the son of my boyhood friend Shake. He had spent two and a half years in Japan as a Mormon missionary. He had received his degree in political science from Brigham Young University, was familiar with JACL through his father, and was looking for a job when the Washington position was brought to his attention.

Ushio was energetic, aggressive, smart, a self-starting, take-charge sort of youngster. He had no shortage of ideas. He proved he was a quick learner while helping me in the final phases of the campaign to repeal Title II.

He was also impatient and ambitious. Not many months after Ushio came to Washington, Mas Satow announced his intention to retire as national director on his sixty-fifth birthday, February 14, 1973. Without consulting me, Ushio applied for Satow's job. When we got around to talking about it, Ushio said it appeared Satow's successor would be either a caretaker type or a radical activist. He said he didn't like the prospect of working for either kind of boss and decided to seek the directorship himself.

I urged Ushio to stay in Washington, where after a few more years of experience he would be in a position to move into some promising government job if he wished, or perhaps find a place in my organization. I warned him of the danger of getting cut up in JACL's internal politics and the burden he would face in converting Satow's comfortable mom and pop style of operation to meet the demands of the computer age. Ushio was not one to be dissuaded. When word got out, his candidacy was bitterly opposed by a young activist group in JACL's Los Angeles office, where posters of Ho Chi Minh, Che Guevara, the Black Panthers, and Cesar Chavez, anathema to conservative Nisei farmers in California's Central Valley, were displayed.

JACL's personnel committee voted 4 to 3 to hire Ushio, and after acrimonious debate the National Council meeting at the 1972 convention in Washington confirmed the appointment. The Los Angeles staff promptly resigned. Since Ushio had been my protégé, so to speak, and he had chosen not to follow my advice, I was careful to steer clear of the controversy.

Ushio took over as national director in San Francisco early in 1973. He ran the office with a firm, aggressive hand, which undoubtedly the organization needed. My part-time employment by JACL had terminated at the end of 1972. With a strong director at headquarters and no representation in Washington for the first time since 1946, the focal point of JACL activity moved to San Francisco. Ushio had declared his independence and adopted a high profile, and my influence in the organization diminished abruptly. Unfortunately, many of the internal problems of which I had warned Ushio surfaced quickly. With every good intention, he tried to broaden JACL's concerns. Inevitably his version of the great leap forward alarmed the conservatives and provoked the activists. He resigned in September 1976 after three and a half turbulent years to take a position in Jimmy Carter's presidential campaign.

Let me emphasize that I initiated the ending of business ties with JACL; there was no effort to push me out the door although a small but vocal faction indicated I was out of step with the new times. But in their view, so was everyone except themselves. I harbored no sense of rejection as JACL forged on in new directions with my best wishes. From my point of view, the big battles had been fought and won and strong foundations were now in place. Many of my comrades in those battles—members of JACL, members of Congress, and others deeply concerned with human rights— had died or gone on to other interests. There was an entirely new generation in Congress unfamiliar with Japanese-American history. I found it tedious, even ridiculous, to have to educate young legislators on the anti-alien land laws, barriers to citizenship, and even the evacuation when I went to talk to them about current Japanese-American issues. Undoubtedly the generation gap was showing. I was embarrassed when I was asked to invite members of Congress to JACL functions, and found later that they had not been given the courtesies that were standard in a more gracious time, such as being met and escorted to their tables. The issues that preoccupied the new JACL leadership, an Asian-American coalition, for example, and bilingual education, didn't arouse my enthusiasm. I felt I had other important matters to tend to, like doing everything possible to solidify relations between the United States and Japan.

Severance of formal ties with JACL freed me to register as a foreign agent and represent Japanese commercial interests more actively. The term "foreign agent" has an unfortunately sinister ring to it. It has absolutely nothing to do with espionage. It simply means that one is representing the legitimate interests of a foreign firm. Many of Washington's most prestigious law offices and public-relations agencies are registered as agents of foreign corporations. In my case, most of the work with Japanese companies involved providing them with specialized information about the status of federal and state legislation and regulations, and commenting on political moods and prospects. If a particular proposal affected a client, we would see that his point of view was presented to the decision-makers.

This involved close contact with the Washington bureaucracy as well as with members of Congress and the White House staff. The election of Japanese Americans to Congress made my work a little easier, but not in the sense that one might expect. Not once have I ever asked them to introduce a bill, or take sides on an issue, that might embarrass them. I believe their greatest asset as members of Congress is their credibility, and I made certain not to do anything to jeopardize it. Many of the bills beneficial to Japan in which I had a hand were introduced at my request by other than the Japanese Americans. It was not that these bills were "bad." I simply wanted to avoid any possibility of a controversy because of racial links. In an ideal world there should be no fear of such controversy, but we have not reached that state and it was simple wisdom not to take chances.

Nisei on the mainland, being younger on the whole than those in Hawaii, were slower to get into politics. I noted with satisfaction that Etsu's little brother Norman, the one I used to bribe with quarters to leave us alone while I was courting her, was taking a lively interest in Democratic politics. He became a member of the San Jose, California, city council in 1967, then served successively as vice-mayor and mayor. He made such a good record that he was elected to Congress from California's Thirteenth District in 1974 to succeed a Republican who was retiring.

Mineta was joined in Congress in 1978 by Robert T. Matsui, Democrat, representing California's Third District which is mainly the city of Sacramento. Matsui, a Sansei, was less than three months old at the time of Pearl Harbor, less than a year old when his family was evacuated. He is an attorney and was a Sacramento city councilman for eight years before running for Congress. He understands virtually no Japanese, while the others are fairly fluent.

The first Japanese American Republican to be elected to Congress was Senator Samuel Ichiye Hayakawa, born in Canada but naturalized after passage of the Walter-McCarran bill. Hayakawa is a renowned semanticist who became a popular American hero when, as president of San Francisco State University, he courageously put down unruly student demonstrations that had virtually taken over the campus. Riding on the wave of that popularity, he ran for the Senate in 1976 and received 3,748, 973 votes, defeating the favored John Tunney by almost a quarter million votes. This was a remarkable showing in a state that for generations had been the fountainhead of anti-Orientalism. Older and more conservative Japanese Americans supported Hayakawa; young liberals were vigorously hostile. Hayakawa was seventy-six years old when his term ended and he did not run for a second term.

In 1986 Patricia Saiki overcame Hawaii's strong Democratic tilt to become that state's first Republican member of the U.S. House and the second Japanese American Republican elected to Congress. A veteran of fourteen years' service in the state legislature, she quickly demonstrated that she will become an important lawmaker. I look forward to knowing her better.

My work brought me in close contact with the earlier Japanese American members of Congress, and I got to know them well. The four incumbent veterans are highly regarded by their colleagues and have established admirable records for intelligence, diligence, and statesmanship.

Inouye as a party loyalist is not only respected by the Democratic leadership, but is part of that leadership. He is inclined to take the broad, national view of issues. Matsunaga, on the other hand, frequently has concerned himself with matters affecting Japanese Americans primarily. (Some of his opponents have referred to him as the senator from Japan.) In a general sense, Mineta's stance is closer to that of Matsunaga while Matsui is more like Inouye.

This is not to deny the broad-gauge, statesmanlike position all four have taken on national issues, nor to downplay their concern for Japanese Americans. They have been elected by a wide cross section of their constituencies—less than one third of the voters in Hawaii are Japanese Americans, and they are an infinitesimal minority in the districts represented by Mineta and Matsui—to speak for them on a wide range of issues. In a less sensitive time, writers used to say of heavyweight champion Joe Louis that he was "a credit to his people." Inouye, Matsunaga, Mineta, and Matsui are a credit to Congress, and to the people of the United States.

Kinship has not given me any special political advantage with Congressman Mineta except for access to his staff. To the contrary, I have gone out of my way to avoid any appearance of special treatment. However, the Minetas are a close-knit clan, and we see each other not infrequently. I encouraged Norman's early interest in politics, have campaigned for him, and vicariously enjoyed his development. In my Utah youth I had vague thoughts of going into politics, but circumstances ended that idea. I have never tried to influence Norman's political thinking, but we have had many long, philosophical talks about government that I think benefited both of us.

Even as members of Congress, Nisei have been victims of the widespread perception that Asians aren't really Americans. Norman has been asked whom he was representing, the Japanese or the Americans, when a transportation subcommittee hearing he was conducting got into a discussion on the superiority of Japanese subway cars. At a White House dinner for a top-level Japanese delegation, Senator Matsunaga and his wife found themselves being ushered by Secretary of State Alexander Haig into an anteroom reserved for Japanese guests. Senator Inouye seldom suffers such misidentification. The prosthesis in place of the right arm he lost in battle is familiar.

I'm particularly fond of a story about Norman that is the flip side of racial stereotyping. President Carter was entertaining Japanese Prime Minister Masayoshi Ohira at the White House. Congressman Mineta thought he might get an invitation, but it didn't arrive. Then on the afternoon of the dinner a frantic social secretary called with apologies and asked Congressman and Mrs. Mineta to attend. Mineta declined. What had happened was that the White House staff had assumed Mineta was of Italian ancestry. When a newspaperman asked Mineta why he hadn't accepted the tardy invitation, he replied: "Oh, I thought Ohira was Irish."

My children, Midori and Michael, grew up in a stimulating environment. Etsu and I often discussed my work and issues of the day over the dinner table. Important Americans and Japanese were entertained in our home. And, as sometimes happens, some of them would shake hands with the children, ask how they were doing in school, and say without thinking that they expected them to be as important as their father when they grew up.

This expression of expectation was something Etsu and I tried hard to avoid. We didn't want to put an undue burden on the children. I had experienced the same problem from another angle in my youth. Family friends would urge my brothers and sisters to study hard and get to be like Mike. My siblings were uncomfortable about comparisons with me, and I didn't like it, but fortunately they learned to live with the knowledge that we are all different.

Etsu and I tried to teach our children that each of us was an individual, that they were different from Etsu and me and from each other. We had different likes and dislikes, different interests and aptitudes, different ways of thinking and doing things, and one wasn't necessarily better or worse than another. For Midori, studies and sports and almost everything else came easily. She was outgoing. Michael had to work hard for his many achievements, and, if anything, we were more proud of his accomplishments because we knew of the effort he had put in.

Midori attended Northwestern University, married Richard Amano of Chicago in 1975, transferred to the University of Pennsylvania and completed her undergraduate work in two years instead of the usual three. She returned to Northwestern and earned a law degree. While her husband was developing a real-estate brokerage, Midori went into private practice. A daughter, Michelle Yoshiko, was born in 1979 and Midori went to work as an attorney for the Small Business Administration so she could have regular hours. Michelle had a striking resemblance to her mother. When Michelle reached school age, the family moved to Washington, where Midori continued to work for SBA. They found an apartment near our home and Michelle attended the same school her mother had. Midori died unexpectedly in the summer of 1986. Etsu and I have never been more devastated.

Michael attended the University of Maryland. Much to his and our delight he made the dean's list in his freshman year. But the early seventies were difficult times for students. Caught up in the turmoil, Michael decided he wanted to leave school and try to find his identity. After spending several years in the Los Angeles area trying to find his niche in life, seven months after Midori's untimely death, Michael also passed away suddenly. While Etsu and I continue to wonder why this double tragedy and the incomprehensible waste of talented young lives, we never have regretted that we adopted them, appreciating how much they enriched our lives and gave us so many happy memories over the three decades they spent with us. I will never forget the time, for instance, when Michael, usually mild-mannered and undemonstrative, clenched his fists and threatened to "beat the hell" out of one of my critics. His support meant more to me than he ever knew.

My larger family also was diminishing. Mother died in 1978 in a Los Angeles nursing home at age ninety-three. When the end was near, I flew out from Washington. Tad, Ike, and Shinko were with us for our last prayers with her. Her mind was clear to the end. She had lived a long, hard, and eventful life. In her way she had helped to build the West and to break down discriminatory barriers. But her greatest monument was the young family she kept together after she was widowed. "Be good to Etsu," she whispered. "She is good wife for you."

Mother asked to be buried in the family plot in Green Hills Memorial Park, overlooking San Pedro harbor. Decades earlier, when the cemetery was opened and plots were being sold through Japanese churches, Mother had insisted that Ike and Hank purchase a site. My eldest brother, Joe, who had encouraged me to stay in college, died in 1970 just before the memorable JACL convention in Chicago and was first to be buried there. He was followed by Ike's wife, Sumi Andow, and then by Iwao Hank, the former paratrooper, in 1976. Father's remains were brought from the cemetery in Salt Lake City and reinterred there. At Mother's bedside we surviving sons agreed that all of us, and our spouses if they wished, would be buried in the Masaoka plot.

Ike, with whom I had shared a bed in boyhood, never recovered fully from his war wounds and died in 1984. Ben Frank, the best man at my wedding, had died in the war. Of the six Masaoka boys, only Tad, the youngest, and I are left. Tad works for the federal Department of Housing and Urban Development in San Francisco, California. My sisters, Shinko Masaoka Nakano and Kiyoko Masaoka Ito, neither in the best of health, live in quiet retirement with their husbands. During the past decade or so, "baby brother" Tad, compassionate and helpful, has voluntarily taken over as "head of the family" and performed far more adequately than I ever could. Every year, he has somehow managed to get away to visit me and to do the repairs and chores around the house I never did, took care of Mother in her final illness, was with Ike in his difficult death agonies, sympathized in our grief over the accidents that took both our children, all the while being a good husband and the splendid father of three admirable children and five grandchildren.

At its 1978 convention, JACL voted to make redress for the injustice, humiliation, and material losses of the evacuation its next organizational goal. Originally called "reparations," the issue had been bubbling for a decade. As a matter of fact, compensation for evacuation losses had been discussed first in 1946. That had been followed by the Evacuation Claims Act, which was a measure to recompense the evacuees for actual material losses. But nothing more was done about seeking damages for the injustice of the evacuation until younger Japanese Americans, some born years after the event, began to push it as the only fitting final chapter to the drama. One goal of the redress campaign approved at the convention was "to remind our nation of the need for continued vigilance and to render less likely the recurrence of similar injustice." I could endorse that kind of objective without reservation.

To make the cost of such a campaign more immediately palatable to the membership, JACL leaders emphasized another goal— to demand $25,000 from the federal government for everyone caught up in the evacuation. I had spent nearly four decades of my life in fighting injustice and making sure something as morally and legally repugnant as the evacuation would never again occur. But the thought of setting a price on the priceless sacrifice of freedom was distasteful. Somehow the whole idea of seeking individual monetary recompense for a sacrifice we had accepted in a time of war was disturbing. I would have much preferred to see JACL's limited resources devoted to getting a reversal of the Supreme Court decisions legalizing the evacuation. In thinking back over the evacuation and its long-term impact on the United States, I was haunted by the poignant warning in Justice Robert H. Jackson's dissent, which will bear repetition so long as men revere law:

> I cannot say, from any evidence before me, that the orders of General DeWitt were not reasonably expedient military precautions, nor could I say that they were. But even if they were permissible military procedures, I deny that it follows that they are Constitutional. If, as the Court holds, it does follow, then we may as well say that any military order will be Constitutional and have done with it. . . . A military order, however unconstitutional, is not apt to last longer than the military emergency. Even during that period a succeeding commander may revoke it all. But once a judicial opinion rationalizes such an order to show that it conforms to the Constitution, or rather rationalizes the Constitution to show that the Constitution sanctions such an order, the Court for all time has validated the principle of racial discrimination in criminal procedure and of transplanting American citizens. The principle then lies about like a loaded weapon ready for the hand of any authority that can bring forward a plausible claim of an urgent need. . . . A military commander may overstep the bounds of constitutionality, and it is an incident. But if we review and approve, that passing incident becomes the doctrine of the Constitution. . . .

Since that time, the *coram nobis* lawsuits filed by volunteer teams of young attorneys on behalf of Gordon Hirabayashi, Fred Korematsu, and Minoru Yasui, have addressed the court issue. They contend that official documents uncovered under the Freedom of Information Act show that government lawyers concealed pertinent information in the original trials and thus adversely affected the outcome. I was also concerned that redress might become a full-blown controversy into which U.S.-Japan relations might be drawn just at a time when trade and other problems were making them difficult. I felt JACL's insistence on individual monetary redress was futile, not only because most of the individuals who suffered financial loss would be dead and gone by the time Congress acted, but also because the demand might frustrate realization of the movement's other goals. I believed that the evacuation was a collective crime against a group, and that compensation should primarily benefit the group through community projects, homes for the elderly, and the like. One additional point bothered me as a matter of strategy. It seemed JACL was setting up heavy odds against itself in making a frontal demand on Congress for nearly $3 billion—that's what would have been involved on the basis of $25,000 per person for the 115,000 evacuees.

Senator Inouye came up with a proposal resolving that last problem, which I endorsed fully. He suggested asking Congress to establish a fact-finding commission to investigate the circumstances that led to the evacuation, and giving the commission the responsibility of recommending appropriate redress if any. Kaz Oshiki, behind-the-scenes veteran of congressional battles, pointed out that redress would have a much better chance of success if it had the backing of distinguished Americans. It made sense to put the onus of proving our case on an impartial creature of Congress. Besides, the commission would provide the first real opportunity to dig into the thinking, the pressures, and the decision-making surrounding the evaluation. The commission proposal eased some of my concerns and I felt the need to become involved in redress for two primary reasons—to make a contribution to the resolution of issues in which I had been involved for so long, and to make certain my input would be included in the record. It's a measure of the extremism among some JACLers that Inouye's proposal was criticized as a ploy to avoid the main issue, which they contended was $25,000 cash on the barrelhead. Senators Inouye, Matsunaga, and Hayakawa and Congressmen Mineta and Matsui were among sponsors of the bills authorizing the Commission on Wartime Relocation and Internment of Civilians. Hayakawa, who had opposed the redress movement, said he supported the commission "because a thorough look at the facts is long overdue."

The bill was approved without incident in the Senate and passed 297 to 109 in the House. That 109 members of the House would vote against a proposal to ascertain the facts of history indicated problems ahead for redress. In signing the measure President Carter said:

> It is designed to expose clearly what has happened in that period of war in our nation when many loyal American citizens of Japanese descent were embarrassed during a crucial time in our nation's history. I don't believe anyone would doubt that injustices were done and I don't think anyone would doubt that it is advisable now for us to have a clear understanding as Americans of this episode in the history of our country. . . .

The outlook of the commission was pretty well determined when President Carter named as presidential members Dr. Arthur S. Flemming, chairman of the U.S. Commission of Civil Rights; Joan Bernstein, former general counsel of the Department of Health and Human Services; and Judge William Marutani of the Philadelphia Court of Common Pleas. The three Senate appointees included a former U.S. senator from Massachusetts, Edward W. Brooke, who was both a black and a Republican. The House appointees included Arthur J. Goldberg, former U.S. Supreme Court justice, former secretary of labor, and U.S. ambassador to the United Nations.

JACL played an active role in lining up witnesses to appear before the commission, but, perhaps in view of my earlier lack of enthusiasm, perhaps because I was a stranger to most of the organization's new inner circle. I didn't figure in their plans. At this point, Go for Broke, Inc., the national Nisei veterans' organization headquartered in San Francisco, asked me to help with its presentation. In a sense, this was a logical progression in my association with the buddies I had urged into battle. Now I would have a role in seeing that their sacrifice would not go unrecognized. I testified on their behalf both before the commission and in hearings on HR 442, the bill to carry out the commission's recommendations for redress.

The commission's hearings proved to be a long-overdue cathartic. Many Nisei had not hesitated to express their feelings about the evacuation experience, but others had kept their anger repressed for decades. Urged to speak by commissioners who indicated that they cared, witness after witness released the unforgotten frustration and humiliation in torrents of emotional testimony.

Chairwoman Bernstein had announced that the hearings would

not be an inquisition or trial, but a fact-finding mission to learn where and how the protections of the law had failed. Nonetheless one witness who had never been evacuated falsely charged that Masaoka and JACL had created the loyalty oath and persuaded WRA to set up segregation camps for those who failed it. This led Judge Marutani to decry "vicious and at times irresponsible and reckless attacks" on fellow ethnic members, an action he aptly described as "ethnic hara-kiri."

John J. McCloy came under considerable criticism when he testified that he thought the evacuation was "reasonably undertaken and thoughtful and humanely conducted," and that the program was "carried out in accordance with the best interests of the country considering the conditions, exigencies and considerations which then faced the nation." In other words, he said he and others involved were doing what they thought was best for their country—our country—in a time of peril.

This and other testimony confirmed what I have long felt: the evacuation was not due to military necessity, nor was it an intentionally malicious act. It was the result of ignorance about our minority, insensitivity about racial differences within the American mosaic, and a total lack of attention to the democratic safeguards embodied in the Bill of Rights when applied to what was perceived as lesser citizens.

The commission put it another way. After denying military conditions were involved, it said that "the broad historical causes which shaped these decisions were race prejudice, war hysteria and a failure of political leadership."

The Bernstein Commission's hearings led to an excellent, thoroughly documented report titled *Personal Justice Denied*. I commend it for your reading. The commission came up with a number of recommendations:

- It recommended that Congress pass a joint resolution, to be signed by the president, acknowledging that a grave injustice had been done to Japanese Americans and offering the nation's apologies.
- It recommended a presidential pardon for all those convicted of violating curfew and evacuation orders, and of convictions based on refusal to accept treatment that discriminated on the basis of race or ethnicity.

- It recommended review of any remaining complaints of inequity in entitlements due to the wartime detention.
- It recommended that Congress appropriate funds for humanitarian, research, and public-educational activities so that the events surrounding the evacuation will be remembered.
- With the exception of one member, Congressman Dan Lundgren, it recommended that Congress appropriate $1.5 billion to be used to provide compensation of $20,000 to each of the approximately 60,000 surviving evacuees, with the balance of the fund being used for the activities covered in the previous item.

The fund would be administered by a board whose majority would be Japanese Americans appointed by the president and confirmed by the Senate.

Since I now have no reservations about individual payments, which are likely to prove a formidable barrier to congressional approval, I feel these to be worthy recommendations. A House bill, HR 442, was drawn up to implement the proposals, and JACL has succeeded in getting more than 135 congressmen to co-sponsor it. Almost single-handedly, Senator Matsunaga has persuaded 71 of his colleagues to join in co-sponsoring S 1009, companion to HR 442. A number of others have indicated they endorse everything about the bill except the individual payments. JACL contends strongly that monetary compensation for damages is the "American way," that apologies are easy to make but the real impact of this historical tragedy will not be felt unless substantial money is involved.

I look on the $20,000 as a worthy solatium rather than indemnification, a solatium to express the regrets of our fellow Americans over a national wrong. However, there is precedent for compensation for loss of individual freedom on a mass scale. The War Claims Act compensated American civilians $60 for each month they were held prisoner by Japanese armed forces during World War II. The coverage was extended to American civilians held by North Koreans, and the compensation raised to $150 monthly for those held by Communist forces in Southeast Asia.

Law Researcher John Nakahata makes this trenchant observation: "Because Japanese American citizens have never been compensated for their losses of bodily freedom, they are, ironically, in a worse position than if they had been detained by the enemy. Had a Japanese American been interned by the Imperial Japanese government after the outbreak of war, for instance, he could have been compensated [by the United States] for the loss of bodily freedom under the American War Claims Act. As an American citizen, however, who was incarcerated in the United States by the U.S. government in contravention to the protections enunciated in the Bill of Rights, he has yet to have his injury financially acknowledged by the U.S. government.''

More recently, during Vietnam War protests in Washington, D.C., in 1971, some 7,000 protestors were confined behind fences in Robert J. Kennedy Stadium for up to four days. A district court awarded damages of $2 million and payments ranging from $50 to $1,800 were made to some 1,200 protesters for illegal deprivation of freedom. In 1942, we were cooperating with the government's war effort, not opposing it, when we were imprisoned. Additionally to the point, in 1968 when we faced budgetary and fiscal constraints, Congress approved legislation to provide extra compensation to American civil servants and military who were hostages and/or victims of Middle East terrorism.

After studying the precedents in law and practice involving monetary compensation as substitutionary relief for damages or other grievances against government, I am now convinced that individual redress in the token amount of $20,000 per living evacuee is more than justified, particularly considering the conservative recommendations of the commission. Moreover, I am now persuaded that monetary restitution may well establish a beneficial and precautionary precedent for the future by requiring justifications for arbitrary actions and making the price for such transgressions so expensive and costly that no official or agency can afford to be stampeded as they were in our case in 1942 to authorize the deprivations of our rights, privileges, and immunities as citizens. No one had to explain or justify ''military necessity.'' No one had to consider the impact on us, the victims. And no one had to determine or even estimate the amount that would be due us for the denial of basic, constitutional rights. If money talks, and I think it does, we should make the price of racial discrimination, prejudice, and bigotry so high none can afford to indulge in it.

Remember, in our instance, the commission proposes compensation not for victims of foreign governments but for American citizens victimized by our own government. Certainly justice is on our side. But justice delayed remains justice denied.

Finally, I would add the recommendation of Eugene Rostow of the National Defense University, formerly dean of the Yale School of Law, to amend the National Apology suggestion with an amendment petitioning the Supreme Court to review and reverse its totally discredited decisions in the so-called evacuation test cases at its first opportunity.

But while money may be a major stumbling block in these austere times, friends in Congress have warned that the apology may be an even larger problem. At least three presidents—Harry Truman, Gerald Ford, and Jimmy Carter—have expressed regret at various times that the injustice of the evacuation was allowed to take place. It may be difficult to persuade Congress, which is habitually critical of the administration, to admit officially that the government of the United States did wrong in what was perceived to be defense of the country in time of war. To have HR 442 and S 1009 die on this point would be an enormous tragedy.

In this, the 100th Congress, in the Bicentennial Commemoration of the Constitution of the United States and its Bill of Rights, this would be the most appropriate year ever to redress our grievances of World War II, which constitute grim and melancholy reminders of the most flagrant and gross abuse and violations of our Federal Charter since the Civil War more than a century ago. This is the year for the Congress, the administration, and the people to "Go For Broke" to demonstrate that the Constitution is still a living document by enacting HR 442 and S 1009 into law.

Chapter 20

In Business

At the time I first visited Japan, Dentsu, the giant Japanese advertising agency was headed by charismatic, energetic, visionary Hideo Yoshida. I met him again when he came to Washington with his Nisei interpreter, George Yoshioka. At dinner one night Yoshida came up with a fascinating idea. Dentsu would open a liberally staffed and financed Washington office to handle advertising, public, and government relations for any Japanese firm interested in exploring the then unfamiliar American market, and for any American firm interested in doing business in Japan. Yoshida invited me to head this operation. We discussed this idea at a number of subsequent meetings with growing enthusiasm. I saw no reason why it wouldn't work.

Despite his commitment to the scheme Yoshida was unable to sell it to his directors before his untimely death in the early sixties. His colleagues felt his plans were too grandiose, premature, and costly. Dentsu did establish a New York agency some years later and I was among the founding directors. Our single most ambitious effort was a thirty-two page rotogravure supplement, titled *Japan Salutes America on Its Bicentennial*. It carried a message of friendship and good will and twenty million copies were distributed July 4, 1976, with the *New York Times, Washington Post, Chicago Tribune, Houston Post, Denver Post, San Francisco Examiner and Chronicle, Los Angeles Times,* and *Honolulu Star-Bulletin and Advertiser*. While Dentsu sold the advertising to Japanese firms, I had a hand in assembling the editorial material, contracting for the printing, and arranging the distribution. If Yoshida's concept of a superagency had been developed, it is likely U.S.-Japan trade would have taken a different and smoother course since he was committed to building trade in both directions. It certainly would have altered my plans.

My first substantial Japanese client was the Japan Cotton Spinners Association headed by Yasuo Tawa. General MacArthur's headquarters had encouraged early revival of the textile industry as a means of supplying Japanese and other East Asian needs, to help meet the American demand for inexpensive fabrics, to provide a source of foreign exchange so that Japan could pay for purchases of American goods, and to provide a market for the chronic U.S. surplus of raw cotton.

All these objectives were being met, Tawa said, but he explained in some bewilderment that there was growing opposition in the United States toward imports of Japanese fabrics. There was no rational economic reason for this. My research showed that the Japanese share of the American market was infinitesimal. Japanese textile imports compared to domestic American production was 0.56 percent in 1953, 0.67 percent in 1954, 1.17 percent in 1955, and reached a high of 1.7 percent in 1956. That year, according to figures from the American Cotton Textile Manufacturers Association, U.S. output was 11,592 million square yards. Total imports from all countries amounted to only 188 million square yards, of which Japan's share was 75 percent. Further, said Tawa, the value of Japanese cotton goods entering the United States was less than one-tenth the value of the raw cotton Japan was buying from American farmers.

Until this time I had assumed cotton cloth was simply cotton cloth. As I dug into the problem of developing quota restraints, I discovered there were different restrictions for categories and subcategories such as piece goods, household goods, wearing apparel, and knit goods, that there were such things as gray (unfinished) goods, and finished fabrics such as ginghams, velveteens, poplins, percales, chambrays, voiles, sateens, all covered by different regulations. Later, as many different kinds of synthetic fibers were developed and blended with natural fibers, the regulations became even more complex.

Early on, I realized that if I was to be of use to Tawa, I needed to educate myself. I gathered every book and report I could find on textile matters and read them all. I visited mills in the South and talked to workers and townspeople to learn their problems. I discovered state restrictions such as a legislation requiring retailers to announce in "plain, fully visible" window signs that they were dealing in Japanese textiles.

Since much of the protectionist arguments were based on old stereotypes and exaggerated fears, one of our first moves was to establish an information center to publish a newsletter and distribute fact sheets. Not coincidentally, it was called the Japan United States Textile Information Service (JUSTIS).

Meanwhile, I became acquainted with the amiable Robert L. Jackson, executive vice president of the American Textile Manufacturers Institute, who was spearheading the drive against Japanese goods. We were to become friendly competitors. Jackson had been sent to help Japan rebuild its spinning industry and had many friends there. One day he confided that his mission had erred in helping Japan to develop an industry geared to supply Americans rather than the needs of undeveloped East Asian nations. When I cited figures about Japan's tiny share of the American market, he said he was more concerned with the Japanese potential rather than current sales.

To limit imports from Japan, the U.S. textile industry sought "voluntary" curbs. Meanwhile, Secretary of State John Foster Dulles announced he had advised Japan to "exercise restraint" in textile exports and not attempt to capture so much of the U.S. market that the industry would be injured.

This was the beginning of the so-called textile wars, which have continued to this day. The first skirmish was conceded by the Japanese in May 1956, when Japan agreed to quotas on shipments of velveteens, ginghams, and dollar (cheap) blouses. None of this made sense to me and I told my Japanese employers as much. Velveteens were produced by a single American company and most of the supply was being imported from Italy. Even though the bulk of U.S. gingham was being manufactured in inefficient old mills, Japanese imports totaled only a small percentage of the supply. As for the dollar blouses, American importers had anticipated a market for colorful and inexpensive wear, but I felt, rightly as it turned out, the demand would fall off as consumers moved into higher-quality merchandise.

From the beginning I advised the Japanese that quotas were disadvantageous, but I had to go along when the government decided to accept them rather than face the possibility of restrictive legislation.

Kojiro Abe, the chairman of the Japan Cotton Spinners Association, explained the industry's position: "We did this [accepted the quotas], not as an admission of the validity of the charges made against us, but in the spirit that even though our industry might suffer materially, the international friendship and comity involved between our two nations transcended the problem of any single industry, no matter how vital to Japan."

Sadly, the goodwill was not reciprocated by Americans. There seemed to be no end to U.S. demands for restrictions. These demands were particularly unfair since the balance of payments was heavily in favor of the United States at that point in history. In 1956, according to Commerce Department figures, U.S. exports to Japan totaled $998 million compared to $558 million in imports from Japan. Not until 1965—nine years later—did Japan show a trade surplus. Trade has increased steadily since then, and so has Japan's favorable balance despite continued restrictions.

I had warned my textile clients that if they gave up any part of their market share, it wouldn't be American mills with their Civil War era equipment that would fill the void. American buyers would go to other sources such as Hong Kong, South Korea, Taiwan, Malaysia, even Africa, for their merchandise. Japanese cotton textile exports to the United States were $84.1 million in 1956; by 1960 they had dropped to $74.1 million. But in that same period imports from Hong Kong rose from virtually nothing to $63.5 million. I took no pleasure in seeing my prediction come true. Compared to the 75 percent share of the import market it had at the time quotas were imposed, Japan's share today is about 8 percent.

Japanese acceptance of quotas signaled weakness. American producers quickly applied to the Tariff Commission for "escape clause" relief for a variety of products ranging from cotton typewriter ribbons to Wilton carpets. I represented Japanese exporters in many of the quasi-legal commission hearings, demonstrating that imports from Japan were not the major cause of the problem. Manmade fabrics such as nylon and new uses for plastics and paper were moving in on an inefficient American industry. As the maneuvering became more legalistic, technical, and complex, requiring the skills of attorneys and industry experts, I withdrew from the pleadings, limiting my work to preparation of data to be submitted to the trade commission.

The fact that the U.S. textile industry achieved its goals politically through bilateral agreements after failing to win administrative relief within existing law is of utmost significance. I advised my clients that quota restrictions were an insidious way in which Japan was called upon to penalize itself, that they violated not only the principles of free trade to which the United States was committed but also international agreements to which both were partners. Once the principle of quotas was accepted for any item, it tended to be extended to other products. This led inevitably to cheating American consumers by restricting their choices and increasing prices.

By the end of the Eisenhower administration in 1960, nineteen industries in addition to the bellwether cotton lobby had secured restraints against Japan. The products included such varied items as frozen tuna, plywood, wood screws, clinical thermometers, stainless-steel flatware, umbrellas, porcelain and earthenware dinner sets, silk scarves and mufflers, woolen hooked rugs, and paper cups. Many of my friends in the federal government were embarrassed to explain how such restrictions were justified. Subsequently, steel, color television sets, and automobiles were among the big-ticket items placed under quotas. I will have more to say about this later in this chapter. In my opinion, practically all the restrictions were agreed to by the Japanese in the spirit of goodwill enunciated by Kojiro Abe.

However, the most costly result of trade restrictions is the damage it does to domestic industry. While saving a few jobs temporarily, quotas become a crutch for unimaginative management. Sheltered from competition, the operators have little incentive to replace obsolete plants and equipment. Protectionism inhibits competition and innovation.

I know that I irritated many Tokyo officials by insisting it should not be taken for granted that any president would sign protectionist legislation even if Congress passed it. Apparently neither Japanese government nor industry wanted to gamble, preferring to believe a bird in the hand is worth two in the bush. In their negotiations the Japanese were at a disadvantage since they were represented by bureaucrats and career diplomats, while the United States team included hardheaded businessmen and specialists. Additionally, since Japan was the "seller" and America the "buyer," the preponderance of bargaining power was in U.S. hands.

Ironically, even as one arm of the Eisenhower administration was trying to block Japanese textiles, the government was arranging for the Export-Import Bank to loan the Japanese millions of dollars annually to purchase American cotton. Export-Import Bank loans were designed to spur sale abroad of expensive manufactured items, such as aircraft. A special interpretation, in which I had a part, had to be arranged to cover sales of an agricultural product like cotton. Japan purchased millions of bales of cotton, usually at more than the world price, with U.S. loans, repaying every cent with interest, until the program was killed during the Carter administration.

Noting developments south of the border, Canada soon sought similar protectionist measures against both Japanese and American textiles. The Japanese retained me to appear before the Canadian Board of Tariffs in Ottawa. This time the United States was in the position of trying to maintain an open market. I found myself co-operating with representatives of the mammoth U.S. industry, which sometimes dumped more surplus textiles in Canada in less than a single week than the Japanese exported in an entire year.

Despite their ability to flood the Canadian market, it was obvious that American mills were badly in need of modernizing. Philosophically, I could defend temporary restrictions on Japanese goods if Americans took advantage of the respite to update their plants. To ensure that this would be done, I came up with a proposal that when the two countries agreed quota protection was necessary, the quotas be linked to a firm, supervised timetable for plant improvement. Under this plan a textile mill or steel plant would be given five years, for example, to make its facilities competitive, after which presumably it would no longer need or deserve protection. The Japanese agreed this was a good idea in principle, but deferring to the idea that it was better not to interfere with another nation's domestic policy, declined to use it as a bargaining chip. Americans I talked to said they saw no reason to bring it up so long as the Japanese did not. So an idea that might have enabled U.S. industries to reconstruct their plants died aborning.

American Big Steel, for one, saw no merit whatever in the proposal to modernize. The mill operators were more concerned with paying quarterly dividends to stockholders than investing profits in plant improvement. The result was that steelmakers overseas—first in war-devastated Europe and Japan, then in Korea, Taiwan, Brazil, and India—built new automated mills employing techniques that, even discounting lower labor costs, could produce steel far more cheaply than the antiquated American mills. Big Steel ultimately signaled defeat by diverting capital into buying businesses unconnected with steel.

Japan revealed its vulnerability again in later negotiations over a sweeping pact called the Multi Fiber Agreement (MFA). In response to industry objections, both houses of the Japanese Diet adopted a resolution against acceptance of the MFA. The United States then countered by linking the solution of a highly sensitive Japanese political issue, the reversion of Okinawa and other Ryukyu islands, to the MFA. In a private White House conversation President Nixon, implementing an election pledge to textile interests, was rumored to have sought Prime Minister Eisaku Sato's acceptance of the MFA agreement by promising to see that Japan regained the islands seized by the United States during the war.

(At the White House dinner following this reported conversation, Nixon brought Sato over to me and said I had done more for the good of the Japanese than any other American. The prime minister responded that he was well aware of this.)

When I saw Sato in Tokyo a short time later, I asked about the reports that he had promised Nixon to solve the textile problem. He replied in the roundabout manner for which he was famous: "I, too, seem to have heard rumors to that effect." In other words, yes.

Faced with the overwhelming internal political need to regain sovereign territory, Sato opted to accept the unfavorable textile pact in return for Okinawa and the Ryukyus. Many Japanese resented being forced into such a hard choice. They felt betrayed by the United States after so many years of hard but fair negotiations. The American textile industry won its war, but almost at the cost of continued amicable and mutually advantageous relations with an important Pacific partner.

Since the MFA and its successor pacts were signed, Japan largely has been able to avoid American criticism by concentrating on higher priced, better designed, more fashionable goods. Yet I often wonder what could have been done to avoid the confrontations that marked the textile negotiations. An American friend who participated in many of the meetings tells me that, in retrospect, he believes the acrimony over a relatively minor item such as textiles could have been prevented by trade-offs. He believes constructive agreements benefiting both nations would have resulted if, for instance, the United States had offered market concessions in return for Japanese acceptance of textile protectionism, and the Japanese had been requested to provide greater access to certain of their markets. The furor a few years later over Japanese limits on imports of American beef and oranges are other examples of serious disputes over products that do not loom large in the overall picture. I am not enough of an economist to know whether my friend's idea would work, but certainly its possibilities need careful examination.

President Nixon was responsible for jolting the Japanese on at least three other occasions. The first so-called Nixon Shock came on July 15, 1971, when he reversed long-standing policy and visited Communist China without extending the courtesy of forewarning friends and allies. A month later he delivered the second and third shocks, suspending dollar conversion into gold and thereby upsetting the international monetary system, and slapping a temporary 10 percent surcharge on all imports to combat the American economic recession.

When the news hit I was in Tokyo, preparing to leave for Hawaii on the last leg of my round-the-world trip with my family. Etsu and the children flew on to Honolulu while I immersed myself in conferences with Japanese clients. Years earlier, when I had expressed concern about the consequences to Japan of certain economic legislation under consideration, a senator had said: "Don't worry, Mike. The Japanese will come out of this better than we will. They always find a way out."

They not only survived the Nixon Shocks in good shape, but learned from the experience so that they were able to take in stride the later oil shocks, which rocked the world economy, even though they import 99 percent of their petroleum.

One of my key responsibilities during the textile wars was to keep Toyosaburo Taniguchi informed. Taniguchi was now chairman of the Japan Cotton Spinners Association, first president of the Japan Textile Federation which represented the entire industry, and the only Japanese to be elected president of the International Textile

Manufacturers Association headquartered in Switzerland. He was a gracious gentleman of the old school and we developed what virtually amounted to a father-son relationship.

In 1976, even after years of strenuously opposing U.S. trade restrictions, he asked me to arrange for the presentation to the American people of his priceless collection of one hundred paintings of famous mountains. The paintings were given to the Freer Gallery of Art of the Smithsonian Institution as a token of appreciation for American postwar generosity and admiration for its democracy in the Bicentennial of our independence.

My involvement in textile problems led inevitably to other facets of business between the United States and Japan, one being a seat on the board of the Bank of Tokyo Trust Co. in New York City from 1973 until I reached mandatory retirement age. Unlike the Bank of Tokyo, which operates a highly successful "retail" operation in California through its California First banks, Bank of Tokyo Trust is a "wholesaler" specializing in large loans to major U.S. and Japanese business ventures. The board included such prestigious members as chief executive officers of giant national and international corporations, senior partners of Wall Street law firms, international bankers, and men who had served the government at sub-Cabinet level.

While making contributions to the board in the areas of public opinion, and public and government relations, I also was privileged to gain insights into the rarified atmosphere of international finance in which Japan is playing an increasingly more important role. At the same time I learned something of the background of Japanese industry, and about how thoroughly they research a project before they commit themselves.

Take one of my clients, Toyota Motors. It began as a builder of textile machinery. Its automatic looms were so far superior to anything then in use that the British, at the time world leaders in the textile industry, bought them. In 1935 the Toyoda (a phonetic change from Toyota) Automatic Loom Works organized an automobile division with the £100,000 from sale of patent rights. Two years later it began to turn out trucks. In January 1947, Toyota produced its first passenger car, a small and economical model for the Japanese market. In 1958 Toyota entered the American market with its top-of-the-line Crown model. It was an utter failure. The Crown did not have the power, speed, or stamina to meet American requirements. Toyota engineers went back to work. Six years later they were back with a line of small cars and trucks designed specifically for the American market and their success is history.

In 1981, under tremendous pressure from the Reagan administration, the Japanese government agreed to "voluntary quotas" reducing automobile shipments. Early that year when talks of quotas first surfaced, I hurried to Tokyo with sheafs of reports and documents to back up my urgings that Toyota resist. The company succeeded only in getting a slightly higher ceiling than the Japanese government was ready to accept.

The ultimate loser in this high-stakes fandango was the American consumer. With a restricted supply of new cars, U.S. manufacturers raised prices. So did the Japanese. American builders improved their plants, but also diluted their capital by paying brazenly big bonuses to their executives. While decrying foreign competition, the U.S. Big Three were importing Japanese-built cars for sale under their own brand names, and to top it all, they succeeded in getting them included in the overall quota. I was particularly irritated that while the clamps were being put on Japanese cars, imports were authorized for new car builders in Korea, Brazil, Malaysia, Taiwan, and Yugoslavia.

Some Americans have complained that Japan unfairly fails to provide a "level playing field" in the matter of access to markets. Nevertheless, Ambassador Mike Mansfield has asserted that Japanese markets are not as closed as many Americans allege, nor are they as open as the Japanese contend.

I find it deplorable that the trade imbalance between the two nations is seen as war, that Japan having lost militarily is gaining revenge economically. I see trade as the peaceful exchange of goods and services, which will continue only if both parties benefit. It should not be considered a zero game in which gains on one side equal the losses on the other.

Latest figures show that our worldwide trade deficit amounts to about $170 billion, of which Japan is responsible for one third despite efforts on both sides to trim it to more modest proportions. Regardless of statistics, however, there is no logical reason to expect trade between any two nations to be balanced. Balance is a precarious thing that fluctuates. During the first fifteen years of postwar trade with Japan the United States enjoyed substantial surpluses. The reversal of roles is not comforting.

The nature of the two-way trade makes balance unlikely if not impossible. Lacking natural resources, Japan imports massive quantities of raw materials and foodstuffs from the United States, and fuels from elsewhere. Japan lives by exporting manufactures. The United States, with the world's highest living standards, has the biggest and hungriest market for manufactured goods. Given this structural situation, there is a built-in tendency for Japan to have a surplus. It should be recognized that the problem is neither ethical nor moral. Much of Japan's earnings is coming back to the United States in investments. In a world where most countries need more capital for development than domestic savings can support, it is well that somebody is generating the funds from which investments can be made.

One key reason for Japan's economic success has been its ability to convert technology into desirable consumer products. Not long after the war Sony purchased rights to an American invention whose only use was believed to be in hearing aids. Sony used it to build transistor radios. The first video tape recorders, which revolutionized the television industry, were priced around $100,000 and Americans correctly viewed them as too costly for home use. The Japanese found a way to manufacture them for a fraction of the cost and developed a $10-billion-a-year home-entertainment market. (While the Japanese have excelled at quality production and management, they are not without inventiveness. Former President Jimmy Carter conferred the Presidential Award and International Hall of Fame World Award on Dr. Yoshiro Nakamatsu who is said to have 2,360 patents, compared to 1,093 issued to Thomas Edison.)

Philip Trezise, former assistant secretary of state for economic affairs, endorses a quote about "technorivalry" from an academician he knows: "Japanese activities in any market have always led to improvements in product quality, value, service, and design. Their cost-reduction efforts have lowered prices, raised demand, and increased consumer benefits. Japanese industry is the most powerful force for industrial progress in the world today."

As an American, however, I contend very strongly that our trade deficit with Japan is much too large. Even as I acknowledge Japanese efforts to reduce the deficit, I believe Japan owes it to the

United States to cut its protectionism and liberalize imports even further, eliminate administrative guidance and other nontariff impediments to commerce, provide greater access to manufactured goods, and reverse its cultural-industrial pattern of encouraging exports to promoting imports. Protectionism in Japan, as in the United States, is on behalf of a few against the many.

I am disturbed by the perception, justified in some cases, that Japan has failed to reciprocate fully in opening its markets to American products. Senator Robert Packwood of Oregon has expressed my concerns well in reference to the Northwest's lumber.

"The Japanese are shipping a lot of automobiles to the United States, and when we grumble about unemployment, they say they're helping the American consumer," he told me a few years ago. "Besides, they say, American cars burn too much gasoline, they're undependable and their quality is poor. They're right. But when we go to the Japanese and urge them to buy our timber because it's cheaper than theirs, better, and it helps the Japanese consumer, who's badly in need of housing, they say their domestic lumber industry is small and needs to be protected. There's something unfair about a one-sided argument."

While both sides use the same arguments to try to protect their industries, it is frustrating that the Japanese seem to succeed more often than we do. They will have to liberalize their import policies much more than they have done so far.

At the same time I support Japan's constitutional antiwar stance despite protests that Japan's economic successes are at the expense of America's defense umbrella. I would like to see Japan, the only nation to have suffered nuclear devastation, given the opportunity to demonstrate the possibility of a peaceful, prosperous planet without arms. Japan is the only country with the credibility and ability to try. For a safer and saner world, it should be encouraged to achieve this goal.

There is not space enough to list my clients, all of whom subscribe generally to my views about trade. If they had widely divergent ideas, I would suggest they seek other counsel. There is an immense amount of money being spent in Washington by foreign interests for lobbying and it is not suprising that Japan, as the leading overseas trading partner, tops the list. Unfortunately for me, I have seen little of those funds. In contrast to retainers of hundreds of thousands of dollars being asked and paid to lobbyists, only two clients pay my company as much as $50,000 a year. It goes without saying that I am not wealthy, speculation to the contrary notwithstanding.

The competition among lobbyists is little short of astounding. In fact, many individuals have used government employment or service in a highly visible public job as a stepping-stone to the lucrative lobbying business. Among those who have taken this route to gain Japanese clients, and their former affiliations, are Michael Deaver, one of President Reagan's top advisers; William Fulbright, chairman of the Senate Foreign Relations Committee; William Colby, CIA director; Richard V. Allen, national security adviser; Robert Strauss, chairman of the Democratic National Committee; William Eberle, chief trade representative; Stanton Anderson, assistant secretary of state. There are many others.

The Japanese must share the blame for the inflated cost of lobbying. Just as they insist on brand names and high quality when they buy personal items, they are willing to pay top dollar for consultants likely to get them access to the seats of power. Harold Malmgren, former deputy trade representative, told me he was approached by Japanese interests when he was an untried beginner just getting into the lobbying business. He asked what they could pay. He was floored when they offered $300,000 a year. Late in 1986 a well-known Japanese politician with aspirations for the prime ministership paid one of Washington's leading lobbyists $250,000 for a week's work to arrange appointments with high-level congressional and administration figures. The politician wanted most of all to meet President Reagan, but that was one man the lobbyist couldn't deliver. Without that meeting the politician's trip would have been considered a failure. In desperation and some embarrassment the Japanese embassy asked me and, as I learned later, Senator Spark Matsunaga, for help. We attacked the problem from several directions and finally were able to get him into the Oval Office. Of course there was no charge.

I do not wish to give the impression that working with the Japanese was easy, or that our relations were always tranquil. The biggest problem was getting to know them, learning to understand what they really were thinking about my suggestions for things that needed to be done. They seemed to comprehend the reasons underlying my strategy. They used all the right words. They seemed to agree with my philosophy, but frequently I sensed there was an element missing and that I just wasn't getting through to them.

I think this was a cultural gap rather than one involving simple communications. Many times I wondered that the two nations could work with understanding at topmost levels when I was having problems at mine. There's another dimension to the understanding gap. They never seemed willing to tell me everything they had in mind. In negotiating import quotas, for example, I could never get from them what they considered their bottom line. I told my clients that as their advocate I had to know their limitations as well as their aspirations. The responses invariably were vague and unhelpful.

Another major problem I encountered was Japanese failure, or rather the perception of failure, to follow up on agreements. It's the same difficulty experienced by a series of frustrated U.S. trade negotiators. One of them said to me: "The Japanese are so courteous, they seem to be so understanding, and so damned agreeable, we come home thinking we've won the fight. But after two or three months, or even a year, nothing happens. We get the commitments, but there's no action."

There's a rather simple explanation for this aggravating problem. It has its roots in cultural differences. Americans are impatient and it is our nature to expect immediate results. Delay frustrates us. Prolonged negotiations preceded by chitchat bore us. We say time is money. After we finish one task we want to hurry on to other challenges. That attitude is reflected in the popularity of instant foods. Our credit system—buy now, pay later—permits instant gratification of our desires. Americans establish businesses in Japan, or introduce a product, and are disappointed if they fail to realize profits the first year. They come home complaining about the impossibility of breaking into the Japanese market.

On the other hand, the Japanese with their long history have learned patience. Negotiations are not to be hurried; like a sumo wrestling match, all the traditional formalities must precede the action. The Japanese prefer to proceed slowly and cautiously, but after they have weighed their options and decide to move, they move. From their point of view, they are acting on their promises to liberalize trade and are carrying out their part of the bargain even if no action is visible. They know it will take time to see results, and they expect Americans to understand. Yet when results do not appear quickly, Americans are inclined to charge bad faith. And the Japanese are hurt, confused, and resentful.

I was caught in the middle of a number of these situations before I understood the reason for the problem. Then it became my role to defend our Japanese clients, explaining the situation to their American counterparts while urging the Japanese to proceed with all possible dispatch. The Japanese disinclination to bargain proved to be another problem. Americans start high, or low, as the case may be, and negotiate toward the middle. The Japanese would arrive at what they considered a fair position and place it on the table from the very beginning. In effect, it was a nonnegotiable matter. It took some time for both sides to figure that out.

The Japanese were hard taskmasters, demanding as much in performance from Masaoka and Associates as they did of their own people. They knew what they wanted and they expected me to deliver. In many cases their expectations were unrealistic; I had to explain that Congress had its own agenda and no amount of pressure would change its thinking overnight. Interestingly enough, when for various reasons I was unable to influence legislation or to get a favorable interpretation of regulations, the cultural differences were apparent in the subtlety of their expressions of displeasure. No one pounded the table or shouted into the telephone. They were as polite and proper as usual but I knew, I just knew, from their demeanor when they were dissatisfied.

I don't recall ever being criticized openly by a Japanese client. The criticism is indirect. Dissatisfied clients usually complain to me about the lavishly paid American firm heading up the campaign, but with the clear implication that I should have done something to ensure success. Invariably, they expect more of me and my firm, for less pay, than of Caucasian firms. To put it bluntly, this is a subtle form of reverse racial discrimination softened by gentle language: "We appreciate what you are doing, but I'm afraid we wish for better results" or "We hope you can succeed with renewed efforts as the results are not quite what we expected."

On the other hand, I learned there is danger in being too successful. Some years ago the United States passed special tariff-preference legislation to help developing nations. Exporters like South Korea, Hong Kong, and Taiwan were allowed to bring in binoculars duty-free while the Japanese were paying 20 percent customs. Japanese manufacturers asked me to help them. I found no binoculars were being manufactured in the United States. Therefore there was no logic in protecting a nonexistent industry by taxing Japanese binoculars alone. I brought this to official attention. Before long Japanese binoculars gained equal treatment.

That brought Japanese manufacturers of telescopes to my door asking help in getting duty-free status for their chief product, telescopic sights for sporting guns. This time I found a number of American firms still make telescopic gunsights. Imports would be highly competitive. I'm not sure I was ever able to explain to the satisfaction of Japanese telescope manufacturers why I couldn't get them the same deal as I'd gotten for the binocular people.

My policy is to evaluate the odds and discuss them frankly with clients. Perhaps they feel that, in the Japanese tradition, I am covering myself when I say it will be "very difficult," which in the Japanese idiom means "no can do." Likely as not, there will be a lot of bowing and smiling and *Onegai itashimasu* (literally "I beg of you," but with a meaning closer to "Please do your best").

Rather than any spectacular triumph I was able to achieve for Japanese clients, my success must be measured by the steady growth of trade to the benefit of both countries. Assuming that my contributions toward development of this trade have been substantial, people have asked whether I've experienced any "guilt" that the Japanese have been so successful.

Not at all. Recognizing that Japanese competition has been painful for some segments of America, I am confident nonetheless that we are a better and stronger country as a result of that trade. Take automobiles. Today we are building better, more efficient, more durable cars as a direct result of competition. Detroit had allowed itself to become fat and sloppy. Its design and engineering had become substandard, more concerned with tailfins than performance. The industry tolerated poor workmanship from employees who were capable of better. Management wasn't managing; it simply passed along unbridled costs to the consumer. Then the Japanese came in with well-designed, fuel-efficient, durable cars assembled by people who cared about craftsmanship. American consumers, quick to recognize value, bought millions of imports. Faced with the reality that it had to compete or face extinction, Detroit did what the

Japanese had done: studied and adopted many of the competition's techniques and cleaned up its act. Today the automobile industry is healthier, with a place for both Americans and Japanese, and the consumer has benefited.

I don't think anyone can argue that Americans have not gotten their dollar's worth in buying Japanese goods. At the same time, Japan's profits have enabled it to import vast amounts of U.S. farm products, improving Japanese living standards as well as providing a badly needed market for the beleaguered American farmer. For example, Japan buys 70 percent of American beef exports, 40 percent of pork exports, 28 percent of feed-grain exports, 22 percent of soybean exports plus huge quantities of wheat, citrus fruits, cotton, chickens, and tobacco.

It is difficult not to admire what Japan has accomplished. Rising from the ashes of military defeat, the Japanese have created—to be sure with American help in the early postwar years—an economy second only to that of the United States. (Nonmilitary American Marshall Plan aid to sixteen European nations totaled approximately $22 billion; U.S. aid to Japan was $2.6 billion.) And since Japan is virtually without natural resources, its success was built largely on the skills, intelligence, and energy of the people.

The economic friction is of great and continuing concern to all Americans of Japanese ancestry. It poses delicate problems that affect us as a group, and often each of us as individuals. While we have amply proved our right to our American heritage, we must not seek to evade our identity as Americans with a certain affinity, if you will, with Japan. That link caused us grave problems in the past, and we were helpless to overcome them. But now under other circumstances that affinity can be employed to serve our country.

I have been fortunate to have had a role in trying to improve relations between Japan and the United States. Yet is it not realistic to believe that Japanese Americans, simply on the basis of ethnic origins, are in a position to close the Pacific understanding gap. Back in a time when the Nisei were young and idealistic, there was grandiose talk of Japanese Americans bridging the Pacific. We know now that was only a hopeful pipe dream. Aside from a few notable individuals who have made successful careers of Japanese-American relations, Nisei as a group have become so Americanized that few have the expertise to make a meaningful contribution. Such a bridge is so complex and difficult a project that veteran statesmen of both countries are still trying to build it. So it is unrealistic to expect us, simply because of ethnicity, to provide either the wisdom or the insights that magically will solve the problems.

But at a more modest level, there is much that we can do in keeping channels of communication open between our government and the Japanese government, between us as grass-roots Americans and the people of Japan. We can express our concerns to our elected representatives, to the Department of State, to Japanese consular and diplomatic representatives in the United States, and to our Japanese friends. Out of such dialogue will come not necessarily solutions but the beginning of understanding that must be the basis for resolution of our problems.

I believe as does Ambassador Mike Mansfield that the Japanese-American bilateral relationship is the most important in the Free World. And I want to keep it that way, friendly, strong, and mutually advantageous.

Chapter 21
Quiet Diplomacy

After the peace treaty was signed in 1951, Japan reopened its gray stone embassy at 2520 Massachusetts Avenue N.W. Tokyo was under heavy self-imposed pressure to select just the right man as its first postwar envoy, someone firm but not too aggressive, polished but sincere, and able to hold his own in discussions with State Department officials. The nominee would have to be acceptable to the Americans, and it was preferable that he should not have held a high position in the prewar foreign service. The ministry, still struggling to regain the status it had lost to the militarists during the war, went outside its close-knit ranks to find that man. It selected Eikichi Araki, former governor of the Bank of Japan, who not only understood economics but had a good command of English.

One day I received a call from the embassy saying Ambassador Araki wished to see me. He pelted me with questions. How did I gauge the American public attitude toward Japan? What was the congressional mood toward his country? Would Japan be an issue in the upcoming elections? If not, what would be the main concerns? After the long years of Democratic control, what were General Eisenhower's prospects in the presidential election? How would the Korean War affect the American outlook toward Asia?

"Please be completely candid with me, Masaoka-san," the ambassador said. "As you know, one of my functions is to evaluate American public opinion, and your views, not only as a Japanese-American leader but as an American businessman, are highly valued."

We talked occasionally, and perhaps the most important suggestion I gave him was that if Japan was to succeed in the trade it needed to rebuild the nation, it had to overcome its prewar image as producer of cheap and flimsy goods. "Raise your quality and don't cut prices just to make a sale," I urged him. "Americans don't want junk from Japan or anywhere else."

About this time I began to get invitations from middle-level officials from the State Department's Japan desk to have lunch or drop by for a chat. They were interested primarily in my opinion of how certain U.S. policies under discussion would be received in Japan. Protesting that my knowledge was limited, I answered as best I could. Eventually I found that through my business contacts, visits with Japanese friends, conversations with Japanese embassy officials, the information fed me by my State Department contacts, and a great deal of reading, I was becoming fairly knowledgeable about U.S.-Japanese commercial affairs and political relationships.

Ambassador Araki was exceptionally effective in a difficult situation. He was the first and last of noncareer ambassadors from Japan, and those who followed were of varying personalities, styles, and diplomatic skills. On the whole they represented the highest type of Japanese, for they had passed rigid entrance examinations and worked their way up the Foreign Ministry's bureaucracy. Following are capsule evaluations of some of Araki's successors.

The second ambassador was Sadao Iguchi, who had been ambassador to Canada. He had worked closely with U.S. Occupation officials in Japan, was fluent in English, and did not need the kind of assistance Araki sought. He represented his country well.

Masayuki Tani, the third envoy, had served in Germany before the war and his style was too rigid to fit well with Americans. The critical textile talks started during his tenure.

Koichiro Asakai was next, coming to Washington from the Philippines. Some members of Congress asked why Japan had chosen an envoy whose last post was in such a small nation. What they didn't understand was that because of bitterness built up during the war, the Philippines posed an acid test for Japan's ambassador. Asakai proved to be such an able representative in trade and security matters that he was kept in Washington longer than any envoy until Yoshio Okawara many years later.

Ryuji Takeuchi, who succeeded Asakai, had been Araki's chief deputy. I had first met him when he arrived in Washington as head of a mission before the peace treaty. Takeuchi was the first ambassador to raise objections on his own, instead of pleading he would have to confer with Tokyo, when he thought the United States was being unreasonable. That was a long step toward normalization. Takeuchi also liked to meet with members of Congress and I was often the go-between.

He was followed by Takezo Shimoda, who later became Japan's commissioner of professional baseball after completing service as a Supreme Court justice. Shimoda was the first to ask that the Japanese flag be displayed together with the Stars and Stripes on the platform at joint U.S.-Japan functions, and that "Kimigayo," the Japanese national anthem, be played along with "The Star Spangled Banner." While these may seem to be small matters, they were symbolic of Japan's growing confidence.

Next was Nobuhiko Ushiba, probably the most effective overall. He liked to say he had visited each of the fifty states at least once during his tenure. He spoke English well enough, accepted numerous speaking engagements, and enjoyed chatting with strangers during his travels.

Takeshi Yasukawa, a quiet but highly skilled diplomat, followed. He brought the volatile MFA textile negotiations, which had threatened to disrupt relations, to a satisfactory but not popular conclusion.

His successor, Fumihiko Togo, became the first occupant of the magnificent new embassy residence in Washington. The soft-spoken Togo was overshadowed somewhat by his wife, Ise, daughter of a former foreign minister, who became one of the capital's most popular hostesses. Madame Togo proved Japan had completed her comeback on diplomacy's social front just as she had in the world marketplace.

Early on, I began to suspect that before leaving Tokyo for the Washington post each ambassador had been instructed to meet occasionally with me. Regardless of whether there were specific instructions, the embassy cultivated this relationship. Our meetings were usually informal, freewheeling discussions about U.S.-Japanese relations, with both parties expressing frank opinions. When the ambassador was someone I had first known as a middle-level officer during an earlier Washington assignment, we could be even more candid. This was the case with Togo's successor, Yoshio Okawara, a six-footer whose previous post was Australia. He had a friendly way of calling people by their first names, and his easygoing style helped him weather some difficult years over growing trade problems.

Many in Washington were surprised when Nobuo Matsunaga was named Okawara's successor. He had never served in the United States and his previous assignment had been Mexico. Although it is too early to pass judgment, obviously Matsunaga was given his government's most important overseas assignment because he was considered the best man in his Foreign Ministry class.

In my estimation and that of those with whom I work, the Japanese embassy is to be ranked among the top five of the almost one hundred in Washington for its effectiveness, service, and successes. This speaks well of its ambassadors and staff.

My exchange of views with embassy personnel was not in one direction alone. I was talking with the State Department's Japan experts about as often as I was meeting the Japanese. That relationship began with calls for assistance. "I met with the economics minister at the embassy today and he told me something very interesting," a State Department friend might say. "I'm not quite sure exactly what he meant. Let me run it by you and you tell me what you think." In time I found myself being asked for opinions on policy proposals. "This is what we're thinking of doing," a Japan desk officer might say. "We aren't quite sure what the reaction might be. What is your personal opinion? Why don't you sound out some of your Japanese friends and let us know how they react?"

My State Department contacts knew I was talking frequently with the embassy staff—in fact, I was encouraged to cultivate these relationships—and the Japanese knew I had friends in the State Department. Every time I went to Japan, which often was several times a year, I would touch base at the U.S. embassy, and the Japanese invited me to meet both the foreign minister and the prime minister.

Let me state clearly that I was no simple rumormonger carrying tales from one side to the other at their bidding. I was privy to confidences because my contacts knew I would be discreet. Credibility was my stock-in-trade and it could be maintained only by discretion. In effect, I had become an informal, unofficial conduit for transmitting trial balloons, an honest broker with the confidence of both sides who could help them communicate without facing the possibility of embarrassment if things didn't work out. It was not a role I had sought; it just developed. At certain periods the work took considerable time, but I was never offered a consultant's fee, nor did I ask for payment. I felt that whatever I could do to help the professionals would be my contribution to better understanding between the United States and Japan. There was routine work the embassy would contract out, and my firm got its share, but I preferred to keep consulting on a personal and nonprofessional basis.

In part for this service, I have been decorated twice by the emperor of Japan. The first time was in 1968. I was in Tokyo representing the Japan America Society in the Meiji Centennial celebration when I received a message from Foreign Minister Takeo Miki that the government wished to present me an award. Without any inkling that anything like this was under way, I asked my friend Tamotsu Murayama, the reporter, what I should do.

"A decoration is pretty big stuff here," he said in his characteristically straightforward manner. "They usually don't give one to anybody less than seventy years old. How old are you, fifty-three? I bet they aren't going to give you a high-class decoration because you're too young. Mike, don't accept a low-class decoration, like fifth or sixth grade. You know why? Lots of Issei have those. If you accept the same kind, you'll set a precedent and it will be harder for other Nisei to get a high-class decoration. You know what? I'll go to the Foreign Ministry and tell my friends there you want a high-class decoration."

I wasn't accustomed to looking a gift horse in the mouth but Tamotsu wasn't to be dissuaded. I was awarded the Order of the Rising Sun, Third Grade, an unusually high decoration, particularly for someone my age and a civilian. Prime Minister Eisaku Sato placed the ribbon around my neck. Later he teased me about all the trouble I had caused by demanding an upgraded award, which was the highest possible for a private citizen for services to the people of Japan. A few years ago in a ceremony at the embassy in Washington I was honored to receive the Order of the Sacred Treasure, Second Grade, a decoration usually reserved for ambassadors and other top-level government officials who have rendered particularly meritorious service. If Tamotsu were living, he would have been pleased that I am among the very few Americans to have been awarded two decorations. Incidentally, the White House has presented me with two commendations "in recognition of exceptional services to others, in the finest American tradition."

In June 1980, my partner, Sam Ishikawa, died. He had run the New York office semiautonomously. Getting office affairs in order preparatory to closing it created great personal stress, which probably led to my first heart attack. Fortunately it was minor. My doctors gave the usual warnings about getting regular exercise—my weight was never much of a problem—watching my diet, and getting my blood pressure down. Later that year I felt well enough to accept an invitation from the Japanese embassy to fly to Tokyo to brief the new prime minister, Zenko Suzuki, on U.S. affairs from an American's viewpoint. Suzuki's foreign experience was extremely limited, and his aides felt he would benefit from views other than those of the Foreign Ministry.

I completed the mission but suffered my second heart attack before I could fly home. In itself it was no more serious than the first one, but it frightened me. When I returned to Washington I was put on medication, went on a strict diet, rested regularly, and walked up to three miles a day.

I felt fine, but on Christmas Eve, 1980, I was stricken again. Etsu rushed me to the hospital, where double-bypass surgery was performed without delay after a third heart attack. The doctors had disquieting news. While the surgery was successful, they reported the heart muscle had weakened to the point where it could not pump an adequate amount of blood. For the rest of my life activities would be restricted.

By 1982 I felt well enough to attend JACL's convention in Gardena, California. Historical revisionists had taken to attacking the organization's wartime performance, and I had been asked to review that era at what was billed as a "Redress workshop." The "From the Frying Pan" column in the *Pacific Citizen* caught the essence of that event:

> It was well worth the price of admission and more to witness the return of the vintage Mike Masaoka, nearly felled two years ago by a serious heart attack followed by double-bypass surgery. Masaoka had been vilified, unfairly blamed by a few revisionists for selling Japanese Americans down the river into desert WRA camps 40 years ago. Now, at a so-called Redress workshop, he had been asked to recall the details that led to decisions in the fateful spring of 1942.

So Masaoka rose to speak, a white-maned lion, recounting events of four decades ago without benefit of notes, orating with the fire of his long-ago youth. It was a performance made virtuoso by his sincerity.

JACL had been accused of seizing the reins of power in the Japanese American communities. Masaoka pointed out the Issei leadership had been imprisoned by the FBI under the war powers act, leaving their people drifting, afraid, confused. There was no group capable of moving into the breach to provide assurance and leadership and the role went by default to a young, inexperienced JACL.

JACL had been accused of "negotiating" a role for itself with a government intent on evacuating the Japanese Americans. There was no negotiating, Masaoka pointed out, only a desperate rearguard action to head off disaster simply because no one—the civilian government, the military, the Japanese Americans themselves—seemed to know in the confusion and hysteria of the time what was transpiring.

And what about the decision to seek the right to military service? Masaoka had no apologies, only pride that the Nisei stepped forward to offer their lives after JACL successfully petitioned the federal government for the privilege of defending their country. More than any single action, the military sacrifices of the Nisei insured them a place in the nation after the guns were stilled.

Masaoka made his most telling points when he asked about the intent of JACL's detractors. He admitted to errors of judgment but not of venality. He asked what point there was in blaming the JACL leadership of 40 years ago without acknowledging the greed, the blatant racism, the ignorance, the malign intent of those who stirred latent prejudices to engineer the evacuation of Japanese Americans and who succeeded in changing simple removal to semipermanent confinement behind barbed wire.

Masaoka spoke for an hour and a half and no one stirred or moved to leave, or even coughed. When it comes to passionate oratory, Masaoka knows no peer and this warm night he was at his best. Those who had known Masaoka in his younger days were first astonished, then delighted, that the years had slid away and the old skills were being revealed for a new generation of JACLers to listen and marvel and be educated to the facts of a long-ago tragedy by the man who was at the center of the maelstrom.

Mike Masaoka's report of JACL, as it were, will not silence the criticism. But his presentation of the facts, his interpretation of events as he saw them, will explain what he and his colleagues did, and why they did it. And if there continue to be attacks on his motives, it will not be on the basis of lack of information. . . .

In a sense I was once again like the biblical Moses reasoning with the doubters. In a sense, I was telling my people not to despair, that our sacrifice had been worthwhile. The doubters, as well as those who believed as I did, knew that we were close to the promised land of racial justice, full legal equality, and impartial opportunity. We needed to struggle just a little more to witness America living up to its promise. Moses did not live to see the promised land. Would I?

The effort expended in my speech was more than my body could stand. My heart faltered again, and I spent three weeks in a Los Angeles hospital before I was permitted to fly home to Washington. Since then I have been in and out of hospitals, being treated by one cardiologist after another, one neurologist after another, being subjected to one medical regimen after another. I even tried acupuncture and experienced a measure of relief. But my health has not been restored. My work schedule has been severely restricted, and I depend on a faithful and able office staff to carry on.

As much as I am able, I remain in touch with Japanese and Japanese American friends. The most frequent question asked by the Japanese is about the trade imbalance. Why, they ask, is the United States so upset when Japan is simply putting into practice the lessons she learned from Americans? There is a two-word answer: too successful. Japan has been too successful, and Americans need a breathing spell in which to restore the balance. Do not doubt that the balance will be restored; the issue is how long it will take, at what price and sacrifice, and with what bruised feelings.

There is a Japanese ethical concept called *on-gaeshi,* the obligation to repay a moral debt. There is no doubt in my mind that Japan does indeed owe the United States a moral debt for the generous treaty ending hostilities, the security that enabled the Japanese to rebuild their nation, the open market that resulted in her astonishingly successful industrial and economic buildup, and, above all, the creation of a democratic society. Now the time has come for *on-gaeshi* through cooperation and restraint in solving their problems so the two nations can continue to progress as friends rather than bitter rivals. Economic forces have been likened to supertankers—they take a long time to build up momentum, after which it takes a long time to change course. The rhetoric must be muted while the modifying forces begin to take effect. Once again there is danger of misunderstanding; the word "adversarial" used to describe confrontation over trade problems has been translated in the Japanese press to mean the warlike stance of enemies. Of course we know the English connotation falls short of that, but do the Japanese?

Japanese Americans frequently ask where we go from here. Within a generation we have moved from Oriental ghettoes to places of respect and influence. Our status has changed from despised and suspected inmates of American-style concentration camps to respected members of society. We have been called the "model minority," a well-intentioned but demeaning reference to our success in fitting into the predominantly Anglo society. So where do we go from here?

This answer is not difficult. The largest part of my career has been devoted to winning a rightful place in our native land for Americans whose ancestry and heritage are Japanese. It is a proud heritage. We have as much to contribute to the American mosaic as Americans of other ethnic backgrounds, and as much right to make that contribution. At the same time I have reservations about Japanese Americans in an Asian-Pacific movement. Of course, we have a deep obligation to do everything we can to help in the adjustment of newcomers to America. They are, after all, the beneficiaries of our struggle to bring equality to immigration and naturalization laws, our efforts to win social and economic justice regardless of race or color. But a multi-ethnic alliance based on common Asian heritage is another matter, beset with problems as well as benefits. In reality, Japanese Americans have more in common with the greater American society than with immigrants from Korea or Taiwan or Indochina, even though we may admire their courage and energy and support their aspirations. As a guide to our future, the old JACL motto is still pertinent: "Better Americans in a Greater America."

Early in 1977, as the Carter administration got under way, a Washington newspaper column published a small item saying that Mike Masaoka was under consideration for appointment as U.S. ambassador to Japan. It was an intriguing idea. Americans of various ethnic backgrounds had been sent as envoys to the country of their ancestry. Why not to Japan?

I wonder how seriously I was being considered. After all, the newspapers were full of speculation about Carter appointments. I wondered if the item had been planted as a trial balloon. The Japanese papers picked up the story, and the Tokyo reaction seemed favorable.

For me the question was whether I wanted the appointment if it was offered. On the one hand, service as ambassador would be a great honor, the crowning achievement. I would be following in the footsteps of a distinguished line of postwar envoys, all of whom I had met. I would be in position to make substantial contributions to American-Japanese friendship. It would be great recognition for Japanese Americans. I was only sixty-one years old at the time, still in robust health and willing to take on a new challenge.

I also had serious misgivings. Perhaps I had been too close to Japan. Without doubt there would be many questions asked during the Senate's confirmation hearings about my relations with Japanese business firms and the Japanese embassy, and I stood the risk of having my answers twisted or misinterpreted by sensation-seekers. There was also the matter of money. The entertainment allowance of American ambassadors in major capitals is not nearly sufficient. Ambassadors are expected to have private means. I did not have that kind of wealth.

I also worried about what would be expected of Etsu and me. If matters did not proceed smoothly, it would be easy for Japan to blame me because I was a Japanese American leaning over backward to be American, and for the Americans to blame me because I was a Japanese American leaning over backward to placate the Japanese. In this kind of situation it would be impossible to separate ethnicity from performance. There was the danger of walking into a no-win situation in which my actions would be under intense scrutiny by both nations. As a private citizen visiting Japan, I could get away with calling the prime minister ''Uncle.'' As ambassador, such a faux pas could well be a newspaper sensation. Even more would be expected of Etsu. She would be expected to be sensitive to every nuance of Japanese culture and criticized if she fell short.

My friends were of little help as I sought counsel. Some urged me to take the assignment if it was offered. Some said I would be foolish to accept. In the end I did not have to make a decision. The job was never offered me. Veteran Senator Mike Mansfield, who had not sought reelection, was nominated. I was elated for him. Mansfield had taken a lively interest in foreign affairs, particularly the Far East. He had the confidence of Congress and the respect of Tokyo. He proved to be a superb choice. Without doubt he has been our most effective ambassador to Tokyo in the postwar era, and that is saying a great deal in view of the uniformly high caliber of our representation.

How close was I to appointment? I have no way of knowing but have heard that I was in the final three. Neighbors told me that they were questioned by federal agents making the usual security checks before appointment to government positions. I have also heard that Mansfield had considered me for his deputy chief of mission.

Would I have taken either job if offered? That is a hard question to answer. All things considered, I think I would have declined with deep and sincere regret. The ambassadorship would pose too many problems that I could not cope with because they were beyond my control. The deputy's post would require a knowledge of State Department procedures with which I was not familiar, and being an administrator would be no fun if I could not have an active role in policy.

In the memorable testimonial banquet in my honor at the 1970 JACL convention in Chicago, U. Alexis Johnson, under secretary of state for political affairs, had written of me: "In your lifetime of service, you have been an unofficial American ambassador. We are proud to have Americans like you representing the United States."

For me, that is honor enough.

Chapter 22

Into Tomorrow

Late one afternoon my collaborator, Bill Hosokawa, and I were talking about the future of America's relations with Japan when suddenly he jumped up and switched on his tape recorder. What follows is the transcript of our spontaneous discussion, which turned out, I think, to be an apt way of concluding a story which began nearly three quarters of a century earlier on the shores of the Great Salt Lake.

Hosokawa: You were just saying, Mike, that one of the main sources of trouble at this time is that the United States and Japan are strong competitors producing the same kinds of manufactured goods, like automobiles, computers, and other high-tech items. The United States has the edge in natural resources, but Japan has overcome that to a degree by great skill in technology and production. What about the future of relations between the two countries, and of the Pacific Rim?

Masaoka: You remember that in its youth the United States had problems with the various states competing against each other. Yet we were able to establish a framework that became a nation. In a somewhat like manner the Pacific Rim countries can work out a relationship that will be a logical extension of the industrial civilization that started in Europe. What we have on the Pacific Rim is three tiers of countries. There are the industrialized nations like the United States, Canada, and Japan. In the second tier are the developing areas, like Mexico, South Korea, Taiwan, Hong Kong, and Singapore. And finally there are all the others with all their varied problems of unemployment, population surplus, little literacy, poverty, et cetera. What we need is a system to bring all of them together. The United States and Canada on one side of the Pacific, and Japan on the other, are the natural leaders for the new Pacific Rim era, exchanging technology, passing on their know-how to the less developed countries, turning the natural resources of areas like China and South America into the goods necessary to raise living standards of the entire area.

Hosokawa: I think what you're saying is that the United States and Japan need each other, not as rivals, but as partners in developing the Pacific Rim.

Masaoka: Right. And that gets us back to the point that Japan must not rearm. Asian nations, remembering what happened in World War II, will not accept the leadership of a remilitarized Japan. I still hope that Japan can show the rest of the world that it's possible to be a power without arms.

Hosokawa: That's a great ideal. . . .

Masaoka: But you've got to have ideals to start with. One of the problems now is that too many things are bilateral. That's because it's easier that way. The relationship between the United States and Japan must be made multilateral—bring in other nations—otherwise you're going to have constant competition and confrontations. If we start working together to develop other nations to our mutual benefit, maybe the old economic theory of comparative advantage can be brought into play. If we can start afresh, knowing the errors of the past, I believe we can establish a new cooperative regional relationship. Sure, it's idealistic, but we have to start somewhere and we might as well start with ideals.

Hosokawa: I think you're totally right. The Latin American countries need a lot of help and they're a huge potential market for the United States, just as Southeast Asia is a market for Japan. I don't see why the two countries cannot cooperate in developing the entire Pacific Rim. And I think you make a very good point about the need for more than a bilateral relationship. But it still bothers me that the great preponderance of the responsibility for maintaining a defense against Soviet aggression lies with the United States. Japan contends it provides bases and helps pay for them, and that there's great domestic hostility toward rearming. That's true. But how can we reconcile this inequity between the two countries?

Masaoka: Japan may not be carrying enough of the defense load, but maybe Japan can do its share in other ways without compromising its no-war constitution. For example, by providing the kind of aid that will enable undeveloped countries to become more stable, more democratic, less vulnerable to Communist insurrection. Stability will strengthen the whole region without the kind of military escalation we're seeing in Central America.

Hosokawa: As I read you, you're talking about economic foreign aid, which will raise the general standard of living, which will create a society more able to resist Communist subversion.

Masaoka: Yes, that would be a far more productive way for Japan to spend its money than for arms. Let's say Japan doubles its military spending under U.S. pressure. What does it have then? Not much. What good is a second-rate army with toy tanks and a navy with nothing larger than destroyers? An ever-rising standard of living and a commitment to the free-enterprise system are stronger shields against subversion than a couple of divisions. Let's go back to the early days of this country again. The states weren't equal in resources. We had underdeveloped states that were mostly wilderness; we had industrial states and farming states. They had differences and they had to make adjustments. But they didn't resort to war. They remembered what Ben Franklin said about the states hanging together or they'd hang separately. So they worked together. Well, the same situation exists in the Pacific Basin, and if we've learned anything from the experience of the United States, we ought to be smart enough to apply it to the area.

Hosokawa: You're extending the domestic dilemma into a global context and I think that's right. Let me shift the thinking just a bit. Ambassador Mansfield keeps referring to the Century of the Pacific. That's an articulation of history in that the modern world had its origins in Europe and the great British Empire spread around the globe, but in the postwar era the United States changed from the arsenal of democracy to the economic arsenal, financing projects all over the world, providing the goods the world needed. And now the contention is that the center of dynamism is shifting to Japan . . .

Masaoka: And the Pacific. I say that because Japan lacks the resources to become a genuine power. Japan lacks the American landmass. Japan is heavily dependent on the rest of the world, and American markets and resources in particular. It's a natural partnership. I don't think the United States will ever slip the way Great

Britain did, because it has the resources of an entire continent. I think there's logic in the United States and Japan combining their assets and their efforts.

Hosokawa: Wouldn't that relegate the United States to a colony of Japan, the source of food, manpower, and other resources to feed the Japanese industrial machine?

Masaoka: No. The United States is doing a lot of that now, but that's because it's a two-way competition. We have to remember that Asia is a huge, untapped storehouse of natural resources, possibly greater than that of the Americas. Logically, Japan would focus on Asia, and the United States would pay more attention to South and Central America, where there's great opportunity for development. But there's plenty of opportunity in the Pacific Basin for everybody. The two powers don't have to be confrontational.

Hosokawa: So far, Mike, we've been talking about the economy of the Pacific Basin. You have some broader ideas about developing this relationship.

Masaoka: Economics is just part of it. There has to be social, cultural, educational, scientific interaction. Everything. The United Nations, despite its faults and weaknesses, gives us an idea about what is possible in international cooperation. It won't be easy and it will take time. You remember when President Kennedy said that in ten years we'd have men on the moon. The nation poured its resources and its scientific know-how into the project and we put men on the moon. Is it any less important to create a world of peace and prosperity? The Pacific Rim is right for this kind of effort. This is the kind of effort that demands the all-out cooperation of all nations. We need to work at the art of peace, and there's a perfect geographic framework in the Pacific Basin where we can get it under way. Let economics be the base. The people need a decent standard of living. Provide that, and you can build education and everything else on top of that. Once you get an economic foundation in place, the rest will come. And who are the logical leaders? The United States and Japan.

Postscript

Why does one write an autobiography? For various reasons, including the hope that the story of one man's life and times will be instructional to his contemporaries and those who follow.

There is a frieze on the National Archives building in Washington that proclaims "Past Is Prologue." To carry that thought a step further, if we do not know our history, we are condemned to repeat our mistakes. For this reason I have put an account of my experiences on paper.

My life has covered nearly three quarters of mankind's most tumultuous century. One small but critically significant episode within that period was our nation's hysterical and shamefully bigoted treatment of its citizens of Japanese extraction. Perhaps a recounting of that experience, with which I was deeply involved, will help to make certain that we have put such capricious disregard for human rights behind us forever.

I was first urged to write about my experiences after passage of the Walter-McCarran Immigration and Naturalization Act in 1952 over President Truman's veto. Without false modesty, I can claim that I had a major role in this legislation. In its way, it was as significant as the Civil Rights Act of a subsequent decade in asserting the equality of all peoples in the eyes of United States law. I consider passage of this legislation my most important achievement.

Yet, for various reasons, I resisted authorship. More recently, however, it became apparent the record was vanishing with the death of many of my associates who shared leadership in the common cause. New generations, uninformed, were indifferent to the story of aberrations which the democratic system had remedied. So I decided it was time to write the book.

One of my major problems was a lack of the voluminous notes essential to a biography. A bitter World War II experience with the Dies Un-American Activities Committee of Congress broke me of the practice of keeping careful records. Committee agents, without warrants of any kind, had raided JACL's Washington office after I had entered military service, confiscated letters and information files, and used material out of context to accuse me of un-American activity. Their charges were preposterous, of course, but after that I kept my paperwork at a minimum.

Nonetheless, there is much printed matter—books, newspaper files, letters, congressional reports—to backstop my recollections. What concerns me more than lack of notes is that the constraints of space have forced me to select only those incidents and activities most vivid in memory. While this may be the essence of an auto-biography, I also worry that many deserving events and individuals have been overlooked. For this, I apologize.

I was fortunate in having as collaborator, Bill Hosokawa, a skilled writer, nationally recognized veteran newspaper editor, and perhaps the foremost popular historian of the Japanese American experience. His familiarity with our history enabled him to ask deeply probing questions that forced me to think, questions that have added to the candor of my account and that put events in perspective. This project would not have been possible without his help and this book is as much his as mine.

Although the manuscript is now in the publisher's hands as this is written, I wish to make a few additional points in this postscript.

- I believe my most important achievement, as I have indicated earlier, was persuading Congress to eliminate racial discrimination from immigration and naturalization laws, thereby making the assertion that Asians were entitled to share the American dream.
- My most difficult decision was to urge cooperation with the federal government in the suspension of our rights as Americans as our patriotic contribution to the war effort. We were told this was a matter of military necessity and we had no way of disputing that contention, nor could we risk the possibility of bloodshed if we stood on our rights and resisted military orders. The cooperation

was with evacuation from the West Coast; detention was not a part of Executive Order 9066 and is a totally separate issue. Please pardon the fact that I cannot resist the opportunity to remind others that in spite of hindsight, and the criticisms and condemnations over the years, none of the critics, detractors, and debunkers, including those of Japanese origin, have come up with a viable, workable, and constructive alternative to avoid or prevent the evacuation process.

• My worst mistake was believing in the absolute integrity of the Constitution. Neither I nor anyone in the JACL leadership suspected that our citizenship would be rendered a mere scrap of paper under pressures generated by war hysteria. This experience taught me the need for perpetual vigilance in defending our rights.

• My greatest hope is that we have laid a foundation for world peace, with dignity, equality, freedom, and opportunity for all.

Since I have told you what I have done, it may be appropriate to outline my personal agenda for the balance of the time remaining to me. It is based on my lifelong efforts:

To continue the fight for civil and human rights of all Americans, and for all others everywhere.

To promote harmony and mutually advantageous relations between the United States, the land of my birth and citizenship, and Japan, the land of my ancestry.

To help in JACL's ongoing fight for redress from the injustice Japanese Americans suffered as a result of their government's action in World War II.

To help make the Japanese American Experience exhibit, titled "A More Perfect Union: Japanese Americans and the Constitution," at the National Museum of American History of the Smithsonian Institution, in connection with the Constitution's bicentennial, the success it deserves to be.

To promote a heroic monument commemorating the "Go for Broke" sacrifice of Japanese American servicemen in World War II, to be erected on the Avenue of Heroes at Arlington National Cemetery. To help bring together the National Japanese American Historical Society and the Japanese American National Museum in their efforts to preserve a record of the Japanese American experience.

To eliminate anti-Asian intimidation and violence.

In the more than four decades since Etsu and I moved to Washington there have been extraordinary changes in Congress, particularly in its attitudes. Although it is not possible to identify and thank every member who joined me in common causes over the years, I feel obliged to name a few for special acknowledgment with apologies to those I cannot mention. Among those who stand out in memory, and in no particular order, are:

Senators Elbert Thomas, Arthur Watkins, Wallace Bennett, Frank Moss of Utah; Alan Cranston, Sheridan Downey, Thomas Kuchel of California; Warren Magnuson, Henry Jackson of Washington; Everett Dirksen, Paul Douglas of Illinois; Mike Mansfield of Montana; Pat McCarran of Nevada; Hiram Fong of Hawaii (I will have more to say about others from our newest state); Hubert Humphrey of Minnesota; Jacob Javits of New York; Philip Hart of Michigan; Clifford Case of New Jersey; Hugh Scott of Pennsylvania; Barry Goldwater of Arizona; J. William Fulbright of Arkansas.

Among members of the House: Francis Walter of Pennsylvania; Walter Judd and Bill Frenzel of Minnesota; Sidney Yates of Illinois; Emanuel Cellar of New York; Carl Albert of Oklahoma; Tom Foley of Washington; Sam Rayburn and James Wright of Texas; Peter Rodino of New Jersey; Don Edwards, Chet Holifield, George P. Miller, Cecil King, Edward Roybal of California; William Dawson, Walter Granger, David King of Utah; Bill Alexander, Wilbur Mills of Arkansas; Robert Kastenmeier, Clement Zablocki of Wisconsin; Joseph Farrington, Jack Burns of Hawaii; Morris Udall of Arizona; Hale Boggs of Louisiana; Sam Gibbons of Florida; Thomas Curtis of Missouri.

From my point of view the most vital change in Congress is the election of Americans of Japanese ancestry. In addition to their performance of duties with intelligence and dedication, they have brought a new perspective reflecting the growing importance of Asia and Asian Americans. Their abilities have won them important leadership positions.

I would not be surprised to see Daniel Inouye of Hawaii elected Senate majority leader. He has been named chairman of the Senate

Select Committee on the Iran-Contra Affair, and his hearings may be the most important of the decade. (He has been mentioned as a vice-presidential possibility.) I would not be surprised to see Norman Mineta named speaker of the House some day. Spark Matsunaga is in line for the chair of the powerful Senate Finance Committee. Congressman Robert Matsui is a likely candidate to step one day into the Senate race in California. Patricia Saiki of Hawaii, the only Republican of this group, already has shown strong leadership. I see the probability of other Japanese Americans as well as Asian Americans being elected to Congress on their merits, for the ethnic vote is much too small to elect them on the basis of ethnicity alone.

Although all those named above have been kind and helpful, I wish to pay special tribute to Senator Matsunaga, a legislator whose skills and interests lie in many fields. He has initiated more statutes of benefit to those of Japanese ancestry than any other member of Congress. In addition to being a poet in two languages, he was the principal sponsor of the National Peace Institute Foundation. He has been a close friend and is recognized as probably the hardest-working member of Congress. Author of two published books, he has honored me by introducing me to visiting Japanese as his *Ni-san,* "big brother."

Regrettably, I am unable to name the thousands of Americans who came to our support during the evacuation and the period of imprisonment. I am well aware that many of them faced social and commercial ostracism, and even physical violence, for having had the courage to stand up for justice when justice, as applied to Japanese Americans, was unpopular. To them I say, Thank you. I hope we have justified your confidence in our loyalty.

There have been many days and sleepless nights of remembering events and people, mostly people who influenced my life. People like Judge James Wolfe who became a sort of surrogate father after my own father died. Senator Elbert Thomas, who kindled my interest in government. My comrades in JACL battles—the wise and thoughtful Saburo Kido; George Inagaki, my closest friend; Mas Satow, who covered my rear while I worked in Washington; Hito Okada, who somehow found the money to keep JACL alive during the evacuation years; Larry Tajiri, who combined a newspaperman's realism with a flaming liberalism—all dead now. Dillon Myer, the kind and intensely humane director of the War

Relocation Authority, who hated the side of his job that required him to be a jailkeeper. Joe Itagaki, the mess sergeant who saw that I was fed and went with me in search of my brother Ben Frank's body. Bob Pirosh, whose sensitivity and understanding made the movie *Go for Broke* a living memorial to the men of the 442nd Regimental Combat Team.

My long disability renewed my sense of appreciation for Etsu, wife, helpmate, companion, uncomplaining guardian of my welfare, tireless supporter of causes that interested me, reliable sounding board for testing my ideas. Although she is American through and through, she combines her American strength, initiative, and independence with the finest qualities of Japanese womanhood, which are loyalty, dependability, compassion, and thoughtfulness. I know that in my preoccupation with matters that I considered important, I neglected her, took her presence and support for granted. I failed to tell her of my appreciation for the contributions she made to the fullness of my life. Doctors tell me she has literally kept me alive this past decade. I am not demonstrative; I did not tell her as often as I should have that I love her. Here in print I wish to tell her that.

There are others whose friendship I treasure, and whom I have been unable to treat adequately in this book because there is so much to say about them and so little space in which to say it: Edward J. Ennis, whom I first met soon after war's outbreak, when he was a young attorney serving as chief of the Justice Department's Alien Enemy Control Unit. In a sense we were on opposite sides at the time. But I detected kindness, humanity, and understanding. After the war, when he returned to private practice, Ed Ennis became extremely helpful in our efforts to prevent unfair deportation and to win citizenship for the Issei. Ennis served as chairman of the board of the American Civil Liberties Union and was a sympathetic witness when the Commission on Wartime Relocation and Internment of Civilians held its hearings. But more than all that, I value him as a friend and the godfather of my children. Nor must I forget to mention Walter Judd and Francis Walter, the congressmen who provided guidance, support and encouragement during the postwar legislative fight for justice.

Then there is James Purcell, the San Francisco attorney who was so angry about the evacuation that he took the Mitsuye Endo *habeas corpus* case to the U.S. Supreme Court without fee, using his own money to meet expenses. The Endo case, which demanded the government show cause why a citizen should continue to be detained after her loyalty had been established, was the only test won in the courts and led to the return of the evacuees to the West Coast. My life is full of "what ifs." What would have happened if, somehow, we had been able to get the Endo case to the courts at the beginning of the evacuation period? Would we have been able to avert that entire shameful and outrageous American tragedy? I wonder.

I must also mention Philip H. Trezise, a friend of later years. I got to know him when he was minister for economic affairs at the U.S. embassy in Tokyo from 1957 to 1961. His thoughtful policies are credited with laying the groundwork for Japan's postwar economic recovery. I had many occasions to meet with him when he was assistant secretary of state for economic affairs. Trezise has a delightfully wry, down-to-earth outlook on the obscure discipline of economics. Our professional contacts developed into personal friendship.

In my book of memories every faithful member of the Japanese American Citizens League is a hero. To acknowledge their support except in the collective is impossible. To paraphrase Winston Churchill, no organization has accomplished so much against such odds with so little in as short a time. Perhaps the most appropriate way to recognize JACL stalwarts is to name the official delegates to the first postwar national convention, held in Denver in the spring of 1946, who voted the mandate for human rights that took me to Washington.

At that convention Saburo Kido stepped down from the presidency and Hito Okada of Salt Lake City took over. Vice-presidents were George Inagaki of Venice, California; Mas Satow then living in Milwaukee, Wisconsin; and Bill Yamauchi of Pocatello, Idaho. Dr. Takashi Mayeda of Denver was secretary and Kay Terashima of Salt Lake City treasurer. The official (voting) delegates were:

Denver—Dr. Mayeda, Minoru Yasui. Salt Lake City—Terashima, Alice Kasai. Mount Olympus, Utah—Tom Matsumori, George Fujii. Pocatello—George Shiozawa, Paul Okamoto. Milwaukee—Mas Satow. San Jose, California—Etsu Masaoka. San Francisco—Joe Masaoka, Kaye Uyeda. Idaho Falls—Eli Kobayashi,

Yukio Inouye. Chicago—Noboru Honda, Dr. Randolph Sakada. North Platte, Nebraska—George Kuroki, Dorothy Wada. Fort Lupton, Colorado—Floyd Koshio, Jack Kobayashi. Ogden—Dr. Mike Horii, Toyse Kato. Magic Valley, Idaho—George Makabe. Pueblo, Colorado—Fred Hidaka. New York City—Yurino Takayoshi, Tom Hayashi. Yellowstone, Idaho—Haru Yamasaki, Stomie Hanami. Greeley, Colorado—Misaye Uno, Roy Uyesaka. Snake River Valley, Idaho—Joe Saito. Boise Valley, Idaho—Tom Takatori.

National JACL was represented by Shigeki Ushio, Murray, Utah; Scotty Tsuchiya, Los Angeles; George Minato, Seattle; Peter Aoki, New York City; Dr. T. T. Yatabe, Chicago; Ben Kuroki, North Platte; Fred Tayama, Stillwater, Oklahoma; Kido, Okada, Inagaki, Yuri Yamashita, and attorneys Edward Ennis and A. L. Wirin.

More than half of these JACLers have passed on. Most of those still living continue to be active in JACL which is a tribute not only to the organization, but to their dedication.

While all of the American ambassadors to the Chrysanthemum Throne in Tokyo have been cordial and helpful, I am particularly indebted to Ambassadors Robert Murphy, Douglas MacArthur III, Edwin Reischauer, U. Alexis Johnson, and Mike Mansfield.

Japanese prime ministers who were most cooperative and personally friendly include Shigeru Yoshida, the first postwar premier, Hayato Ikeda, the economic miracle man, and Eisaku Sato, who won the Nobel Peace Prize and arranged the reversion of Okinawa. Among my foremost friends of long standing in the Diet are Susumu Nikaido and Kiichi Miyasawa, the former having been vice-president of the Liberal Democratic Party and chief cabinet secretary. The latter is now the finance minister, after having served as foreign minister, minister of international trade and industry, etc. Both are potential candidates to be prime ministers. Good luck, to both.

Naming all the Japanese who helped me to understand their country is another impossibility. I have mentioned the roles of some, like Toyosaburo Taniguchi, the grand old man of the textile industry. During the battle over textile quotas, Takashi Murayama, Makoto Kosugi, and Ichiro Hayashi were invaluable sources of information about their industry and Japanese business customs.

Some of my most valuable friends in Japan were American-born. I have mentioned George Togasaki and Tamotsu Murayama. Shig Kameda and Kats Nohara, natives of Hawaii, became Japan Air Lines executives and often worked closely with me. George Harada, from California's Central Valley, as president of Suntory International went out of his way to be helpful, as did Ed Noda, Toyosaburo Taniguchi's personal interpreter who became president of Toyobo's New York office.

Among the younger Japanese with whom I was associated is Juichiro Takada, a Columbia-educated businessman who became a surrogate "Japan son" to Etsu and me. Shuzo Ishikawa, now a director of Dentsu, and George Yoshioka helped to carry out their president Yoshida's dream of internationalizing their advertising agency. At the other end of the age scale, Konosuke Matsushita, the nonagenarian founder of Matsushita Electric, has not forgotten our first meeting during my initial trip to Japan. He keeps in touch.

Because of my many friends in Japan's career civil service, I hesitate to mention any of them. However, I must name three recent embassy ministers who during their Washington stay demonstrated both brilliance and great understanding of the need for continuing friendly Japanese-American ties. They are Ken Kunihiro and Hiroshi Fukuda, now executive assistants to Prime Minister Yasuhiro Nakasone, and Makoto Watanabe, deputy director general of the North American Affairs Bureau. They surely are destined for top jobs in Japan's foreign service.

In my time, encouraging progress has been made in the human rights of all peoples. While there is much to be accomplished, even in the United States, Moses Masaoka can now visualize the Promised Land of human dignity and equality. We may not reach it in my lifetime, but I would like to believe that I helped to bring the reality closer.

Now, in the twilight of our lives, Etsu and I, who have worked in tandem for what we thought was the greater good, want to thank all who were responsible for the opportunity to serve. Few have ever enjoyed the tremendous experiences granted us and we are most grateful for the moral, financial, and other support and cooperation so generously extended us. Our leadership may not always have been inspired, or the most effective. But we tried our very best. For our mistakes and errors and there were many, we humbly apologize. For our successes and honors, and there were a few, we happily share them with you. We may not reach the Promised Land before sunset, but we certainly tried in the best "Go For Broke" spirit of the World War II volunteers and of those of Japanese ancestry since time began. Perhaps in the Great Beyond, we shall all meet again.

To our minds, there is nothing more appropriate than to conclude our postscript with the moving sentiments of the Japanese American Hymn. The words are by Marion Tajiri and the music by Marcel Tyrrel.

> There was a dream my father dreamed for me,
> A land in which all men are free.
> Then the desert camp with watchtowers high,
> Where life stood still 'mid sand and brooding sky.
> Out of the war in which my brothers died,
> Their muted voices with mine cried,
> This is our dream, that all men shall be free,
> This is our creed, we'll live in loyalty.
> God help us rid the land of bigotry,
> That we may walk in peace and dignity.

—MIKE M. MASAOKA

Washington, D.C.
March 1, 1987

Index